Advances in Security and Payment Methods for Mobile Commerce

Wen-Chen Hu
University of North Dakota, USA

Chung-wei Lee
Auburn University, USA

Weidong Kou
Chinese State Key Lab. of Integrated Service Networks, China

IDEA GROUP PUBLISHING

Hershey • London • Melbourne • Singapore

Acquisitions Editor:	Mehdi Khosrow-Pour
Senior Managing Editor:	Jan Travers
Managing Editor:	Amanda Appicello
Development Editor:	Michele Rossi
Copy Editor:	Ingrid Widitz
Typesetter:	Jennifer Wetzel
Cover Design:	Lisa Tosheff
Printed at:	Yurchak Printing Inc.

Published in the United States of America by
    Idea Group Publishing (an imprint of Idea Group Inc.)
    701 E. Chocolate Avenue, Suite 200
    Hershey PA 17033
    Tel: 717-533-8845
    Fax: 717-533-8661
    E-mail: cust@idea-group.com
    Web site: http://www.idea-group.com

and in the United Kingdom by
    Idea Group Publishing (an imprint of Idea Group Inc.)
    3 Henrietta Street
    Covent Garden
    London WC2E 8LU
    Tel: 44 20 7240 0856
    Fax: 44 20 7379 3313
    Web site: http://www.eurospan.co.uk

Library of Congress Cataloging-in-Publication Data

Advances in security and payment methods for mobile commerce / Wen Chen Hu,
Chung-Wei Lee and Weidong Kou, editors.
        p. cm.
    Includes bibliographical references and index.
    ISBN 1-59140-345-6 (h/c) -- ISBN 1-59140-346-4 (s/c) -- ISBN 1-59140-347-2 (eisbn)
    1. Mobile commerce--Security measures. 2. Business enterprises--Computer
networks--Security measures. I. Hu, Wen Chen, 1960- II. Lee, Chung-Wei, 1965- III.
Kou, Weidong.
    HF5548.34.A37 2004
    658.4'78--dc22

                                                                        2004016285

British Cataloguing in Publication Data
A Cataloguing in Publication record for this book is available from the British Library.

All work contributed to this book is new, previously-unpublished material. The views expressed in
this book are those of the authors, but not necessarily of the publisher.

Advances in Security and Payment Methods for Mobile Commerce

Table of Contents

Section II: Mobile Commerce Security

Section III: Mobile Commerce Payment Methods

Section IV: Ad Hoc Mobile Commerce Security and Payment Methods

Preface

Introduction

With the introduction of the World Wide Web, electronic commerce has revolutionized traditional commerce and boosted sales and exchanges of merchandise and information. Recently, the emergence of wireless and mobile networks has made possible the admission of electronic commerce to a new application and research subject: mobile commerce, which is defined as the exchange or buying and selling of commodities, services, or information on the Internet through the use of mobile handheld devices. In just a few years, mobile commerce has emerged from nowhere to become the hottest new trend in business transactions. In fact, the growth of mobile handheld devices has been more rapid than the growth in any previous technology.

Yet, one of the biggest impediments to the growth of mobile commerce has been a lack of consistency in security and payment methods and an absence of consensus on technology standards. Various wired or electronic commerce security and payment methods have been modified and applied to mobile commerce, but experience shows that simply adapting those solutions to mobile commerce is not feasible. Different methods and approaches must be taken to enforce mobile commerce security and secure payment methods. Many novel security and payment technologies, therefore, have been proposed and applied to mobile commerce and they are highly diverse and broad in application. This book attempts to provide a comprehensive study of mobile commerce security and payment methods and address the complex challenges facing the mobile commerce industry.

This book contains high-quality research, and industrial and practical articles in the areas of mobile commerce security and payment methods from both academics and industrialists. It includes research and development results of lasting significance in the theory, design, implementation, analysis, and application of mobile commerce security and payment methods. It could be used for a textbook of an advanced computer science (or related disciplines) course and would be a highly useful reference book for IT professionals.

Organization

The issues related to mobile commerce security and payment methods are wide and varied, and this book has benefited from contributions by authors with a range of backgrounds. To help readers better understand this book, it is divided into four major sections and a brief overview of each chapter is given below.

Section I

This section describes the fundamentals of mobile commerce security and payment methods and includes four chapters on the general concepts, reputation and trust, intrusion detection, and a secure authentication infrastructure.

Chapter I, *Mobile Commerce Security and Payment Methods*, is by Chung-wei Lee, Weidong Kou, and Wen-Chen Hu. This chapter provides a comprehensive overview of mobile commerce security and payment methods. A secure mobile commerce system must have the following properties: (i) confidentiality, (ii) authentication, (iii) integrity, (iv) authorization, (v) availability, and (vi) non-repudiation. It discusses the security issues related to the following three network infrastructures: (i) wireless local area networks, (ii) wireless wide area networks, and (iii) WAP. Among the many themes of mobile commerce security, mobile payment methods are probably the most important. A typical mobile payment process includes: (i) registration, (ii) payment submission, (iii) authentication and authorization by a content provider, and (iv) confirmation. This chapter also describes a set of standards for mobile payments.

Chapter II, *Reputation and Trust*, is authored by Li Xiong and Ling Liu. The authors introduce reputation systems as a means of facilitating trust and minimizing risks in m-commerce and e-commerce in general. They presents PeerTrust, an adaptive and dynamic reputation based trust model that helps participants or peers to evaluate the trustworthiness of each other based on the community feedback about participants' past behavior.

Chapter III, *Intrusion Detection and Vulnerability Analysis of Mobile Commerce Platform*, is authored by Changhua Zhu and Changxing Pei. Intrusion detection and vulnerability analysis play the same important roles in wireless infrastructure as in wired infrastructure. This chapter first gives the methods and technologies of intrusion detection and vulnerability analysis. It then gives the security issues in various wireless networking technologies, analyzes the vulnerability of the enabling technologies for the mobile commerce platform, and proposes a distributed wireless intrusion detection & vulnerability analysis (WID&VA) system that can help to address the identified security issues.

Chapter IV, *A Secure Authentication Infrastructure for Mobile Users*, is authored by Gregor v. Bochmann and Eric Zhen Zhang. This chapter first explains the requirements for an authentication infrastructure for electronic commerce, identifying the partners involved in e-commerce transactions and the trust relationships required. An improved authentication protocol, which provides trust relationships for mobile e-commerce users, is then presented. Its analysis and comparison with other proposed authentication protocols indicate that it is a good candidate for use in the context of mobile e-commerce.

Section II

This section discusses issues related to mobile commerce security and includes four chapters on policy-based access control, XML-based trust negotiations, mobile agents, and secure multicast.

Chapter V, *Policy-Based Access Control for Context-Aware Services over the Wireless Internet*, is authored by Paolo Bellavista, Antonio Corradi, and Cesare Stefanelli. The spreading wireless accessibility to the Internet stimulates the provisioning of mobile commercial services to a wide set of heterogeneous and limited client terminals. This requires novel programming methodologies to support and simplify the development of innovative service classes. In these novel services, results and offered quality levels should depend on both client location and locally available resources (context). Within this perspective, this chapter motivates the need for novel access control solutions to flexibly control the resource access of mobile clients depending on the currently applicable context. In particular, it discusses and exemplifies how innovative middlewares for access control should support the determination of the client context on the basis of high-level declarative directives (profiles and policies) and distributed online monitoring.

Chapter VI, *A Comprehensive XML Based Approach to Trust Negotiations*, is authored by Elisa Bertino, Elena Ferrari, and Anna Cinzia Squicciarini. Trust negotiation is a promising approach for establishing trust in open systems like the Internet, where sensitive interactions may often occur between entities at first contact, with no prior knowledge of each other. This chapter presents Trust-X, a comprehensive XML-based XML framework for trust negotiations, specifically conceived for a peer-to-peer environment. It also discusses the applicability of trust negotiation principles to mobile commerce, and introduces a variety of possible approaches to extend and improve Trust-X in order to fully support mobile commerce transactions and payments.

Chapter VII, *Security Issues and Possible Countermeasures for a Mobile Agent Based M-Commerce Application*, is authored by Jyh-haw Yeh, Wen-Chen Hu, and Chung-wei Lee. With the advent of wireless and mobile networks, the Internet is rapidly evolving from a set of connected stationary machines to include mobile handheld devices. This creates new opportunities for customers to conduct business from any location at any time. However, the electronic commerce technologies currently used cannot be applied directly since most were developed based on fixed, wired networks. As a result, a new research area, mobile commerce, is now being developed to supplement existing electronic commerce capabilities. This chapter discusses the security issues related to this new field, along with possible countermeasures, and introduces a mobile agent based solution for mobile commerce.

Chapter VIII, *Secure Multicast for Mobile Commerce Applications: Issues and Challenges*, is authored by Mohamed Eltoweissy, Sushil Jajodia, and Ravi Mukkamala. This chapter identifies system parameters and subsequent security requirements for secure multicast in m-commerce. Attacks on m-commerce environments may undermine satisfying these security requirements, resulting, at most times, in major losses. A set of common attacks and the core services needed to mitigate these attacks are discussed first. It then provides efficient solutions for secure multicast in m-commerce. Among these services, authentication and key management play a major role. Given the varying requirements of m-commerce applications and the large number of current key management schemes, it also provides a set of performance metrics to aid m-commerce system designers in the evaluation and selection of key management schemes.

Section III

Section III covers the issues related to mobile commerce payment methods and includes three chapters on the subjects of mobile payment introduction and overview, micro-payments, and a mobile payment service SeMoPS, respectively.

Chapter IX, *M-Payment Solutions and M-Commerce Fraud Management*, is by Seema Nambiar and Chang-Tien Lu. The shift from physical to virtual payments has brought enormous benefits to consumers and merchants. For consumers it means ease of use. For mobile operators, mobile payment presents a unique opportunity to consolidate their central role in the m-commerce value chain. Financial organizations view mobile payment and mobile banking as a way of providing added convenience to their customers along with an opportunity to reduce their operating costs. This chapter starts by giving a general introduction to m-payment by providing an overview of the m-payment value chain, life cycle and characteristics. The second section reviews competing mobile payment solutions that are found in the marketplace. Different types of mobile frauds in the m-commerce environment and solutions to prevent such frauds are discussed in the last section.

Chapter X, *Multi-Party Micro-Payment for Mobile Commerce*, is authored by Jianming Zhu and Jianfeng Ma. This chapter introduces a new micro-payment scheme that is able to apply to multi-party for mobile commerce, which allows a mobile user to pay every party involved in providing services. The micro-payment, which refers to low-value financial transactions ranging from several cents to a few dollars, is an important technique in m-commerce. Their scheme is based on the hash function and without any additional communication and expensive public key cryptography in order to achieve good efficiency and low transaction costs. In the scheme, the mobile user releases an ongoing stream of low-valued micro-payment tokens into the network in exchange for the requested services.

Chapter XI, *SeMoPS: A Global Secure Mobile Payment Service*, is authored by Stamatis Karnouskos, András Vilmos, Antonis Ramfos, Balázs Csik, and Petra Hoepner. Many experts consider that efficient and effective mobile payment solutions will empower existing e- and m-commerce efforts and unleash the true potential of mobile business. Recently, different mobile payment approaches appear to the market addressing particular needs, but up to now no global mobile payment solution exists. SEMOPS is a secure mobile payment service with an innovative technology and business concept that aims to fully address the challenges the mobile payment domain poses and become a global mobile payment service. They present a detailed description of the approach, its implementation, and features that diversify it from other systems. They also discuss on its business model and try to predict its future impact.

Section IV

The issues related to mobile commerce security and payment methods are wide and disparate. This section consists of three chapters on digital signatures and smart cards.

Chapter XII, *Remote Digital Signing for Mobile Commerce*, is authored by Oguz Kaan Onbilger, Randy Chow, and Richard Newman. Mobile agents (MAs) are a promising technology, which directly address physical limitations of mobile devices such as limited battery life, intermittent and low-bandwidth connections, with their capability of providing disconnected operation. This chapter addresses the problem of digital contract signing with MAs, which is an important part of any mobile commerce activity and one special challenging case of computing with secrets remotely in public. The authors use a multi-agent model together with simple secret splitting schemes for signing with shares of a secret key carried by MAs, cooperating to accomplish a trading task.

Chapter XIII, *A Mobile Coalition Key-Evolving Digital Signature Scheme for Wireless/Mobile Networks*, is authored by Quanxing Zhang, Chwan-Hwa "John" Wu, and J. David Irwin. A scheme is proposed in this chapter to apply a secure digital signature scheme in a mobile-IP environment and treats the three entities in a dynamic path as either foreign agents (FA), home agents (HA) or mobile agents (MA), such that a coalition is formed containing each of the individual agents. Each agent has a pair of keys: one private and one public. The private key is evolving with time, and the public key is signed by a certification authority (CA). All the private keys of the three agents in the coalition are needed to sign a signature. Furthermore, all the messages are signed and verified. The signature is verified against a public key, computed as the product of the public keys of all three agents, and readily generated when a new dynamic path is formed.

Chapter XIV, *Smart Card Based Protocol for Secure and Controlled Access of Mobile Host in IPv6 Compatible Foreign Network*, is authored by R.K. Ghosh, Abhinav Arora, and Gautam Barua. This chapter presents a proposal to combine the advantages of IPSec and smart cards in order to design a new protocol for secure bi-directional access of mobile hosts in an IPv6 foreign network using smart cards. The protocol, called mobile authentication protocol (MAP), builds a security association needed for IPsec. An access router in a foreign network contacts an AAA (authentication, authorization and accounting) server in order to authenticate and authorize a mobile host that approaches the router to access services. The access router then acts as a gateway for all subsequent service requirements of the mobile host.

Acknowledgments

The successful accomplishment of this book is a credit to all chapter authors' excellent contributions. Also, the chapter authors did considerable reviewing of each other's work. Other reviewers who helped review and comment on chapters also have our thanks. Special thanks go to the staff at Idea Group Publishing, especially to Mehdi Khosrow-Pour, Jan Travers, and Michele Rossi. The biggest thanks go to our family members for their love and support throughout this project. Finally, this work is supported by the NSFC Grant 90304008.

Wen-Chen Hu
Chung-wei Lee
Weidong Kou
April 17, 2004

Section I

Fundamentals of Mobile Commerce Security and Payment Methods

Chapter I

Mobile Commerce Security and Payment Methods

Chung-wei Lee, Auburn University, USA

Weidong Kou, Chinese State Key Lab. of Integrated Service Networks, China

Wen-Chen Hu, University of North Dakota, USA

Abstract

Without secure commercial information exchange and safe electronic financial transactions over mobile networks, neither service providers nor potential customers will trust mobile commerce. Various mobile security procedures and payment methods have been proposed and applied to mobile commerce, and this chapter attempts to provide a comprehensive overview of them. A secure mobile commerce system must have the following properties: (i) confidentiality, (ii) authentication, (iii) integrity, (iv) authorization, (v) availability, and (vi) non-repudiation. This chapter discusses the security issues related to the following three network paradigms: (i) wireless local area networks, (ii) wireless wide area networks, and (iii) WAP. Among the many themes of mobile commerce security, mobile payment methods are probably the most important. A typical mobile payment process includes: (i) registration, (ii) payment submission, (iii) authentication and authorization by a content provider, and (iv) confirmation. This chapter also describes a set of standards for mobile payments.

Introduction

With the introduction of the World Wide Web, electronic commerce has revolutionized traditional commerce and boosted sales and exchanges of merchandise and information. Recently, the emergence of wireless and mobile networks has made possible the extension of electronic commerce to a new application and research area: mobile commerce, which is defined as the exchange or buying and selling of commodities, services, or information on the Internet through the use of mobile handheld devices. In just a few years, mobile commerce has emerged from nowhere to become the hottest new trend in business transactions. Despite a weak economy, the future of mobile commerce is bright according to the latest predictions:

- Figure 1 shows the growth in demand for handheld computing devices (not including smart cellular phones) through 2007, as predicted by the research firm In-Stat/MDR (PalmInfocenter.com, 2003).

- It is estimated that 50 million wireless phone users in the United States will use their handheld devices to authorize payment for premium content and physical goods at some point during the year 2006. This represents 17% of the projected total population and 26% of all wireless users (Reuters, 2001).

- Mobile commerce is an effective and convenient way of delivering electronic commerce to consumers from anywhere and at any time. Realizing the advantages to be gained from mobile commerce, companies have begun to offer mobile commerce options for their customers in addition to the electronic commerce they already provide (The Yankee Group, 2002).

Regardless of the bright future of mobile commerce, its prosperity and popularity will be brought to a higher level only if information can be securely and safely exchanged among end systems (mobile users and content providers). Applying the security and payment technologies for electronic commerce to mobile commerce has been proven to be a futile

Figure 1. Forecast of demand for mobile handheld computing devices (not including smart cellular phones)

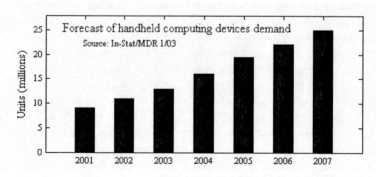

effort because electronic commerce and mobile commerce are based on different infra-structures (wired vs. wireless). A wide variety of security procedures and payment methods, therefore, have been developed and applied to mobile commerce. These technologies are extremely diverse and complicated and a comprehensive discussion on them is still absent. This chapter attempts to provide a comprehensive overview of mobile commerce security and payment methods. It is organized into four sections. The first section introduces the fundamentals of mobile commerce security and payment methods. Mobile commerce security and payment methods are detailed in the second and third sections, respectively. The last section summarizes the discussions in this chapter.

Security and Payment Methods

Foremost, the theme of this chapter, mobile commerce security, is defined as the technological and managerial procedures applied to mobile commerce to provide the following properties of mobile commerce information and systems:

- *Confidentiality*: The information and systems must not be disclosed to unautho-rized persons, processes, or devices.

- *Authentication*: Ensures parties to a transaction are not impostors and are trusted.

- *Integrity*: The information and systems have not been altered or corrupted by outside parties.

- *Authorization*: Procedures must be provided to verify that the user can make the requested purchases.

- *Availability*: An authorized user must have timely, reliable access to information in order to perform mobile commerce transactions.

- *Non-repudiation*: Ensures a user cannot deny they performed a transaction; the user is provided with proof of the transaction and the recipient is assured of the user's identity.

These procedures involve a variety of policies and processes, along with the hardware and software tools necessary to protect the mobile commerce systems and transactions and the information processed, stored, and transmitted by them.

Among the many issues that arise with mobile commerce security, mobile payment methods are probably the most important. They are the methods used to pay for goods or services with a mobile handheld device, such as a smart cellular phone or an Internet-enabled PDA. A typical payment scenario is as follows:

1. A user registers for the services via an Internet-enabled mobile handheld device.
2. The user submits his/her payment.

3.   The content provider settles down the request by performing authentication and authorization to the user as well as contacting a wireless service provider and a financial institution.

4.   A confirmation of the completed transaction is delivered to the user.

Requirements of Mobile Commerce Security and Payment Methods

It is first necessary to examine what kind of features mobile commerce security and payment methods are expected to have in order to conduct effective and efficient mobile commerce transactions and what kind of challenges may be faced in the process of developing new mobile commerce security and payment methods. The requirements for mobile commerce security and payment methods are:

1.   Confidentiality, authentication, integrity, authorization, availability, and non-repudiation must be rigorously enforced.

2.   They should be interoperable for most systems.

3.   They should be acceptable by the current or future systems with reduced cost.

4.   They should allow content providers to provide affordable, easy-to-use, efficient and interoperable payment methods to users.

5.   No mobile commerce transactions are deferred or deterred because of the deployment.

Mobile Commerce Security

The emerging wireless and mobile networks have extended electronic commerce to another research and application subject: mobile commerce. Mobile commerce applications are built on top of the existing network infrastructure consisting of wired networks, such as the Internet; wireless networks, such as wide area 3G cellular networks and Wi-Fi wireless local area networks (WLAN). Therefore, security issues in mobile commerce are tightly coupled with network security.

Security Basics

Without security of the underlying networking technologies, mobile commerce will be beyond our imagination. Network security usually involves communications of two or more participating entities. However "security" covers many different aspects. In this section we focus on those features that are most important to mobile commerce systems.

Security Services

A mobile commerce system needs to provide security services to its participating entities so that business can be conducted successfully in electronic form.

- *Authentication.* Before business transactions can be performed, the participating entities (usually the sender and receiver) must confirm the identity of each other. This service prevents an unauthorized third party from masquerading as one of the legitimate parties. Authentication is usually achieved using network-based authentication protocols.

- *Data confidentiality/secrecy.* In an electronic business transaction, it is assumed that only the sender and intended receiver(s) will be able to comprehend the transmitted messages in cleartext. Providing data confidentiality prevents eavesdroppers or interceptors from understanding the secret communication. It is usually accomplished using computer-based cryptographic encryption and decryption computation.

- *Data integrity.* No transmitted message should be altered accidentally or maliciously without this being detected at the receiver side of a mobile commerce system. With this security feature, an interceptor is not able to fool the receiver by modifying the content of a message in transmission. Adding secure electronic signatures to messages provides data integrity.

- *Non-repudiation.* Mobile commerce transactions are official business deals. Neither the sender nor receiver should be able to deny the existence of a legitimate transaction afterwards. That is, the sender can prove that the specified receiver had received the message and the receiver can prove that the specified sender did send the message. This is usually done using digital signature techniques.

- *Availability.* The availability of a mobile commerce system ensures that legitimate users can access the business service reliably and securely. The system should be designed so that it can minimize the impact of the notorious denial-of-service (DoS) attacks, which can cause mobile commerce services to become unstable or unusable for long periods of time. Deploying network security devices such as firewalls and configuring them along with associated protocols properly is the key to ensuring service availability.

Security Mechanisms

Security services in the modern world take advantage of advances in computation technology (both hardware and software). To achieve these security goals, digital data are encrypted and decrypted based on cryptographic algorithms. There are two categories of cryptographic algorithms: symmetric key systems and asymmetric key systems.

- *Symmetric key systems.* In this category, the sender and receiver of a security session both own the same digital key. The sender encrypts messages using this key and then sends it over to the receiver through the public network. The receiver decrypts the received messages using the same key. This digital key, however, is never transmitted over the network in cleartext, thus preventing a third party from obtaining it and thus compromising the secure communication. To agree upon this symmetric key requires both sides to use outside channels, such as a telephone conversation, or a specially designed key distribution center (KDC). The data encryption standard (DES), triple-DES (3DES), and advanced encryption standard (AES) are symmetric key systems.

- *Asymmetric key systems.* These are also called **public key systems**. Unlike in symmetric key systems, a participating entity in an asymmetric key system uses two keys — a public key that is accessible to everyone in the world and a private key known only to itself. Applying one or both of these two keys in different orders to data messages provides security services such as authentication and digital signature. The famous RSA algorithm is an example of an asymmetric key system.

Mobile Security

Mobile security is a crucial issue for mobile commerce. Without secure commercial information exchange and safe electronic financial transactions over mobile networks, neither service providers nor potential customers will trust mobile commerce systems. From a technical point of view, mobile commerce over wireless networks is inherently insecure compared to electronic commerce over wired networks. The reasons are as follows:

- *Reliability and integrity*: Interference and fading make the wireless channel error prone. Frequent handoffs and disconnections also degrade the security services.

- *Confidentiality/Privacy*: The broadcast nature of the radio channel makes it easier to tap. Thus, communication can be intercepted and interpreted without difficulty if no security mechanisms such as cryptographic encryption are employed.

- *Identification and authentication*: The mobility of wireless devices introduces an additional difficulty in identifying and authenticating mobile terminals.

- *Capability*: Wireless devices usually have limited computation capability, memory size, communication bandwidth, and battery power. This will make it difficult to utilize high-level security schemes such as 256-bit encryption.

Security issues span the whole mobile commerce system, from one end to the other, from the top to the bottom network protocol stack, from machines to humans. We will focus only on issues exclusively related to mobile/wireless technologies. Lacking a unified wireless security standard, different wireless technologies support different aspects and levels of security features. We will thus discuss some well-known wireless network standards and their corresponding security issues (Tanenbaum, 2002).

Network Infrastructure and Security

Network infrastructure provides essential voice and data communication capability for consumers and vendors in cyberspace. Evolving from electronic commerce (EC) to mobile commerce (MC), it is necessary for a wired network infrastructure, such as the Internet, to be augmented by wireless networks that support mobility for end users. Mobile commerce is possible mainly because of the availability of wireless networks. User requests are delivered to either the closest wireless access point (in a wireless local area network environment) or a base station (in a cellular network environment). Although the wired network is not essential in a mobile commerce system, most mobile commerce servers reside on wired networks and user requests are frequently routed to these servers using transport and/or security mechanisms provided by wired networks. However, our interests in this section focus on the unique aspects of mobile commerce network infrastructure, which is a wireless mobile network; therefore we have chosen to omit any discussion of wired networks.

Wireless communication capability supports mobility for end users in mobile commerce systems. Wireless LAN and WAN are major components used to provide radio communication channels so that mobile service is possible. In the WLAN category, the Wi-Fi standard with 11 Mbps throughput dominates the current market. It is expected that standards with much higher transmission speeds, such as IEEE 802.11a and 802.11g, will replace Wi-Fi in the near future. Cellular networking technologies are advancing at a tremendous pace and each represents a solution for a certain phase, such as 1G, 2G, and 3G, in a particular geographical area, such as the United States, Europe, or Japan. Compared to WLANs, cellular systems can provide longer transmission distances and greater radio coverage, but suffer from the drawback of much lower bandwidth (less than 1 Mbps). In the latest trend for cellular systems, 3G standards supporting wireless multimedia and high-bandwidth services are beginning to be deployed. WCDMA and CDMA2000 are likely to dominate the market in the future.

Wireless Local Area Network and Security

Devices used in wireless local area network (WLAN) technologies are lightweight (easy to carry) and flexible in network configuration. Therefore, WLANs are suitable for office networks, home networks, personal area networks (PANs), and ad hoc networks. In a one-hop WLAN environment, where an access point (AP) acting as a router or switch is a part of a wired network, mobile devices connect directly to the AP through radio channels. Data packets are relayed by the AP to the other end of a network connection. If no APs are available, mobile devices can form a wireless ad hoc network among themselves and exchange data packets or perform business transactions as necessary.

In Table 1, major WLAN technologies are compared in terms of their maximum data transfer rate (channel bandwidth), typical transmission range, modulation techniques,

Table 1. Major WLAN standards

Standard	Maximum Data Rate	Typical Range (m)	Modulation	Frequency Band
Bluetooth	1 Mbps	5 – 10	GFSK	2.4 GHz
802.11b (Wi-Fi)	11 Mbps	50 – 100	HR-DSSS	2.4 GHz
802.11a	54 Mbps	50 – 100	OFDM	5 GHz
HyperLAN2	54 Mbps	50 – 300	OFDM	5 GHz
802.11g	54 Mbps	50 – 150	OFDM	2.4 GHz

and operational frequency bands. The various combinations of modulation schemes and frequency bands make up different standards, resulting in different throughputs and coverage ranges. A detailed coverage of modulation techniques is beyond the scope of this chapter, but interested readers can refer to Chapter III of the book by Pahlavan and Krishnamurthy (2002).

In general, Bluetooth technology supports very limited coverage range and throughput. Thus, it is only suitable for applications in personal area networks. In many parts of the world, the IEEE 802.11b (Wi-Fi) system is now the most popular wireless network and is used in offices, homes, and public spaces such as airports, shopping malls, and restaurants. However, many experts predict that with much higher transmission speeds, 802.11a and 802.11g will replace 802.11b in the near future.

- *Wi-Fi security.* The security of the IEEE 802.11 WLAN standard is provided by a data link level protocol called Wired Equivalent Privacy (WEP). When it is enabled, each mobile host has a secret key that is shared with the base station. The encryption algorithm used in WEP is a stream cipher based on RC4. The ciphertext is generated by XORing the plaintext with a RC4 generated keystream. However, recently published literature has discovered weaknesses in RC4 (Borisov, Goldberg & Wagner, 2001; Fluhrer, Martin & Shamir, 2001; Stubblefield, Ioannidis & Rubin, 2002). The next version, 802.11i, is expected to have better security by employing an authentication server that separates authentication process from the AP.

- *Bluetooth security.* Bluetooth provides security by using frequency hopping in the physical layer, sharing secret keys (called passkeys) between the slave and the master, encrypting communication channels, and controlling integrity. Encryption in Bluetooth is a stream cipher called "E_0," while for integrity control a block cipher called "SAFER+" is used. However, "E_0" has potential weaknesses (as described in Biryukov, Shamir & Wagner, 2000; Jakobsson & Wetzel, 2001) and "SAFER+" is slower than the other similar symmetric-key block ciphers (Tanenbaum, 2002).

Wireless Wide Area Network and Security

The most important technology in this category is the cellular wireless network. Cellular system users can conduct mobile commerce operations through their cellular phones.

Under this scenario, a cellular phone connects directly to the closest base station, where communication is relayed to the service site through a radio access network (RAN) and other fixed networks.

Originally designed for voice-only communication, cellular systems are evolving from analog to digital, and from circuit-switched to packet-switched networks, in order to accommodate mobile commerce (data) applications. Table 2 lists the classifications of standards in first generation (1G), second generations (2G, 2.5G), and third generation (3G) wireless cellular networks. 1G systems such as the advanced mobile phone system (AMPS) and total access control system (TACS) are becoming obsolete, and thus will not play a significant role in mobile commerce systems. The global system for mobile communications (GSM) and its enhancement general packet radio service (GPRS) have mainly been developed and deployed in Europe. GPRS can support data rates of only about 100 kbps, but its upgraded version — enhanced data for global evolution (EDGE) — is capable of supporting 384 kbps. In the United States, wireless operators use time division multiple access (TDMA) and code division multiple access (CDMA) technologies in their cellular networks.

Currently, most of the cellular wireless networks in the world follow 2G or 2.5G standards. However, there is no doubt that in the near future, 3G systems with quality-of-service (QoS) capability will dominate wireless cellular services. The two main standards for 3G are Wideband CDMA (WCDMA), proposed by Ericsson, and CDMA2000, proposed by Qualcomm. Both use direct sequence spread spectrum (DSSS) communication technique in a 5-MHz bandwidth. Technical differences between them include a different chip rate, frame time, spectrum used, and time synchronization mechanism. The WCDMA system can inter-network with GSM networks and has been strongly supported by the European Union, which calls it the Universal Mobile Telecommunications System (UMTS). CDMA2000 is backward-compatible with IS-95, which is widely deployed in the United States.

In a wireless cellular system, a wired network called a radio access network (RAN) is employed to connect radio transceivers with core networks. Two examples of existing RAN architectures are UMTS Terrestrial Radio Access Network (UTRAN) (UTRAN overall description, 1999) and IOS (MSC to BS interface inter-operability specification, 1999). UTRAN is the new radio access network designed especially for 3G UMTS.

Table 2. Major cellular wireless networks

Generation	Radio Channels	Switching Technique	Standards (Examples)
1G	Analog voice channels Digital control channels	Circuit-switched	AMPS TACS
2G	Digital channels	Circuit-switched	GSM TDMA
		Packet-switched	CDMA
2.5G	Digital channels	Packet-switched	GPRS EDGE
3G	Digital channels	Packet-switched	CDMA2000 WCDMA

The architecture and components of UMTS and UTRAN can be found in Vriendt et al. (2002). At the highest level, the UMTS network structure consists of the core network (CN) and UTRAN. The network subsystem (NSS) of GSM/GPRS is reused as much as possible in UMTS CN. Two service domains are supported in CN, circuit switching (CS) and packet switching (PS). By moving the NSS transcoder function from the base station subsystem to the core network, CS provides voice and circuit-switched data services. Evolving from GPRS, the packet-switched service provided by PS optimizes functional relationships between CN and UTRAN. UTRAN consists of radio network subsystems (RNS). Each RNS includes one radio network controller (RNC) and one or more Node B (base station). The RNC controls the logical resources for Node Bs in the UTRAN. Node B manages radio transmission and reception of one or more cells and provides logical resources to the RNC.

- *GSM security.* The Subscriber Identity Module (SIM) in the GSM contains the subscriber's authentication information, such as cryptographic keys, and a unique identifier called international mobile subscriber identity (IMSI). The SIM is usually implemented as a smart card consisting of microprocessors and memory chips. The same authentication key and IMSI are stored on GSM's network side in the authentication center (AuC) and home location register (HLR), respectively. In GSM, short messages are stored in the SIM and calls are directed to the SIM rather than the mobile terminal. This feature allows GSM subscribers to share a terminal with different SIM cards. The security features provided between GSM network and mobile station include IMSI confidentiality and authentication, user data confidentiality, and signaling information element confidentiality. One of the security weaknesses identified in GSM is the one-way authentication. That is, only the mobile station is authenticated and the network is not. This can pose a security threat, as a compromised base station can launch a "man-in-the-middle" attack without being detected by mobile stations.

- *UMTS security.* UMTS is designed to reuse and evolve from existing core network components of the GSM/GPRS and fix known GSM security weaknesses such as the one-way authentication scheme and optional encryption. Authentication in UMTS is mutual and encryption is mandatory (unless specified otherwise) to prevent message replay and modification. In addition, UMTS employs longer cryptographic keys and newer cipher algorithms, which make it more secure than GSM/GPRS.

WAP and Security

Beyond the link-layer communication mechanisms provided by WLANs and cellular networks, the wireless application protocol (WAP) is designed to work with all wireless networks. The most important technology applied by WAP is probably the WAP Gateway, which translates requests from the WAP protocol stack to the WWW stack, so they can be submitted to Web servers. For example, requests from mobile stations are sent as a URL through the network to the WAP Gateway; responses are sent from the

Web server to the WAP Gateway in HTML and are then translated to WML and sent to the mobile stations. Although WAP supports HTML and XML, its host language is WML (wireless markup language), which is a markup language based on XML that is intended for use in specifying content and user interfaces for mobile stations. WAP also supports WMLScript, which is similar to JavaScript but makes minimal demands on memory and CPU power because it does not contain many of the unnecessary functions found in other scripting languages.

WAP security is provided through the wireless transport layer security (WTLS) protocol (in WAP 1.0) and IETF standard transport layer security (TLS) protocol (in WAP 2.0). They provide data integrity, privacy, and authentication. One security problem, known as the "WAP Gap," is caused by the inclusion of the WAP gateway in a security session. That is, encrypted messages sent by end systems might temporarily become clear text on the WAP gateway when messages are processed. One solution is to make the WAP gateway resident within the enterprise (server) network (Ashley et al., 2001), where heavyweight security mechanisms can be enforced.

Mobile Commerce Payment Methods

With the development of commerce, there has been a tremendous evolution in the methods of payment, from the seashell of ancient times to coins and notes, from writing checks to online banking. The emergence of e-commerce has revolutionized the traditional methods of payment. With the help of mobile devices, the dream of "transaction without cash on the move" has come true. Mobile payment enables the transfer of financial value and corresponding services or items between different participators without factual contract. The mobile device can be a wireless communication device, such as a mobile phone, a PDA, a wireless tablet, or a mobile computer. Mobile payment can be divided into two categories, generally according to the amount of transaction value. One is micro-payment, which defines a mobile payment of approximately $10 or less, often for mobile content such as video downloads or gaming. The other is macro-payment, which refers to larger value payments.

Mobile Payment Scenarios

Mobile telecommunications has been so successful that the number of mobile subscribers has risen to one billion worldwide by the end of 2002. In 2003, 60 million users spent more than $50 billion on mobile services. One survey predicted that combined e-commerce and m-commerce volumes would grow from $38 billion in 2002 to $128 billion in 2004. Accompanying the increase in subscriptions, there are evolutions in more sophisticated devices, encouraging the emergence of new applications, which include enhanced messaging services (EMS) and multimedia messaging services (MMS). In these applications, consumers have more options such as the downloading of images, streaming video, and data files as well as the addition of global positioning systems (GPS) in mobile phones, which will facilitate location-based mobile commerce and furthermore provide more feasibility to mobile payment methods.

There are four players in a mobile payment transaction. The mobile consumer (MC) subscribes to a product or service and pays for it via their mobile device. The content provider/merchant (CP/M) provides the appropriate digital content, physical product, or service product to the consumer. The payment service provider (PSP), which may be a network operator, a financial institution, or an independent payment vendor, controls the payment process. The trusted third party (TTP) administers the authentication of transaction parties and the authorization of the payment settlement. In fact, the different roles can be merged into one organization, for example a network bank, which is capable of acting as CP/M, PSP, and TTP at the same time. In a more general sense, a PSP and TTP can be performed by the same organization.

Content Download

In this scenario, the consumer orders the content he/she wants to download from a content provider. The content provider then initiates the charging session, asking the PSP for authorization. The PSP authorizes the CP/M, and then the download starts. The transaction can be settled by either a metered or pricing model. The metered content includes streaming services. The consumers are charged according to the metered quantity of the provided service, for example interval, the data volume or gaming sessions. In a pricing model, the consumer is charged according to the items downloaded completely. A content purchase is also available via a PC Internet connection, where the mobile device will be used to authorize the payment transaction and authenticate the content user.

Point of Sale

In this scenario, services or the sale of goods are offered to the mobile user on the point of sale location instead of a virtual site, for example a taxi service. The merchant (e.g., the taxi driver) will initiate the payment at the point of sale. The PSP asks the mobile user to directly authorize the transaction via a SMS pin, or indirectly via the taxi driver through a wireless Bluetooth link. The process is also applicable to a vending machine scenario.

Content on Device

In this payment scenario, the user has the content preinstalled in his/her mobile device, but he/she should be granted a license to initiate the usage of the content, for example the activation of on-demand gaming service. The license varies with usage, duration, or number of users, and determines the value that the consumer should pay for the desired content.

Mobile Payment Methods

Mobile Payment Operations

In a card transaction, there are usually four stages, including set-up and configuration, the initiation of the payment, authentication of the user, and completion of the payment. In the mobile payment environment, the payment methods can share the same dynamics. Within the four stages, there exist certain kinds of operations among the four parties, and not all the operations may be needed, depending on the stages and scenarios.

- *Registration.* There is a communication between the MC and CP/M that ensures that the content is accessible. During this stage, the MC uses a personal identification number (PIN) for identification and authentication. The MC obtains service details such as the category of payment, the characteristic of the content, as well as the confirmation of the payment after the service. During this operation, an identity number is allotted to the consumer, which uniquely defines the identity of the CP/M during each transaction and a service is initiated. In general, this operation ensures the security of the payment.

- *Charging.* Once the registration is completed, the CP/M submits the authentication and authorization requests to the PSP, initiating the charging session. At the end of every service or time interval, the content provider asks for a charging operation. The PSP settles the payment according to the default scheme, notifying both parties. This is usually presented to mobile consumers in the form of a receipt.

- *Request authorization and authentication.* Before the start of a charging session, the mobile consumers must confirm that they are willing to pay for the service. This authorization request is often sent from the PSP in the form of a contract. The contract will describe the conditions and agreements between the MC and the CP/M. The charging session is initiated by the acceptance of the contract. The MC is also requested to authorize the PSP. This can be settled by submitting the PIN from the MC. Authorization and authentication are completed using the same request. Authorization includes the authentication by PIN.

- *User authentication.* The PSP will notify the authentication result of the MC to the CP/M. If the return of authorization request from the MC is positive, the PSP sends the CP/M a session ID, signaling the initiation of a charging session. It is vital to perceive the difference between micro- and macro-payments, since the security required in the two types is distinct from each other. For example, authentication for every macro-payment transaction through a trusted financial entity is extremely important, whereas network authentication, such as SIM, may be sufficient for micro-payments that only use the operator's infrastructure.

Out-of-Band Payment Method

In the "out-of-band" model, content and operation signals are transmitted in separate channels; for example credit card holders may use their mobile device to authenticate and pay for a service they consume on the fixed line Internet or interactive TV. This model usually involves a system controlled by a financial institution, sometimes collaborating with a mobile operator. There are two typical cases:

- *Financial institutions.* A great number of banks are conducting research to turn the individual mobile into a disbursing terminal. Payments involved in the financial transaction are usually macro-payments. Various methods can be deployed to ensure the authentication of payment transaction. In credit card payments, dual slot phone is usually adopted. Other approaches include PIN authentication via a SIM toolkit application and the use of a digital signature based on a public key infrastructure (PKI) mechanism that demand the 2.5G (or higher) technology.

- *Reverse-charge/billed SMS.* In reverse-billed premium rate SMS, the CP/M deliver content to mobile telephone handsets (ICSTIS, n.d.). Customers subscribe to a service and are charged for the messages they receive. This payment model allows consumers to use SMS text messages to pay for access to digital entertainment and content without being identified. In this application, however, it is the SMS message receiver who is charged, instead of the sender of the SMS message. There are a considerable number of vendors who offer the reverse-charge/billed MSM service payment models.

"In-Band" Payment Method

In this method, a single channel is deployed for the transfer of both content and operation signals. A chargeable WAP service over GPRS is of this kind. Two models of this in-bank payment are in use, namely, subscription models and per usage payment models, with the amount of the payment usually being small, that is, micro-payments. In-band transactions include applications such as video streaming of sports highlights or video messaging.

Proximity

Proximity payments involve the use of wireless technologies to pay for goods and services over short distances. Proximity transactions develop the potential of mobile commerce, for example, using a mobile device to pay at a point of sale, vending machine, ticket machine, market, parking, and so forth. Through short range messaging protocols such as Bluetooth, infrared, RFID, contactless chip, the mobile device can be transformed to a sophisticated terminal that is able to process both micro and macro payments (DeClercq, 2002).

Mobile Payment Standardization

Common Issues of Mobile Payment Standards

Mobile payment enables users to globally conduct payment transactions without physical contact. Unfortunately, regional distinctions and market dynamics often lay barriers for its development. A set of standards is required for all of the four parties. Dominant corporations are competing for the advance of their own standards, which will contribute to their competition with their rivals. Among different standards, the common issues addressed are:

- *Security*. The fraud holds back the usage and trust of consumers and merchants in the integrity of the payment network. In addition, it also adds the cost of operation. Therefore, increased security is vital for the development of mobile payment method to address these issues. The main security elements include those identified in the "Security and Payment Methods" section of this chapter, such as confidentiality, authentication, integrity, authorization, availability, and non-repudiation.

- *Interoperability*. This strengthens any global payment system, ensuring that any participating payment product can be used at any participating merchant location.

- *Usability*. According to the study on the consumers' consumption behavior, MC do not like to change their major habit and tend to opt for the products that are user-friendly. This fact lays the requirement for usability.

Standardization of the Payment Lifecycle

Abiding by the payment standards, the MPF (mobile payment forum) is working on the standardization of the phases in the mobile payment lifecycle, namely device set-up and personalization, payment initiation, authentication and payment completion:

- *Set-up and configuration*. When the mobile device is purchased, the owner who wants to get access to the mobile services should set up the payment mechanism in the mobile environment. Set-up and configuration could take place over a mobile network or the Internet, or they can be done physically.

- *Payment initiation*. In this step, payment information is transmitted to the merchant over a network.

- *Authentication*. The authentication of the user is essential for any payment transaction. The MPF is considering two-way messaging authentication and SAT (SIM Alliance/Application Toolkit) authentication applications. The SAT authentication standardization includes defining a set of minimum requirements for authentication; hence the cost of band can be considerably retrenched.

- *Payment completion.* This process takes place after the cardholder's details have been authenticated and the transaction is authorized. In the normal physical transaction, this involves the printing of a receipt for the user to confirm that the money has been transferred. In the mobile environment, the MPF is currently studying issues about the format and storage of digital receipts.

Summary

It is widely acknowledged that mobile commerce is a field of enormous potential. However, it is also commonly admitted that the development in this field is constrained. There are still considerable barriers waiting to be overcome. Among these, mobile security and payment methods are probably the biggest obstacles. Without secure commercial information exchange and safe electronic financial transactions over mobile networks, neither service providers nor potential customers will trust mobile commerce. Various mobile security procedures and payment methods have been proposed and applied to mobile commerce, and this chapter has provided a comprehensive overview of them.

A secure mobile commerce system must have the following properties: (i) confidentiality, (ii) authentication, (iii) integrity, (iv) authorization, (v) availability, and (vi) non-repudiation. Mobile commerce security is tightly coupled with network security; however, lacking a unified wireless security standard, different wireless technologies support different aspects and levels of security features. This chapter therefore discussed the security issues related to the following three network paradigms: (i) wireless local area networks, (ii) wireless wide area networks, and (iii) WAP.

Among the many themes of mobile commerce security, mobile payment methods are probably the most important. These consist of the methods used to pay for goods or services with a mobile handheld device, such as a smart cellular phone or an Internet-enabled PDA. A typical mobile payment process includes: (i) registration, (ii) payment submission, (iii) authentication and authorization by a content provider, and (iv) confirmation. This chapter also described a set of standards for mobile payments. Dominant corporations are competing for the advance of their own standards, which will contribute to their competition with their rivals. Among different standards, the common issues addressed are: (i) security, (ii) interoperability, and (iii) usability. Current mobile payment standardization has mainly been developed by several organizations, as follows:

- *Mobey Forum (2002):* Founded by a number of financial institutions and mobile terminal manufacturers, Mobey Forum's mission is to encourage the use of mobile technology in financial services.

- *Mobile Payment Forum (2002):* This group is dedicated to developing a framework for standardized, secure, and authenticated mobile commerce using payment card accounts.

- *Mobile electronic Transactions (MeT) Ltd. (2002)*: This group's objective is to ensure the interoperability of mobile transaction solutions. Its work is based on existing specifications and standards, including WAP.

References

Ashley, P., Hinton, H., & Vandenwauver, M. (2001). Wired versus wireless security: The Internet, WAP and iMode for e-commerce. In *Proceedings of Annual Computer Security Applications Conferences (ACSAC).*

Biryukov, A., Shamir, A., & Wagner, D. (2000). Real time cryptanalysis of A5/1 on a PC. In *Proceedings of the 7th International Workshop on Fast Software Encryption.*

Borisov, N., Goldberg, I., & Wagner, D. (2001). Intercepting mobile communications: The insecurity of 802.11. In *Proceedings of the 7th International Conference on Mobile Computing and Networking.*

DeClercq, K. (2002). *Banking sector.* Lessius Hogeschool.

Fluhrer, S., Martin, I., & Shamir, A. (2001). Weakness in the key scheduling algorithm of RC4. In *Proceedings of the 8th Annual Workshop on Selected Areas in Cryptography.*

ICSTIS (The Independent Committee for the Supervision of Standards of Telephone Information Services). (n.d.). Reverse-billed premium rate SMS. Retrieved February 17, 2004 from: *http://www.icstis.org.uk/icstis2002/default.asp?node=6*

Jakobsson, M., & Wetzel, S. (2001). Security weaknesses in Bluetooth. *Topics in Cryptography: CT-RSA 2001* (pp. 176-191). Berlin: Springer-Verlag.

McKitterick, D., & Dowling, J. (2003). State of the art review of mobile payment technology. Retrieved from *http://www.cs.tcd.ie/publications/tech-reports/reports.03/TCD-CS-2003-24.pdf*

Mobey Forum. (2002). Retrieved October 10, 2002 from: *http://www.mobeyforum.org/*

Mobile electronic Transactions (MeT) Ltd. (2002). Retrieved November 22, 2002 from: *http://www.mobiletransaction.org/*

Mobile Payment Forum (2002). Enabling secure, interoperable and user-friendly mobile payment. Retrieved from: *http://www.mobilepaymentforum.org/pdfs/mpf_white paper.pdf*

MSC to BS interface inter-operability specification. (1999). *CDMA Development Group.* CDG-IOS v. 3.1.1.

Pahlavan, K., & Krishnamurthy, P. (2002). *Principles of wireless networks: A unified approach.* Upper Saddle River, NJ: Prentice Hall.

PalmInfocenter.com. (2003). PDA market still poised for growth. Retrieved December 10, 2003 from: *http://www.PalmInfocenter.com/view_Story.asp?ID=5050*

Reuters. (2001). The Yankee Group publishes U.S. mobile commerce forecast. Retrieved October 16, 2003 from: *http://about.reuters.com/newsreleases/art_31-10-2001_id765.asp*

Stubblefield, A., Ioannidis, J., & Rubin, A.D. (2002). Using the Fluhrer, Martin, and Shamir attack to break WEP. In *Proceedings of the Network and Distributed Systems Security Symposium.*

Tanenbaum, A.S. (2002). *Computer Networks* (4th ed.). Upper Saddle River, NJ: Prentice Hall.

UTRAN overall description. (1999). *3GPP.* TS 25.401 v3.3.0, R-99, RAN WG3.

Vriendt, J.D., Lainé, P., Lerouge, C., & Xu, X. (2002). Mobile network evolution: A revolution on the move. *IEEE Communications Magazine, 40*(4), 104-111.

WAP (Wireless Application Protocol). (2003). Open Mobile Alliance Ltd. Retrieved November 21, 2002 from: *http://www.wapforum.org/*

The Yankee Group. (2002). Over 50% of large U.S. enterprises plan to implement a wireless/mobile solution by 2003. Retrieved November 6, 2003 from: *http://www.yankeegroup.com/public/news_releases/news_release_detail.jsp?ID=PressReleases/news_09102002_wmec.htm*

Chapter II

Reputation and Trust

Li Xiong, Georgia Institute of Technology, USA

Ling Liu, Georgia Institute of Technology, USA

Abstract

This chapter introduces reputation systems as a means of facilitating trust and minimizing risks in m-commerce and e-commerce in general. It first illustrates the importance of reputation systems in m-commerce by analyzing a list of risks through example scenarios and discusses a number of challenges of building an effective and robust reputation system in e-commerce applications. It then describes PeerTrust, an adaptive and dynamic reputation based trust model that helps participants or peers to evaluate the trustworthiness of each other based on the community feedback about participants' past behavior. It also presents some initial experiments showing the effectiveness, benefit and vulnerabilities of the reputation systems. Finally it discusses a few interesting open issues.

Introduction

Mobile commerce (m-commerce) communities create enormous opportunities for many, as participants (or peers) can purchase products, access information, and interact with each other from anywhere at any time. However, they also present risks for participants as they are often established dynamically with unknown or unrelated participants. The open nature of such presents a big challenge for accountability. As in general e-commerce, the participants have to manage the risk when interacting with other participants. In other words, in addition to its wireless communication layer risks, m-commerce is also faced with all the application layer risks in general e-commerce. For example, a Palm Pilot user may encounter a virus attack by downloading the Liberty Trojan masquerading as an innocent program for PalmOS from other malicious users, which will wipe out all the contact information. Techniques such as smart cards solve part of the problem by authentication but cannot answer the question of which players are more trustworthy. It is very important for users to be able to quantify and compare the trustworthiness of different participants so they can choose reliable and reputable ones to interact with and filter out the unreliable ones to reduce risk.

Application and Risk Scenarios

We first analyze the risks through several m-commerce example scenarios and illustrate the importance of reputation based trust systems.

M-commerce communities can be built on top of either traditional client-server architecture or peer-to-peer wireless network. In the first case, mobile devices are connected to fixed networks through a wireless gateway in order to access the services in the wired Internet. It essentially replaces desktop computers with mobile devices in the traditional e-commerce communities and allows users to order products and access information from anywhere and at any time. Several important classes of applications have been identified, including transaction-based applications such as mobile auction and mobile shopping, communication-based applications such as mobile advertising and mobile alerts, and entertainment-based applications such as mobile music and software downloading (Varshney, 2002). M-commerce communities can be also built on top of a P2P network. They are typically formed by a group of mobile devices under the same service coverage that have a common mission or interest. All members or peers communicate over wireless channels directly without any fixed networking infrastructure. Such type of infrastructure is receiving growing attention for commercial applications, such as team collaboration applications, networking intelligent sensors and cooperative robots.

Most m-commerce security techniques or analyses deal with security concerns specific to the wireless communication such as privacy and authenticity of wireless communications (Chari, 2001). However, the application layer risks in general e-commerce are also manifested in m-commerce. Mobile clients or peers have to face potential threats or risks when interacting with unknown or unfamiliar service providers or other peers. We summarize the risks and threats as follows:

- *Transaction Specific Risks*. For example, in mobile auctions scenario, buyers are vulnerable to potential risks because malicious sellers may provide incomplete or distorted information or fail to deliver goods.

- *Malicious SMS Messages*. Applications such as mobile advertising and mobile alerts typically send advertising and alerts to mobile users using short messaging service (SMS) messages or short paging messages. A malicious service provider or participant may send out malicious SMS messages that hide nefarious instructions.

- *Virus Attack.* Consider the mobile software-downloading scenario where a mobile user is asking for a resource from the network. An adversary can respond by a fake resource with the same name as the real resource the original user is looking for, but the actual file could be a virus. The first wireless virus has been discovered in PalmOS, which is called PalmOS/Phage[1], and it will infect all third-party applications on the PDA device. Other wireless virus examples include the PalmOS/LibertyCrack[2] Trojan that arrives masquerading as a crack program for an application called Liberty, which allows PalmOS devices to run Nintendo GameBoy Games. When run, however, the Trojan attempts to delete all applications from the handheld and then reboot it.

- *DoS Attack.* The first cell phone virus hacked users of GSM mobile phones and broadcasted a disparaging remark through SMS[3]. Although the virus caused no damage, it foreshadowed a potential DoS attack. If an adversary can disseminate a worm that send out millions of such messages, it could deluge cell phones with them, thereby overwhelming the short message system.

Reputation Systems

Reputation systems (Resnick, 2000) provide attractive techniques to address the above listed risks by facilitating trust and minimizing risks through reputations. Concretely, they help participants to evaluate trustworthiness of each other and predict future behaviors of participants based on the community feedback about the participants' past behavior. By harnessing the community knowledge in the form of feedback, these systems help people decide who to trust, encourage trustworthy behavior, and deter dishonest participation. Reputation systems are important for fostering trust and minimize risks in two ways. First, by collecting and aggregating feedback about participants' past behavior, they provide a way for participants to share their experiences and knowledge so they can estimate the trustworthiness of other participants with whom they may not have personal experiences and in turn they can avoid malicious participants to reduce risk. Second, the presence of a reputation system creates the expectation of reciprocity or retaliation in future behavior, which in turn creates an incentive for good behavior and discourages malicious behavior.

Building such reputation-based systems for m-commerce communities presents a number of challenges. The main one is how to develop an effective trust model that computes an accurate trust value for each participant even with possible strategic malicious behaviors of participants. This essentially applies to general e-commerce communities at large. Dellarocas (2003) provides a latest survey for research in game theory and economics on the topic of reputation. Most of the game theoretic models assume that stage game outcomes are publicly observed. Online feedback mechanisms, in contrast, rely on private (pair-wise) and subjective ratings of stage game outcomes. This introduces two important considerations. One is incentive for providing feedback and the other is the credibility or the truthfulness of the feedback.

A variety of online community sites have reputation management built in, such as eBay, Amazon, Yahoo! Auction, Edeal, Slashdot, and Entrepreneur.com. Even though they facilitate the trust among users to some extent, they also have some common problems and vulnerabilities. Most of these systems use a simple sum or average of the ratings as the reputation value of a user. For example, eBay uses a summation of positive and negative feedback. It fails to convey important subtleties of online interactions such as whether these feedback ratings come from low-value transactions and whether the feedback ratings are honest. It is important to develop effective metrics that aggregate feedback into a meaningful trust value as an estimate of the trustworthiness of participants by incorporating all the subtleties of online interactions. We discuss below the research challenges of developing an effective trust model in detail.

- *Differentiating dishonest feedback.* An important difficulty in aggregating feedback into a single value is dealing with dishonest feedback and various attacks to the reputation system itself. Malicious participants may provide false or misleading feedback to badmouth other participants and to fool the system. Things are made much worse if a group of malicious participants collude to boost each other's ratings and damage others' ratings. An effective trust metric has to differentiate dishonest feedback from honest ones and be robust against various malicious manipulations of participants.

- *Context and location awareness.* Another important consideration is the context and location awareness, as many of the applications are sensitive to the context or the location of the transactions. For example, the functionality of the transaction is an important context to be incorporated into the trust metric. Amazon.com may be trustworthy on selling books but not on providing medical devices.

- *Incentive to provide feedback.* Lastly, there is a lack of incentive for participants to provide feedback. It is even more so in m-commerce communities where mobile users may not bother to provide feedback at all due to the power limitations of their mobile devices and their on-the-road situation.

The other important challenge is related to how to build the supporting infrastructure to collect, aggregate and distribute feedback and reputation information.

- *Efficient and scalable reputation data dissemination.* There are two alternative ways for reputation data dissemination, namely centralized and decentralized. A trust model can be implemented by either scheme. For example, in the m-commerce communities that are built on top of client-server architecture, a centralized trust server (wireless access provider or other independent service provider) can be deployed to collect, aggregate and distribute reputation information. In the peer-to-peer wireless network, the P2P nature of this type of network makes the traditional centralized solution unfeasible, as there is no centralized server or database. Various P2P data location schemes such as broadcast based scheme and distributed hash table based schemes can be used to store and look up the reputation data. Data replication has to be considered in order to address the dynamics of the network such as members leaving and joining the network and potential malicious behaviors of the peers.

- *Secure trust data transmission.* There are a number of known security threats at the wireless communication layer. The reputation system infrastructure has to guarantee the secrecy and integrity of the reputation data during their transmission. Encryption based wireless security solutions such as WAP WTLS[4] and PKI[5] schemes can be used in the implementation to ensure reputation data are securely transferred.

Bearing these research issues in mind, we developed PeerTrust (Xiong, 2003) as a dynamic and adaptive reputation based trust system for participants or peers to quantify and compare the trustworthiness of each other. The rest of the chapter focuses on the trust model. The next section describes the PeerTrust model. Technical details including the illustration of the trust metrics in the context of e-commerce and m-commerce applications will be provided. The section followed presents some initial experiments evaluating the trust model. The last section concludes the chapter by a summary and points out some future research opportunities.

The Trust Model

The main focus of PeerTrust approach is the design and development of a dynamic trust model for aggregating feedback into a trust value to quantify and assess the trustworthiness of participants or peers in e-commerce communities.

Trust Parameters

A peer's trustworthiness is defined by an evaluation of the peer it receives in providing service to other peers in the past. Such reputation reflects the degree of trust that other peers in the community have on the given peer based on their past experiences. We identify five important factors for such evaluation: (1) the feedback a peer obtains from other peers, (2) the feedback scope, such as the total number of transactions that a peer has with other peers, (3) the credibility factor of the feedback source, (4) the transaction context factor for discriminating mission-critical transactions from less or non-critical ones, and (5) the community context factor for addressing community-related characteristics and vulnerabilities. We now illustrate the importance of these parameters through a number of example scenarios.

Feedback in Terms of Amount of Satisfaction

Reputation-based systems rely on feedback to evaluate a peer. Feedback in terms of amount of satisfaction a peer receives during a transaction reflects how well this peer has fulfilled its own part of the service agreement. Some existing reputation based systems use this factor alone and compute a peer u's trust value by a summation of all the feedback u receives through its transactions with other peers in the community. For example, buyers and sellers in eBay can rate each other after each transaction (+1, 0, -1) and the overall reputation is the sum of these ratings over the last 6 months.

We can clearly see that these feedback-only metrics are flawed. A peer who has performed dozens of transactions and cheated 1 out of every 4 cases will have a steadily rising reputation in a given time duration whereas a peer who has only performed 10 transactions during the given time duration but has been completely honest will be treated as less reputable if the reputation measures are computed by a simple sum of the feedback they receive. It is been proved that binary reputation mechanisms will not function well and the resulting market outcome will be unfair if judgment is inferred from knowledge of the sum of positive and negative ratings alone (Dellarocas, 2001).

Number of Transactions

As described above, a peer may increase its trust value by increasing its transaction volume to hide the fact that it frequently misbehaves at a certain rate when a simple summation of feedback is used to model the trustworthiness of peers. The number of transactions is an important scope factor for comparing the feedback in terms of degree of satisfaction among different peers. An updated metric can be defined as the ratio of the total amount of satisfaction peer u receives over the total number of transactions peer u has, that is, the average amount of satisfaction peer u receives for each transaction.

However, this is still not sufficient to measure a peer's trustworthiness. When considering reputation information we often account for the source of information and context.

Credibility of Feedback

The feedback peer u receives from another peer v during a transaction is simply a statement from v regarding how satisfied v feels about the quality of the information or service provided by u. A peer may make false statements about another peer's service due to jealousy or other types of malicious motives. Consequently a trustworthy peer may end up getting a large number of false statements and may be evaluated incorrectly even though it provides satisfactory service in every transaction.

We introduce the credibility of feedback as a basic trust building parameter, which is equally important as the number of transactions and the feedback. The feedback from those peers with higher credibility should be weighted more than those with lower credibility. We have developed two mechanisms for measuring the credibility of a peer in providing feedback. The concrete formulas will be discussed later.

Transaction Context Factor

Transaction context is another important factor when aggregating the feedback from each transaction as we have discussed earlier because of the context and location awareness of mobile transactions. For example, when a mobile user is trying to compare potential services, the previous feedback from a mobile user who was using the same device and was in the same location to access the service should be weighted more than those from a regular user accessing the service from a desktop computer at home.

Other general transaction context such as the value and functionality are also important. For example, the size of a transaction should be incorporated to give more weight to the feedback from larger transactions. It can act as a defense against some of the subtle malicious attacks, such as when a seller develops a good reputation by being honest for small transactions and tries to make a profit by being dishonest for large transactions. It can be seen as a simplified mechanism for more sophisticated risk management in e-commerce (Manchala, 2000).

Community Context Factor

Community contexts can be used to address non-transaction specific issues. One example is to add a reward for peers who submit feedback. This can to some extent alleviate the feedback incentive problem. As another example, it can be also used to incorporate historical information, and reputation from other applications or communities.

General Trust Metric

We have discussed the importance of each of the five trust parameters. In this section we formalize these parameters, present a general trust metric that combines these parameters in a coherent scheme, and describe the formula we use to compute the values for each of the parameters given a peer and the community it belongs to.

Given a recent time window, let $I(u,v)$ denote the total number of Interactions performed by peer u with v, $I(u)$ denote the total number of interactions performed by peer u with all other peers, $p(u,i)$ denote the other participating peer in peer u's ith transaction, $S(u,i)$ denote the normalized amount of Satisfaction peer u receives from $p(u,i)$ in its ith transaction, $Cr(v)$ denote the Credibility of the feedback submitted by v, $TF(u,i)$ denote the adaptive Transaction context Factor for peer u's ith transaction, and $CF(u)$ denote the adaptive Community context Factor for peer u. Let α and β denote the normalized weight factors, the Trust value of peer u, denoted by $T(u)$, is defined as follows:

$$T(u) = \alpha * \frac{\sum_{i=1}^{I(u)} S(u,i)*(Cr(p(u,i))*TF(u,i))}{\sum_{i=1}^{I(u)} Cr(p(u,i))*TF(u,i)} + \beta * CF(u)$$

The first term is a weighted average of amount of satisfaction a peer receives for each transaction. The weight $(Cr(p(u,i))*TF(u,i))$ takes into account the credibility of feedback source to counter dishonest feedback, and transaction context to capture the transaction-dependent characteristics. This history-based evaluation can be seen as a prediction for peer u's likelihood of a successful transaction in the future. A confidence value can be computed and associated with the trust metric that may reflect the number of transactions, and the standard deviation of the ratings depending on different communities and requirements. The second term adjusts the first term by an increase or decrease of the trust value based on community-specific characteristics. The α and β parameters can be used to assign different weights to the feedback-based evaluation and community context in different situations. For instance, they can be assigned properly so the trust value is set to be either the feedback-based evaluation when the peer has enough transactions or a default value otherwise.

Important to note is that this general trust metric may have different appearances depending on which of the parameters are turned on and how the parameters and weight factors are set. The design choices depend on characteristics of online communities. It is a non-trivial problem to choose the optimal parameters in practice. Different users may also choose different settings based on their own preferences and have their own view of the universe. We emphasize that the first three parameters — the feedback, the number of transactions, and the credibility of feedback source are important basic trust parameters that should be considered in computing a peer's trustworthiness in any communities. We illustrate next how the basic parameters can be collected or determined and how the adaptive parameters can be set.

The Basic Metric

We first consider the basic form of the general metric as shown below by turning off the transaction context factor $(TF(u,i)=1)$ and the community context factor $(\alpha=1$ and $\beta=0)$. It computes the trust value of a peer u by a weighted average of the amount of satisfaction peer u receives for each transaction.

$$T(u) = \frac{\sum_{i=1}^{I(u)} S(u,i)*Cr(p(u,i))}{\sum_{i=1}^{I(u)} Cr(p(u,i))}$$

The feedback in terms of amount of satisfaction is collected by a feedback system. PeerTrust uses a transaction-based feedback system, where the feedback is bound to each transaction. The system solicits feedback after each transaction and the two participating peers give feedback about each other based on the transaction. Feedback systems differ with each other in their feedback format. They can use a positive format, a negative format, a numeric rating or a mixed format. *S(u,i)* is a normalized amount of satisfaction between 0 and 1 that can be computed based on the feedback.

Both the feedback and the number of transactions are quantitative measures and can be collected automatically. Different from these two, the third parameter — credibility of feedback — is a qualitative measure and needs to be computed based on past behavior of peers who file feedback. Different approaches can be used to determine the credibility factor and compute the credible amount of satisfaction. One way is to solicit separate feedback for feedback themselves. This makes the reputation system more complex and adds more burdens on users. A simpler approach is to infer or compute the credibility value of a peer implicitly. We discuss two such credibility measures.

The first one is to use a function of the trust value of a peer as its credibility factor recursively so feedback from trustworthy peers are considered more credible and thus weighted more than those from untrustworthy peers. We refer to the basic trust metric that uses the Trust Value of a peer recursively as its credibility Measure as PeerTrust TVM metric and it is defined as follows:

$$T(u) = \frac{\sum_{i=1}^{I(u)} S(u,i) * T(p(u,i))}{\sum_{i=1}^{I(u)} T(p(u,i))}$$

This solution is based on two assumptions. First, untrustworthy peers are more likely to submit false or misleading feedback in order to hide their own malicious behavior. Second, trustworthy peers are more likely to be honest on the feedback they provide. It is widely recognized that the first assumption is generally true but the second assumption may not be true at all time. For example, it is possible that a peer may maintain a good reputation by performing high quality services but send malicious feedback to its competitors. In this extreme case, using a function of trust value to approximate the credibility of feedback will generate errors. This is because the reputation-based trust in PeerTrust model is established in terms of the quality of service provided by peers, rather than the quality of the feedback filed by peers.

The second credibility measure is for a peer *w* to use a personalized similarity measure to rate the credibility of another peer *v* through *w*'s personalized experience. Concretely, peer *w* will use a personalized similarity between itself and another peer *v* to weight the feedback by *v* on any other peers. Let *IS(v)* denote the Set of peers that have Interacted with peer *v*. To measure the feedback credibility of peer *v*, peer *w* computes the feedback similarity between *w* and *v* over *IS(v)* ∩ *IS(w)*, the common set of peers they have interacted with in the past. If we model the feedback by *v* and the feedback by *w* over the common set of peers as two vectors, the credibility can be defined as the similarity between the two feedback vectors. Particularly, we use the root-mean-square or standard deviation (dissimilarity) of the two feedback vectors to compute the feedback similarity. We refer to the basic metric that uses the Personalized Similarity as the credibility Measure as PeerTrust PSM metric and it is defined as follows:

$$T(u) = \frac{\sum_{i=1}^{I(u)} S(u,i) * Sim(p(u,i), w)}{\sum_{i=1}^{I(u)} Sim(p(u,i), w)}$$

where

$$Sim(v, w) = 1 - \sqrt{\frac{\sum_{x \in IS(v) \cap IS(w)} (\frac{\sum_{i=1}^{I(x,v)} S(x,i)}{I(x,v)} - \frac{\sum_{i=1}^{I(x,w)} S(x,i)}{I(x,w)})^2}{|IS(v) \cap IS(w)|}}.$$

This notion of local or personalized credibility measure provides great deal of flexibility and stronger predictive value as the feedback from similar raters are given more weight. It may also act as an effective defense against potential malicious collusions. Given the observation that peers in a collusive group give good ratings within the group and bad ratings outside the group, the feedback similarity between a peer v in the collusive group and a peer w outside the group will be low, which will effectively filter out the dishonest feedback by peer v for peer w.

Given that one of the design goals of PeerTrust model is to emphasize the roles of different trust parameters in computing trustworthiness of peers, in the rest of the chapter we will use the above two measures as examples and study their effectiveness, benefit and vulnerabilities. We believe that the study of what determines the precision of credibility of feedback is by itself an interesting and hard research problem that deserves attention of its own.

Adapting the Trust Metric with Context Factors

We have discussed the motivations and scenarios for incorporating the adaptive context factors into our general trust metric. In this section we give two examples of adapting the metric using the transaction and community context factor respectively.

Incorporating Transaction Contexts by Transaction Context Factor

Various transaction contexts, such as the size, category, or time stamp of the transaction and the location information of the transacting peer can be incorporated into the metric. For example, an adapted metric that incorporates the size of a transaction i in terms of the Dollar amount of the payment, denoted by $D(u,i)$, is defined below so the feedback for larger transactions are assigned more weight than those for smaller ones:

$$T(u) = \frac{\sum_{i=1}^{I(u)} S(u,i) * Cr(p(u,i)) * D(u,i)}{\sum_{i=1}^{I(u)} Cr(p(u,i)) * D(u,i)}$$

Providing Incentives to Rate by Community Context Factor

Several remedies have been suggested to the incentive problem of reputation systems such as market-based approaches and policy-based approach in which users will not receive rating information without paying or providing ratings. However, implementing these approaches might stifle the growth of online communities and fledgling electronic markets. In PeerTrust, the incentive problem of reputation systems can be alleviated by building incentives or rewards into the metric through community context factor for peers who provide feedback to others. An adapted metric can be defined below with a reward as a function of the ratio of total number of Feedback peer u give others, denoted as $F(u)$, over the total number of transactions peer u has during the recent time window. The weight factors can be tuned to control the amount of reputation that can be gained by rating others.

$$T(u) = \alpha * \frac{\sum_{i=1}^{I(u)} S(u,i) * Cr(p(u,i))}{\sum_{i=1}^{I(u)} Cr(p(u,i))} + \beta * \frac{F(u)}{I(u)}$$

Evaluation

We performed some initial experiments to evaluate PeerTrust model and show its feasibility, effectiveness, and benefits. The first one evaluates effectiveness of PeerTrust model in terms of its computation error against malicious manipulations of peers in two settings. The second one demonstrates the importance and benefit of supporting reputation based trust in a P2P community by allowing peers to avoid untrustworthy peers using the reputation based trust scheme.

Simulation Setup

Our initial simulated community consists of N peers and N is set to be 128 in most experiments. The game theory research on reputation introduced two types of players

(Dellarocas, 2003). One is commitment type or a long-run player who would always cooperate because cooperation is the action that maximizes the player's lifetime payoffs if the player could credibly commit to an action for the entire duration. In contrast, a strategic type corresponds to an opportunistic player who cheats whenever it is advantageous for him to do. We split peers into these two types in our simulation, namely, good peers and strategic or malicious peers. The percentage of malicious peers is denoted by k. We have one experiment with varying k to show its effect and otherwise k is set to be 25%.

The behavior pattern for good peers is to always cooperate in transactions and provide honest feedback afterwards. While it is a challenging task to model peers' malicious behavior realistically, we start with two malicious behavior patterns to study the robustness of PeerTrust metrics, namely non-collusive setting and collusive setting. In non-collusive setting, malicious peers cheat during transactions and give dishonest ratings to other peers, that is, give bad rating to a peer who cooperates and give good rating to a peer who cheats. A malicious peer may choose to occasionally cooperate in order to confuse other peers and fool the system. We use *mrate* to model the rate that a malicious peer acts maliciously. We have one experiment varying *mrate* to show its effect on trust computation effectiveness, and otherwise *mrate* is set to 100%. In collusive setting, malicious peers act similarly to those in non-collusive setting, and in addition, they form a collusive group and deterministically help each other by performing numerous fake transactions and give good ratings to each other.

We use a binary feedback system where a peer rates the other peer either 0 or 1 according to whether the transaction is satisfactory. The number of transactions each peer has during the latest time window, denoted by I, is set to be 100 for all peers. For comparison purpose, we compare PeerTrust metrics to the conventional approach, referred to as Conventional, in which an average of the ratings is used to measure the trustworthiness of a peer without taking into account the credibility factor. All experiment results are averaged over five runs of the experiments.

Effectiveness against Malicious Behaviors of Peers

The objective of this set of experiments is to evaluate the effectiveness and robustness of the trust metrics against malicious behaviors of peers. The experiments proceeds as peers perform random transactions with each other. After 6,400 transactions in the community, that is, an average of 100 transactions for each peer, a good peer is selected to evaluate the trustworthiness of all other peers. Each experiment is performed under both non-collusive and collusive settings described earlier. We compute the trust computation error as the root-mean-square (RMS) of the computed trust value of all peers and the actual likelihood of peers performing a satisfactory transaction, which is 1 for good peers and (1-*mrate*) for malicious peers. A lower RMS indicates a better performance.

For the first experiment, we vary the percentage of malicious peers (k) and set the malicious rate to 1 (*mrate*=1). Figure 1 represents the trust computation error of different PeerTrust algorithms and the conventional approach with respect to k in the two settings.

Figure 1. Trust computation error with respect to percentage of malicious peers in non-collusive setting (left) and collusive setting (right)

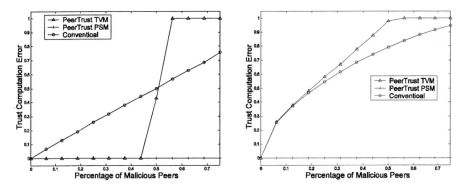

We can make a number of interesting observations in the non-collusive setting. First, the performance of the conventional approach drops almost linearly when k increases. Without taking into account the credibility of feedback source, it is very sensitive to malicious peers who provide dishonest feedback. Second, PeerTrust TVM stays effective when k is less than 50%. Using trust values of peers recursively as the weight for their feedback, they are able to filter out dishonest feedback and make correct trust computations. However, the error becomes 100% when k is greater than 50%, which indicates they completely make wrong evaluations by mistaking good peers as untrustworthy and malicious peers as trustworthy. This is particularly interesting because it shows that malicious peers are able to fool the system by overriding the honest feedback provided by good peers when they are the majority. Last, PeerTrust PSM stays effective even with a large percentage of malicious peers. This confirms that the personalized similarity based credibility acts as a very effective measure to filter out dishonest feedback. The collusive setting also presents interesting observations. Both conven-

Figure 2. Trust computation error with respect to malicious rate of malicious peers in non-collusive setting (left) and collusive setting (right)

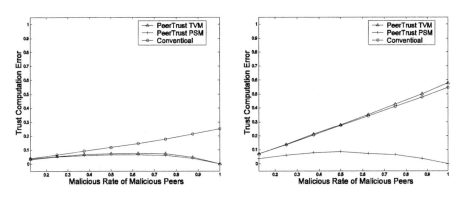

tional metric and PeerTrust TVM metric are extremely sensitive to collusive attempts that dishonestly provide feedback even when the number of malicious peers is very small. On the other hand, PeerTrust PSM metric, as we have expected, acts as a very effective defense against collusion by filtering out dishonest feedback from the collusive group.

For the second experiment, we vary the malicious rate (*mrate*) and set the percentage of malicious peers to 25% (*k*=25%). Figure 2 compares the trust computation error of PeerTrust metrics and the conventional metric with respect to *mrate* in the two settings. Again we can make a number of interesting observations in both settings. First, the performance of the conventional approach drops when *mrate* increases. Second, both PeerTrust TVM and PSM metrics have a slightly dropped performance when the malicious rate is less than 100%. This indicates that malicious peers are able to confuse the system a little when they occasionally cooperate and give honest feedback. The collusive setting shows similar results but to a larger extent.

Benefit of Trust Based Peer Selection

This set of experiments demonstrates the benefit of using a reputation based trust system in which peers compare the trustworthiness of peers and choose the peer with the highest trust value to interact with. A transaction is considered successful if both of the participating peers cooperate. We define successful transaction rate as the ratio of the number of successful transactions over the total number of transactions in the community up to a certain time. A community with a higher transaction success rate has a higher productivity and a stronger level of security. The experiment proceeds by repeatedly having randomly selected good peers initiating transactions. In a community that has a reputation system, the source peer selects the peer with the highest trust value to perform the transaction. Otherwise it randomly selects a peer. The two peers then perform the transaction and the transaction succeeds only if the selected peer cooperates. The experiment is performed in both non-collusive setting and collusive setting. We show the benefit of utilizing a reputation based trust system that uses conventional and PeerTrust metrics compared to a community without any trust system.

Figure 3 shows the transaction success rate with regard to the number of transactions in the community in the two settings. In the non-collusive setting, we can see an obvious gain of the transaction success rate in communities equipped with a trust mechanism. This confirms that supporting trust is an important feature, as peers are able to avoid untrustworthy peers. We can also see different trust metrics benefit the community to a different extent. This shows a similar comparison to the previous experiment. It is worth noting, however, that the system using conventional metric achieves a transaction success rate close to 100% even though its trust computation error is much higher than 0, shown in Figure 1. This is because even if the computed trust values do not reflect accurately the likelihood of the peers being cooperative, they do differentiate good peers from bad peers in most cases by the relative ranking. In the collusive setting, we can see that the transaction success rate is 0 for the system using conventional and PeerTrust TVM metric. This indicates that malicious peers are able to completely fool these trust schemes by collusion and render the system useless, even worse than the system without

Figure 3. Benefit of reputation based trust scheme in non-collusive (left) and collusive setting (right)

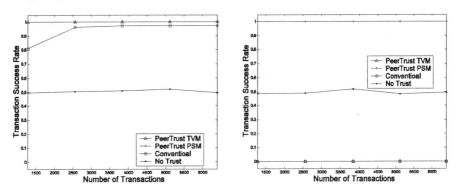

a trust scheme. However, the system still benefits from PeerTrust PSM metric significantly and shows robustness against the collusion.

Conclusion and Future Trends

We discussed reputation and trust and described PeerTrust model for building reputation based trust systems for e-commerce including m-commerce applications. It alleviates or avoids some of the security risks we discussed earlier by helping participants to choose reputable participants and avoid untrustworthy ones. For example, the simplest version of a virus attack would be that an adversary delivers a virus to a good peer or member. With a reputation based trust mechanism in place, the peer who receives the malicious content will be able to submit a negative feedback about the malicious peer and help other peers to avoid it in the future.

Not surprisingly, a reputation-based trust mechanism also introduces vulnerabilities and problems by itself. Common attacks are known as shilling attacks, where adversaries attack the system by submitting fake or misleading ratings to confuse the system as we have discussed earlier. Further, participants can amount attacks on the trust management system by distributing tampered with trust information. PeerTrust tries to minimize such security weaknesses. For example, the use of the credibility factor of the feedback source can be seen as an effective step towards handling fake or misleading ratings. The ability to incorporate various transaction and community contexts can also act against some of the subtle attacks. Furthermore, by combining the proposed trust metric and the secure trust data transmission built on top of public key cryptographic algorithms, it prevents distribution of tampered with trust information and man in the middle attack.

There remain many interesting research problems, some of which are listed below:

- *Collusion among participants.* Unfortunately there is so far no mechanism that can completely prevent this type of attack. Developing mechanisms that are robust to collusion among participants is currently an active area for research.

- *Lack of portability of reputation between systems.* This limits the effectiveness of reputation systems. For example, if a mobile user travels to a foreign network, he or she would become a newcomer in that network and lose all his/her reputation in his or her home network. Efforts are currently underway to construct a more universal framework in e-commerce research. However, it is yet to receive a global acceptance.

- *Get rid of bad history through reentry.* Another risk mainly in the P2P community is that peers can easily discard their old identity and adopt a new one through reentry to get rid of the bad history. Potentially there are two classes of approaches to this issue: either make it more difficult to change online identities, or structure the community in such a way that exit and reentry with a new identity becomes unprofitable (Friedman, 2001).

- *One-time attack.* The proposed trust building techniques are based on experiences. Therefore, a peer that has been consistently reliable can perform an unavoidable one-time attack. Although trust metrics can be adapted to quickly detect a malicious participant's bad behavior, it is very hard if not impossible to fully prevent this type of attack.

We believe efforts for promoting reputation and trust play an important role in m-commerce security, which is a key to the acceptance and general deployment of m-commerce applications.

Acknowledgments

We would like to thank the reviewer of this chapter and the editors of the book for their valuable comments.

This work is partially supported by the National Science Foundation under an CISE ITR grant, an CISE CCR grant, a grant from DoE SciDAC. Any opinions, findings, and conclusions or recommendations expressed in this material are those of the author(s) and do not necessarily reflect the views of the National Science Foundation or DoE.

References

Chari, S., Kermani, P., Smith, S., & Tassiulas, L. (2001). Security issues in m-commerce: A usage-based taxonomy. *E-Commerce Agents, LNAI 2033*, 264-282.

Dellarocas, C. (2001). Analyzing the economic efficiency of eBay-like online reputation reporting mechanisms. *3rd ACM Conference on Electronic Commerce*.

Dellarocas, C. (2003). The digitization of word-of-mouth: Promise and challenges of online reputation mechanism. *Management Science, 49*(10), 1407-1424.

Friedman, E., & Resnick, P. (2001). The social cost of cheap pseudonyms. *Journal of Economics and Management Strategy, 10*(1), 173-199.

Manchala, D.W. (2000). E-commerce trust metrics and models. *IEEE Internet Computing, 4*(2), 36-44.

Resnick, P., Zeckhauser, R., Friedman, E., & Kuwabara, K. (2000). Reputation systems. *Communications of the ACM, 43*(12), 45-48.

Varshney, U., & Vetter, R. (2002). Mobile commerce: Framework, applications and networking support. *ACM/Kluwer Journal on Mobile Networks and Applications, 7*(3), 185-198.

Xiong, L., & Liu, L. (2003). A reputation-based trust model for peer-to-peer eCommerce communities. *IEEE Conference on Electronic Commerce*.

Endnotes

[1] PalmOS/Phage.963 virus. *http://vil.nai.com/vil/content/v_98836.htm*

[2] PalmOS/LibertyCrack virus. *http http://vil.nai.com/vil/content/v_98801.htm*

[3] Funny SMS Messages. *http://www.free-sms-messages.com/viruses.html*

[4] Wireless Application Protocol Forum. WAP Wireless Transport Layer Security. Version 06-Apr-2001.

[5] Wireless Application Protocol Forum. WAP Public Key Infrastructure. Version 24-Apr-2001.

Chapter III

Intrusion Detection and Vulnerability Analysis of Mobile Commerce Platform

Changhua Zhu, Xidian University, China

Changxing Pei, Xidian University, China

Abstract

Intrusion detection and vulnerability analysis play the same important roles in wireless infrastructure as in wired infrastructure. In this chapter we briefly present the methods and technologies of intrusion detection and vulnerability analysis. Then we give the security issues in various wireless networking technologies, analyze the vulnerability of the enabling technologies for the mobile commerce platform, and propose a distributed wireless intrusion detection & vulnerability analysis (WID&VA) system that can help to address the identified security issues. Finally, we conclude this chapter and discuss the future trends.

Introduction

Combining with current wireless communications infrastructure, wireless computing infrastructure and mobile middleware, mobile commerce provides consumers with secure, faster and personalized services and is becoming one of the most important wireless applications. Mobile commerce is a vast area of activity comprised of transactions with monetary value conducted via a mobile device. These transactions may involve intangible goods, such as applications and information delivered to the mobile device in digital format, as well as tangible goods that are purchased using the mobile device but delivered separately. More and more people prefer m-commerce services and enjoy themselves by these prompt services.

On the other hand, compared with wired networks, wireless networks have no central control scheme and determinate boundary, which provide many chances for the intruders to attack the networks. Mobile data can be copied, sniffed, or lost. Wireless terminals and network platforms can also be deceived, and attacked passively (decryption) or actively (unauthorized communications).

Typical systems of wireless infrastructure for m-commerce platform include cellular networks (e.g., GSM), WLAN (wireless local area networks, e.g., IEEE 802.11), wireless MAN (metropolitan area networks, e.g., IEEE 802.16), HomeRF, WPAN (wireless personal area networks, e.g., Bluetooth) and the combination of them (e.g., GPRS (general packet radio service) /WLAN). In GSM circuit-switched data (CSD), GPRS and EDGE (enhanced data rates for global evolution), the A5 algorithm is applied to encrypt the radio link data and the A3/A8 algorithm is applied for the authentication. There exists a common weakness that has been reported that both A5 encryption algorithm and A3/A8 authentication algorithm can be easily broken. This means that the attacker can calculate the private key of a consumer and duplicate the SIM (subscriber identity module) card. In GSM, there is no authentication against networks, no end-to-end security scheme, and no explicit integrity protection on the air link. Barkan, Biham, and Keller (Barkan, Biham & Keller, 2003) from Technion Institute of Technology in Haifa (Israel) described a ciphertext-only attack on A5/2 that requires a few dozen milliseconds of encrypted off-the-air cellular conversation and finds the correct key in less than a second on a personal computer. They described new attacks on the protocols of networks that use A5/1, A5/3 or even GPRS. UMTS has explicit integrity protection on the air link, uses the publicly reviewed encryption algorithm (KASUMI), conducts the authentication between mobile terminal and network, and encrypts transmitted data within a base station. However, UMTS has not been widely implemented and will not be likely accepted worldwide in the near future. In addition, with the increasing capability of the intruders, new security weaknesses of wireless cellular networks may be discovered.

The wireless application protocol (WAP) offers additional and advanced layers of security, where wireless identity module (WIM) may carry asymmetric keys, certificates, and perform WTLS (wireless transport layer security) authentication and signature operations. The WAP has a special security layer, WTLS, in the WAP protocol stack, and it supports PKI (public key infrastructure). However, it is well known that decryption and re-encryption between WTLS and SSL/TLS (secure sockets layer/transport layer security) occur in the WAP gateway. This means that the data are exposed to intruders. The intruders can access private authorization information through packet sniffing (so-called WAP GAP).

WLAN is easy to be broken-in because the network must send beacon frame with information that can be used by hackers, and this provides necessary clues for intrusion. Intruders can penetrate into the WLAN anywhere by using high sensitivity antennas. Subscribers might be deceived by unauthorized APs (access points). Because of limited bandwidth, the resource of WLAN may be exhausted by non-authorized traffic, and APs can be blocked. This is a so-called DoS (denial of services) attack. Fluhrer, Mantin and Shamir analyze the weakness of RC4 stream cipher that is applied to traffic between wireless access points and stations by WEP (wired equivalent protocol) and declare that WEP can be cracked within 15 minutes (Fluhrer, Mantin & Shamir, 2001). On the other hand, WEP can merely protect the initial data of the subscriber and network. It cannot encrypt the supervision and control frames. Therefore, it provides chances of being deceived by fraud frames. In addition, many subscribers have not really implemented WEP although it is a default option in many WLAN products. This allows an intruder to easily puzzle the ARP table, to obtain the MAC address, to find the existence of AP, and to perform vicious attacks in absence of selection of encryption code and authentication method together with the possibility of wireless data being captured and modified.

There is no such thing as a 100% secure system and there is no silver bullet (Lee, 2003). Some computer security breaches cannot be prevented using access and information flow control techniques. These breaches may be a consequence of system software bugs, hardware or software failures, incorrect system administration procedures, or failure of the system authentication. Cryptographic methods have their own problems. Passwords can be cracked, users can lose their passwords, and entire crypto-systems can be broken. Even a truly secure system is vulnerable to abuse by insiders who abuse their privileges. It has been seen that the relationship between the level of access control and user efficiency is an inverse one, which means that the stricter the mechanism is, the lower the efficiency becomes. Vicious attackers always seek the flaw of system for various aims and want to intrude on the system deliberately. Given that there is no absolutely secure system, intrusion detection and vulnerability analysis are very important, particularly for wireless applications such as mobile commerce.

Intrusion detection techniques can play a significant role in the detection of computer misuse in such cases. An intrusion is defined by Heady et al. (Heady et al., 1990) as any set of actions that attempt to compromise the integrity, confidentiality, or availability of a resource. An earlier study done by Anderson (Anderson, 1980) uses the term "threat" in the same sense and defines it to be the potential possibility of a deliberate unauthorized attempt to access information, manipulate information, or render a system unreliable or unusable. The objectives of intrusion detection include: identify intruders (unauthorized access, misuse by internal personnel or external person); distinguish intrusion behaviors from normal behaviors; detect and monitor successful break-in; and provide immediate information for counterworking. Vulnerability is defined as a design flaw, defect or misconfiguration that can be exploited by an attacker. Vulnerability analysis is a process to check the security state of a system and its components. Vulnerability analysis system can scan and analyze network system (servers, routers, fireworks, operation system, network application processes), test and report weakness and vulnerability before hacker, and suggest the remediation and security methods. It strengthens network security. Vulnerability scanners focus on static configuration, while intrusion detection searches temporary misuse or anomaly scenarios. Vulnerability scanners can search a known NFS (network file system) weakness through checking services and configuration of a remote system and make administrators find the weakness or holes before intrusion occurs. But for the same weakness, an intrusion detection system cannot report this until attackers attempt to utilize this weakness. So, wireless intrusion detection and vulnerability analysis must be strongly enforced by network administrator for secure m-commerce platforms.

In this chapter we will briefly present various methods and technologies of intrusion detection and vulnerability analysis in wired and wireless networks. Then we give the security issues in various wireless networking technologies, analyze the vulnerability of the enabling technologies for the mobile commerce platform, and propose a distributed wireless intrusion detection & vulnerability analysis (WID&VA) system to address the identified security issues. And we also show the future trends of intrusion detection and vulnerability analysis of m-commerce platform.

Intrusion Detection

There are two types of methods for intrusion detection: one is misuse detection, and the other is anomaly detection.

Misuse Detection

The concept behind misuse detection schemes is that there are ways to represent attacks in the form of a pattern or a signature so that even variations of the same attack can be detected. This means that these systems are not unlike virus detection systems — they can detect many or all known attack patterns, but they are of little use for as yet unknown attack methods. An interesting point to note is that anomaly detection systems try to detect the complement of "bad" behavior. Misuse detection systems try to recognize known "bad" behavior. The main issues in misuse detection systems are how to write a signature that encompasses all possible variations of the pertinent attack, and how to write signatures that do not also match non-intrusive activity.

Misuse detection looks primarily for recognized patterns of attack. The major methods can be given as follows: rule-based production/expert systems (Bace, 2000), state transition analysis (Ilgun, Kemmerer & Porras, 1995), model-based intrusion detection (Garvey & Lunt, 1991), pattern matching (Kumar, 1995; Kumar & Spafford, 1994), using conditional probability to predict misuse intrusions (Kumar, 1995), keystroke monitoring (Sundaram, 1996), and information retrieval (Anderson & Khattak, 1998). Table 1 shows the main idea of each misuse detection method.

Anomaly Detection

Anomaly detection techniques assume that all intrusive activities are necessarily anomalous. This means that if we could establish a "normal activity profile" for a system, we could, in theory, flag all system states varying from the established profile by statistically significant amounts as intrusion attempts. However, if we consider that the set of intrusive activities only intersects the set of anomalous activities instead of being exactly the same, we find a couple of possibilities: (1) Anomalous activities that are not intrusive are flagged as intrusive. (2) Intrusive activities that are not anomalous result in false negatives (events are not flagged intrusive, though they actually are). This is a dangerous problem, and is far more serious than the problem of false positives. The main issues in anomaly detection systems thus become the selection of threshold levels so that neither of the above two problems is unreasonably magnified, and the selection of features to monitor. Anomaly detection systems are also computationally expensive because of the overhead of keeping track of, and possibly updating several system profile metrics.

Anomaly detection searches for deviations from normal user or system behavior patterns, from usage of computer or network resources. The major methods can be given as follows: statistical methods (Lunt, Tamaru & Gilham, 1992), haystack (Smaha, 1988), feature selection (Crosbie & Spafford, 1995; Doak, 1992), Bayesian statistics (Cheuing, et al., 1999; Farshchi, 2003), Bayesian classification (Cheeseman, Stutz & Hanson, 1991), time-based inductive machine (Teng, Chen & Lu, 1990), instance based learning techniques (Lane & Broadley, 1999), neural networks (Fox et al., 1990; Ryan, Lin & Miikkulainen, 1998), support vector machine method (Nguyen, 2002), information-theoretic measures (Lee & Xiang, 2001), and so forth. Table 2 shows the main idea of each anomaly detection method.

Other methods belong to neither misuse nor anomaly detection methods, several of which are as follows: artificial immune theory (Forrest et al., 1997; Hofmeyr, Forrest & Somayaji, 1998), genetic algorithm (Crosbie & Spafford, 1995), data mining (Lee, 1999), and so forth. Another interesting method is honey pot. It traps tempt intruders into areas which appear attractive, worth investigating and easy to access, taking them away from the really sensitive areas of the systems (The Honeynet Project, 2003).

Table 1. Misuse detection methods illustration

Misuse detection methods	Main idea
Rule-based expert system	If-then rules sets. If part: the conditions requisite for an attack
State transition analysis	Attacks are represented as a sequence of state transitions of the monitored system
Model-based	Combines models of misuse with evidential reasoning
Pattern matching	Encodes known intrusion signatures as patterns that are matched against audit data
Conditional probability	Analyzes the conditional probability, P(Intrusion I event pattern), of a sequence of external events
Keystroke monitoring	Pattern match for specific keystroke sequences that indicate an attack
Information retrieval	Uses information retrieval techniques to index audit trails

Table 2. Anomaly detection methods illustration

Anomaly detection methods	Main idea
Statistical method	Observes the behavior of subjects and generates profiles for them, and anomaly detector generates the variance of the present profile from the original.
Feature selection	Determines the subset that accurately predicts or classifies intrusions given a set of heuristically chosen measures.
Bayesian statistics	Estimates the conditional probability with which anomaly intrusion occurs by using Bayes' theorem from n measures.
Bayesian classification	By using Bayesian classification, the data collected are divided into different classes, which are applied to infer anomaly users and events.
Time-based inductive machine	Uses a time-based inductive machine to capture users' behavior patterns that are expected to provide prediction for anomaly events.
Instance based learning	Applies instance based learning to learn users' normal behavior from temporal sequence data.
Neural networks	Trains the neural net on a set of representative commands sequences of a user. The variance of the user behavior from his or her profile can predict intrusion.
Support vector machine	Trains the support vector machine on different types of attacks and normal data, then separates normal and intrusive patterns.
Information-theoretic measures	Uses the information theoretic measures, for example entropy, to understand the characteristics of audit data and build anomaly detection models.

Intrusion Detection System

Traditionally, IDS systems are divided into two categories: network-based and host-based IDS. Network-based systems (NIDS) passively or actively listen on the network, and capture and examine individual packet flowing through a network. In contrast to firewalls, NIDS can analyze the entire packet, not just IP addresses and ports. They are able to look at the payload within a packet, to see which particular host application is being accessed, and with what options, and to raise alerts when an attacker tries to exploit a bug in such code, by detecting known attack signatures. Host-based intrusion detection systems (HIDS) are concerned with what is happening on each individual host. They are able to detect actions such as repeated failed access attempts or changes to critical system files, and normally operate by accessing log files or monitoring real-time system usage. To ensure effective operation, host-based IDS clients have to be installed on every host on the network, tailored to specific host configuration. Host-based IDS do not depend on network bandwidth, but are used for smaller networks, where each host dedicates processing power towards the task of system monitoring. As mentioned, these systems are host dependent, and can considerably slow down the hosts that have IDS clients installed.

In order to interoperation of various IDS products, components and other security products, DARPA (The Defense Advanced Research Projects Agency) and IDWG (Intrusion Detection Working Group) of IETF (Internet Engineering Task Force) proposed a series of drafts of IDS, which include IDMEF (intrusion detection message exchange format), IDXP (intrusion detection exchange protocol) and tunnel profile (Curry & Debar, 2003; Feinstein, Matthews & White, 2002).

Vulnerability Analysis

Vulnerabilities in a system can generally be broken down into five categories: physical/
environmental, network/connectivity, platform/operating system, application/service,
and human/policy. The vulnerabilities that come from these five categories always act
together, which adds the burden of vulnerability evaluation. A good vulnerability
scanner should be able to detect all well-known vulnerabilities and should be easily
updated when new vulnerabilities are identified. In addition, a vulnerability scanner
should itself be well protected and resistant to subversion, as it could be altered by an
intruder to give false results. Common scanning tools include: Security Profile Inspector
(SPI), Internet Security Scanner (ISS), Security Analysis Tool for Auditing Networks
(SATAN), Tiger, Sscan, Nmap, Computer Oracle and Password System (COPS), Tripwire,
and so forth.

Network-Based and Host-Based Vulnerability Scanners

There are generally two types of vulnerability scanning tools: network-based and host-
based (Shostack & Blake, 1999). Network-based scanning tools send probe traffic to
various network hosts and devices with the goal of gathering information that will
indicate whether those systems have holes that can be exploited. They work by checking
the network interfaces of remote systems, searching the vulnerable services and
reporting possible vulnerability, for example port scanners, war dialers, and weakness
scanning for special applications and services. Network-based vulnerability scanners
depend on signatures or fingerprints. If new vulnerability occurs, an attacker can intrude
the network before the signature is renewed. Host-based scanning tools run on each host
to scan for a wide range of system problems, including: unauthorized software, unauthorized accounts, unprotected logins, weak passwords, dormant viruses, and inappropriate
access permissions. A would-be intruder endeavors to exploit these types of vulnerabilities in an attempt to compromise the integrity, confidentiality, or availability of a
resource. Host-based scanning tools are applied to audit the security weakness of hosts
or servers related, for example configuration of using limit of hosts or servers, security
schemes, shared file systems, and so forth.

Credentialed and Non-Credentialed Methods for
Vulnerability Analysis

According to the way by which related information is obtained, the methods of
vulnerability analysis can be divided into two categories (Bace, 2000). One is credentialed, and the other is non-credentialed. The difference between them is how the
information is obtained (credential or non-credential). The credentialed methods assumed that some access to system, for example using the data resources, such as file
contents, configuration information and status information, are legal. The information

is obtained from resources that have not been broken-in, in other words, from state query and profile checking for standard system. The advantage of the credentialed method is that it can quickly find the backdoors, strange data files and other traces left by hackers. In addition it is more accurate and reliable than the non-credentialed method. Vulnerability analyzer works by using non-credentialed method, acts as attacker, and marks and records the system response for these attacks. It can monitor user and network behaviors and assess vulnerability related with network services. The advantages of the non-credentialed method are that it is independent of platforms, and a single analyzer can support multiple OS platforms.

Vulnerability Analysis Systems

Qu et al. (Qu et al., 2002) present an agent based network vulnerability analysis framework and show how the framework can be used to analyze and quantify the system vulnerability under a distributed denial of service (DDOS) attack scenario. Their approach can be described in terms of three steps: (1) *vulnerability metrics* – identify the metrics to be used to analyze the network vulnerability; (2) *system state characterization* – define the thresholds to be used to characterize the node/system state to be in one of three states: normal state, uncertain state, and vulnerable state and (3) *vulnerability index evaluation* – evaluate the vulnerability of the network or application with respect to the vulnerability metrics defined in the first step. The vulnerability index can also be used as an indicator to trigger proactive and survivable methodologies to aid fast recovery at the earliest possible stages.

Lye and Wing (Lye & Wing, 2002) present a game-theoretic method for analyzing the security of computer networks. They view the interactions between an attacker and the administrator as a two-player stochastic game and construct a model for the game. Using a non-linear programming, they compute Nash equilibria that give the administrator an idea of the attacker's strategy and a plan for what to do in each state in the event of an attack. Finding more Nash equilibria thus allows the administrator to know more about the attacker's best attack strategies.

Ramakrishnan and Sekar (Ramakrishnan & Sekar, 1998) propose a model-based vulnerability analysis system where the security-related behavior of each system component is modeled in a high-level specification language. These component models can then be composed to obtain all possible behaviors of the entire system. Finding system vulnerability can be implemented by analyzing these behaviors using automated verification techniques to identify scenarios where security-related properties (such as maintaining integrity of password files) are violated. The model-based approach can automatically seek out and identify known and as-yet-unknown vulnerabilities.

Swiler, Phillips and Gaylor (Swiler, Phillips & Gaylor, 1998) propose a graph-based network vulnerability analysis system, which is based on the idea of an attack graph. Each node in the graph represents a possible attack state. A node will usually be some combination of physical machine(s), user access level, and effects of the attack so far, such as placement of Trojan horses or modification of access control. Edges represent a change of state caused by a single action taken by the attacker or actions taken by an unwitting assistant (such as the execution of a Trojan horse). They propose a method that can automatically generate the graph. Once the attack graph has been generated, high-risk attack paths can be determined by using shortest-path algorithm. If a probability or cost is attached to each arc, a shortest-path algorithm can find the attack path with lowest cost or highest probability of success, provided the success probabilities can be modeled as independent. The major advance of this method over other computer-security-risk methods is that it considers the physical network topology in conjunction with the set of attacks.

Distributed Wireless Intrusion Detection & Vulnerability Analysis (WID&VA) System

Intrusion Detection of Wireless Networks

Intrusion detection of wireless network can utilize the foregoing methods applied in wired networks. But intrusion detection in wireless network has characteristics of its own. It must work as the following two tiered: detecting wireless attacks and detecting IP based attacks. The wireless IDS focuses primarily on wireless attacks and does not perform IP-based intrusion detection. We can put a NIDS at the wireless AP (for WLAN infrastructure mode) or at the Gateway GPRS Support Node (GGSN in GPRS) to detect wireless born IP based attacks.

Several wireless network IDS have been proposed, typical systems of which for WLAN are: Whiff intrusion detection system (Ameter, Griffith & Pickett, 2002), WIDZ (WIDZ, 2003), IBM Wireless Intrusion Detection Extension (WIDE) (Lackey, Roths & Goddard, 2003), and so forth. Zhang and Lee outline several fundamental issues with wireless ad hoc networks for intrusion detection and they propose an architecture in which all nodes act as independent IDS sensor and can act independently or cooperatively (Zhang & Lee, 2000). Kachirski and Guha propose a distributed intrusion detection system for ad hoc wireless networks based on mobile agent technology (Kachirski & Guha, 2003). Anjum, Subhadrabandhu and Sarkar consider the signature detection technique and investigate the ability of various routing protocols to facilitate intrusion detection when the attack signatures are completely known (Anjum, Subhadrabandhu & Sarkar, 2003). They show that reactive ad hoc routing protocols suffer from a serious problem due to which it might be difficult to detect intrusions even in the absence of mobility. Mobility makes the problem of detecting intruders harder.

Notare et al. (Notare et al., 2000) present an intrusion detection system in wireless communication networks, and propose adding more security services in order to avoid specific violations, in particular cloning mobile phones. Their main approach to identify fraud calls is to classify the mobile phone users into a set of groups according to their log files in which all relevant characteristics that identify the users are stored, for example where, at what time, and from where the calls were made, and so forth. Samfat and Molva (Samfat & Molva, 1997) propose an intrusion detection architecture for mobile networks (IDAMN) in which the normal user's normal behavior profile (e.g. velocity, place) or signature is built up and intrusion detection can be performed in the visited location and within the duration of a typical call.

Vulnerability Analysis of Wireless Networks

Vulnerability Analysis of WLAN

The current 802.11 standard defines two security protocols: shared key authentication was designed to provide secure access control, and WEP encryption was designed to provide confidentiality. The SSID and station MAC addresses are transmitted in the clear, they do not provide any meaningful security, and are trivially bypassed. There are several security issues with these protocols. Most importantly, WEP and shared key are optional, and turned off by default in Access Points. The 802.11 signal can travel surprisingly large distances from the access point, allowing the hackers to connect from outside the building, such as from a parking lot, or from the street. If, as is often the case, the wireless network is connected directly to a corporate intranet, this gives the hackers direct access to the intranet, bypassing any Internet boundary firewalls. In addition, wireless network operating in ad hoc mode introduces some new security problems that include the following: easy theft of nodes, vulnerability to tampering, limited computational abilities, battery powered operation and transient nature of services and devices, and so forth.

Here let's give a fast look at general attacks to WLAN and possible countermeasures. Generally there are several kinds of attacks, as follows:

- *Sniffing*. Network Stumbler (IEEE 802.11 sniffer, free for Windows platform, Ministumbler for PDA supported by WinCE, and Kismet for Unix) can be applied to sniff nearby AP, show ESSID, and measure the strength of signal whether WEP is used or not. In order to prevent being sniffed the session should be encrypted anywhere, and secure shell (SSH), not telnet, secure copy (SCP) or FTP should be applied. In addition, broadcast function should be closed and unauthorized users should be refused. We hope TKIP (temporal key integrity protocol) will remove these problems.

- *Spoofing and unauthorized access*. Once the attacker knows primitive plain text and encrypted text, he or she may create mendacious message because he/she can easily crack the encryption key used to encrypt the response message. In addition, he or she can also forge MAC address. In order to overcome this problem authentication is needed, such as RADIUS (remote authentication dial-in user service).

- *Network hijack*. Hacker may pretend to be a host, and give response for a known host so that correspondence information can be obtained. It can also pretend to be a rogue AP and obtain useful information of mobile stations. To decrease the probability with which a network is hijacked we can configure static MAC/IP address, check the ARP (address resolution protocol) request, authenticate the user identity by RADIUS, and set up dynamical firewalls.

- *DOS/Flooding attack.* These attacks can incur frequency conflict and interference to a useful signal. In another way large numbers of illegal identities authentication are requested. The result that comes with this is that a legal user cannot utilize the networks. To reduce the influence of DOS/flooding attack all signals in wireless network must be monitored (e.g. using Netstumbler) so that related methods such as changing the frequency channel can be done immediately.

From the foregoing analysis results, combining VPN (virtual private network) technology with WLAN is a good choice. IPsec in VPN can be applied to prevent data from being sniffed and analyzed, and to avoid the attacks based on security holes of the WEP algorithm. In addition, tunneling technology and subscriber authentication can further decrease the security risk of WLAN.

Vulnerability Analysis of Cellular Networks

Problems with GSM security include (Gadaix, 2001): only provides access security; communications and signaling traffic in the fixed network are not protected; does not address active attacks, whereby some network elements (e.g. BTS: base station) can be modified to implement attacks; only as secure as the fixed networks to which they connect; lawful interception only considered as an afterthought; terminal identity cannot be trusted; difficult to upgrade the cryptographic mechanisms; and lack of user visibility (e.g., does not know if encrypted or not). The attacks on GSM networks may include (Gadaix, 2001):

- *Eavesdropping.* This is the capability that the intruder can eavesdrop signaling and data connections associated with other users. The required equipment is a modified MS.

- *Impersonation of a user.* This is the capability whereby the intruder sends signaling and/or user data to the network, in an attempt to make the network believe that they originate from the target user. The required equipment is again a modified MS.

- *Impersonation of the network.* This is the capability whereby the intruder sends signaling and/or user data to the target user, in an attempt to make the target user believe they originate from a genuine network. The required equipment is modified BTS.

- *Man-in-the-middle.* This is the capability whereby the intruder puts itself in between the target user and a genuine network and has the ability to eavesdrop, modify, delete, re-order, replay, and spoof signaling and user data messages exchanged between the two parties. The required equipment is modified BTS in conjunction with a modified MS.

- *Compromising authentication vectors in the network.* The intruder possesses a compromised authentication vector, which may include challenge/response pairs, cipher keys and integrity keys. This data may have been obtained by compromising network nodes or by intercepting signaling messages on network links.

Compared with GSM, 3G provide some changes for secure networks. A change was made to defeat the false base station attack. The security mechanisms include a sequence number that ensures that the mobile can identify the network; key lengths were increased to allow for the possibility of stronger algorithms for encryption and integrity; mechanisms were included to support security within and between networks; security is based within the switch rather than the base station as in GSM. Therefore links are protected between the base station and switch; integrity mechanisms for the terminal identity (IMEI) have been designed in from the start, rather than that introduced late into GSM. Although in 3G systems new authentication and encryption techniques are developed, hackers or attackers will search weakness continuously. There is no absolutely secure system.

WAP Gap and Security Holes in WTLS

Though WTLS is supposed to provide privacy, data integrity and authentication for WAP, there are some potential security problems in it (Mao, Hui & Williams, 2003). The WTLS supports a 40-bit XOR MAC, which works by padding the message with zeros, dividing it into 5-byte blocks and xoring these blocks together. In fact, XOR MAC may be unable to provide the message integrity protection if stream ciphers are used, regardless of the key length. Some of the alert messages used in the protocol are sent in plaintext. An attacker may replace an encrypted datagram with an unauthenticated plaintext alert message with the same sequence number without being detected. There are other security flaws in WTLS such as a chosen plaintext attack, a message forgery attack, and so forth. A sufficient security level is always a compromise between the usability and the strength of the used encryption method. Since WTLS has been developed to support a very wide range of mobile devices, the weakest device cannot support heavy encryption because of the limitations of CPU, memory and bandwidth resources. There is no point in using over 50% of the limited resources for encryption and decryption. For WTLS, the security level is always a trade-off with the usage of limited resources.

WAP 2.0 uses TLS instead of WTLS due to requiring end-to-end security with all-IP based technology in order to overcome the WAP gateway security breaches. WAP 2.0 overcomes this problem by using TLS tunneling to support end-to-end security. Current WIM supports TLS client authentication, and ongoing work to define support for TLS session handling in WIM. The user's key pairs and certificates/certificate ids can be stored in WIM. In addition, WIM also has optional cryptographic functions.

We should collect new information about related m-commerce component such as operation system software, encryption algorithm, authentication scheme, and so forth. New leakages or weakness can be reported, which need to be upgraded, patched, or replaced. With new protocols and new techniques continuously occurring, the success probability of attackers is decreasing, but the risk will always exist. Special guidelines for security management must be built in any network environment.

As wired electronic commerce, the possible threats from inside are important problems in wireless networks. In m-commerce platform, database server must be separated with internal networks and internal firewall should be set up. Web servers and data servers with important data, for example order, customer information, transaction, key, and sensitive information, must be scanned frequently. User identities and passwords should be controlled using special rules. Especially important files and logs should be checked carefully against internal attacks. For internal attacks, detailed and normative security guidelines are necessary.

Distributed WID&VA System

Based on the foregoing discusses we will present a new wireless intrusion detection and vulnerability analysis system for m-commerce platforms. The distributed architecture is adopted in the proposed system. There are two main components: one is remote monitoring station (RMS), and the other is wireless intrusion detection and vulnerability analysis center (WID&VA center). The two components have special communication modules to exchange data and control message, as shown in Figure 1.

Remote monitoring station, as shown in Figure 2, works in the wireless access networks, key nodes, or internal networks of companies, and so forth. That is to say, all the nodes and links, through which data are generated during m-commerce applications, are the objects that need to be monitored. RMS can be deployed on WLAN in a hotel, company, hospital, or school, and so forth. In this scenario, data pre-processing, intrusion detection engine, rules bases generation and maintenance, and local decision engine operate on a mobile station or wired computer connected with access point or base station. We suggest that data mining, artificial immune, and genetic algorithm should be

Figure 1. Distributed wireless intrusion detection & vulnerability analysis system

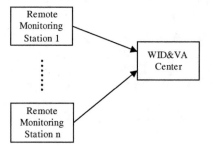

Figure 2. Remote monitoring station

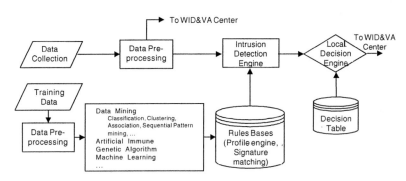

applied. Of course other methods can also be used. In data mining, classification, clustering, association rule mining, and sequential pattern mining are mainly adopted.

The data collection schedule is the important part in WID&VA system. As shown in Figure 3, more data need to be collected than wired IDS. Event logs from the terminals in client end (e.g., mobile terminals or portable PCs, PDAs.), accessing and forwarding nodes, or the Web servers and database server in server end are transported to a local detection computer. This process might need to load probe software/program on them. The distribution of wireless signal, especially strongest and weakest places, is more important data for seeking potential attacks. Location information (the environment and structure of building) can help to determine the place of the intruders. If necessary all packets can be captured by a mobile station with special software or by the access point (or base station). In addition, some data can be obtained by active measurement or probe, for example delay, packet loss, and so forth. The research results on wireless network measurement (includes visiting network management information base) and analysis can be directly applied to WID&VA system. Moreover, the interference measurement is another important content. In GSM, logs file and message stored in MSC (mobile switching center), HLR (home location register), VLR (visiting location register) and AC (authentication center) is very important to detect accuracy and efficiency. In 2.5/3G mobile communication systems, with the convergence of cellular networks and computer networks, occurrence of smart phone and adoption of IP technology in core network, the method of data collection used in wired networks can also be applied.

In addition, in order to countermeasure for low-tech fraud such as call forwarding to premium rate numbers, bogus registration details, roaming fraud, terminal theft, and multiple forwarding, fraud management systems should look for (Gadaix, 2001): multiple calls at the same time, large variations in revenue being paid to other parties, large variations in the duration of calls, such as very short or long calls, changes in customer usage, perhaps indicating that a mobile has been stolen or is being abused, and monitoring the usage of a customer closely during a "probationary period".

Figure 3. Data collection in cellular networks/WLAN/WPAN

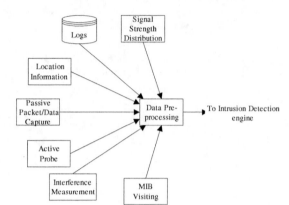

Because a complete m-commerce transaction may cross several networks operated by different services providers, the results obtained by different RMS must be analyzed as a whole. So another main component is distributed WID&VA center, as shown in Figure 4. It receives the detection results and necessary data that come from other RMS. Then final result can be obtained. The data mining, artificial immune, and genetic algorithms are also applied in the center. According to the global decision engine, the related alarms are transmitted to system administrators, the results are recorded in system logs and detailed reports can also be generated. In order to reduce the loss produced by success intrusion, immediate response is required.

Both RMS and WID&VA center can initiate a vulnerability assessment. The analysis result obtained by each RMS can be gathered and a final assessment conclusion made.

Figure 4. Distributed WID&VA center

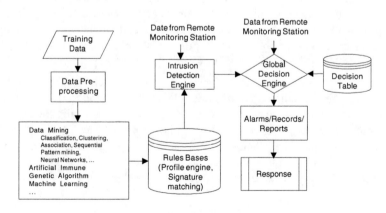

Conclusion and Future Trends

Although more hardened base stations and mobile terminals, better encryption algorithms and authentication schemes will be designed, IDS and vulnerability analysis are still needed. And more methods and technologies of intrusion detection and vulnerability analysis applied in wired networks can be extended to m-commerce platforms. Biology technologies, intelligence computing, machining-learning, and so forth can also be used to smart wireless devices; for example voice verification can be applied to identify unauthorized using.

Intrusion detection is not limited in wireless networks infrastructure; higher-layer application such as Web services, data services, and even transaction content, can also provide useful information about a wicked break-in or intrusion. And with the development of wireless networks, intrusion detection systems will combine the wireless intrusion detection with wired intrusion detection. Another important direction is that intrusion detection component may be integrated in wireless infrastructure before m-commerce application begins.

There is a combat between IPS (intrusion prevention system) and IDS. Some think IPS is enough for network security and suggest that IDS should be replaced by IPS. NFR Security Inc. suggests that intelligent intrusion management (IIM) represents the next generation of intrusion detection and prevention technology that will address prevailing issues of current generation products (Yee, 2003). Its technical framework encompasses three fundamental areas — smart detection, advanced management, and trusted prevention. Smart detection advances the current detection technology by employing a hybrid detection model that incorporates a combination of pattern matching signatures, protocol anomaly detection, and statistically based heuristics. The intelligent mapping layer provides enterprise context for making decisions on the nature and relevance of an attack. The net effect is the dramatic reduction of false positives and earlier detection of true attacks. Advanced management incorporates facilities for simplified deployment such as bootable appliances, "lights out" remote installation/update, and single point management control. It also offers fine-grained control over alert management and visualization facilities. Trusted prevention eliminates the concerns of current generation prevention technology by utilizing a multi-dimensional model for prevention that allows a graceful transition to intrusion prevention with detection facilities offered by IIM to prevent malicious traffic. As the IIM learning system gains a baseline of trusted detection parameters, the user may migrate to an inline appliance model. The combination of detection with prevention is a good way by which the results that come from success attacks can be greatly decreased, and intrusions may be alarmed or avoided at an earlier time.

With the development of m-commerce, new challenges will be encountered continuously. Purely dependence on known encryption, authentication, authorization, audit mechanism is not enough to stop the intruders. Intrusion detection and vulnerability analysis will still be important for a long time.

Acknowledgment

This work is supported by NSFC (National Natural Science Foundation of China) (grant number: 60132030). We would like to thanks Dr. Weidong Kou for his helpful suggestion and instruction.

References

Ameter, C.R., Griffith, R.A., & Pickett, J.K. (2002). WHIFF—Wireless intrusion detection system. Foundstone, Inc. and Carnegie Mellon University. Retrieved September 27, 2003, from *http://www.foundstone.com/index.htm?subnav= resources/ navigation.htm&subcontent=/resources/whitepapers.htm*

Anderson, J.P. (1980). *Computer security threat monitoring and surveillance.* Technical Report. James P Anderson Co., Fort Washington, PA.

Anderson, R., & Khattak, A. (1998). The use of information retrieval techniques for intrusion detection. *First International Workshop on Recent Advances in Intrusion Detection (RAID '98)*, Louvain-La-Neuve, Belgium.

Anjum, F., Subhadrabandhu, D., & Sarkar, S. (2003). Signature based intrusion detection for wireless ad-hoc networks: A comparative study of various routing protocols. *Vehicular Technology Conference, Wireless Security Symposium*, Orlando, FL.

Bace, R.G. (2000). *Intrusion detection.* Indianapolis: Macmillan Technical Publishing.

Barkan, E., Biham, E., & Keller, N. (2003). Instant ciphertext-only cryptanalysis of GSM encrypted communication. *Proceedings of Crypto 2003*, Santa Barbara, CA.

Cheeseman, P., Stutz, J., & Hanson, R. (1991). Bayesian classification with correlation and inheritance. *Proceedings of 12th International Joint Conference on Artificial Intelligence*, Sydney, Australia, 692-698.

Cheung, S., Crawford, R., Dilger, M. et al. (1999). *The design of grids: A graph-based intrusion detection system.* University of California, Davis, No CSE-99-2.

Crosbie, M., & Spafford, E. (1995). Applying genetic programming to intrusion detection. *Proceedings of the AAAI 1995 Fall Symposium on Genetic Programming*, Cambridge, MA, pp.1-8.

Curry, D., & Debar, H. (2003). Intrusion detection message exchange format data model and extensible markup language (XML) document type definition. *draft-ietf-idwg-idmef-xml-10.txt*

Doak, J. (1992). *Intrusion detection: The application of feature selection—A comparison of algorithms, and the application of a wide area network analyzer.* Master's Thesis. Department of Computer Science, University of California, Davis.

Farshchi, J. (2003). Statistical based approach to intrusion detection. Intrusion detection FAQ. Retrieved September 25, 2003, from *http://www.sans.org/resources/idfaq/ statistic_ids.php*

Feinstein, B., Matthews, G., & White, J. (2002). The intrusion detection exchange protocol (IDXP). *draft-ietf-idwg-beep-idxp-07*

Fluhrer, S., Martin, I., & Shamir, A. (2001). Weakness in the key scheduling algorithm of RC4. *Proceedings of the 8th Annual Workshop on Selected Areas in Cryptography,* Toronto, Ontario, Canada.

Forrest, S., Hofmeyr, S.A., & Somayaji, A. (1997). Computer immunology. *Communications of the ACM, 40*(10), 88-96.

Fox, K.L., Henning, R.R., Reed, J.H., & Simonian, R. (1990). A neural network approach towards intrusion detection. *Proceedings of the 13th National Computer Security Conference,* Washington, DC, pp. 125-134.

Gadaix, E. (2001). GSM and 3G security. *http:// opensores.thebunker.net/pub/mirrors/ blackhat/presentations/bh-asia-01/gadiax.ppt*

Garvey, T.G., & Lunt, T.F. (1991). Model based intrusion detection. *Proceeding of the 14th National Computer Security Conference,* Washington, DC, pp. 372-385.

Heady, R., Luger, G., Maccabe, A., & Servilla, M. (1990). The architecture of a network level intrusion detection system. Technical Report CS90-20. Department of Computer Science, University of New Mexico.

Hofmeyr, S., Forrest, S., & Somayaji, A. (1998). Intrusion detection using sequences of system calls. *Journal of Computer Security, 6,* 151-180.

The Honeynet Project. (2003). Retrieved 2003 from *http://www.honeynet.org/misc/ project.html*

Ilgun, K., Kemmerer, R.A., & Porras, P.A. (1995). State transition analysis: A rule-based intrusion detection approach. *IEEE Transactions on Software Engineering, 21*(3), 181-199.

Kachirski, O., & Guha, R. (2003). Effective intrusion detection using multiple sensors in wireless ad hoc networks. *Proceedings of the 36th Hawaii International Conference on System Sciences,* Big Island, Hawaii, pp. 57.1.

Kumar, G. (1995). *Classification and detection of computer intrusions.* PhD dissertation. Purdue University.

Kumar, K., & Spafford, E. (1994). A pattern matching model for misuse intrusion detection. *Proceedings of the 17th National Computer Security Conference,* National Institute of Standards and Technology (NIST), Baltimore, MD.

Lackey, J., Roths, A., & Goddard, J. (2003). Wireless intrusion detection. Retrieved April 2003, from *http://www.ibm.com/services/continuity/recover1.nsf/files/ Downloads_MSS/$file/ibm+wide.pdf*

Lane, T., & Brodley, C.E. (1999). Temporal sequence learning and data reduction for anomaly detection. *ACM Transactions on Information and System Security, 2*(3), 295–331.

Lee, S. (2003). *Trends and predictions on IT security.* Part of the 'Security & Trust' month organized by IDA, Sensecurity Institute.

Lee, W. (1999). *A data mining framework for constructing features and models for intrusion detection systems.* PhD dissertation. Columbia University.

Lee, W., & Xiang, D. (2001). Information-theoretic measures for anomaly detection. *Proc. of the 2001 IEEE Symposium on Security and Privacy*, Oakland, CA, pp.130-143.

Lunt, T., Tamaru, A., Gilham F. et al (1992). A real-time intrusion detection expert system (IDES). Technical report. SRI International, Menlo Park, CA.

Lye, K., & Wing, J.M. (2002). Game strategies in network security. Retrieved from *http://reports-archive.adm.cs.cmu.edu/ anon/2002/CMU-CS-02-136.pdf*

Mao, S., Hui, D., & Williams, R. (2003). Wireless networking security. Retrieved from *http://www.ee.virginia.edu/~rdw/EE68601/WirelessMobileIPSec2.pdf*

Nguyen, B.V. (2002). An application of support vector machines to anomaly detection. CS681 (Research in Computer Science - Support Vector Machine) Report. Ohio Univ. Retrieved September 26, 2003, from *http://www.math.ohiou.edu/~vnguyen/papers/papers.htm*

Notare, M.S.M.A., Boukerche, A., Cruz, F., & Westphall, C.B. (2000). An intrusion detection system to mobile phone networks. *EXPO2000-Feira de Hannover.*

Qu, G., Modukuri, J.R., Hariri, S., & Raghavendra, C.S. (2002). A framework for network vulnerability analysis. *IASTED International Conference on Communications, Internet and Information Technology (CIIT-2002)*, St. Thomas Virgin Islands.

Ramakrishnan, C.R., & Sekar, R. (1998). Model-based vulnerability analysis of computer systems. *Second International Workshop on Verification, Model Checking, and Abstract Interpretation, VMCAI'98*, Pisa, Italy.

Ryan, J., Lin, M.J., & Miikkulainen, R. (1998). Intrusion detection with neural networks. *Advances in Neural Information Processing Systems, 10*. Cambridge, MA: MIT Press.

Samfat, D., & Molva, R. (1997). IDAMN: An intrusion detection architecture for mobile networks. *IEEE Journal on Selected Areas in Communications, 15*(7), 1373-1380.

Shostack, A., & Blake, S. (1999). Towards a taxonomy of network security assessment techniques. *Proceedings of 1999 Black Hat Briefings,* Las Vegas, NV.

Smaha, S. (1988). Haystack: An intrusion detection system. *Proceedings of the 4th Aerospace Computer Security Applications Conference*, Orlando, FL, pp.37-44.

Sundaram, A. (1996). An introduction to intrusion detection. ACM Crossroads 2.4. *http://www.acm.org/crossroads/xrds2-4/intrus.html*

Swiler, L.P., Phillips, C., & Gaylor, T. (1998). A graph-based network-vulnerability analysis system. *Proceedings of the 1998 Workshop on New Security Paradigms,* Charlottesville, VA, pp. 71-79.

Teng, H., Chen, K., & Lu, S. (1990). Adaptive real-time anomaly detection using inductively generated sequential patterns. *Proceedings of 1990 IEEE Computer Society Symposium on Research in Security and Privacy,* Oakland, CA, 278-84.

WIDZ. (2003). The wireless intrusion detection system. Retrieved September 27, 2003, from *http://www.loud-fat-bloke.co.uk/tools.html*

Yee, A. (2003). The intelligent IDS: Next generation network intrusion management Reserved, NFR Security, Inc. Retrieved July 2003, from *http://www.nfr.com/resource/downloads/The_Intelligent_IDS.pdf*

Zhang, Y., & Lee, W. (2000). Intrusion detection in wireless ad hoc networks. *Proceedings of the Sixth Annual International Conference on Mobile Computing and Networking (MobiCom'2000)*, Boston, MA.

Chapter IV

A Secure Authentication Infrastructure for Mobile Users

Gregor v. Bochmann, University of Ottawa, Canada

Eric Zhen Zhang, University of Ottawa, Canada

Abstract

The requirements for an authentication infrastructure for electronic commerce are explained by identifying the partners involved in e-commerce transactions and the trust relationships required. Related security requirements are also explained, such as authentication, access rights, payment credentials, anonymity (in certain cases), and privacy and integrity of message exchanges. Then several general authentication schemes and specific protocols are reviewed and their suitability for mobile users is discussed. Finally, an improved authentication protocol is presented which can provide trust relationships for mobile e-commerce users. Its analysis and comparison with other proposed authentication protocols indicate that it is a good candidate for use in the context of mobile e-commerce.

Introduction

With the introduction of the World Wide Web, electronic commerce has begun to enhance the traditional commerce practice in the exchange of merchandise and information. Recently, the emergence of wireless networks and mobile devices has introduced further commodities for using telecommunication services and electronic commerce transactions on the go. Mobile commerce may be defined as the exchange or buying and selling of commodities, services or information on the Internet through the use of mobile handheld devices. However, in this chapter we take a little larger view of mobile commerce by including the notion of "mobile users," which means that the user may be in a foreign country, in an unusual environment and may use, for the electronic commerce session, any device that happens to be available, for instance a workstation in a hotel business lounge or the handheld device belonging to a friend.

While many aspects of **mobile** commerce are identical to the same aspects of normal electronic commerce, in general, there are certain aspects that are specific to mobile commerce. These aspects are either related to the limitations of handheld devices, such as (a) the limited computation power of most handheld devices related to CPU power and battery life and (b) certain limitations of the communication bandwidth, which depends on the particular wireless networking technology in use, or related to the notion of "mobile users," such as (c) the security implications of using unknown ad hoc devices that are locally available and (d) the fact that the user may need to be authenticated by a foreign organization that provides network access facilities and other services within the foreign domain where the user temporarily resides.

In this chapter, we principally deal with the problem of user authentication and the establishment of trust relationships between the different parties involved in an electronic commerce transaction. In this context, we consider specifically the aspects (c) and (d) above which are specific to mobile commerce. To a lesser degree we are also concerned with aspect (a) and (b).

In second section, we explain the requirements for an authentication infrastructure for electronic commerce by identifying the partners that are typically involved in transactions and the trust relationships that are required. We also describe the security requirements, such as authentication, access rights, payment credentials, anonymity (in certain cases), as well as the traditional requirements such as privacy and integrity of message exchange. Then we review in the third section first the three general schemes for authentication, namely authentication based on a shared key, on public/private key pair, and on biometric information. After this introduction, we review certain authentication protocols that are currently in use or proposed, and discuss their applicability to electronic commerce applications and in particular to the requirements of mobile users as identified by points (c) and (d) above.

In the fourth section, we then propose a secure authentication protocol for mobile user that (1) combines ease of password-based authentication with the power of public key technology, (2) can be executed on an ad hoc device that happens to be available in the environment of the mobile user, and (3) provides authentication support for (i) the normal electronic commerce transactions, (ii) for obtaining the necessary transmission resources from the local Internet service provider (ISP) (e.g., to view a high-quality video from some given video-on-demand server), and (iii) for authentication to arbitrary third parties (e.g., for a secure IP-telephone conversation). The protocol is based on a password-based user identification procedure performed by the authentication authority where the user is registered, and also involves an agent of the foreign domain where the mobile user is visiting. The use of public key technology is limited in order to satisfy the limitations of handheld devices concerning computing power and battery life.

We believe that the authentication protocol described and analyzed in the fourth section contains a number of interesting features that make it suitable as an alternative to the other authentication protocols that can be used for mobile commerce, as explained in the conclusions.

Requirements for Authentication Infrastructure

In order to discuss the requirements for authentication in mobile e-commerce applications, we start with the presentation of a typical application scenario. We then identify specific roles played by the different parties involved and discuss the trust relationships between the parties and other security requirements.

Example Scenario

We consider the following scenario of a mobile user of e-commerce facilities: Bob has a subscription to an e-learning course with company Teach-Inc. Now Bob is on a business trip in a hotel in Paris and uses a rented portable computer in his hotel room to study another chapter of the subscribed course. Then he checks the balance of his personal account at his Bank in Canada and buys some food for delivery from the nearby Paris-Bistro restaurant. The next day, he travels through Paris. After an IP-telephone conversation with his friend Alice using his handheld PDA/phone through a wireless Internet connection available in a shopping center, he decides to do some money transfer from his Montreal account using the same PDA device. Then he uses the PDA to watch an adult movie from an Internet video store.

Generic Roles in E-Commerce

In order to clarify the discussion of security requirements, we first try in the following to identify the major parties and their roles within the e-commerce environment from a generic point of view. We identify the following basic roles:

1. *User*: This is the person (or agent) that takes initiatives for e-commerce transactions. In the context of mobile e-commerce, it is typically a person on the move, using a mobile terminal, such as a PDA or mobile phone, or a fixed terminal that is publicly available or belongs to third parties (e.g., a visited friend) not involved in the transaction. In our scenario, Bob is the user.

2. *Service provider*: This is an organization or a person that provides a service that the user is interested in. It includes the computer through which the service is effectively provided. In many cases, the service transaction also involves real goods, such as the delivered food in our example. The service may involve a fee to be paid by the user, or may be freely available. Examples of service provides in our example are: the Teach-Inc company, the restaurant, the bank, the video store, and the long-distance telephone company used for the telephone call with Alice.

3. *Network access provider*: This is the organization that provides network access to the mobile user. Although this may be considered a service provider, we distinguish this role because of the special role of the network access service and the related security requirements (to be discussed below). Unlike other service providers, the network service provider either provides free service for all users, as for instance the wireless Internet service provider in the shopping center, or will provide at least initial free access to any new user to allow his/her identification and/or establishment of payment procedure.

4. *Third parties*: These are other persons or organizations that participate in the transaction initiated by the user. For instance, if we consider the telephone conversation of Bob with Alice as a transaction, Alice plays the role of a third party.

In addition, there are certain parties that play the role of providing appropriate references about the user. We can identify the following reference roles:

1. *Credit reference*: This is a role typically played by a credit or debit card organization. For example, Bob may use a credit card or some equivalent electronic version as payment instrument for his transactions with the restaurant or the video store.

2. *Authentication authority*: This could be an authority that attests that the person in our scenario is Bob XYZ that lives in Ottawa at 300 Stewart Street, or an authority that attests Bob's age to allow him the viewing of an adult movie. This role is also played by the government of Canada when it emits Bob's passport, which is required for the visit to Paris.

Various Trust Relationships

Depending on the particular e-commerce application, different trust relationships are required between the different parties involved. Based on our example scenario, we identify the following most important relationships between the generic roles:

Authentication

Applications that involve personal data of the user require the authentication of the user by the service provider. Inversely, the user usually also wants to authenticate the service provider so that he/she could be assured that he/she is dealing with a trustworthy party. Furthermore the transaction may involve the exposure of additional personal information. This is the case when Bob accesses his banking service. Mutual authentication is usually also required between the user and any third party, especially in the case of a communication service. An example is the telephone call between Bob and Alice.

Access Rights

Many e-commerce services could in principle be provided to anonymous users; that is, the service provider does not need to authenticate the user. For instance, Teach-Inc does not really care whether it is Bob that accesses the e-learning course, as long it is assured that the user has obtained the access rights to the course (through some previous transaction in which some access permit would have been established, probably against payment). Another example is Bob's viewing of a video; here the service provider must satisfy the policy that adult movies can only be seen by users of a certain age. In Canada, the user's driver's license is typically used as a reference for checking the age of a person. For e-commerce purposes, a public key authentication certificate may also include such information.

Payment Credentials

Payment is an essential part of the e-commerce framework. Payment methods can be classified into cash-based methods and methods based on payment credentials, such as credit and debit cards. The latter payment methods involve a credit institution as a third party that asserts that the service provider will be paid the amount due as long as this amount is within the user's credit limit. All transactions in our example scenario involve payment, except for the viewing of the online course for which the access rights were obtained through an earlier transaction during which Bob subscribed to the particular course. Payment may also be involved for the use of communication services, including network access, unless this service is provided free of charge.

Other Security Requirements

In addition to authentication, access control and payment credentials discussed above, e-commerce applications often have other security requirements, such as the following:

Privacy of Communication

The communication between the user and the service provider, and possibly the other parties participating in the transaction, should remain private, that is, should be protected from leaking out to other parties not involved in the transaction. Sometimes, certain information should only be available to specific parties in the transaction, as for instance in the SET protocol for electronic credit/debit card payment, where the store will see the details of the goods purchased by the user, but not the credit institution.

Integrity of Message Exchanges

Message integrity ensures that messages exchanged between the parties involved in a transaction are not changed during transmission either through transmission errors or intruders.

Verifiable Signatures

Signed messages or documents are required in case of important transactions. The signature by user A of a given message becomes significant if the signature is verifiable in the following sense: The receiver of the message can verify that the message was signed by user A, and the user cannot repudiate the signing of the message; that is, a third party playing the role of an arbiter may be able to determine whether it was user A that signed the message or some other person.

Anonymity

As mentioned above, many services could in principle be provided to anonymous users. In certain situations, anonymity becomes a user preference or requirement. For instance, in many situations the user does not want any other person to know that he/she is buying certain goods. In other situations, the user may not want to be recognized, or the user wants his or her presence in the particular geographical area to remain secret. In order to allow an anonymous user to participate in e-commerce applications, it is nevertheless required to verify access rights or payment credentials. It is therefore important that these references can be provided without interfering with the user's anonymity.

Review of Authentication Methods

In this section we discuss authentication methods and protocols, and how they could be used for mobile applications. Before reviewing existing authentication protocols, we briefly present the major generic approaches to authentication. Finally, we discuss some common issues, such as the need for an authentication authority for mobile users getting involved in new relationships, and the need for trusting the software in the devices that the mobile user may happen to use.

Generic Approaches to Authentication

Generally, authentication is accomplished through a sharing secret between user and authentication server. The server could be a stand-along workstation that is in charge of authentication or a module integrated into a multi-functional server. In terms of type of shared secrete, the authentication methods can be cataloged into three sub-catalogs: symmetric authentication, asymmetric authentication and biometrics authentication.

Authentication Based on a Shared Secret

Also called symmetric authentication, this approach to authentication is based on a secret key that is shared among two parties or more. Typically, these parties are the user and a service provider. Basically, mutual authentication is realized between the two parties by the exchange of messages that are encrypted by a symmetric encryption algorithm using the shared secret as the key. By decrypting the message with the same key, the other party can verify that the sender is in possession of the secret key. If the key is not exposed, correct authentication is assured. The common password authentication schemes currently used by most servers are based on this principle.

The major challenge of this approach is key management, especially key distribution and the strength of the key. The approach is suitable for centralized systems where a central server each potential users. Key distribution is accomplished when the user first registers him/herself at the central server. Although applying the same key for message encryption/decryption repeatedly increases the possibility of breaking the key, the strength of the key could be improved by changing the password periodically based on pre-built agreements between the user and the server.

Authentication Based on Public Keys

Also called asymmetric authentication, this approach is based on a public/private key pair. Authentication is based on the possession of the private key, and the other parties in the transaction would use the public key for encrypting or decrypting messages. A public/private key pair provides for the authentication of the party having the private key; for the authentication of the other party, another private/public key pair is required. For instance, a server could authenticate a user by sending some random number encrypted by the public key of the user, which could only be decrypted using the private key; the user should then return the decrypted random number to the server as proof of his or her identity.

Public/private key technology also provides for verifiable signatures. Normally, the message to be signed is hashed and the hash value is encrypted with the private key, which results in the signature that is sent together with the original message. By decrypting the signature with the public key and comparing the result with the hash value of the received message, the recipient of the message verifies the signature. This verification can be performed by any party having received the message and the signature. Since only the sender has a copy of the private key, he or she cannot repudiate the signing of the message.

In order to provide reliable information about the public keys of various users and organizations, a public key infrastructure (PKI) is provided, which consists of a collection of authentication authorities that give out signed authentication certificates, which include the public key of the user or service provider together with certain attributes, such as the name and possibly the address, employment, age, and so forth.

Authentication Based on Biometric Information

Instead of creating big random numbers that serve as shared or private/public keys, this approach is based on biometric information that is characteristic of the user. Examples are of such information are fingerprints, eyeball scans and DNA recognition. This authentication approach cannot be used for authenticating organizations. Like the shared key in the case of symmetric authentication, the biometric information of the registered users is stored in the database of a central server that represents the authentication authority. Authentication is performed by reading again the biometric information on the individual and comparing the result with the value stored in the database.

Discussion

The public/private key approach to authentication is basically much more suitable for e-commerce applications because, once a user is registered with an authentication authority based on PKI, he/she can be authenticated by any other party without any pre-established relationship. In contrast, shared key and biometric authentication requires a pre-established relationship with the party by whom the user wants to be recognized. In addition, the public/private key approach provides at the same time for verifiable signatures, which are very important for many e-commerce application.

Unfortunately, the algorithms performing public/private key encryption are much less efficient that shared-key encryption algorithms. This is of concern for mobile devices that usually have lower CPU power and battery limitations. Therefore one usually tries to limit the use of public/private key technology for mobile devices as much as possible.

Another issue is the secure storage of the private key. The public/private keys are much longer than password and cannot be remembered by the human user. Therefore they must be stored in computer-readable form and only be accessible and usable by the user that owns it. In the case of mobile commerce, the key may either be stored in a personal mobile device (PDA or mobile phone) belonging to the user, or in a small card (e.g., smart card, SIM card or SD memory card) readable by the device used by the user.

Existing Security Protocols

We mention in this section a number of security protocols that could be applied for mobile commerce applications and shortly discuss their benefits and limitations.

Radius

The Radius mechanism using CHAP (challenge handshake authentication protocol) (Simpson, 1996) is widely used by Internet service providers to give point-to-point protocol access with mobility (AbdelAziz, 2000). The example shown below indicates that this kind of protocol is not compatible with our mobile commerce requirements. The Radius-CHAP message exchanges are presented in Figure 1. The protocol uses a challenge value CV. K is a key shared by the network access server (NAS) and the authentication authority, called Radius Server.

The user first communicates with the NAS to be given a challenge value. The user gives the answer (res) that is forwarded by the NAS to the Radius server. The latter checks the validity of res. The authentication answer is included in the reply.

The NAS and the Radius server are supposed to know and to trust each other. And the link between them is supposed to be secure. Anonymity cannot be provided with this scheme. Moreover, the NAS generates the random challenge value CV and sends it to the user in plaintext along with a CHAP identifier (called 'msgID' in the figure), which allows attackers to perform a chosen plaintext attack by guessing the password to calculate $H(pwd, msgID, CV)$ and comparing the result with the value 'res' included in the message. Radius was designed for centralized network infrastructure and fails to meet the requirement for mobile users.

Figure 1. RADIUS-CHAP message exchange

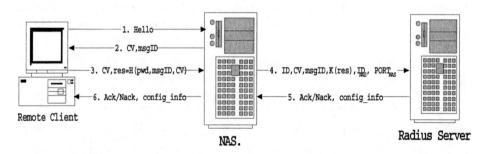

Figure 2. Getting and using Initial Ticket (Kohl, Neuman & Tso, 1994)

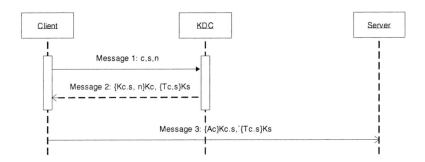

Kerberos

Like in the case of Radius, Kerberos uses a centralized authentication server where the shared password of the user is stored. This server plays the role of a centralized key distribution center (KDC) to assist in key management (Steiner, Neuman & Schiller, 1988). A ticket or authenticator is issued by the authentication server to the user for service access control as shown in Figure 2.

The ticket will be used to authenticate the user at the server providing the service and to generate a sub-session key. Anonymity cannot be provided since the client has to send out his/her identity as well as required services in clear to the KDC. This information is sent unencrypted and could be listened to by any third party sitting on the communication path.

The major challenge Kerberos faces is the first message exchange between clients and the KDC. In the scenario above, when Bob comes to the shopping center, he has no knowledge about the KDC. How could he make sure that the KDC he talks to is a real trustable KDC instead of a fake one sitting in the middle and trying to damage? Moreover, since Bob is a foreign user for the KDC in Paris, how could a secret key be distributed between them prior to authentication? While Kerberos has the function of providing a ticket for services in a foreign domain, this mechanism is impractical, especially when the user's visit is unpredictable.

SSL

SSL stands for Secure Sockets Layer and is renamed by IETF as TLS (*ftp://ftp.isi.edu/in-notes/rfc2246.txt*) (Transport Layer Security). Originally developed by Netscape, SSL is especially used by Web browsers to provide authentication and privacy for sensitive Web applications. SSL contains various options for authentication including several versions of public/private key authentication. The protocol also provides for a fresh shared session key that can be used for encrypting the messages exchanged over the session.

XML Security Extensions

Security Assertion Markup Language (SAML) (*http://www.xmltrustcenter.org/saml/ docs/draft-sstc-core-12-final.pdf*) is the first industry standard for enabling secure e-commerce transactions through the eXtensible Markup Language (XML). Independent of any particular platform, SAML enables companies to securely exchange authentication and authorization information with customers, vendors and suppliers, while the XML Key Management Specification (XKMS) (*http://www.verisign.com/resources/gd/ xml/xkms/xkmsv1-1.pdf*) efficiently manages digital signatures and encryption. A supplement, XMLPay (*http://www.verisign.com/resources/gd/xml/xmlpay/xmlpay.pdf*), provides further facilities for payment transactions to build trust-supported B2B and B2C e-commerce.

Smart Cards and SIM Card

Many types of smart cards and the SIM card used with mobile phones contain an authentication certificate including the public key of the user (owner of the card) and some attributes (e.g., user name) and the associated private key. For security reasons, the private key will never be communicated through the card reader interface. Instead, any message to be encrypted or decrypted with the private key is transferred to the card and the result of the operation is returned to the card reader. Thus, any device that can interface with the card could perform an authentication handshake with a remote party through which the owner of the card would be identified as the user.

Other Protocols

SSH (*http://www.ieft.org/ids.by.wg/secsh.html*) is a protocol that provides secure access over insecure channels to remote server computers, including file transfer and a command line interpreter. Two versions of the protocol are available. SSH1 provides both server and user authentication, while SSH2 only provides user authentication, but it is more secure. The Diffie Hellman Algorithm (*http://www.rsasecurity.com/rsalabs/faq/3-6-1.html*) is used to negotiate a shared secret key.

SHTTP was designed to secure only HTML (Hypertext Markup Language) Web pages. Server and client preferences and security constraint are negotiated for each Web page or set of pages. The client-side public key certificates are optional, "as it supports symmetric key-only operation mode" (*http://www.ietf.org/proceedings/99jul/I-D/draft-ietf-wts-shttp-06.txt*).

There are also extensions of the IP protocol for mobility (Glass et al., 2000) and security (*http://www.ietf.org/html.charters/ipsec-charter.html*); however, the security framework at the IP level is not very useful for mobile commerce applications.

Discussion of the Requirements for Mobile Commerce

Comparing the authentication and other security requirements for mobile commerce discussed in the second section with the authentication methods described above, we come to the following conclusions:

1. The public/private key technology is the preferred method for authentication since it only requires the registration of the user with a single authentication authority and allows authentication to third parties without any pre-established relationship. It also provides a simple scheme for signatures.

2. The public/private key technology utilizes some form of PKI which consists of a collection of registration authorities that provide signed public key certificates that contain the public key of a user together with certain user attributes.

3. In addition, commerce applications require other forms of references, such as payment credentials and other kinds of certification, such as proof of age, proof of competence, and so forth. Similar to public key certificates, such references could also be provided in the form of signed documents that contain just the necessary information, signed by an appropriate certification agency. For instance, a credit credential would be signed by a bank. In an extreme case, when the user wants to remain anonymous, the credit credential destined for a network access provider in a foreign domain may contain the following information: "Communication charges up to an amount of 10$ will be covered for the current user." (See the fourth section for a more detailed example.)

4. Among the existing authentication protocols, SSL and smart cards appear to be most interesting for mobile commerce; however, they do not provide support for payment credentials and other references for users that want to remain anonymous.

Concept of a Home Directory

We have seen in the earlier subsections that, whatever the authentication scheme chosen, each user has to register in at least one authentication authority. In our work on quality of service management for distributed multimedia applications and mobile users (El-Khatib, Hadibi & Bochmann, 2003), we identified the need for what we called a "home directory" where the user profile and preferences are stored. In the case of IP telephony, the home directory would also play the role of the user's proxy agent; that is, it would be the place to where incoming communication requests would be sent, since the user profile would contain information about the device through which the user (who may be on the move) would accept such a request at the given time.

We note that such a home directory may also include user preferences concerning commerce applications. It may also be sensible to combine such a home directory with the function of the authentication authority mentioned above.

Need for Trusted Software

One of the difficulties with mobile commerce is the fact that the user may use a device that is locally available, like for example the portable computer Bob rented from the hotel. In such a case, there is the problem of trusting the software running on that device. Trusting software, in general, is problematic. As early as 1984, Ken Thompson stated, "You can't trust code that you did not totally create yourself" (Thompson, 1984). In the case of the software residing in a device locally available, we could normally assume that it contains standard software; however, it is not excluded that, for instance, the previous user inserted a piece of code performing some extra tasks, such as recording all activities of the subsequent users and sending a log of these activities to a given destination for espionage, for instance. If the device contains a smart card interface and the smart card is used by the user, the malicious software may also send additional encoding and decoding commands to the smart card as part of a fake transaction with some third party without the knowledge of the legitimate user.

It is difficult to systematically exclude these possibilities of fraud. One way to reduce these risks is to download certified software from trusted service providers. However, the fraudulent software operating system that performs the download and verification of the certification may download a fraudulent software version from some other source and present to the user a window that (falsely) attests to the successful checking of the certification. It appears that we can only hope that such things would occur only very infrequently.

Password-Based Authentication for Mobile Users with Support for Public Key Technology

In the following, we describe a new authentication protocol for mobile users which is based on a secret password shared between the user and the authentication authority and supports the creation of a new public/private key pair for which the authority provides an authentication certificate and the private key is stored in the device the user happens to use at that time. After providing an architectural overview and describing how the protocol would be used, we provide a detailed description of the protocol, discuss its properties, analyze its robustness against security attacks and discuss possible design choices for the detailed definition of the protocol.

Architecture Overview and Design Objectives

Let us consider part of the usage scenario described in the second section: While Bob is on a business trip in Paris, he has an IP-telephone conversation with his friend Alice using his handheld PDA/phone through a wireless Internet connection which is available in a shopping mall provided by a third party, say France Telecom. We may identify the following security concerns in this context: (a) France Telecom wants to see payment credentials for the cost of providing the telecommunications facilities to Bob. However, Bob may want his presence in Paris to remain unknown and therefore requires anonymity. (b) Bob may want to authenticate France Telecom to be sure that he uses a trustworthy carrier, although he should use end-to-end encryption to ensure the privacy of the telephone conversation. (c) To persuade Alice to accept the incoming call that claims to be from Bob, Bob's PDA must be authenticated to Alice as belonging to Bob, and vice versa. Note that the authentication procedure at Bob's side is symmetrically identical with Alice's side, and the authentication between Bob and Alice is the same as between Bob and France Telecom; we could therefore only focus on how Bob and France Telecom authenticate each other. The architecture of the authentication protocol between the latter two is shown in Figure 3.

Figure 3 provides an architectural overview including the different parties involved in this scenario. Besides the parties mentioned above, the figure also shows Bob's home agent and a certification authority. Bob's home agent plays the role of Bob's authentication authority, while the certification authority is part of the public key infrastructure (PKI) and allows the foreign agent and Bob's home agent to authenticate one another based on certificates of their public keys provided by the certification authority. The certificate of the foreign agent may also be used by Bob to check the authentication of *France Telecom* in our example scenario.

The main design objectives for the proposed authentication protocol are the following:

1. The user's authentication is based on a secret password that is shared between the user and the home agent.

2. The protocol leads to the creation of a new public/private key pair that can be used for the authentication of the user. The private key will reside on the device that the user is currently using and an authentication certificate signed by the home agent is provided for the new public key.

3. A trust relationship is established between the home agent and the foreign agent based on reciprocal authentication, and payment credentials for the user are transmitted by the home agent to the foreign agent.

4. The user may remain anonymous for the foreign agent.

We note that the use of a secret password for authentication has the advantage that it is easily implemented with a relatively short password (of a length of approximately 6 to 10 characters) that the user can remember. The authentication based on public key technology requires a much longer private key that must be stored in some device or card carried by the user. This makes it difficult for the mobile user to use any device that may be locally available. On the other hand, public key technology is essential for authentication to third parties and for the generation and verification of signatures. This is the reason for the second design objective. The main characteristic of this new authentication protocol is therefore to combine the use of a password with public key authentica-

Figure 3. Architectural overview

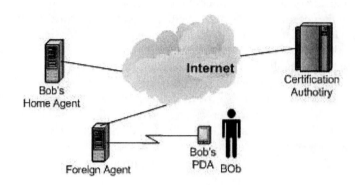

tion. The new public/private key pair generated by the authentication protocol may be used for authentication to third parties, for instance for Bob's telephone conversation with Alice, and allows the user to generate verifiable signatures.

We note that the Radius protocol also uses password-based authentication, but it does not provide the creation of a public key certificate for authentication to third parties. Also, it assumes that the network access server (NAC), which corresponds to the foreign agent in our architecture, is associated with a single radius server, while our protocol foresees inter-working with a variety of different home agents throughout the world.

Objective (3) is important. In fact, no initial trust relationship is assumed between the user and the foreign agent. However, when the authentication protocol completes success-fully, the home agent will have authenticated the foreign agent, and the resulting trust is indirectly available to the user. On the other hand, the user may remain completely anonymous to the foreign agent (as stated in Objective (4)). In fact, the payment credentials, in the form of a ticket T, are directly transmitted by the home agent. This ticket may also be used by the user to obtain services from other service provides within the foreign domain.

It is important to note that the protocol is structured in such a way that the user side of the protocol, also called personal agent (PA), is realized by software that runs on the device that the user happens to use within the foreign domain. This device may be his/her own PDA, but it may also be any device that happens to be available. The user has to trust the integrity of the software that represents the PA, but it does not have to trust the foreign agent.

Protocol Description

Protocol Overview

The message exchanges of the authentication protocol are shown in Figure 4. One can identify the following three steps:

1. A locally broadcast preliminary message (number 1) provides information about the FA, for example the FA's IP address and its public key. This information allows the user to start the following authentication exchange.

2. The user (here Bob, or his personal agent, PA) sends an authentication request to the FA (message 2). The request is encrypted by a randomly generated session key Ks_1, which is protected by the FA's public key. The FA uses its private key to get the session key and the information about Bob's home agent, including its address.

3. The FA then forwards the authentication request to the HA after having removed the encryption with the session key (messages 3). Depending on the outcome of the authentication, the HA either replies a positive authentication response (messages 3.1 and 3.1.1) or a negative response (messages 3.2 and 3.2.1). These messages include information about the reasons for either success or failure. The foreign agent recognizes the message and also forwards the information to Bob. In the message from the FA to the user, this information is encrypted with a session key Ks_2, while the message exchanges between the FA and the HA pass through an encrypted connection.

4. The authentication between Bob and the FA is successfully achieved if the message 3.1.1 is received; otherwise the NACK value in the message 3.2.1 will indicate the reason of the refusal. The NACK value is determined by the HA; Bob can have confidence that the FA did not change the value in the message 3.2.1 by calculating $H(HV_1, N_2, NACK, pwd)$ and comparing it with the value of HV_2 received from the FA.

Detailed Protocol Description

The sequence of message exchanges of the protocol are shown in Figure 4, and the various information fields of the messages are indicated. We give in the following an explanation of the abbreviations used.

* ID_X denotes the unique identifier of the user X (for instance: *Bob@domain.net*)

* KU_X: public-key of user X

* KR_X: private-key of user X

* Ks: a session key (symmetric key)

- *K(M)* means *M* is encrypted using key *K*

- *N*: a nonce

- *SecCx*: a secure connection, for example realized through TLS

- *CSR*: Certificate Signing Request (defined in PKCS#10 standard)

- *CERT$_X$*: Certificate of user *X* (defined in X.509)

- *pwd*: password of the user

Some particular values are defined as follows:

- $HV_1 = H(ID_B, CSR_B, N_1, pwd)$ is calculated by Bob and can be used by the FA as a session identifier

- $HV'_1 = H(ID_B, CSR_B, N_1, pwd)$ is calculated by the HA and is compared with HV_1

- $HV_2 = H(HV'_1, N_2, NACK, pwd)$ in negative case and $H(HV'_1, N_2, ACK, pwd)$ in positive case

- Ks_1: session key, is randomly chosen by Bob and only used in message 2

- $Ks_2 = H(N_1, N_2, Ks_1)$ is a session key, in which N_2 is selected by the HA and used between PA and FA after the authentication.

- $Ks_3 = H(N_1, N_3, pwd)$ is a session key selected by the HA and only known by the PA and HA.

Each of the messages shown in the figure is further explain in the following.

Figure 4. Message exchanges of the authentication protocol

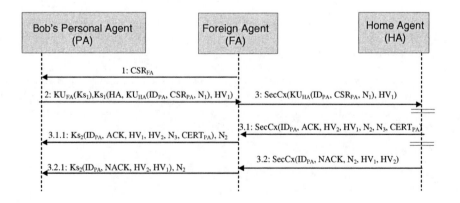

- *Message 1 – Service agent advertisement*: A broadcast message in the local domain informs Bob about the location and the digital certificate of the FA. This could be realized through existing protocols, such as the Dynamic Host Configuration Protocol (DHCP) or Jini.

- *Message 2 – Authentication request*: Bob's device executes the following steps in order to prepare this message:

  1. Bob generates a random number N_1 and a certificate-signing request (*CSR*) according to the PKCS#10 standards (RSA Laboratories, 1993). To perform the *CSR*, Bob generates a pair of public and private keys KU_{PA} and KR_{PA} on his terminal. KR_{PA} is stored on the terminal in a secure key store and is never sent over the network. The *CSR* includes KU_{PA} and a proof of possession of the private key. Bob encrypts his identity information along with N_1 and CSR_{PA}, using a public key of his HA KU_{HA} retrieved from an available standard authentication authority on his terminal.

  2. Bob generates a digest, called HV_1, of all the above information and the password *pwd*.

  3. Bob then selects a random session key Ks_1 that is used to encrypt all the above information HV_1 as well as the information of his HA. This will allow the FA to forward HV_1 to the HA. Ks_1 is then encrypted with FA's public key, which was obtained from the FA's certificate included in Message 1.

- *Message 3 – Forwarded Authentication request*: The following steps relate to the forwarding of the authentication request to the HA:

  1. The FA receives Message 2, decrypts $KU_{FA}(Ks_1)$ using KR_{FA}, and then decrypts $Ks_1(ID_{HA}, KU_{HA}(ID_{PA}, CSR_{PA}, N_1), HV_1)$.

  2. With the help of $ID_{HA,}$ the FA establishes a secure connection with Bob's HA and sends $KU_{HA}(ID_{PA}, CSR_{PA}, N_1), HV_1$.

- *Authentication by the HA*: The HA receives Message 3, computes its own digest HV_1' and compares it with HV_1. If they are equal, authentication succeeds and an "ACK" (acknowledgment) is returned; otherwise a "NACK" (negative acknowledgment) is returned.

- *Message 3.1 – Authentication reply - Ack*: The HA performs the following steps:

  1. HA signs Bob's *CSR* and generates two random numbers N_2, N_3.

  2. Using the current secure connection established with the FA, the HA sends back a message including the answer of the authentication process (ACK), the hash value HV_1 sent by Bob that uniquely identifies the request, and security material for Bob $(ID_{PA,} N_2, N_3, HV_2, CERT_{PA})$.

- *Message 3.1.1 – Forwarded Authentication reply - Ack*: The FA performs the following steps:

    1. FA receives Message 3.1, calculates Ks_2 encrypts ID_{PA}, ACK, HV_2, HV_1, N_3 and $CERT_B$ with Ks_2 and transmits it together with the nonce N_2 in clear as Message 3.1.1.

    2. Bob receives this message. He computes $Ks_2 = H(N_1, N_2, Ks_1)$ and decrypts Ks_2 $(ID_{PA}, ACK, HV_1, N_3, HV_2, CERT_{PA})$. He also computes $Ks_3 = H(N_1, N_3, pwd)$.

    Bob now shares a security association with FA based on the shared key Ks_2, and with HA based on the shared key Ks_3. He can establish a security association with a new party or sign a document using $CERT_{PA}$ and KR_{PA}.

- *Message 3.2 – Negative Authentication Reply - Nack*: the HA performs the following steps:

    1. HA generates a random number N_2.

    2. HA prepares a "NACK" answer that includes a rejection reason (e.g., "revoked user" or "password expired") and the hash value HV_1 that identifies Bob's request. It then computes $HV_2 = H(HV'_1, N_2, NACK, pwd)$.

    3. Using the current secure connection established with the FA, the HA sends back the answer including N_2, the answer of the authentication process (NACK), HV_1 sent by Bob, and HV_2, which serves as a proof of answer and ID_{PA}.

- *Message 3.2.1 – Negative Authentication Reply Forwarded - Nack*: the FA performs the following steps:

    1. FA receives Message 3.2. It computes $Ks_2 = H(N_1, N_2, pwd)$ and encrypts ID_B, ACK, HV_1 and $HV2$ with Ks_2 and transmits it together with N_2 in clear text as Message 3.2.1.

    2. Bob receives this message, calculates Ks_2 and decrypts $Ks_2 (ID_B, NACK, HV_1, HV_2, N_2)$ and then computes $HV'_2 = H(HV_1, N_2, NACK, pwd)$ to check that this authentication answer actually comes from the HA.

    Bob now knows that his request has been rejected and he has received the reason.

Discussion

This protocol was inspired by a similar protocol described in Dupre-la-Tour, Bochmann, and Chouinard (2001); however, it contains the following improvements compared to the protocol of:

1. Minimal usage of public key technology at the PA side to satisfy the limitation of computing capability and battery power of mobile devices. Through the authentication protocol, public key encryption is used only twice in Message 2. After the initial authentication, there is a session key shared between Bob's PA and the FA (Ks_2), as well as between the PA and the HA (Ks_3). Further negotiation will be based on these session keys using symmetric key operation.

2. A hash value is included to prevent that a misbehaving third party may introduce itself between two nodes, such as HV_1, HV_1', and HV_2.

3. The mobile user relies on his/her HA to authenticate the FA. Since Bob does not have a root certificate, his PA could not verify the FA certificate sent in Message 1. Instead, the PA will send an encrypted request to the FA which should then be forwarded to the HA. If the FA could not be authenticated by the HA, the secure connection between these two parties could not be established. Without the secure connection, the request would not be sent. Therefore the PA would time-out after waiting for a reply message from the FA. Such a time-out indicates that the FA may have failed to get authentication.

4. Anonymity option: The user's anonymity can be guaranteed by hiding the user information from the FA and using tickets provided by the FA to gain access to services within the domain of the FA. The anonymity option implies the following modifications to the protocol. In the case of a positive acknowledgment, Message 3.1 now becomes SecCx (ACK, HV_1, N_2, N_3, Ks_3 ($CERT_{PA}$)) and Message 3.1.1 becomes Ks_2 (ACK, HV_1, N_3, T, Ks_3 ($CERT_{PA}$)), N_2. We note that ID_{PA} is removed from these two messages. Instead of sending $CERT_{PA}$ in clear, it is now encrypted with a shared session key Ks_3 which is only known by the PA and the HA. A ticket T is created by the FA and sent to the PA to be used for local service access. The service server would validate the ticket and provide service upon validation regardless of who presents the ticket. In the case of a negative reply, Message 3.2 becomes SecCx (NACK, N_2, HV_1, HV_2), and Message 3.2.1 becomes Ks_2(NACK, HV_2, HV_1), N_2. As in the previous case, ID_{PA} is removed from these two messages.

Verification of the Authentication Requirements

In case of positive authentication, all six possible cross-authentications between the three parties take place:

1. Bob authenticates the FA: Bob trusts the HA to authenticate FA. After decrypting Message 3.1.1 or 3.2.1, he knows that FA received HV_2 from HA because that value could only be computed knowing the password. That means HA authenticated FA previously when establishing the secure connection SecCx.

2. Bob authenticates the HA: After decrypting Message 3.1.1 or 3.2.1, Bob knows that the HA computed HV2, because the HA is the only agent that knows the password.

3. The FA authenticates the HA: The FA checks the certificate of the HA before sending Message 3 when establishing the secure connection.

4.   The FA authenticates Bob: After receiving Message 3.1 or 3.2, the FA knows the authentication answer of the HA and trusts the authentication done by the HA. In addition Bob can decrypt Message 3.1.1 if and only if he recovers Ks_2 from N_2. If he does so and uses Ks_2 to communicate later with the FA, the latter knows he shares some information with the HA.

5.   The HA authenticates Bob: After receiving Message 3, the HA compares HV_1 with HV_1' to check Bob's password.

6.   The HA authenticates the FA: The HA checks the certificate of the FA when FA tries to establish a secure connection.

In the case of a negative response, Bob is sure that the answer was prepared by HA because of the following reasoning. After receiving Message 3.2.1, Bob checks that the negative answer was made by the HA by computing HV_2. The latter value could have been computed only by HA and is related to Bob's initial request because of the presence of HV_1. This check is useful to verify that no third party is misbehaving in the middle between Bob and the HA. The presence of ACK/NACK in the HV_2 computation is useful to check that the middle party did not change the reason of acceptance or rejection.

Consideration of Typical Security Attacks

We discuss in the following a few typical security attacks and how the protocol copes with them.

1.   Spoofing attack of a malicious user: A malicious user, says Eve, may try to usurp Bob's identity. Authentication information is included in HV_1 sent by Bob to the FA in Message 2. Since Eve does not know Bob's password, the HA while calculating HV_1' finds a different value and does not authenticate Eve as Bob. In message 3.2, the HA sends the authentication result to the FA so that the FA knows that Bob (actually Eve) is not authenticated.

2.   Spoofing attack of servers (the FA, the HA) is denied by the systematic use of digital certificates. Bob relies on the HA to authenticate the FA (see Section 4.2).

3.   Replay attacks of an authentication request are impossible owing to the nonce. If an attacker tries to replay messages or a rogue FA tries to replay messages, this will be detected by the HA that keeps all successful logins for a given time period (e.g., a few days). Even if the attack is not detected by the HA, a malicious user replaying the request message could not decrypt Message 3.1.1 because he/she would require the knowledge of the key K_{S2}, which can only be calculated with the knowledge of K_{S1}, which is generated by Bob.

4.   Denial of service (*DoS*) attacks would consists of sending rogue authentication request that would consume both bandwidth and processing time at the FA and the HA. Such an attack can be realized more easily by simultaneously mass replay attacks. It would make the HA compute all the key material for each request. Denial of service is a general and open issue for any service on the Internet.

Comments on the Detailed Design of the Protocol

The description of the authentication protocol given in the fourth section represents, in some sense, an "abstract protocol; that is, only the logical meaning of the message parameters is described, while the coding of these parameters is left undefined. It is important to note, however, that a complete protocol specification (describing all requirements for an implementation) should also include the definition of the parameter encoding and the description of the cryptographic functions that are used. It is clear that the choice of these cryptographic functions has a strong impact on the level of security that can be obtained by the given "abstract protocol". In the following, we give some comments on the possible choices.

Private-key algorithms should be chosen such that the length of the key can be adapted to the computational power of the mobile terminal. Triple-DES, Blowfish and AES (Advanced Encryption Standard) are such algorithms. Elliptic Curve Cryptography (ECC) should preferably be used for public-key encryption, rather than RSA, to make use of its shorter key length at equal security level.

Secure connections could be set up in several ways since both FA and HA own a digital certificate. TLS (Transport Layer Security), IPsec (IP security), IKE (Internet Key Exchange) or any secure link establishment protocol could be used between the two agents.

Note that the protocol satisfies all the requirements when executed on a user-owned mobile device. However, when executed on any device that may be locally available to the mobile user, there are two common problems (which are not related to this particular protocol): (a) The user has to trust the integrity of the software (as explained in the third section), and (b) the private key generated by the protocol may be left on the device and used by other people, if the user does not properly terminate the application.

Concluding Discussion

We gave an introduction to the authentication requirements for electronic commerce by identifying the commerce partners and required trust relationships, and by describing the security requirements including authentication, access rights, payment credentials, and anonymity (in certain cases). We also reviewed existing paradigms for authentication and corresponding protocols, and discussed their suitability for electronic commerce applications. We considered in particular the requirements stemming from user mobility, which include the security implications of using unknown ad hoc devices that are locally available and the fact that the user may need to be authenticated by a foreign organization that provides network access facilities and other services within the foreign domain where the user temporarily resides.

We then proposed a secure authentication protocol for mobile users that combines the ease of password-based authentication with the power of public key technology, and can be executed on an ad hoc device. It provides authentication support (i) for electronic commerce transactions, (ii) for obtaining the necessary transmission resources from the local Internet service provider (ISP) and (iii) for authentication to arbitrary third parties. We believe that this authentication protocol contains a number of interesting features that make it suitable as an alternative to the other authentication protocols that are currently in use. In fact, this authentication protocol is not limited to electronic commerce applications, but could be used as well for other distributed applications, such as IP telephony and multimedia teleconferencing.

We note that in the context of electronic commerce and other applications, there is not only the need for authentication of users and services, but also a need for obtaining other kinds of references, such as payment credentials, age certifications, or competence certificates. Such references may be provided in the form of signed certificates, similar to authentication certificates, but containing different information attributes. It is also important to allow the user of commerce applications to remain anonymous; for this case one has to foresee certificates that do not contain the name of the user, nor other identifying information. An example is a payment credential for an anonymous user who is only identified to the commerce server by a random number without any other significance.

We finally note that the use of ad hoc devices that may be available in the local environment of the mobile user poses certain security threats, since it is very difficult to ensure the security of the software that runs on such a computer. For the present purposes, we assume that this risk can be kept sufficiently small by using certified software downloaded over the Internet. However, future research may identify methods for closing the remaining loopholes.

References

AbdelAziz, B. (2000). Using IKE and radius with MobInTel. Technical report. University of Ottawa, Ottawa, Canada.

Dupré-la-Tour, I., Bochmann, G.v., & Chouinard, J.Y. (2001). A secure authentication infrastructure for mobile communication services over the Internet. In R. Steinmetz et al. (Eds.), *Communications and Multimedia Security Issues of the New Century (Proc. IFIP Working Conf. CMS'01, Darmstadt)* (pp. 405-416). KluwerAcademic Publication.

El-Khatib, K., Hadibi, N., & Bochmann, G.v. (2003). Support for personal and service mobility in ubiquitous computing environments. *EuroPar*.

Glass, S., Hiller, T., Jacobs, S., & Perkins, C. (2000). Mobile IP authentication, authorization, and accounting requirements. Request for Comments, RFC 2977, the Internet Engineering Task Force.

Kohl, J.T., Neuman, B.C., & Tso, T.Y. (1994). *The evolution of the Kerberos authentication system. Distributed open systems* (pp. 78-94). IEEE Computer Society Press.

RSA Laboratories. (1993). PKCS #10: Certification request syntax standard. Technical report.

Simpson, W. (1996). Challenge handshake authentication protocol (CHAP). Request for Comments, RFC 1994, the Internet Engineering Task Force.

Steiner, J.G., Neuman, B.C., & Schiller, J.I. (1988). Kerberos: An authentication service for open network systems. *Proceedings of the Winter 1988 Usenix Conference.*

Section II

Mobile Commerce Security

Chapter V

Policy-Based Access Control for Context-Aware Services over the Wireless Internet

Paolo Bellavista, University of Bologna, Italy

Antonio Corradi, University of Bologna, Italy

Cesare Stefanelli, University of Ferrara, Italy

Abstract

The spreading wireless accessibility to the Internet stimulates the provisioning of mobile commercial services to a wide set of heterogeneous and limited client terminals. This requires novel programming methodologies to support and simplify the development of innovative service classes. In these novel services, results and offered quality levels should depend on both client location and locally available resources (context). In addition, it is crucial to manage the frequent modifications of resource availability due to wireless client movements during service provisioning. Within this perspective, the chapter motivates the need for novel access control solutions to flexibly control the resource access of mobile clients depending on the currently applicable context. In particular, it discusses and exemplifies how innovative middleware for access control should support the determination of the client context on the basis of high-level declarative directives (profiles and policies) and distributed online monitoring.

Introduction

Recent advances in wireless networking and the growing number of wireless-enabled portable devices create new promising commercial opportunities. In-Stat/MDR estimates that more than 465 million mobile device units will be built and shipped in 2004, with an annual increase of more than 7%, and a similar rise expectation for the next years (Reeds, 2003). A primary commercial challenge is to exploit this enlarging market to ubiquitously provide mobile users with both traditional Internet services and innovative location-dependent mobile commerce applications.

Service providers and wireless network operators have to face new and challenging technical issues toward the seamless integration of wireless clients with the traditional fixed Internet. This scenario, called *wireless Internet* in the following, already starts to exhibit research and commercial solutions to support network connectivity (Bos, 2001; Perkins, 1999). However, provisioning commercially mature mobile services over the global and open wireless Internet requires addressing complex and different issues, such as configuration management, service content adaptation, access control, accounting, dynamic un/installation of infrastructure/service components, and interoperability. The research in several of these areas is still at its beginning; it starts to recognize the need for novel and flexible middleware solutions (Bellavista, 2002a).

In particular, the wireless Internet calls for novel methodologies to support and simplify the development of innovative service classes where results and offered quality levels depend on the *context*; that is, the logical set of resources that a client can access due to provisioning environment properties, such as current client location, security permissions, access device capabilities, user preferences and trust level, runtime resource state, and mutual relationships with currently local users/terminals/resources (Bellavista, 2003a). Some simple forms of context determination, such as the ones associated with traditional security permissions, are not new for distributed systems. The novelty here is that the frequent mobility of wireless Internet clients makes it crucial to manage the recurrent context variations, and the consequent service reconfiguration at provision time. In fact, the context depends on both quite static aspects, for example, the local authorization rules and the client device characteristics, and very dynamic aspects, for example, the client location and the provision-time state of involved resources.

In other words, the wide heterogeneity, the changing network topology/connectivity and the resource shortage/discontinuities typical of the wireless Internet stress the relevance of context awareness and of developing context-adaptive services. However, the complexity of designing, implementing, and deploying context-aware mobile services potentially limits the rapid emergence of this new service market. Therefore, there is a growing request for highly flexible and innovative middleware to facilitate the development and runtime support of context-aware wireless Internet services. In particular, in this chapter we motivate and discuss the necessity of novel security middleware solutions to perform enhanced forms of access control. Such an access control exploits the flexible definition and the dynamic determination/update of user contexts during service sessions.

For instance, a mobile stock trading service should allow its mobile users to operate via laptops connected to Wi-Fi hotspots, via PDAs connected to Bluetooth Local Infotainment Points (BLIP), and via GSM phones receiving simple SMS-based communication. Access control middleware should assign differentiated contexts depending on differentiated classes of users, access terminals and connectivity technology. On the basis of context, clients should have visibility of alternative trading service interfaces. In addition, access control solutions should update contexts (and service provisioning accordingly) in response to client mobility and user class of service. If a bronze user moves to a very congested wireless cell, she should simply lose visibility of the trading service. A gold user, instead, should have priority and transparently access a service gateway that downscales the service results to either text files or SMS messages. The result is a reduced modality of service provisioning that does not aggravate too much the network congestion situation.

The chapter aims at identifying the main requirements, functions and technical challenges associated with innovative context-aware security middleware for wireless Internet access control. In particular, it claims that flexible access control should determine the client context depending on different types of high-level declarative metadata (profiles and policies) and on the runtime state of the provisioning environment. Profiles and policies can represent, respectively, the characteristics of users/terminals/resources and the resource/service management strategies, in a cleanly separated way from the service implementation. The online resource monitoring is crucial to enable the runtime shaping of contexts in response to the frequent modifications of resource availability due to wireless client mobility. Access control middleware based on both metadata and online monitoring can determine and impose differentiated contexts (and consequently differentiated and tailored service behaviors) with no need to modify the application logic. As a relevant side effect, this favors middleware/service component reusability in different deployment scenarios (Bellavista, 2003b).

As an example of context-aware access control solution, the chapter presents the architecture and the most relevant implementation aspects of Wireless Internet Context-aware access Control (WICoCo). WICoCo is the Java-based security solution for access control in CARMEN (Bellavista, 2003b). WICoCo addresses two primary state-of-the-art challenges for context-aware access control: how to enforce user/service requirements expressed at a high level of abstraction in terms of declarative metadata, and how to achieve full visibility of monitoring information in a portable way.

In addition, to smooth the relevant discontinuities in resource availability at the wired-wireless edges of the wireless Internet, WICoCo provides mobile clients with mobile middleware proxies that work over the fixed network infrastructure on their behalf (and in their vicinity). WICoCo proxies determine the client contexts and mediate any client access to resources. They are implemented in terms of mobile agents (MAs) and can follow the provision-time movement of clients, where and when needed (Fuggetta, 1998).

Context-Aware Service Provisioning over the Wireless Internet

The wireless Internet scenario exhibits several peculiar characteristics that need to be considered in service provisioning. Mobility of users and access devices is pushed to the extreme. Users can connect to the network from ubiquitous points of attachment and wireless portable devices can roam by maintaining continuous connectivity (Bos, 2001). Frequent disconnections of users/devices are rather common operating modes that can occur either voluntarily to reduce connection costs and to save battery or accidentally due to the loss of wireless connectivity.

Moreover, the wireless Internet exhibits a high degree of heterogeneity of both access devices (in terms of screen size and resolution, computing power, memory, storage, operating system, and supported software) and networking technologies (IEEE 802.11a/b/g, Bluetooth, IrDA, GPRS, and UMTS). In addition, this heterogeneity seems not only a temporary aspect due to the novelty and immaturity of the technology, but is expected to last in the open and global wireless Internet.

These distinctive features of mobility and heterogeneity pose new challenging issues and undermine several assumptions of traditional distributed services. Traditional service provisioning relies on a relatively static characterization of the context. For instance, resource availability is typically independent of both the user current location and the access device properties (location and heterogeneity transparency). Changes in the set of accessible resources are relatively small, rare, or predictable (Roman, 2000). On the contrary, in the wireless Internet, it is crucial to consider rapidly changing contexts and to frequently reorganize service provisioning in response to context modifications. Client mobility requires solutions that properly and promptly handle changes of client location, modifications in locally accessible resources, temporary disconnection, and changing network topology. In addition, users can change their portable access devices, with different wireless technologies, even at runtime. All the above elements require context-aware service management at provision time.

Service provisioning in the wireless Internet requires the full visibility of location information. For instance, middleware/service components should be aware of the location of both users and involved resources to forward stock trading transaction requests to the server, instances that minimize the current client/server distance. Middleware/service components should also have visibility of different kinds of system-level data, such as the access device characteristics and the currently available wireless bandwidth, respectively, to customize service provisioning and to guarantee effective resource usage. These aspects are particularly crucial in wireless provisioning environments because of the scarcity and the high cost of resources. System-level data should be propagated up to the middleware/application level to dynamically determine the applicable context for the user during her session and to perform service configuration and delivery accordingly. For instance, middleware/service components should be aware of the congestion state of both the replicated stock trading service components and the local wireless network. This awareness enables the forwarding of transaction requests to the server instances by balancing the network/service load and, therefore, by minimizing the client connection time.

In summary, the handling of context information in the wireless Internet is complicated by the frequent variations in the provisioning environment, primarily due to client mobility and heterogeneity at provision time. Context variability significantly increases the complexity and the costs of designing, developing and deploying wireless Internet services, thus slowing down their widespread diffusion. As a consequence, context-aware services call for middleware support infrastructures. There is the need for nontraditional middleware with full context visibility and capable of automating service reconfiguration depending on dynamic context changes. These middleware should interact with the underlying execution environment to collect relevant information for context determination, for example, current location of users/devices, resource state, user preferences, and device characteristics. This information should be processed at provision time to identify the applicable contexts, their evolution, and the most appropriate service management operations.

Context-Aware Access Control: Requirements and Solution Guidelines

Traditional security solutions for access control, in both centralized and distributed systems, are all based on the main concept of associating permission information with either the potentially accessible resources (as in access control lists) or the potentially accessing clients (as in capabilities) (Sandhu, 1996). These permissions rule resource accesses in a simple way, by denying/allowing different access modes, for example, read/write/execute, to different clients depending on the client identity or grouping. In traditional systems, access control solutions are usually provided at the operating system level. They evaluate the applicable permissions at runtime, typically at any client access request in the case of access control lists and at the starting of the client session when adopting capabilities.

We claim that the traditional security solutions for access control are not flexible enough for mobile commerce services over the wireless Internet, where it is crucial to distinguish access control on the basis of a wide variety of information, and not only to consider the client identity. For instance, the set of resources that a client can access should also depend on user preferences, characteristics of currently used access terminals, subscribed services, and associated trust level (Bellavista, 2003a). In addition, resource accessibility should also take into account the congestion state of the provisioning environment at resource request time. When addressing quality of service issues for mobile commerce services over best-effort networks, it is crucial to operate access control decisions that depend on the expected quality perturbations produced by newly accepted requests. This is necessary to avoid compromising the established service level agreements on the already admitted active sessions.

Moreover, novel security solutions should support the possibility to modify access control decisions and with the maximum degree of flexibility, even by affecting already established service sessions. Let us think about the case of a gold user who enters a congested wireless cell. It could be reasonable to reduce the set of accessible resources of "already-in" bronze users, even if they have already achieved the access to those resources. For instance, bronze users could be automatically rebound to downscaled service components, which are less resource-consuming.

Last, but not least, we claim that access control decisions should also impact on the resource visibility itself provided to the client, in order to suggest (and simplify) the most suitable client-resource binding depending on the client characteristics and the provision-time conditions. This customized visibility could significantly reduce the complexity of developing mobile commerce services for the wireless Internet. It is the access control support that becomes in charge of proposing only the resource bindings that best fit the specific management goals chosen, for example, best-effort quality support, resource load balancing, and limitation of the client connection time.

In other words, we claim that access control solutions for mobile commerce over the wireless Internet should be context-aware. Security supports for the wireless Internet should also assume the burden of dynamically establishing the user context, of determining the applicable resource visibility, and of automatically reconfiguring the provided services with no (or little) impact on the implementation of mobile commerce clients and servers. Let us note that context-aware access control middleware can significantly simplify the realization of context-dependent mobile services by allowing developers to continue to implement context-transparent traditional service components (Bellavista, 2003b).

Providing such an access control middleware is particularly challenging and complex. The client mobility, the wide heterogeneity of clients and wireless technologies, and the openness of the provisioning environment are only the most evident among the numerous tricky aspects to address. This multiplicity of issues is producing a plethora of research projects and prototypes, each one proposing different partial solutions in the general area of context-aware resource visibility in mobile computing environments (Schilit, 2002). Most important, some first common guidelines of solution are starting to emerge. On the one hand, there is a growing interest in specifying access control rules and resource management strategies in a cleanly separated way from the service implementation. This can be done by adopting different kinds of high-level metadata to describe clients, resources, and service management requirements, and by interpreting/enforcing them at service provision time, as introduced in the third section. On the other hand, the significant discontinuity in resource availability (and costs) between the wired infrastructure and the wireless access cells is pushing towards the exploitation of proxy middleware components, as illustrated in the third section.

Profile and Policy Metadata

The need for a clean separation of concerns between context determination (and context-based service management) and application logic implementation starts to be widely recognized (Roman, 2000). Two main types of approaches are possible to achieve such separation in a flexible way. The first is to define separated programming meta-levels in charge of mobility management and service adaptation. These meta-levels interwork with the actual service implementation by exploiting reflection techniques (Capra, 2003). The second possibility is to specify high-level metadata describing the characteristics of the involved service entities and the goals of service management. The evaluation and enforcement of these metadata require middleware facilities for monitoring and event distribution. Reflection represents an interesting solution guideline for context-aware mobile commerce services, but is difficult to integrate with legacy systems usually implemented in non-reflective programming languages. On the contrary, profile/policy-based approaches, as the WICoCo one extensively described in the fourth section, can apply also to legacy services, independently of their implementation language. For these reasons, in the following we will only focus on metadata-based solutions for context management.

Context-aware access control solutions can significantly benefit from the adoption of metadata to represent both the context characteristics and the choices in service behavior at a high level of abstraction, with a clean separation between service management and service logic (Huber, 1996). Among the different possible types of metadata, profiles and policies are considered of increasing interest (Heflin, 2003). Profiles represent characteristics, capabilities and requirements of users, devices, resources, and service components. They should guide the determination of the applicable context, for example, by allowing a client device to have visibility of a service component if and only if the client can visualize the format of the results produced by that component. Several research efforts are attempting to identify well accepted formats for the most common access devices. They are encouraging the adoption of standards for profile representation, in order to favor resource reusing and sharing in the open wireless Internet (W3C, 2002).

Policies express the choices ruling system behavior, in terms of the actions that subjects can/must perform upon resources. Policies are maintained completely separate from system implementation details; they are expressed at a high level of abstraction to simplify their specification by system administrators, service managers, and even final users. Some recent policy-based systems distinguish two different kinds of policies (Moffett, 1993): authorization policies and obligation ones. The former specify the actions that subjects are allowed to perform on resources depending on various types of conditions, for example, subject identity and resource state. The latter define the actions that subjects must perform on resources when triggered by the occurrence of specified conditions.

Figure 1 shows a possible metadata taxonomy, and two examples of obligation policy and device profile. The depicted taxonomy is the one adopted in the WICoCo solution, as more extensively described in the fourth section, where we will show how the different types of metadata are relevant to determine the applicable context and to update it flexibly during service provisioning.

Middleware Proxies

In context-aware security solutions for access control, it is crucial to adopt middleware proxies that execute over the fixed Internet on the behalf of wireless mobile clients. Middleware proxies are located along the service flow path between the clients and the

Figure 1. The metadata taxonomy adopted in WICoCo

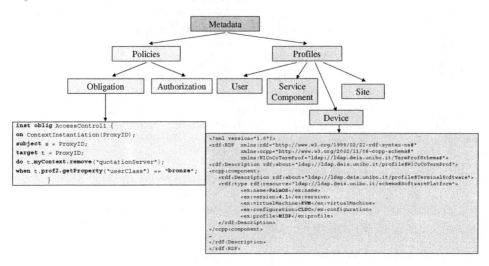

server, typically in the proximity of the clients they work for, as depicted in Figure 2 (Bellavista, 2003a).

Proxies are demonstrating their effectiveness in playing the general role of assisting mobile clients in their current access locality, by smoothing the problems due to both intermittent and limited bandwidth wireless connections. For instance, proxies can asynchronously perform complex queries on wired resources and can downscale service results to fit the access device visualization capabilities (Hwang, 2003). In particular, by focusing on context-aware access control, proxies can perform, over the wired network, the possibly complex computations needed to determine the applicable contexts, and should work as intermediaries in the client access to any resource currently included in its context.

Mediating service accessibility via proxies, however, requires any participating wireless locality to enable the proxy-based support for any possible visiting client. This could be impracticable in the open wireless Internet where highly heterogeneous unpredictable types of clients are willing to access different and statically unforeseen mobile commerce services. In fact, these clients usually require differentiated support behaviors and different capabilities to interpret the applicable metadata. Any a priori installation of all possible middleware proxies in all possible access localities is to be considered definitely unfeasible in an open provisioning environment. For these reasons, there are a few state-of-the-art research projects that propose the adoption of the mobile agent (MA) technology to implement wireless Internet middleware proxies (Bellavista, 2003b; IKV, 2003). MA-based proxies can follow the client movements from a wireless access locality to another one during service provisioning, also by preserving the session state thanks to the MA peculiar capability to migrate both behavior and reached state of execution at runtime (Fuggetta, 1998).

Figure 2. Middleware proxies mediating the mobile client access to wireless Internet services

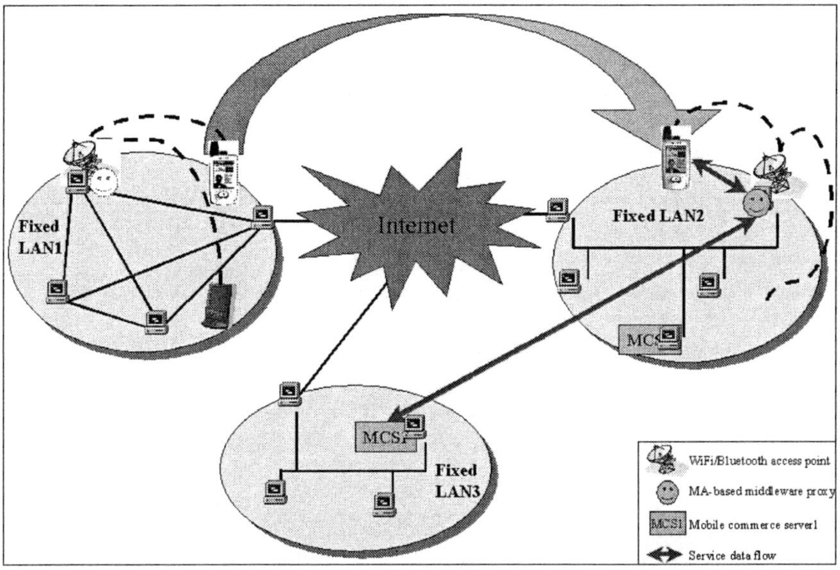

In the next section, we will exemplify how the proxy-based WICoCo middleware can dynamically determine and update the applicable context depending on different forms of metadata, and how WICoCo proxies use the applicable context to rule the client access control to mobile commerce services over the wireless Internet.

WiCoCo Middleware

Along the previously sketched design guidelines, we have developed WICoCo, a flexible and portable middleware for context-aware access control in the wireless Internet. This section describes the main characteristics of WICoCo primarily to point out how the combined adoption of different kinds of metadata, mobile code, and portable implementation technologies can lead to very flexible access control solutions. This flexibility is needed to fit the specific properties of the open and heterogeneous wireless Internet provisioning environment. In our opinion, the WICoCo design and implementation can represent a useful experience to exemplify, with an actual middleware prototype, the state-of-the-art guidelines of solution emerging in this novel challenging field.

WICoCo is the access control security solution adopted in CARMEN, an MA-based flexible middleware for adaptive service provisioning to mobile wireless clients (Bellavista, 2003b). The CARMEN middleware is designed according to the layered architecture shown in Figure 3. CARMEN is based on a general-purpose MA platform called SOMA, which supports the mobility of both code and reached execution state of middleware components. The CARMEN facilities provides mechanisms and tools to address the most common issues in context-aware service provisioning to wireless clients: a rich and articulated naming system (the *identification*, *discovery* and *directory* facilities) (Bellavista, 2001); a *location* facility that integrates heterogeneous tracking solutions for IEEE 802.11b and Bluetooth; a *monitoring* facility that allows observing indicators at the application and system level to achieve full visibility of context changes (Bellavista, 2002b); and an *event manager* facility to distribute context-related events to interested CARMEN components, even mobile (Bellavista, 2003b).

WICoCo works on top of the above facilities, and consists of two main components: the context manager (CM) and the metadata manager (MM). CM determines dynamically the client context, mediates the client access to resources in the applicable context via specialized MA-based proxies, and transparently performs service adaptation in the case of context modifications. MM supports the specification, modification, and checks for correctness, installation, and evaluation of the different kinds of WICoCo metadata. To better understand how WICoCo performs context-aware access control, in the following we will focus on the description of the two WICoCo components, CM and MM, and of the monitoring/location facilities responsible for sensing context changes.

Context Manager

CM is the WICoCo component responsible for dynamically establishing the context of any client, thus determining its resource visibility. In particular, WICoCo exploits MA-based mobile proxies, working over the fixed network on behalf (and in proximity) of their wireless clients, to determine the applicable contexts and to mediate any client access to resources.

To dynamically determine the applicable context object for a client, CM firstly merges the list of resources in the client access locality, obtained via the discovery facility, and the list of globally available resources, retrieved via the directory facility. Then, CM discards resources from the merged set depending on the metadata included in the applicable user/

Figure 3. The CARMEN layered architecture

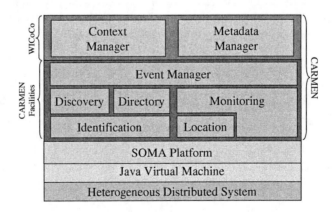

device/service component profiles (see the fourth section). For instance, if the device profile specifies that the Web browser on the access terminal can visualize only c-HTML pages, stock trading service components that provide only XML-based stock information are automatically removed from the context.

The obtained resource set is the result of the combination of local/global resource availability and applicable profile metadata, that is, user desiderata, access device capabilities, and service component characteristics. To obtain the applicable context, this resource set is subject to further restrictions and discarding due to the enforcement of the access control policies (see the fourth section). The result is a context object listing all the resources currently accessible to one client. CM represents a context object as a container of tuples, any tuple corresponding to an accessible resource and including a unique resource identifier, a resource descriptor, and additional information to properly manage the resource binding in case of client mobility. The context object is automatically updated anytime a client requests a resource access and anytime an event in the provisioning environment triggers a modification in the applicable context. In fact, events may trigger the enforcement of WICoCo access control policies, thus affecting the resource visibility, as detailed in the following.

The WICoCo MA-Based Proxies

WICoCo provides any user, at the starting of her service session, with a personal mobile proxy that migrates over the fixed network and follows the user movements among wireless localities at service provision time. The mobile proxy acts as the intermediary between the user wireless device and the accessed resources. The access permission/denial depends on the currently applicable context, which the proxy determines by exploiting the CM facilities.

We claim the suitability of the MA technology to implement mobile proxies for context-aware access control. WICoCo exploits SOMA to implement proxies as SOMA agents and to provide them with execution environments, called places, which offer the basic services for MA communication and migration. Places typically model nodes and can be grouped into domains that correspond to network localities, for example, local area networks with IEEE 802.11b/Bluetooth access points providing wireless connectivity to WiFi/Bluetooth portable devices (Figure 4a). CARMEN middleware facilities are available in any domain. Proxies run on places in the domain where the associated users and the corresponding wireless companion devices are currently connected.

WICoCo associates one proxy for each user, with a 1-to-1 mapping; proxies follow their associated users in their movements among different domains, carry the applicable context and the reached service state, and make it possible to migrate whole service sessions. As shown in Figure 4b, proxies retrieve the profiles of their companion devices (and of the profile associated users) at their instantiation via MM (see the fourth section). Let us note that the proxies need to ask for profiles only once, at the starting of the service session, being the profiles part of their state, which is maintained even after migration. Only the modification of the associated profiles triggers a corresponding event and a new profile request.

Proxies are designed to refer, at start up, only to CM and MM, without any direct resource access. They request their contexts by passing profile information to the CM component in their domain, as depicted in Figure 3b. After context determination, CM returns back to the proxy a context object listing the identifiers of all accessible resources, either active

Figure 4. (a) WICoCo places and domains; (b) the deployment of WICoCo middleware components in one wireless access locality

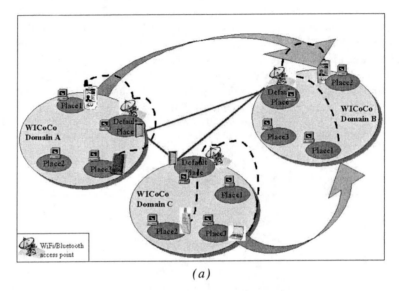

(a)

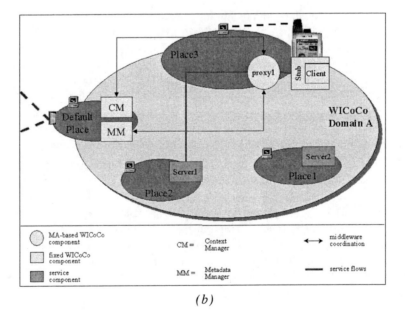

(b)

or passive. At the beginning, all resources in the context are passive. A resource becomes active when the user requests to access it. For any active resource, the context object includes a resource identifier (the only information maintained for passive resources), the binding management strategy to apply in case of client migration, and a reference object that implements the chosen binding. WICoCo supports four different binding strategies (resource movement, copy movement, remote reference, and rebinding). The proxies dynamically re-qualify resource bindings, with no impact on the client/server implementation (Bellavista, 2003b). Any modification of interest in the provisioning environment produces the notification of a monitoring event to both CM and the involved proxies; the notified proxies usually react by interrogating their local CM to update their context objects.

Proxies interact with an additional type of middleware components: device-specific stubs. The stub is the only middleware component required to run on the wireless device, locally wraps the service-specific client, and connects to the responsible proxy to send/ receive service requests/results. Let us observe that the adoption of proxies over the fixed network and of lightweight clients on the portable devices permits to exploit the MA-based access control also when providing mobile commerce services to limited devices that cannot host MA execution environments.

Metadata Manager

MM is in charge of supporting the specification of all the different kinds of metadata depicted in the taxonomy of Figure 1. User profiles maintain information about personal preferences, interests, security requirements, and subscribed services for any WICoCo registered user. Device profiles report the hardware/software characteristics of the supported access terminals. Service component profiles describe the interface of available service components as well as their properties relevant for dynamic binding to mobile clients, for example, type/format of provided results. Site profiles are a resource group abstraction, and list all the resources available at one WICoCo host. WICoCo adopts standard formats for profile representation: the W3C Composite Capability/ Preference Profiles (CC/PP) for user/device profiles (W3C, 2002), the Web Service Description Language (WSDL) for the service component interface description (Curbera, 2002), and the Resource Description Framework (RDF) for the site collections of resources (Decker, 2000).

In addition, MM permits to specify access control policies as high-level declarative directives that affect the context determination and its runtime modification. WICoCo access control policies include not only traditional authorization policies, but also obligation policies. Authorization policies define the actions that clients are allowed to perform on resources and are triggered by resource access requests. Obligation policies, instead, specify the actions that clients and middleware/service components must perform on resources when specified conditions occur. The enforcement of obligation policies is event-triggered. For instance, a NetworkOverload (threshold) event, notified by the CARMEN Event Manager in response to the request of the monitoring facility (described in the following section), can trigger an obligation that updates the contexts of clients in the network locality, by removing the mobile stock trading service from bronze user contexts. WICoCo policies are written in the Ponder language and maintained completely separate from both application logic and middleware implementation details (Imperial, 2003).

MM supports not only the metadata specification/update but also the dynamic distribution, installation and enforcement of the access control policies. It is organized in two logical modules: the specification module, and the policy enforcer. The specification module exploits the tools developed within the Ponder project for editing, distributing, updating, removing, and browsing policies (Imperial, 2003). In addition, it provides tools for transforming high-level policy specifications into platform-enforceable Java policy objects. When a new policy object is created, it is registered in the directory facility and distributed to the interested MA-based proxies. The policy enforcer retrieves newly instantiated policy objects and parses them to retrieve relevant information: events, subjects, targets and actions. Then, on behalf of policy subjects, it registers the significant events to the event manager. It actually enforces the policies, when needed, by interpreting the applicable policy specifications. Policy interpretation consists in policy parsing, controlling the dynamic conditions for policy applicability, extracting the policy actions, and accordingly activating the specified context management operations.

Portable Middleware Facilities for Monitoring and Location

For any context-aware middleware, it is definitely crucial to have full visibility of the whole information that characterizes the provisioning environment, for example, the state of distributed resources and service components. This full visibility is difficult when operating on global scenarios with highly heterogeneous access terminals, communication technologies, and resources. The visibility goal further complicates in an open deployment scenario where the middleware portability must be considered essential.

The WICoCo access control aims at full portability, if possible not depending on the heterogeneous characteristics of the resources and of the operating systems involved. In addition, WICoCo has the objective of dynamically installing and propagating its middleware infrastructure (primarily its proxies) where and when needed at runtime, and to this purpose operates on top of a Java-based MA platform. The choice of Java simplifies dynamic portability. Almost all the recent MA platforms are built on top of the standard Java Virtual Machine (JVM) both to exploit the Java class loading features and to enable the MA portable migration in open environments (Bellavista, 2001). However, the Java choice can make it very hard to achieve the needed level of system state visibility. In the following, we show how WICoCo achieves the full awareness of monitoring and location information in a portable way, without imposing any modification to the standard JVM. The monitoring/location visibility solution in WICoCo is presented as an example, also applicable to other context-aware middlewares and to other application domains. The primary solution guideline is to achieve some forms of portability through the design of modular middleware infrastructures consisting of dynamically selected plug-ins.

Monitoring Facility Implementation

The monitoring facility enables the online observation of the state of resources and service components. It achieves the visibility of different kinds of monitoring data at different levels of abstraction. At the application level, it dynamically interacts with the JVM to gather detailed information about the execution of Java-based service components. At the kernel level, it enables the access to system indicators at the monitored target, such as CPU/memory usage of active processes and available network bandwidth. To overcome the transparency imposed by the JVM, the monitoring facility exploits extensions of the Java technology: the JVM Profiler Interface (JVMPI) (SUN, 2003a) and the Java Native Interface (JNI) (Gordon, 1998). In addition, it integrates with external standard monitoring entities of large adoption in network management, that is, Simple Network Management Protocol (SNMP) agents (Stallings, 1998).

JVMPI provides an interface to indicate to the JVM which are the application-level events of interest for monitoring purposes. After this initialization phase, JVMPI can be exploited to collect, filter and analyze the events produced by Java applications, for example, method invocation and object allocation. On the contrary, WICoCo obtains kernel-level monitoring data, such as CPU usage and incoming network packets, via SNMP agents that export local monitoring information in their standard management information bases (MIBs). To enable also the monitoring of non-SNMP hosts, the monitoring facility exploits JNI to integrate with platform-dependent monitoring mechanisms. Details about how to perform Java-based online monitoring by exploiting JVMPI, SNMP, and JNI, together with details about the implementation of the monitoring facility are available elsewhere (Bellavista, 2002b).

Here, instead, we focus on the fact that, in absence of a standard uniform support for online monitoring in Java, the monitoring portability is achieved via a modular architec-

Figure 5. The architecture of the portable monitoring facility

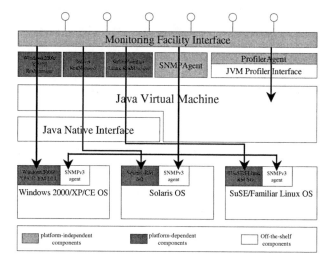

ture. The facility integrates three different components (ProfilerAgent, SNMPAgent, and *ResManager) and dynamically links the mechanisms and plug-ins fitting the monitoring target (see Figure 5). ProfilerAgent provides the JVMPI-based monitoring of Java resources and is portable on any host with the standard JVM. SNMPAgent acts as an SNMP manager that interrogates the monitored target to obtain the state of non-Java resources (Bellavista, 2002b). The *ResManager classes achieve kernel-level monitoring visibility via the JNI-based integration with native monitoring libraries, implemented with the same interfaces for different platforms. The monitoring facility binds to the correct monitoring mechanisms (and possibly loads the correct native library) for the monitored target. At middleware deployment time, the facility exploits the site profile to choose which monitoring modules to install. In that way, the modular implementation of the facility achieves portability over a large set of deployment scenarios and permits the installation of the middleware components only where specifically needed. The result is to provide a uniform monitoring interface independently of the platform heterogeneity.

Location Facility Implementation

Similar considerations about portability via dynamic composition of alternative modules apply to the location facility. At the state of the art, there is no application-level API for cell location visibility in wireless networks accepted by any vendor and spread across the most common operating systems. This is producing vendor/technology-specific solutions, which significantly slow down the emergence of a wide market of location-dependent wireless Internet services. Our approach is to develop a portable location facility via the dynamic composition of different implementation mechanisms, automatically downloaded and deployed depending on the system characteristics of wireless access points and client devices.

The WICoCo Location provides online visibility of the associations between access terminals and WiFi/Bluetooth wireless cells. On the one hand, middleware-level location visibility is required to enable the development of location-dependent services, without affecting the client/server implementation (Bellavista, 2002a). In the case of Wi-Fi connectivity, the location facility exploits the monitoring information that IEEE 802.11 access points make available via standard SNMP MIBs (Gast, 2002). In particular, the access point is configured to notify an intra-domain SNMP trap anytime a new portable device associates with the local wireless locality. This permits the location component to have the online visibility of all the associated wireless access devices, and, in particular, to sense any new device entering the controlled domain. In the case of Bluetooth-based access points, the facility exploits the portable Java API for Bluetooth to obtain the list of the devices currently connected to the network locality (JCP, 2003; Johansson, 2001).

On the other hand, it is sometimes useful to have portable location visibility also at the client side, that is, at client stubs. In the case of WiFi-enabled clients hosting Linux, the location facility provides a Java API, based on the Linux Wireless Extensions, to obtain the access points currently in visibility and some related communication-level information, such as received signal strength (Debian, 2003). If the clients host Windows CE3.0/CE.NET, the facility exploits the Network Driver Interface Specification User-mode I/O

(NDISUIO), which is platform-dependent but portable on any network vendor implementation, to obtain the same information as in Linux (MSDN, 2003). Finally, in the case of Bluetooth connectivity, the facility takes advantage of the Java API for Bluetooth.

As for the monitoring facility, at middleware deployment time the facility exploits the terminal and site profiles to choose which location mechanisms to install at either the fixed network or the access terminal, depending on the type of wireless connectivity and on the operating system. Specialized MAs dynamically install the needed location modules over the fixed network; at the wireless devices, the client stubs exploit the standard code upload mechanisms of the Java 2 Micro Edition.

Mobile Stock Trading Case Study

To exemplify how the WICoCo access control operates during a service session and how it facilitates the development of context-aware services, this section provides some design and implementation insights of a mobile stock trading service (MSTS). MSTS allows mobile users with their wireless devices to roam among different wireless localities while continuing to operate on up-to-date stock quotations. In addition, MSTS can immediately notify abrupt quotation changes to interested users independently of their current location. It is the WICoCo middleware that handles all the complexity associated with access control and changing resource visibility: the access control support is in charge of context determination and modification in response to user mobility, terminal heterogeneity, and time-evolving resource availability. Context management does not affect the implementation of MSTS-specific clients and servers, which are transparently realized as in traditional distributed systems.

The WICoCo-based MSTS prototype allows users to browse stock quotations and to buy/sell stocks. The transactional properties of buying/selling operations are not the primary focus of the prototype and are not currently supported. We have deployed MSTS in a distributed environment consisting of several local area networks with either IEEE 802.11b or Bluetooth access points. Each locality is modeled as a WICoCo domain that hosts the middleware facilities and an MSTS server, called "quotationServer," that maintains updated stock quotations. In addition, each domain provides execution environments for the proxies of the MSTS users currently connected to that locality.

Let us observe that in the MSTS case the "quotationServer" instances in the different domains are exact replicas of the quotation information. In different application scenarios, WICoCo can easily support the deployment of location-dependent services by exploiting domain servers with different domain-related data, for example, tourist information about local buildings and restaurants.

Users can access MSTS via wireless devices where only the device-specific MSTS clients and the associated client stubs are installed. We have currently implemented clients and client stubs for portable devices with either the J2ME/CLDC/MIDP suite and Wi-Fi connectivity, or PalmOS and Bluetooth. MSTS clients allow the users to subscribe to the service, to specify the list of stock quotations of primary interest, and to successively modify the profile information. In order to start the service session, the

Figure 6. Excerpts from the MSTSProxy code

```
class MSTSProxy extends WICoCoProxy {
...
void init() {
... UserProfile prof1 = Directory.getProfile(userID);
    DeviceProfile prof2 = Directory.getProfile(deviceID);
    Context myContext = CM.getContext(prof1,prof2);
    StockInfoList resID;
    try {
        resID = (StockInfoList) myContext.getResource(
            "quotationServer"); }
    catch (NotInContextException exception) { ... }
... }
void run() {
... if (isConnected==true) results = resID.downloadAll();
    visualizer(results);
    ... }
void onMSTSResUpdate() {
... if (isConnected==true) results = resID.downloadAll();
    visualizer(results);
    ... }
... }
```

users must pass an authentication phase. A successful authentication associates the user with both a unique user identifier and a unique device identifier corresponding to the currently used terminal. User and device identifiers are cleanly separated in WICoCo to allow the same user to change her access device (nomadic user mobility) by maintaining the same active service session.

After the authentication, the MSTS user is associated with a newly instantiated and personal WICoCo proxy. Figure 6 shows an excerpt from the simple and reusable code of the MSTSProxy, which subclasses the general-purpose WICoCoProxy. At the instantiation, the proxy executes the init() method to retrieve the profiles of both the user and her current device from the directory facility. Examples of CC/PP-compliant profiles for users and terminals are reported in the annex. We have used the CC/PP standard XML schemas to represent the device software platform characteristics and the supported data formats, while we had to define our schema extensions to maintain the user information of interest for MSTS, for example, the user belonging to the silver class and her stocks of primary interest. After the profile retrieval, the proxy commands CM to determine the context object myContext. As described in the previous sections, CM dynamically determines the context by applying different kinds of metadata. Starting from the set of locally and globally visible resources, CM removes the items with resource profiles incompatible with the user/terminal ones. For instance, in the case of the device profile in the annex, service components providing only XML-based results are removed from the context because the access terminal only supports txt, c-HTML, and mp3-based data formats.

Then, all the obligation policies for access control triggered by the *ContextInstantiation* event are enforced. For instance, the enforcement of AccessControl1 in Figure 7a forbids bronze users to access MSTS by removing quotation server resources from their contexts. After the policy enforcement, the determination of the session-start context is completed, and the context is sent to the proxy. Let us observe that access control actions such as the one specified in AccessControl1 could have been obtained also in a more traditional way, by defining an equivalent authorization policy to deny the access of bronze users to quotation servers. Even if the access control result is the same, the two alternative solutions have some differences. In the case of authorization policies, the user context would have included the quotation server instances; an access request to a quotation server would have produced a runtime evaluation of the access control permission. By enforcing AccessControl1, the resource visibility itself is completely hidden to the proxy (and therefore to the client). Thus, the MSTS client cannot even try to request that resource during the service session. This results in a little increase in the context determination overhead at session initialization, but reduces the runtime overhead for access denial. Most important, this intrinsically provides context-aware differentiated views of available resources, thus simplifying the resource binding decisions to the proxy and avoiding useless denials at runtime.

Once the context is determined, the proxy invokes the getResource("quotationServer") method on myContext. If the context includes a resource called "quotationServer," the invocation makes that resource active in the context, and returns back the resID resource descriptor to the proxy. If there is no resource with the given name in the applicable context, the exception handling produces a pop-up window in the MSTS client. The pop-up tells the user that the MSTS service is not accessible in her current wireless locality.

After the initialization and after any migration to a new domain, the proxy executes its run() method: if the user device is connected, the proxy requests the downloading of all stock quotation information from resID and then invokes visualizer() to push the received results to the client. Figure 6 shows that the update of an MSTS resource triggers the same actions described above. Obviously, it is reasonable to think also to alternative lighter solutions that assign to the user the responsibility of pulling the possibly updated results when desired. To this purpose, it is sufficient to specify a void on MSTSResUpdate() method. Other proxy threads, not shown in the code excerpt, serve in the visualization of the stock quotations of primary interest indicated in the user profile and in the handling of user-entered queries/purchases/sales for specific stocks.

Without any impact on the design and implementation of the MSTS server, client and proxy, WICoCo permits to flexibly specify different access control policies, for different deployment domains, even depending on the resource state at policy enforcement time. All these policies are evaluated dynamically when triggered by either a resource access request or an event notified by the monitoring/location facility, and possibly modify the applicable context during a service session. For instance, Figure 7b reports AccessControl2, which is triggered by the *NewLocation* event notified by the location facility when the user connects to the new domain LocalityID. By simply specifying that policy, a system administrator obtains that, in the LocalityID domain, silver users cannot access MSTS when the average network bandwidth is lower than a threshold. Let us note that, to reduce the overhead due to policy enforcement, in MSTS this potential context update is performed only at the user entrance in a new domain and not at any sensed variation in the local network bandwidth. Similarly, it is possible to simply associate service re-configuration operations at the user entrance in a network locality, by specifying other policies triggered by the *NewLocation* event. The change of domain of attachment is usually one of the most important reasons of context update in wireless Internet services (Bellavista, 2003b).

However, when necessary, it is also possible to specify access control policies that immediately update the contexts in the domain as soon as something changes in the local resource availability. Figure 7c shows AccessControl3 triggered by the *AvgBandUnderThreshold* event notified by the monitoring facility. AccessControl3 denies the MSTS access to one randomly-chosen proxy in the domain if the associated user is silver class, by producing an exception handling similarly to the failure of getResource(). If the local network bandwidth keeps too low even after the policy enforcement, another *AvgBandUnderThreshold* event will be notified, and possibly another proxy will have the MSTS access denied. Alternatively, a system administrator could have decided to update the context of a silver user only when her proxy requests to access the MSTS resource. AccessControl4 in Figure 7d specifies the same actions of AccessControl3 but in terms of an authorization policy triggered by the proxy explicit request of operating on resID. Here we can apply the same performance considerations

Figure 7. Examples of MSTS access control policies: AccessControl1 enforced at context instantiation time (a), AccessControl2 triggered by the user change of domain (b), AccessControl3 enforced in response to a local network traffic change (c), AccessControl4 triggered by a proxy access request to an MSTS resource (d), and AccessControl5 enforced when the local quotation server is overloaded (e)

```
inst oblig AccessControl1 {
on ContextInstantiation(ProxyID);
subject s = ProxyID;
target t = ProxyID;
do t.myContext.remove("quotationServer");
when t.prof2.getProperty("userClass") == "bronze";
        }
```
a)

```
inst oblig AccessControl2 {
on NewLocation(ProxyID,LocalityID)
subject s = ProxyID;
target t = ProxyID;
do t.myContext.remove("quotationServer");
when ((t.prof2.getProperty("userClass") == "silver") &&
        (Monitoring.getAvgBand() > threshold));
        }
```
b)

```
inst oblig AccessControl3 {
on AvgBandUnderThreshold();
subject s = getOneLocalProxy();
target t = s;
do t.myContext.remove("quotationServer");
when t.prof2.getProperty("userClass") == "silver";
        }
```
c)

```
inst auth- AccessControl4 {
subject s = ProxyID;
target quotationServerID;
action downloadAll(), query(),
        onlyPrimaryStocks();
when s.prof2.getProperty("userClass")=="silver";
        }
```
d)

```
inst oblig AccessControl5 {
on QuotationServerOverload(QSID);
subject s = getOneLocalProxy();
target t = s;
do t.myContext.remove(QSID) ->
    t.myContext.add("quotationServerBackup") ->
    t.resID = (StockInfoList) myContext.getResource(
        "quotationServerBackup");
when ((t.prof2.getProperty("userClass") == "silver")
&& (Monitoring.getCPULoad(QSID.host()) > t1)
&& (Monitoring.getMemoryOcc(QSID.host()) > t2));
        }
```
e)

about the differences between obligation and authorization policies that we previously made for context initialization.

Finally, also server state modifications can trigger context modifications and consequent context-aware service adaptations. The AccessControl5 policy in Figure 7e automatically rebinds silver user proxies to an alternative local quotation server, which acts as a slow backup copy of the master quotation server. The policy is triggered when the CPU and the memory usage of the master overcome the thresholds, with the goal of preventing the degradation of the service quality achieved by the gold clients in the locality.

Related Work

Several research efforts have addressed the general issue of middleware to support different forms of mobility in the wireless Internet (user, device, resource, and service component mobility). They face very diverse aspects, from the provisioning of virtual home environments to 3G roaming users, to the effective synchronization of data replicas on mobile devices, and to profile-based content tailoring (Davies, 2002; Mascolo, 2002; Moura, 2002; Roman, 2000). It is relevant to observe that, notwithstanding the wide spectrum of challenges addressed, most solutions recognize the need to consider some forms of context. To this purpose, they propose the adoption of different kinds of metadata to drive the service behavior at runtime, for example, to maintain replica modification flags and multimedia presentations with alternative contents (Agarwal, 2002; Bulterman, 2002). We do not intend to provide here a general survey of the state-of-the-art middleware for context awareness in mobile computing, but only to focus on the access control research that explicitly deals with the primary design guidelines proposed in the chapter, that is, the profile/policy-driven context management, and the exploitation of MA-based middleware proxies.

By focusing on metadata for context-aware access control, a few first research proposals are appearing due to the novelty of the approach. All these projects agree on the crucial relevance to cleanly separate the context-aware access control issues from the application logic implementation, both to favor component reusability and to facilitate service development. Some proposals exploit reflection techniques to define separated programming meta-levels (Capra, 2003). Tanter and Piquer use reflection to define customizable access control strategies to rearrange the associations among service components and needed resources depending on meta-objects (2001). However, the determination of the applicable context is performed only at execution start, and cannot change at provision time. Another interesting approach is FarGo, which supports the programming of context determination rules as separate components (Holder, 1999). Similarly to Tanter (2001), the context is computed and associated to FarGo service components only at the application start. WICoCo has several points in common with the above approaches: it exploits middleware intermediaries to mediate the client access to resources, and it adopts some forms of metadata to separately specify how to determine the applicable context. The primary distinguishing feature, however, is that WICoCo can specify context determination rules in terms of high-level profiles and policies and that these rules can be modified during service provisioning, without any impact on the service implementation.

About policy representation, a wide spectrum of languages with different purposes, expressiveness, and formats have been defined, especially in the network management area, for example, the routing-oriented RPSL, the service monitoring-oriented SRL, and the service path management-oriented PPL (Stone, 2001). Several recent proposals exploit XML as their representation language, to facilitate the adoption in open environments. Among them, the eXtensible Access Control Markup Language (XACML) is the most significant effort of standardization and permits to represent both access control policies and resource access requests/responses (OASIS, 03). Differently from these approaches, Ponder allows the specification not only of authorization policies but also of obligation ones, essential in WICoCo to trigger the context update in response to environment modifications. In addition, Ponder is object-oriented and supports high-level abstractions to model collections of subjects/targets, based on either groups or roles. Let us note that a recent research hot topic is the definition of semantic-based policy languages, for example, KaoS and Rei, which have a further extended expressive power (Tonti, 2003). The Ponder adoption in WICoCo is a reasonable compromise between the very rich expressiveness (and considerable overhead) of semantic-based languages and the simplicity (and reduced expressiveness) of XML-based solutions.

Regarding the adoption of proxies, the solution guideline of interposing security mediators between users and resources is recently emerging in different areas. For instance, in Ajanta, any MA access to resources is controlled by using a proxy-based mechanism at the client side (Karnik, 2000). In a different domain, Foster et al. propose the exploitation of proxies to secure the access to the resources offered by a computational grid (1998). In particular, proxy-based solutions seem suitable for wired-wireless integrated environments to smooth the discontinuities in available resources at the wired-wireless edges. Yoshimura et al. propose statically placed middleware components that perform local monitoring and multimedia adaptation (2002). Ross et al. exploit security proxies to determine the customized resource visibility of wireless clients; device-specific scripts, embedded in the proxy code, determine the visibility decisions (2000). However, also due to the novelty of the MA technology, few researches have proposed MAs to implement access control proxies. The ACTS OnTheMove project has developed a mobile application support environment that provides a statically installed proxy that manages laptop mobility between fixed and wireless networks (Kovacs, 1998). Other MA proposals mainly concentrate on proxies for profile-based virtual home environments (Lipperts, 1999). To the best of our knowledge, WICoCo is original in adopting MA-based mobile proxies working in the fixed network to perform context-aware access control also for resource-constrained terminals that cannot host any version of the JVM.

Lessons Learned and Concluding Remarks

The provisioning of mobile commerce services over the wireless Internet motivates flexible security solutions with full context awareness and capable of properly handling context modifications at runtime. On the one hand, the complexity of context handling and of context-based service management suggests a clear separation of concerns between access control strategies and service logic implementation. This is primary to simplify the implementation of context-dependent adaptive mobile commerce and to promote the reusability of service components. Novel programmable security middleware, integrated with profiles and policies, can provide the required adaptability, while hiding low-level implementation mechanisms. Notwithstanding their high level of abstraction, the metadata evaluation at runtime is demonstrating to introduce an acceptable overhead when coupled with effective and decentralized support solutions that exploit code/state mobility to maintain access control proxies in proximity of their wireless clients.

On the other hand, context-aware access control in an open environment calls for portable mechanisms for online monitoring. Java-based technologies are mature to integrate heterogeneous monitoring solutions within a uniform portable framework with performance results compatible with most mobile commerce applications for the wireless Internet. The SUN attention for the integration of the JVM with monitoring mechanisms is confirmed by the novel management features of the forthcoming JVM1.5 edition, which are expected to further improve the performance of Java-based monitoring (SUN, 2003c).

Acknowledgments

Work supported by the FIRB WEB-MINDS Project "Wide-scale Broadband Middleware for Network Distributed Services" and Strategic IS-MANET Project "Middleware Support for Mobile Ad-hoc Networks and their Application".

References

Agarwal, S., Starobinski, D., & Trachtenberg, A. (2002). On the scalability of data synchronization protocols for PDAs and mobile devices. *IEEE Network, 16*(4), 22-28.

Bakic, A., Mutka, M.W., & Rover, D.T. (2000). BRISK: A portable and flexible distributed instrumentation system. *Software - Practice and Experience, 30*(12), 1353-1373.

Bellavista, P., Bottazzi, D., Corradi, A., Montanari, R., & Vecchi, S. (2004). Mobile agent middlewares for context-aware applications. In I. Mahgoub & M. Ilyas (Eds.), *Handbook of mobile computing*. CRC Press, to be published.

Bellavista, P., Corradi, A., Montanari, R., & Stefanelli, C. (2003a). Dynamic binding in mobile applications: A middleware approach. *IEEE Internet Computing, 7*(2), 34-42.

Bellavista, P., Corradi, A., Montanari, R., & Stefanelli, C. (2003b). Context-aware middleware for resource management in the wireless Internet. *IEEE Transactions on Software Engineering, 30*(2), 1086-1099.

Bellavista, P., Corradi, A., & Stefanelli, C. (2001). Mobile agent middleware for mobile computing. *IEEE Computer, 34*(3), 73-81.

Bellavista, P., Corradi, A., & Stefanelli, C. (2002a). The ubiquitous provisioning of Internet services to portable devices. *IEEE Pervasive Computing, 1*(3), 81-87.

Bellavista, P., Corradi, A., & Stefanelli, C. (2002b). Java for on-line distributed monitoring of heterogeneous systems and services. *The Computer Journal, 45*(6), 595-607.

Bos, L., & Leroy, S. (2001). Toward an all-IP-based UMTS system architecture. *IEEE Network, 15*(1), 36-45.

Bulterman, D.C.A. (2002). SMIL 2.0: Examples and comparisons. *IEEE Multimedia, 9*(1), 74-84.

Capra, L., Emmerich, W., & Mascolo, C. (2003). CARISMA: Context-aware reflective middleware system for mobile applications. *IEEE Transactions on Software Engineering, 29*(10), 929-945.

Curbera, F., Duftler, M., Khalaf, R., Mukhi, N., Nagy, W., & Weerawarana, S. (2002). Unraveling the Web services: An introduction to SOAP, WSDL, and UDDI. *IEEE Internet Computing, 6*(2), 86-93.

Davies, N., & Gellersen, H.-W. (2002). Beyond prototypes: Challenges in deploying ubiquitous systems. *IEEE Pervasive Computing, 1*(1), 26-35.

Debian. (2003). Tools for Manipulating Linux Wireless Extension. Retrieved October 2003, from *http://packages.debian.org/stable/net/wireless-tools.html*

Decker, S., Mitra, P., & Melnik, S. (2000). Framework for the semantic Web: An RDF tutorial. *IEEE Internet Computing, 4*(6), 68-73.

Foster, I., Kesselman, C., Tsudik, G., & Tuecke, S. (1998). A security architecture for computational grids. *5th ACM Conference on Computer and Communications Security* (pp. 83-92). ACM Press.

Fuggetta, A., Picco, G.P., & Vigna, G. (1998). Understanding code mobility. *IEEE Transactions on Software Engineering, 24*(5), 342-361.

Gast, M. (2002). *802.11 Wireless networks: The definitive guide.* O'Reilly.

Gordon, R. (1998). *Essential Java native interface.* Prentice Hall.

Heflin, J., & Huhns, M.N. (2003). The Zen of the Web. *Special Section of IEEE Internet Computing, 7*(5), 30-59.

Holder, O., Ben-Shaul, I., & Gazit, H. (1999). Dynamic layout of distributed applications in FarGo. *21st Int. Conf. on Software Engineering (ICSE'99)* (pp. 163-173).

Huber, H., Jarke, M., Jeusfeld, M.A., Nissen, H.W., & Zemanek, G.V. (1996). Managing multiple requirements perspectives with metamodels. *IEEE Software, 13*(2), 37-48.

Hwang, Y, Kim, J., & Seo, E. (2003). Structure-aware Web transcoding for mobile devices. *IEEE Internet Computing, 7*(5), 14-21.

IKV++ Technologies AG. (2003). enago mobile. Retrieved October 2003, from *http:// www.ikv.de*

Imperial College. (2003). Ponder Toolkit. Retrieved October 2003, from *http://www-dse.doc.ic.ac.uk/Re-search/policies/ponder.shtml*

Java Community Process (JCP). (2003). Java APIs for Bluetooth (JSR-82). Retrieved October 2003, from *http://www.jcp.org/en/jsr/detail?id=82*

Johansson, P., Kazantzidis, M., Kapoor, R., & Gerla, M. (2001). Bluetooth: An enabler for personal area networking. *IEEE Network, 15*(5), 28-37.

Karnik, N.M., & Tripathi, A.R. (2000). A security architecture for mobile agents in Ajanta. *20th Int. Conf. Distributed Computing Systems (ICDCS'00)* (pp. 402-409). IEEE Computer Society Press.

Kovacs, E., Rohrle, K., & Reich, M. (1998). Integrating mobile agents into the mobile middleware. *Mobile Agents Int. Workshop (MA'98)* (pp. 124-35). Springer-Verlag LNCS.

Lee, J. (2000). Enabling network management using Java technologies. *IEEE Communications Magazine, 38*(1), 116-123.

Lipperts, S., & Park, A. (1999). An agent-based middleware: A solution for terminal and user mobility. *Computer Networks, 31*, 2053-62.

Mascolo, C., Capra, L., & Emmerich, W. (2002). Middleware for mobile computing. *Networking 2002 Tutorial papers* (pp. 20-58). Springer-Verlag LNCS 2497.

Microsoft Software Developer Network (MSDN). (2003). *NDIS Features in Windows CE.* Retrieved October 2003, from *http://msdn.microsoft.com/library*

Moffett, J., & Sloman, M. (1993). Policy hierarchies for distributed systems management. *IEEE Journal on Selected Areas in Communications, 11*(9), 1404-1414.

Moura, J.A., Oliveira, J.M., Carrapatoso, E., & Roque, R. (2002). Service provision and resource discovery in the VESPER VHE. *IEEE Int. Conf. on Communications (ICC'02)*. IEEE Computer Society Press.

Organization for the Advancement of Structured Information Standards – OASIS. (2003). eXtensible Access Control Markup Language Standard 1.0 (normative) Specification Document. Retrieved December 2003, from *http://www.oasis-open.org/committees/download.php/2406/oasis-xacml-1.0.pdf*

Perkins, C. (Ed.). (1999). Special section on autoconfiguration. *IEEE Internet Computing, 3*(4), 42-80.

Reed Electronics Group - In-Stat/MDR - Mobile Devices and Components. (2003). Live another day: Year-end review & 2003 handset forecast. Retrieved December 2003, from *http://www.instat.com*

Roman, G.-C., Picco, G.P., & Murphy, A.L. (2000). Software engineering for mobility: A roadmap. *22nd Int. Conf. on Software Engineering (ICSE'00)* (pp. 241-258). IEEE Computer Society Press.

Ross, S.J., Hill, J.L., Chen, M.Y., Joseph, A.D., Culler, D.E., & Brewer, E.A. (2000). A composable framework for secure multi-modal access to Internet services from Ppst-PC devices. *3rd IEEE Workshop on Mobile Computing Systems and Applications* (pp. 171–182).

Sandhu, R., & Samarati, P. (1996). Authentication, access control, and audit. *ACM Computing Surveys, 28*(1), 241-243.

Schilit, B.N., Hilbert, D.M., & Trevor, J. (2002). Context-aware communication. *IEEE Wireless Communications, 9*(5), 46-54.

Schroeder, B.A. (1995). On-line monitoring: A tutorial. *IEEE Computer, 28*(6), 72-78.

Stallings, W. (1998). *SNMP, SNMPv2, SNMPv3, and RMON 1 and 2* (3rd ed.). Addison Wesley.

Stone, G.N., Lundy, B., & Xie, G.G. (2001). Network policy languages: A survey and a new approach. *IEEE Network, 15*(1), 10–21.

SUN Microsystems. (2003a). Java Virtual Machine Profiler Interface (JVMPI). Retrieved October 2003, from *http://java.sun.com/ products/jdk/1.3/docs/guide/jvmpi/ jvmpi.html*

SUN Microsystems. (2003b). Java Management Extensions (JMX). Retrieved October 2003, from *http://java.sun.com/products/JavaManagement/*

SUN Microsystems. (2003c). A Roadmap for Java 2 Platform, Standard Edition (J2SE) 1.5. Retrieved October 2003, from *http://developer.java.sun.com/developer/ technicalArticles/RoadMaps/J2SE_1.5/ j2se_1_5.html*

Tanter, E., & Piquer, J. (2001). Managing references upon object migration: Applying separation of concerns. *21s Int. Conf. Chilean Computer Science Society (SCCC'01)* (pp. 264-272).

Tonti, G., Bradshaw, J.M., Jeffers, R., Montanari, R., Suri, N., & Uszok, A. (2003). Semantic Web languages for policy representation and reasoning: A comparison of KAoS, Rei, and Ponder. *2nd Int. Semantic Web Conf. (ISWC2003)*.

World Wide Web Consortium. (2002). Composite Capability/Preference Profiles (CC/PP). Retrieved December 2002, from *http://www.w3.org/Mobile*

Yoshimura, T., Ohya, T., Kawahara, T., & Etoh, M. (2002). Rate and robustness control with RTP monitoring agent for mobile multimedia streaming. *IEEE Int. Conf. on Communications (ICC'02)*. IEEE Computer Society Press.

Appendix

Examples of CC/PP-compliant profiles for WICoCo users and terminals:

Code excerpts from an MSTS silver user profile

```
<?xml version="1.0"?>
<rdf:RDF  xmlns:rdf="http://www.w3.org/1999/02/22-rdf-syntax-ns#"
          xmlns:ccpp="http://www.w3.org/2002/11/08-ccpp-schema#"
          xmlns:WICoCoTermProf="ldap://ldap.deis.unibo.it/UserProfSchema#">
<rdf:Description rdf:about="ldap://ldap.deis.unibo.it/profile#WICoCoUserProf">

<ccpp:component>
    <rdf:Description rdf:about="ldap://ldap.deis.unibo.it/profile#UserID">
    <rdf:type rdf:resource="ldap://ldap.deis.unibo.it/schema#Identity">
        <ex:name>Paolo Bellavista</ex:name>
        <ex:nickName>Paolo</ex:nickName>
        <ex:city>Bologna</ex:city>
        <ex:userClass>silver</ex:userClass>
        ...
    </rdf:Description>
</ccpp:component>

<ccpp:component>
    <rdf:Description rdf:about="ldap://ldap.deis.unibo.it/profile#StockPrefs">
    <rdf:type rdf:resource="ldap://ldap.deis.unibo.it/schema#Stock">
        <ex:primaryStocks> <rdf:Bag>
                <rdf:li>HP</rdf:li>
                <rdf:li>DaimlerChrisler</rdf:li>
                <rdf:li>IBM</rdf:li>
            </rdf:Bag> </ex:primaryStocks>
    </rdf:Description>
</ccpp:component>

...
</rdf:Description>
</rdf:RDF>
```

Code excerpts from a WindowsCE device profile

```
<?xml version="1.0"?>
<rdf:RDF  xmlns:rdf="http://www.w3.org/1999/02/22-rdf-syntax-ns#"
          xmlns:ccpp="http://www.w3.org/2002/11/08-ccpp-schema#"
          xmlns:WICoCoTermProf="ldap://ldap.deis.unibo.it/TermProfSchema#">
<rdf:Description rdf:about="ldap://ldap.deis.unibo.it/profile#WICoCoTermProf">

<ccpp:component>
    <rdf:Description rdf:about="ldap://ldap.deis.unibo.it/profile#TerminalSoftware">
    <rdf:type rdf:resource="ldap://ldap.deis.unibo.it/schema#SoftwarePlatform">
        <ex:name>WindowsCE</ex:name>
        <ex:version>4.0</ex:version>
        <ex:vendor>Microsoft</ex:vendor>
    </rdf:Description>
</ccpp:component>

<ccpp:component>
    <rdf:Description rdf:about="ldap://ldap.deis.unibo.it/profile#TerminalBrowser">
    <rdf:type rdf:resource="ldap://ldap.deis.unibo.it/schema#Browser">
        <ex:name>Mozilla</ex:name>
        ...
        <ex:formatSupported> <rdf:Bag>
                    <rdf:li>txt</rdf:li>
                    <rdf:li>c-HTML</rdf:li>
                    <rdf:li>mp3</rdf:li>
            </rdf:Bag> </ex:formatSupported>
    </rdf:Description>
</ccpp:component>
...
</rdf:Description>
</rdf:RDF>
```

Chapter VI

A Comprehensive XML Based Approach to Trust Negotiations

Elisa Bertino, Purdue University, USA

Elena Ferrari, Università degli Studi dell'Insubria, Italy

Anna Cinzia Squicciarini, Università degli Studi di Milano, Italy

Abstract

Trust negotiation is a promising approach for establishing trust in open systems like the Internet, where sensitive interactions may often occur between entities at first contact, with no prior knowledge of each other. In this chapter we present Trust-X, a comprehensive XML-based XML framework for trust negotiations, specifically conceived for a peer-to-peer environment. We also discuss the applicability of trust negotiation principles to mobile commerce. We introduce a variety of possible approaches to extend and improve Trust-X in order to fully support mobile commerce transactions and payments. In the chapter, besides presenting the Trust-X system, we present the basic principles of trust negotiation.

Introduction

Computer systems have traditionally had centrally managed security domains. Every entity that can access such systems has one or more identities in that domain. The underlying assumption is that entities in the system already know each other. Therefore, the system relies on party identities to grant or deny authorizations.

As we move towards a globally Internetworked infrastructure, like the Internet, interactions involving strangers are dramatically increasing. In particular, transactions between companies and their cooperating partners or customers are becoming of everyday use. Furthermore, advances in technology enable users to perform commerce transactions through the use of mobile systems, adding new requirements to the traditional scenario. Nowadays, companies of all sizes are able to conduct business without worrying about the territorial market limitations of the past. In such a complex scenario, traditional assumptions for establishing and enforcing access control regulations no longer hold. The entities need not only to authenticate each other, but also to trust each other in order to exchange sensitive information and resources. Interactions are further complicated by the fact that usually the interacting entities belong to different security domains, or can change domains during a transaction if they are mobile users, and/or do not have any pre-existing relationships.

Traditional attempts to establish trust in open systems either minimize security measures or assume that parties are not strangers and can present a local identity to obtain services. According to such paradigm each subject is uniquely identified by an ID (e.g., login name, IP address) that is the means for proving the subject's trustworthiness. However, identity-based methods for establishing trust are not feasible in an environment like the Web. In such an environment, properties other than identity are crucial in determining parties' trustworthiness.

A promising approach in this respect is represented by trust negotiation (TN) (Seamons & Winslett, 2001), according to which trust is established through a mutual exchange of *digital credentials*. Disclosure of credentials, in turn, must be protected by the use of policies specifying which credentials must be received before the requested credential can be disclosed.

A trust negotiation system, thus, relies on digital credentials held by the negotiating parties, with the goal of establishing mutual trust before completing the transaction. This approach allows parties having no pre-existing relationships to confidently perform sensitive interactions.

One of the most interesting applications for trust negotiation systems is represented by e-commerce applications. An e-commerce application typically carries out commercial transactions on the Web, such as buying and selling products, or various other activities, such as supply chain management. Trust negotiation systems represent a powerful means to conduct business transactions, very often characterized by the fact that the interacting entities are unknown to each other and need to establish a sufficient level of trust to complete the transaction. Mobile commerce, in particular, is an important branch of e-commerce requiring additional trust establishment capabilities. In a nutshell, mobile commerce provides consumers with secure, faster and personalized services and is becoming one of the most important wireless applications. Mobile commerce is a vast area of activity comprised of transactions with monetary value conducted via a mobile device. More and more people prefer m-commerce services and truly enjoy these prompt services.

Although the problem of trust negotiations performed using typical desktop computers has been thoroughly explored, the issue of negotiations involving mobile devices is still an unexplored research area. This is a promising and challenging research area, as trust negotiation systems have a number of features that might be exploited to develop efficient and powerful mobile negotiation systems for conducting business transactions.

This chapter is devoted to present the basic principles of trust negotiation and its basic building blocks. Then, as an example of trust negotiation system, we present Trust-$\mathcal{X}$, a framework we have developed providing a comprehensive solution to trust negotiation management. Trust-$\mathcal{X}$ provides both an XML based language for expressing policies and credentials and a methodology and related algorithms for carrying on negotiations. We end the chapter by discussing the applicability of trust negotiation principles to mobile commerce. We introduce a variety of possible approaches to extend and improve Trust-$\mathcal{X}$ in order to fully support mobile commerce transactions and payments. In presenting such approaches we refer to a set of open issues we have identified and that have to be taken into account while redesigning the system.

More precisely, this chapter is organized as follows. Next section summarizes basic concepts underlying trust negotiation. The following two sections are devoted to Trust-$\mathcal{X}$. Then, we survey related work and compares Trust-$\mathcal{X}$ with some of the most relevant proposals in the negotiation area. Finally, we discuss the use of Trust-$\mathcal{X}$ in mobile commerce applications and identify open research issues, and conclude the chapter by outlining future research directions. The chapter also contains an appendix, reporting formal proofs.

Trust Negotiation: Basic Concepts

A trust negotiation consists of a bilateral disclosure of digital credentials, representing statements certified by given entities, which can be used for verifying properties of their holders. Typically, a trust negotiation involves two entities, namely a *client,* that is, the entity asking for a certain resource, and a *server,* that is, the entity owning (or more generally, managing access to) the requested resource. The notion of *resource* comprises both sensitive information and services, whereas the notion of entity includes users, processes, roles, and servers. Resource disclosure is protected by a set of *policies.*

A trust negotiation is basically peer-to-peer: both negotiation entities may possess sensitive resources to be protected and thus must be equipped with a compliant negotiation system. Trust is incrementally built by iteratively disclosing *digital credentials* in order to verify properties of the negotiating parties. Credentials are typically collected by each party in appropriate repositories, also named profiles. Disclosure policies govern access to protected resources by specifying credential combinations that must be submitted in order to obtain authorizations. The overall interaction process between parties is usually carried out through software components such as browsers, user agents, and wrappers (Subrahmanian et al., n.d.).

The fundamental elements of trust negotiations are thus digital credentials and policies, discussed in the remainder of this section.

Digital Credentials

Digital credentials are assertions describing one or more properties about a given subject, referred to as the "owner," certified by trusted credential authorities (CAs). Entities are thus identified and described through a set of *digital credentials*.

Like paper credentials that subjects carry in their wallets, digital credentials state properties about their owners. Typically, a digital credential contains a set of attributes, specified using name/value pairs, that are signed by the issuer's private key and can be verified using the issuer's public key (Stallings, 1999). To achieve unforgeability and verifiability, digital credentials are usually implemented using the X.509 V3 standard for public key certificates. However, since the X.509 certificates were not conceived for online negotiations they do not efficiently support either the notion of attribute or protect privacy. As a result, other formats have been recently proposed that can better support entities' property description (Bertino & Ferrrari, 2003). An example of these proposals will be presented later on in the chapter. Finally, in order to increase privacy guarantee and non-forgeability, alternative certificate formats (Brands, 2000; Persiano & Visconti, 2000) have also been developed. These approaches rely on the possibility of selectively disclosing attributes within credentials, so that only the required subset is disclosed to the counterpart. In particular, to achieve this goal Persiano et al. in 2002 introduced the SPSL protocol extending the transport layer security protocol, whereas Brands introduces a number of techniques for designing private credentials and protocols for issuing and disclosing private credentials.

Disclosure Policies

To automate trust negotiation, each party must specify disclosure policies to regulate access to sensitive resources such as services, data, credentials or even policies themselves. Policies are usually expressed as constraints against the credentials of the interacting parties and their attributes. Further, depending on their contents, credentials themselves may be sensitive and thus their disclosure may be regulated by ad-hoc disclosure policies. For example, a credential may contain non-public attributes about an individual, such as a credit card number.

Disclosure policies, in turn, may be regarded as sensitive information because they are often related to the business and governance processes of organizations. For example, the Web site for a secret joint venture of two companies might be protected by policies that limit access to particular employees of those companies. Outsiders who access the policies may infer information about the type of engagement between the companies, and take advantage of such information. Therefore, recent researchers consider disclosure policies as sensitive as other resources and provide mechanisms for their protection (Winslett & Seamons, 2002).

Besides general purpose policy languages (Damianou, Dulay, Lupu & Sloman, 2001), a number of policy languages especially conceived for encoding security information used in trust negotiations have been proposed (Bonatti & Samarati, 2000; Herzberg & Mihaeli, 2000; Winsborough & Li, 2002). An example of trust negotiation policy language is given in the next sections, where we present X-TNL, the XML based language supported by Trust-X.

Trust-X: A Comprehensive Framework for Trust Negotiations

Trust-X is a system providing a comprehensive approach to all aspects of a negotiation. Building blocks of Trust-X are an XML-based language, named X-TNL, for specifying Trust-X certificates and policies, and an architecture and related algorithms for managing negotiations. In Bertino and Ferrari (2003) we have presented the language for specifying certificates. In this chapter we mainly focus on disclosure policies and present the Trust-X architecture for negotiation management. A Trust-X negotiation consists of a set of phases that are sequentially executed. Trust-X negotiations maximize the protection of the involved resources; indeed, certificates and services are disclosed only after a complete counterpart policy evaluation, that is, and only when the parties have found a sequence of certificate disclosures that makes it possible to release the requested resource. Additionally, both parties can drive the steps of the negotiation by selecting the adopted strategy from a variety of alternative strategies, and thus can better trade-off protection and efficiency.

An Example of Trust Negotiation

We now introduce a basic example of a trust negotiation, which we will use throughout this section as a running example to illustrate the basic functions of Trust-X and its main features.

KTH is a flight company selling electronic flight tickets to travel around Europe. We assume that KTH and all the entities interacting with KTH are characterized by a profile of certificates, describing properties of the owners. Additionally, each party has specified a set of disclosure policies to protect credentials and services.

Alice is a student wishing to purchase a flight ticket to KTH airline. As Alice browses the site, she fills out the booking form on the Web, checking a form box to indicate that

Figure 1. Sketch of a trust negotiation process (In the example, negotiating participants perform a TN in which the client obtains a service after exchanging policies and credentials with the server.)

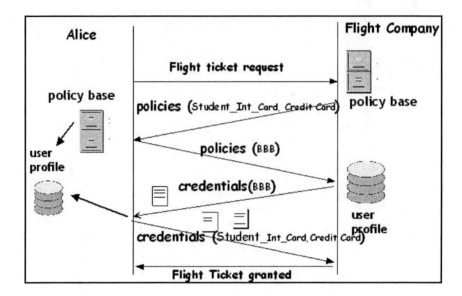

she wishes to take advantage of a special offer. Upon receipt of the reservation request, KTH asks for a valid credit card or her account credential, issued by KTH as a frequent flyer, and a current international student card. Alice has both the account with KTH and a valid credit card. Suppose she does not want to use her account as frequent flyer. She is willing to disclose her student card to anyone under certain privacy guarantees, but she will only show her credit card to members of the Better Business Bureau. Alice may specify such security requirements by means of disclosure policies, exchanged following the protocol sketched in Figure 1. The same can do KTH to express the requirements needed to sell a flight ticket. In the following, we will show how this negotiation can be carried on in the framework of Trust-*X*.

X-TNL Trust Negotiation Language

In this section, we present *X*-TNL (Bertino & Ferrari, 2003), the XML-based language we have developed for specifying Trust-*X* certificates and policies. The language provides a flexible way of qualifying the parties involved in the negotiation, which relies on a distinction between *credentials* and *declarations*. Additionally, it provides an expressive XML encoding of *disclosure policies,* where a disclosure policy regulates the disclosure of a resource by imposing conditions on both credentials and negotiations.

The language we provide has been especially conceived for handling multiple and heterogeneous credentials and it is flexible enough to express a wide range of protection requirements.

We first present the credential language, that is, the language encoding credentials and declarations. Then, we present *X*-TNL *disclosure policies,* that is, policies regulating the disclosure of resources by imposing conditions on the certificates the requesting party should possess.

Credential Language

Constructs of *X*-TNL include the notion of *certificate,* which is the means to convey information about the profile of the parties involved in the negotiation. A certificate can be either a *credential* or a *declaration*. A credential is a set of properties of a party certified by a certification authority, whereas declarations contain information that may help the negotiation process, such as for instance specific preferences of one of the parties, but that do not need to be certified.

As far as credentials are concerned, *X*-TNL simplifies the task of credential specification because it provides a set of templates, called *credential types,* for the specification of credentials with similar structure. In *X*-TNL, a credential type is modelled as a DTD and a credential as a valid document with respect to the corresponding credential type. Each credential is digitally signed by the issuer credential authority, according to the standard defined by W3C for XML signatures. A credential is an instance of a credential type, and specifies the list of property values characterizing a given subject. A Trust-*X* credential is thus a valid XML document conforming to the DTD modelling of the corresponding credential type. Figure 2 shows an example of credential, containing the basic information about a Frequent_Traveller. Note that, as each Trust-*X* credential, the Frequent_Traveller credential has a set of default attributes, namely, SENS, CREDID and CIssuer. The CREDID and CIssuer attributes specify the credential identifier and the identity of the issuer of the credential, respectively. By contrast, the SENS denotes the degree of sensitivity of the information contained in the credential. This attribute takes values from a set v of sensitivity levels, defined according to the considered domain. Throughout the chapter, we assume $v = \{HIGH, NORMAL, LOW\}$.

By contrast, declarations are sets of data without any certification; therefore they are stated by their owner. Declarations can be considered as self-certificates, collecting personal information about the owner. This kind of certificate thus provides auxiliary information that can help the negotiation process. For instance, a declaration named customer_info may describe the habits of a given subject for what concern travels.

In *X*-TNL, we simply define a declaration as a valid XML document. Like credentials, also declarations are structured into declaration types, that is, DTDs to which the corresponding declarations conform. Figure 3 shows the Trust-*X* representation of the customer_info declaration. The declaration describes Alice's personal information about her travels with KTH airlines. This declaration can be used to communicate Alice's personal preferences during negotiation with a KTH Airline.

Figure 2. An example of Trust-X credential

```
<FREQUENT_TRAVELLER  CREDID='12AB', SENS= 'NORMAL'>
<ISSUER HREF='HTTP://WWW.CORRIER.COM'
TITLE=CORRIER\_EMPLOYEES_REPOSITORY/>
      <NAME>
         <FNAME> ALICE   </FNAME>
         <LNAME>  WHITE </LNAME>
      </NAME>
      <ADDRESS> GRANGE WOOD  69  DUBLIN      </ADDRESS>
   <CITIZENSHIP> IRISH </CITIZENSHIP>
      <CARD\_NUMBER CODE=34ABN/>
       <E_MAIL> O.WHITE@YAHOO.COM </E_MAIL>
        <DEPARTMENT>  AGENCY 45 </DEPARTMENT>
  <POSITION> DRIVER </POSITION>
</FREQUENT_TRAVELLER>
```

Figure 3. An example of Trust-X declaration

```
<customer_info>
<name>
<Fname> Alice </Fname>
 <lname >  White</lname>
 </name>   <flight_class> business traveller </flight_class>
 <meal_preferences >
< vegetarian>
</meal_preferences >
<preferred_travelling_time> 9AM-8PM </preferred_travelling_time>
 <favorite_route >  Dublin-Rome </favorite_route>
  <collected_miles> 1220  </collected_miles>
 </customer_info>
```

Data Sets and *X*-Profiles

All certificates associated with a party are collected into its *X*-Profile. To better structure credentials and declarations into an *X*-Profile, each *X*-Profile is organized into *data sets*. Each data set collects a class of credentials and declarations referring to a particular aspect of the life of their owner. For instance, Demographic Data, Education, and Working Experience are examples of possible data sets.[1] For example, Alice's certificates concerning working experiences can be collected in the Working Experience data set. In this group of digital documents we can find Alice's work license number, a digital copy of her last job contract and some uncertified information about her precedent job experiences. Organizing certificates into data sets facilitates their retrieval during negotiation because all certificates collected in the same data set are logically related. Data sets can then be used to refer to a set of homogeneous declarations or credentials as a whole, and this can facilitate their evaluation and exchange during negotiation.

Disclosure Policies Language

Trust-X disclosure policies are specified by each party involved in a negotiation, and state the conditions under which a resource can be released during a negotiation. Conditions are expressed as constraints against the certificates possessed by the involved parties and on the certificate attributes. Each party adopts its own policies to regulate release of local information and access to services. Like certificates, disclosure policies are encoded using X-TNL (Bertino, Ferrari & Squicciarini, 2003). Additionally, Trust-X policies can also be formalized as logical rules. In the following, we present such logical representation, since it makes easier explaining the compliance checker mechanisms and runtime system algorithms.

Before introducing the notion of disclosure policy, we need to introduce some preliminary concepts. We first introduce the notion of *R-Term*. An R-Term univocally denotes a resource offered by a party. A resource can be either a certificate, or a service. By service we mean either an application that the requesting party can execute, for instance for purchasing goods, or an access to protected data, such as for instance medical data. Formally, an R-Term can be considered as a structured object identified by a name and some properties, and is modelled as an expression of the form *resource_name(attribute_list),* where *resource_name* is the name of the resource, and *attribute_list* is a possible empty list of attribute names characterizing the resource. If the resource is a certificate-type the list of properties consists of the attribute and tag names contained in its XML encoding. Resource properties are used to express constraints on the resource release when specifying disclosure policies. We use the dot notation to refer to a specific attribute of a resource, that is, we use $R.a$ to denote attribute a of a resource R. Expressions of the form $R.a$ are called *resource expressions*.

Example 3.1

Examples of R-Terms for our running example are:

1. Flight_Ticket(customerCode, from, to, departure, return, class):

    it denotes an online flight ticket buying service. The service is characterized by a set of attributes required to customize the purchasing, such as the requester code, (if any), the route (attributes from and to), the travelling days (departure date and return date), and the flight category.

2. Frequent_Traveller():

    it denotes the credential type Frequent_Traveller.

We now review the notion of certificate conditions and terms. These concepts have been already presented in our previous work (Bertino, Ferrrari & Squicciarini, 2004) to formally define the Trust-$\mathcal{X}$ policy language. Informally, certificate conditions and terms can be regarded as the building blocks used to compose disclosure policies. More precisely, a certificate condition **C** is an expression of the form **a op expr,** where: **a** denotes an element tag or an attribute name in a certain credential type; **op** is a comparison operator, such as $<, >, =, \neq, \geq$; **expr** can be either a constant or a resource expression, compatible with the type of **a**. Terms, in turn, are expressions of the form **P(C)** or **P( )** where: **P** is a Trust-$\mathcal{X}$ certificate type; and **C** is a list of certificate conditions $C_1...C_n$ against **P**. The form **P( )** denotes a term without conditions.

Example 3.2

The following are examples of terms:

- $\mathcal{T}_1$=CreditCard(Release_year > 1998);

- $\mathcal{T}_2$=Frequent_Traveller(code=Flght_Ticket.customerCode).

- $\mathcal{T}_3$=Id_Card().

$\mathcal{T}_1$ is a term denoting a credit card, containing a certificate condition against the Release_year attribute. Similarly, $\mathcal{T}_2$ is a term for the Frequent_Traveller credential, specifying a credential condition against attribute *code*. Finally, the last term denotes a term without any conditions, that is, *Id_Card*.

In the remainder of the chapter, we say that a certificate $\mathcal{X}$-Cert *satisfies* a term *P(C)*, if $\mathcal{X}$-Cert is of type *P* and satisfies all the conditions specified in *C*. Additionally, given a term, we use the notation P($\mathcal{T}$) to denote the certificate type in $\mathcal{T}$, and C($\mathcal{T}$) to denote the certificate conditions in *P*.

We are now ready to formally define disclosure policies.

Definition 3.1.

Disclosure Policies: A disclosure policy is an expression of one of the following forms:

1. **R←$\mathcal{T}_1$, $\mathcal{T}_2$,...., $\mathcal{T}_n$,** $n \geq 1$, where $\mathcal{T}_1$, $\mathcal{T}_2$,...., $\mathcal{T}_n$ are terms and **R** is the Resource_name component of an R-Term.

2. **R←DELIV,** where **R** is the Resource_name component of an R-Term. These policies are called *delivery policies*.

A disclosure policy specifies which kind of certificates a party should possess in order to obtain access to a resource owned by the other party. Delivery policies are specified for resources that do not contain sensitive information, and can be released whenever requested.

Example 3.3

Consider the negotiation sketched in. As already mentioned, a special fare is offered either to frequent travellers or to students. Suppose that the server already knows frequent customers possessing the Frequent_Traveller credential and has a digital copy of their credit cards. By contrast, flight tickets are available on payment for unknown customers, who have to submit a digital copy of their student international card issued by a state member of EU to obtain a special fare, and a valid credit card. These requirements can be formalized by the following disclosure policies:

- Flight_Ticket←Frequent_Traveller(code=Flght_Ticket.customerCode);

- Flight_Ticket←Student_Int_Card(age<25,issuer=EU),Credit_Card (ExpirationDate>Flight_Ticket.ReturnDate).

In the remainder of this chapter we say that a disclosure policy $R \leftarrow \mathcal{T}_1, \mathcal{T}_2, ..., \mathcal{T}_n$ specified by one of the parties involved in the negotiation is satisfied if the right side elements of the policy are all satisfied by the counterpart $\mathcal{X}$-Profile.

Trust-$\mathcal{X}$ policies are thus defined for protecting both services and certificates. Indeed, the left side element of a disclosure policy can denote either a service identifier or a certificate type. Different expressions having the same element R on the left side denote alternative policies equally valid to obtain R. Terms on the right side of a policy specify conditions for the release of R. Each resource R can be disclosed only if one of the corresponding policies is satisfied. In addition, the disclosure policy language may be adopted to define prerequisite information. Such policies denote conditions that must be satisfied for a resource request to be taken into consideration, and are therefore used at the beginning of the negotiation process, as explained in the next sections.

Trust-$\mathcal{X}$ Architecture

As shown in Figure 4, Trust-$\mathcal{X}$ is composed by several components. Further, Trust-$\mathcal{X}$ architecture is symmetric and peer-to-peer; therefore the terms *client* and *server* are simply used as a convenient way for distinguishing parties during negotiations. The goals of the system components are essentially the following: supporting policy exchange, testing whether a policy is satisfied, and supporting certificate exchange. Each of those functions is executed by a specific module of Trust-$\mathcal{X}$. Facet modules may also be added to make the negotiation easier and faster, but we omit them to focus on the most relevant components. The system is composed of a *policy base*, storing disclosure policies, the $\mathcal{X}$-Profile associated with the party, a *tree manager*, storing the state of the negotiation, and a *compliance checker*, to test policy satisfaction and determine request replies.

Each negotiation participant has a Trust-$\mathcal{X}$ profile of certificates, conforming to the $\mathcal{X}$-TNL syntax summarized in the previous section. Unlike traditional approaches, during a

Figure 4. Trust-X architecture

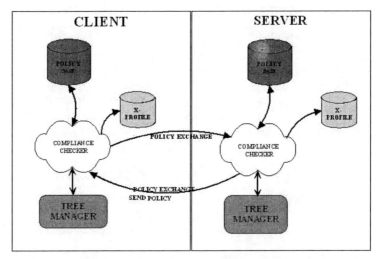

negotiation mutual trust might be established between the client and the server: the client has to show its certificates to obtain the resource, and the server, whose honesty is not always assured, submits certificates to the client in order to prove its trustworthiness before receiving sensitive certificates. Disclosure of information and certificates is regulated by disclosure policies, which are exchanged to inform the other party of the trust requirements that need to be satisfied to advance the state of the negotiation. We elaborate on the trust negotiation process in the following section.

Trust-X Negotiations

In this section we focus on the approach used in Trust-X for policy disclosures during negotiation. Trust-X adopts a cautious strategy, distinguishing between policy exchange and certificates and/or resource disclosure. This distinction results in an efficient and effective protection of all the resources involved during negotiations. Certificates and services are disclosed only after a complete counterpart policies evaluation; that is, only when the parties have found a sequence of certificate disclosure that makes possible the release of the requested resource, according to the disclosure policies of both parties. In the following, we assume that both parties are Trust-X compliant. However, it is also possible to carry on negotiations even between parties that do not adopt the same negotiation language, simply by adding a translation mechanism. A Trust-X negotiation is organized according to the following phases:

- *Introduction*. It is the starting phase of a negotiation. A client contacts a server requiring a resource $\mathcal{R}$. The server may react by asking *prerequisite information*, if necessary. Prerequisite information is general conditions that must be satisfied to start processing the resource request, independently from the result of the request. Moreover, these conditions are usually independent also from the requested resource. For instance, a server providing services only to registered clients, before evaluating the requirements for the requested service, can ask the counterpart for the login name. If the client is not registered there is no reason to further proceed. The introductory phase may also be used to collect information about the client preferences or needs. For instance, in the Flight ticket scenario, the server may ask the customer to submit the customer_info declaration, if any, in order to better satisfy client requirements.[2] If the client does not assume honesty of the server it can, in turn, ask some prerequisite information to the server. Such a phase is therefore composed of a small number of simple messages exchanged between the two parties.

- *Policy evaluation*. During this phase, both client and server communicate disclosure policies adopted for the involved resources. The goal is to determine a sequence of client and server certificates that when disclosed allow the release of the requested resource, in accordance to the disclosure policies of both parties. This phase is carried out as an interplay between the client and the server. During each interaction one of the two parties sends a set of disclosure policies to the other. The receiver party verifies whether its X-Profile satisfies the conditions stated by the policies, and whether its local policy base contains policies regulating the disclosure of the certificates requested by the policies sent by the other party. If the X-Profile of the receiver party satisfies the conditions stated by at least one of the received policies, the receiver can adopt one of two alternative strategies. It can choose to maximize the protection of its local resources, by replying to only one policy at a time, thus hiding the real availability of the other requested resources. Alternatively, it can reply to all the policies in order to maximize the number of potential solutions for negotiation and thus speed up the overall process. Otherwise, if the X-Profile of the receiver party does not satisfy the conditions stated by the received policies, the receiver informs the counterpart that it does not possess the requested certificates. The counterpart then sends an alternative policy, if any, or halts the process if no other policies can be found. The interplay goes on until one or more potential solutions are determined; that is, whenever both client and server determine one or more set of policies that can be satisfied for all the resources and certificates involved. The policy evaluation phase is mostly executed by the *compliance checker*, whose goal is the evaluation of remote policies with respect to local policies and certificates (certificates can be locally available in the X-Profile or can be retrieved through certificate chains), and the selection of the strategy for carrying out the remainder of the negotiation. To simplify the process a tree structure is used, explained in detail in the next section, which is managed and updated by the *tree manager*. Note that no certificates are disclosed during the policy evaluation phase. The satisfaction of the policies is only checked to communicate to the other party the possibility of going on with the process and how the process can actually be executed.

- *Certificate exchange*. This phase begins when the policy evaluation phase determines one or more *trust sequences*[3] to successfully complete the negotiation. A trust sequence determines a list of sets of certificates where the disclosure of each set of certificates in the list represents a condition for a trust release of the certificates following it in the list. Several trust sequences can be determined for the same negotiation and several criteria can then be used by both the client and the server to select one of the possible trust sequences. Examples of these criteria include the number of involved certificates, the sensitivity of their content, the expected length of the negotiation, or the number of certificate chains that need to be traversed. Once the parties have agreed on a sequence, the certificate exchange phase begins. Each party discloses its certificates, following the order defined in the trust sequence, eventually retrieving those that are not immediately available through certificate chains. Functions required to carry out certificate disclosure are: verification of certificate contents, check for revocation, check validity dates, and authentication of ownership (for credentials). The process ends with the disclosure of the requested resource or, if any unforeseen event happens, with an interruption. If the failure is caused by dishonest behavior of one of the parties, for instance a party discloses a revoked certificate, the negotiation fails. Otherwise, if it is due to events not related with parties' trustworthiness, for instance interruption of connection, the negotiation is restarted, repeating certificates exchange. If it is not possible to complete the certificate exchange for the interrupted sequence, one of the alternative trust sequences determined at the beginning of this phase is chosen.

Note that there is a significant difference between the first and the other two phases of a Trust-X negotiation. The introductory phase is executed following a static protocol, since it is simply a fixed exchange of information that is necessary for starting any negotiation involving the considered parties. By contrast, the second and the beginning part of the third phase are dynamic and may evolve in several ways.

Next two sections are thus devoted to the policy evaluation phase and the certificate exchange phase, since they are the most complex and interesting phases of the negotiation process.

Policy Evaluation Phase

In this section, we focus on the key phase of a Trust-X negotiation, that is, the policy evaluation phase. This phase consists of a bilateral and ordered policy exchange. The compliance checker module of each party, upon receiving a disclosure policy, determines if it can be satisfied by querying the local X-Profile. Then, it checks in its policy base the protection requirements associated with the certificates satisfying the policy, if any. The progress of a negotiation is recorded into a specific data structure, called *negotiation tree*, managed by the *tree manager*, which is described in the next section.

Negotiation Tree

A negotiation tree specifies a set of negotiation paths, where each path denotes a possible trust sequence. The path also keeps track of which certificates may contribute to the success of the negotiation, and of the correct order of certificate exchange.

Upon the end of the introductory phase, each party maintains a copy of a negotiation tree, rooted at the requested resource $\mathcal{R}$. The policy evaluation phase ends when at least one trust sequence (corresponding to a path in the tree) is found or there is no compatibility between the policies of the parties. If no trust sequence can be determined the phase ends with a failure message. Otherwise, the subsequent phase is executed.

In defining a negotiation tree we make use of a function, called *Eval,* that receives as input a term $\mathcal{T}$ and an X-Profile, and returns TRUE if the X-Profile contains a certificate satisfying $\mathcal{T}$, and FALSE otherwise.

Definition 4.1.

Negotiation Tree: Let S be a server and C be a client. Let $\mathcal{PB}_s$ and $\mathcal{PB}_c$ be the policy bases associated with S and C, respectively. Let X-$Prof_s$ and X-$Prof_c$ be the X-Profiles associated with S and C respectively. Let $\mathcal{R}$, be the resource requested by C to S. A negotiation tree $NT=<\mathcal{N}, \mathcal{R}, \mathcal{E}>$ for $\mathcal{R}, S$, and C is a finite tree satisfying the following properties:

- $\mathcal{N}$ (the set of nodes) is a set of triples:

$$n=<\mathcal{T}, \ state, \ party>$$

  where:

  - $\mathcal{T}$ is a term;

  - *state* denotes the current state of the node;

  - *party* $E \in \{C, S\}$ denotes whether the node belongs to C or S;

- $\mathcal{R}=<R, \ state, \ S>$ is the root of the tree;

- $\mathcal{E}$ (the set of edges), where each $e \in \mathcal{E}$ has one of the following forms:4

  - simple edge $S\mathcal{E}$: $e=(n_1, n_2)$, $n_1, n_2 \in \mathcal{N}$ belongs to $S\mathcal{E}$ if both the following conditions hold:

  - $[Eval(\mathcal{T}(n_1), X\text{-}Prof_c)= TRUE \wedge \mathcal{T}(n_1) \leftarrow \mathcal{T}(n_2) \in \mathcal{PB}_c$ or $Eval(\mathcal{T}(n_1), X\text{-}Prof_s)= TRUE \wedge \mathcal{T}(n_1) \leftarrow T(n_2) \in \mathcal{PB}_s]$ or $[\mathcal{T}(n_1)= R \wedge R \leftarrow \mathcal{T}(n_2) \in \mathcal{PB}_s]$;

  - $[(Eval(\mathcal{T}(n_1),X\text{-}Prof_c)= TRUE) \wedge (Eval(\mathcal{T}(n_2),X\text{-}Prof_s)= TRUE)] \vee (Eval(\mathcal{T}(n_1), X\text{-}Prof_s)= TRUE) \wedge (Eval(\mathcal{T}(n_2),X\text{-}Prof_c)= TRUE)]$;

- multi edge $M\mathcal{E}$: $e=\{(n, n_1),...., (n, n_k) \} n, n_1,.., n_k \in \mathcal{N}$ belongs to $M\mathcal{E}$ if both the following conditions hold:

- [$Eval(\mathcal{T}(n), X\text{-}Prof_c)= TRUE \wedge \mathcal{T}(n) \leftarrow \mathcal{T}(n_1),..., \mathcal{T}(n_k) \in \mathcal{PB}_c$ or $Eval(\mathcal{T}(n),$ $X\text{-}Prof_s)= TRUE \wedge \mathcal{T}(n) \leftarrow \mathcal{T}(n_1),..., \mathcal{T}(n_k) \in \mathcal{PB}_s$] or [$\mathcal{T}(n)= R \wedge R \leftarrow \mathcal{T}(n_1),$ $...., \mathcal{T}(n_k) \in \mathcal{PB}_s$];

- [$(Eval(\mathcal{T}(n),X\text{-}Prof_c)= TRUE) \wedge (Eval(\mathcal{T}(n_1),X\text{-}Prof_s)= TRUE) \wedge...\wedge (Eval(\mathcal{T}(n_K),$ $X\text{-}Prof_s)= TRUE)$] $\vee$ [$(Eval(\mathcal{T}(n), X\text{-}Prof_c)= TRUE) \wedge (Eval(\mathcal{T}(n_1), X\text{-}Prof_c)=$ $TRUE) \wedge...\wedge (Eval(\mathcal{T}(n_K),X\text{-}Prof_c)= TRUE)$]

- The *state* of a node n can assume one of the following two values:

- **DELIV**, if one of the following conditions holds:

  - [$\mathcal{T}(n) \leftarrow$ DELIV $\in \mathcal{PB}_c \wedge Eval(\mathcal{T}(n),X\text{-}Prof_c)= TRUE$]$\vee$ $\mathcal{T}(n) \leftarrow$ DELIV $\in \mathcal{PB}_s$ $\wedge Eval(\mathcal{T}(n),X\text{-}Prof_s)= TRUE$]

  - if $\exists\, e=(n, n_2) \in \mathcal{SE}$ such that [$state(n_2)=$DELIV] or [$\exists\, e=\{(n, n_1),..., (n, n_k)\}$ $\in \mathcal{ME}$ and $\forall\, i \in [1,k],\ state(n_i)=$DELIV];

- **OPEN**, if one of the following conditions holds:

  - if $e=(n, n_2) \in \mathcal{SE}$ and $state(n_2)=$OPEN;

  - if $\{e=(n, n_1),..., (n, n_k)\} \in \mathcal{ME}$ and $\exists\, i \in [1,k]$ such that $state(n_i)=$OPEN;

  - $\forall\, e=(n,n_1) \in \mathcal{SE}$ if $party(n)=C$ then $party(n_1)=S$ and $\forall\, e=\{(n, n_1),...,$ $(n, n_k)\} \in \mathcal{ME}$ if $party(n)=C$ then $party(n_1)=S,..., party(n_K)=S$, and vice versa.

A negotiation tree is thus a particular tree that evolves during the policy evaluation phase through addition of disclosure policies by one of the parties. Graphically, nodes are represented as labelled circles. Figure 5 shows three steps of the construction of a negotiation tree. The example shows a negotiation tree for our Flight Ticket scenario.

A negotiation tree may contain two different kinds of edges: multi and simple, which are the result of the different kinds of policy that can be expressed in our language. Multi edges are the result of policies having right side elements with more than one term; therefore, these edges model terms in conjunction. By contrast, simple edges are used to model policies having only one term on the left side component of the associated rule.

A simple edge is modelled as a directed line, whereas a multi edge is represented as many edges as the terms in the corresponding policy, linked by an arch. For example with respect to Figure 5, at step 2, the evaluation of policy: $R \leftarrow Credit\_Card(...),$ $Student\_Int\_Card(...)$[5] results in a multi edge connecting node n_1 with nodes n_2 and n_3. The *state* associated with a node denotes the possibility of finding a trust sequence containing the corresponding term. Intuitively, if the state of a node n is DELIV, this means that there exists a trust sequence containing $\mathcal{T}(n)$. In the example above, the request for the server certification from the Better Business Bureau, named *BBB*, does not need further requirements, and thus the corresponding node is tagged DELIV. When

Figure 5. Negotiation tree building

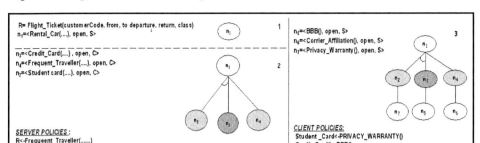

a new node is appended to the tree during the policy evaluation phase, its state is initially set to OPEN, meaning that the tree may evolve, through addition of children to that node. Then, it changes its state to DELIV when at least one of its children has a DELIV state, or there exists a delivery policy associated with its term (meaning that there are no additional protection requirements specified for such term). In case of multi edges it is required that the state of all the linked children be DELIV. With reference to Figure 5, the root node n_1 is labelled OPEN until the evaluation of disclosure policies *Privacy_Warranty←DELIV* (whose corresponding term is in node n_7) and *BBB←DELIV* (whose corresponding term is in node n_5) is completed, as shown in Figure 6.

OPEN nodes may have different evolutions. For instance, suppose that a Web server requires a certificate to a subject proving that the country that issued the subject birth certificate is a legal country. Likely, that kind of certificate does not belong to the birth certificate owner but to the issuer country, and, consequently, it is not immediately available. However, the subject may gather it using a credential chain. The disclosure is not certain, so the corresponding node is set to open. Alternatively, a node may be open also to maximize protection of policies and resources: a party may choose to reply only for one node at a time, without submitting policies for the other resources involved. Consequently, the tree evolves naturally giving priority to those solutions that can be locally solved.

Multi Path and Trust Sequences

The negotiation tree signals a potential trust sequence when it contains a *multi path* composed of all delivery nodes. We use the term *multi path* to outline the fact that the path may include multi edges, and consequently more brothers may be part of a path.1 Valid multi paths are formally defined as follows.

Definition 4.2.

Valid Multi path: Let $NT=<\mathcal{N}, \mathcal{R}, \mathcal{E}>$ be a negotiation tree of height h. A *valid multi path* mp on NT is a partially ordered list of set of nodes $[S_1,...,S_k]$, where $S_i \in 2^N$, $i \in [1,k]$, $k \geq h$ such that:

- $S_1 = \mathcal{R}$;

- The state of each node in S_i, $i \in [1,k]$ is *DELIV*;

- The nodes in each set S_i, $i \in [1,k]$, all refer either to C or S; that is, $\forall n \in S_i$, $i \in [1,k]$, $party(n) = C$ (or $party(n) = S$);

- All the non leaf nodes in the sets belonging to the list are linked either by a simple edge or by a multi edge to one of the nodes in the sets following them in the list. Formally, $\forall S_i, S_{i+1} \in mp$:
  - if $|S_i|=|S_{i+1}|=1$, and the unique node in S_i is a non leaf node, then there must be in $\mathcal{E}$ a simple edge connecting the unique node in S_i to the unique node in S_{i+1};
  - if $|S_i|=1$, $|S_{i+1}| > 1$, and the unique node in S_i is a non leaf node, then there must exist in $\mathcal{E}$ a multi edge connecting the unique node in S_i to all the nodes in S_{i+1};
  - if $|S_i|=m$, $m > 1$, then $\forall n_j \in S_i$, $j \in [1,m]$ such that n_j is a non leaf node:
    - if $|S_{i+1}|=1$, then there must exist in $\mathcal{E}$ a single edge connecting n_j to the unique node in S_{i+1};
    - if $|S_{i+1}|>1$ then there must exist in $\mathcal{E}$ a multi edge connecting n_j to all nodes in S_{i+1}.

Figure 6 shows two multi paths valid for the considered negotiation.

A trust sequence is a list of sets of certificates whose ordered disclosure leads to the grant of the requested resource, assuring at the same time the satisfaction of the disclosure policies of both the involved parties. This sequence can be obtained by simply grouping the sets of nodes composing a valid multi path, starting from the last set of the path, in such a way that the resulting sequence will be composed of as many sets as the height of the tree, each one containing certificates belonging alternatively to client and server party. Formally, a trust sequence is defined as follows.

Definition 4.3.

Trust Sequence: Let S be a server and C be a client. Let $\mathcal{PB}_s$ and $\mathcal{PB}_c$ be the policy bases associated with S and C, respectively. Let $X\text{-}Prof_s$ and $X\text{-}Prof_c$ be the X-Profiles associated with S and C, respectively. Let $\mathcal{R}$, be the resource requested by C to S. A *trust sequence* ts for $\mathcal{R}, S$ and C is a ordered list of sets of certificates $[C_1,...,C_n]$ such that:

- $C_n = \mathcal{R}$;

- For each set C_i, $i \in [1,n-1]$:

Figure 6. Examples of valid multi paths

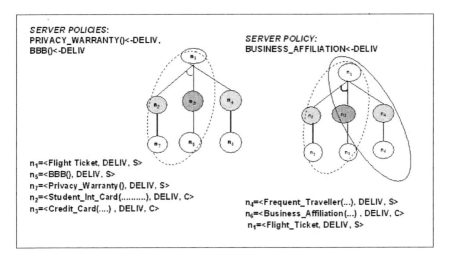

- All the certificates in C_i belong either to C or S;

- If the certificates in C_i belong to C, then the certificates in C_{i+1} belong to S and satisfy a corresponding policy of the form $c_{pi} \leftarrow T_1..T_n$, of C for each $c_{pi} \in C_i$ p=1,...,$|C_i|$. Vice versa, if the certificates in C_i belong to S, then the certificates in C_{i+1} belong to C and satisfy a corresponding policy of the form $c_{pi} \leftarrow T_1..T_n$, of S for each $c_{pi} \in C_i$ p=1,...,$|C_i|$.

Example 3.4

Consider the example in Figure 6. The paths shown in the figure are valid multi paths. In particular, the path on the left side, that is, [{n_1}{n_2, n_3},{n_7},{n_5}], is a valid multi path in that: (1) n_1={R}; (2) The state of each node is DELIV; (3) All the non leaf nodes in the sets belonging to the list are linked either by a simple or by a multi edge to some of the nodes in the sets following them in the list. For instance, {n_1} and {n_2,n_3} are linked by a multi edge, and each node in {n_2,n_3} is linked by a simple edge to a node in a set following it in the list: n_2 is linked to n_7, and n_3 to n_5, respectively. By Definition 3.8, the corresponding trust sequence is: [{BBB, Privacy_Warranty}, {Student_Intl_Card,Credit_Card}, {Flight_Ticket}]. Note that the number of sets of certificates in the trust sequence is equal to the height of the negotiation tree and each set contains certificates, satisfied by a disclosure policy, belonging to C or S, alternatively.

The following theorem states the relationship between a trust sequence and a valid multi path. The formal proof is reported in Appendix.

Figure 7. Example of redundant path and the negotiation tree after the pruning

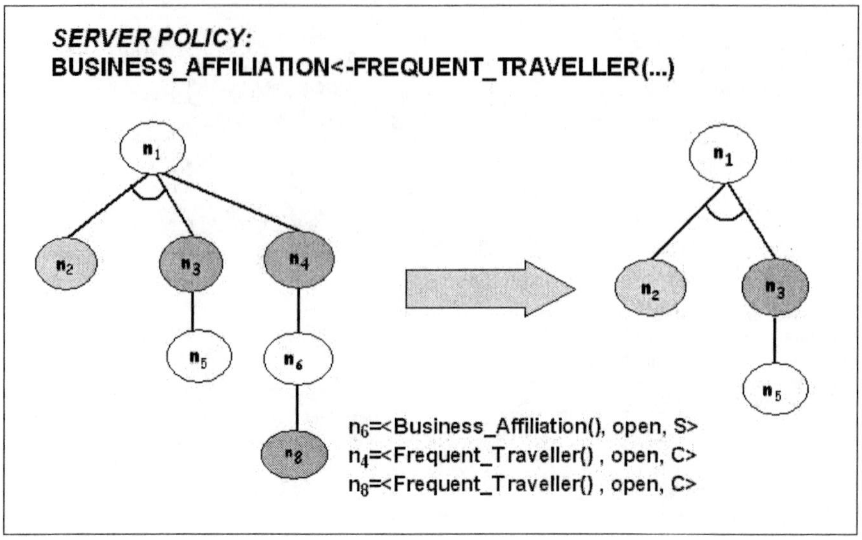

Theorem 1

Let C be a client requesting a resource $\mathcal{R}$ to a server S.

Let NT be the corresponding negotiation tree. For each trust sequence TS=$[C_1,..,C_n=\{R\}]$ associated with the negotiation, there is a valid multi path in NT consisting of all and only the terms satisfied by the certificates in TS. Additionally, for each valid multi path in NT, there is a corresponding trust sequence TS containing all and only the certificates corresponding to terms in the path.

Repeated Nodes Detection

Since parties are not always aware of counterpart policies, the evaluation of some policies can be recursive and create cycles. Repeated terms can be easily detected in the negotiation tree as soon as a term appears twice in the same path. In this case, the *tree manager* prunes the portion of the tree that creates the redundancy. The pruning is executed from the last repeated node (a terminal node) to the first instance of the term found going up towards the tree root. Obviously, each term is pruned only if it does not have any other edge in addition to the edge that creates the redundancy. Figure 7 shows an example of pruning. Suppose that in the negotiation depicted in Figure 5 the server adopts a policy stating that the submission of its Business_affiliation card can be executed only after receiving the Frequent_Traveller badge of the requester. In this case, nodes n_8, n_4 and n_6 are pruned because $\mathcal{T}(n_4)= \mathcal{T}(n_8)$=Frequent_Traveller, and $party(n_4) = party(n_8)$=C.

Note that the presence of many nodes in the negotiation tree referring to the same term $\mathcal{T}(n,)$ and belonging to the same party, does not necessarily denote redundancy. Indeed, if the repeated terms are not in the same path they do not denote a repetition and therefore the tree does not need to be pruned. In such a case the detection of the repetition can be exploited to speed up negotiation tree evolution. More precisely, consider two nodes n_1 and n_2 such that $T(n_1) = T(n_2)$, connected to the root by different paths. If the state of $T(n_1)$ is *DELIV*, it means that a valid multi path rooted at n_1 already exists. A pointer can thus be used to link n_2 to n_1, propagating the state of n_1 to n_2. As a result, n_2 can be immediately managed as a *DELIV* node, without the need of building again the sub tree rooted at n_1. By contrast, if the state of n_1 is *OPEN* and the height of the node is less than the current tree height the link is added anyway, in order to avoid redundant policies exchanges, but the state of both nodes is not modified.

Example 3.5

With reference to the Example in Figure 5, suppose that the privacy warranty is unprotected and the corresponding policy is a delivery policy. As a result, the states of nodes n_2 and n_7 are updated and become DELIV (see Figure 8(a)). Moreover, suppose that the server requires the Student_Int_Card as a document in order to disclose its business affiliation. A new node, labelled n_8, is then added to the tree and linked to node n_2, since it refers to the same term. As a result, the state of n_2 is immediately set as DELIV, thus introducing a new valid multi path, as shown in Figure 8(b).

Certificate Exchange Phase

As remarked in the previous sections, both parties have a complete view of the state of a negotiation and consequently they can both be able to determine valid multi paths. The existence of a valid multi path is thus communicated by the first party that, by processing its policies, detects the path. If more than one valid multi path is determined in the same step, the party analyzes each of them and establishes the associated trust sequences.

Figure 8. Example of link usage (shadowed nodes denote deliv nodes)

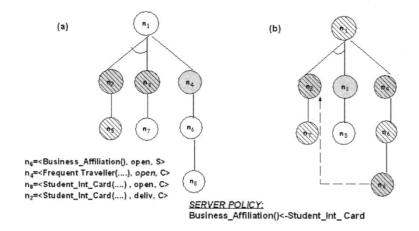

n_6=<Business_Affiliation(), open, S>
n_4=<Frequent Traveller(....), open, C>
n_8=<Student_Int_Card(....) , open, C>
n_2=<Student_Int_Card(....) , deliv, C>

SERVER POLICY:
Business_Affiliation()<-Student_Int_ Card

Then, the party suggests the one it prefers with a Sequence message. Otherwise it signals to the other party the unique valid sequence determined. If the counterpart accepts the suggestion, the two parties begin the exchange of the certificates; otherwise a different sequence is proposed to the counterpart. This interaction goes on until the two parties establish an agreement on a sequence. Once the parties come to an agreement, the certificate exchange phase starts. Each party discloses its certificates, observing the order defined in the sequence. Note that, when a party discloses a set of certificates, it actually discloses one certificate at the time. Upon receiving a certificate, the counterpart verifies the satisfaction of the associated policies, checks for revocation, checks validity dates and authenticates the ownership (for credentials). Eventually, if further information is needed for establishing trust, it is the receiver's responsibility to check for new certificates using credential chains. For example, if a medical certificate was requested and the issuer is an unknown hospital, the receiver party has to check the validity of issuer certificate by collecting new certificates from issuer repository. The receiver then replies with an acknowledgment expressed with an ack message, and asks for the following certificate in the sequence, or whether it has received all the certificates of the set, and it sends a certificate belonging to the following set of certificates in the trust sequence. If no unforeseen event happens, the exchange ends with the disclosure of the requested resource.

Example 3.6

Consider the valid multi paths shown in Figure 8. The corresponding trust sequences are:

[{Very_Sign_Certificate, Privacy_Warranty}, {Student_Int_Card, Credit_Card,},
{Flight_Ticket}] and [{Business_Affiliation}, {Frequent_Traveller}, {Flight_Ticket}].

The two trust sequences are determined by the server party, which is the first who, with its delivery policies, determines two valid multi paths. Assume that the parties agree on the second trust sequence, since it is faster and easier to be executed. Figure 9 shows the messages exchanged by the two parties.

Related Work

Because of the relevance of trust negotiation for Web-based applications, a number of systems and research prototypes have been recently developed (Blaze & Fegeinbamum, 1999; Bonatti & Samarati, 2001; Herzberg & Mihaeli, 2001; Winsborough & Li, 2002), whcih we survey and analyze in what follows and compare with our proposal.

PSPL, proposed by Bonatti and Samarati in 2001, is part of a uniform framework for formulating and reasoning about information release on the Web. It is a protection language for expressing access control policies for services and release policies for client

Figure 9. An example of certificate exchange phase

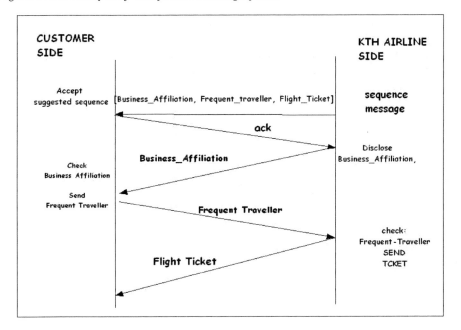

and service portfolios. The language also includes a policy filtering mechanism, to provide policy disclosures and to protect privacy during policy disclosures. The main difference between PSPL and our language is that PSPL only provides a logical definition of the language constructs. Therefore no directly usable language is provided.

The Trust Policy Language (TPL) (Herzberg & Mihaeli, 2001) is an XML-based framework for specifying and managing role-based access control policies in distributed context where the involved parties are characterized by credentials, and digital certificates are used for authentication. There are two versions of TPL: Definite TPL (DTPL), and TPL itself. DTPL is a subset of TPL that excludes negative rules, and it is therefore monotonic.

TPL credentials, like Trust-$\mathcal{X}$ credentials, contain a reference to the site associated with the issuer. However, no protection for sensitive credentials is provided by TPL, since credentials are assumed to be accessible to anyone.

Reference site of issuers contained in credentials is used as a starting point for a collector-controlled search for relevant supporting credentials. One of the most important features of TPL is, indeed, the support of credential chain discovery, which is not yet fully supported by our system.

KeyNote (Blaze & Feigenbaum, 1999) is the most well known trust management language. It was designed to work for a variety of large and small scale Internet-based applications. It provides a single, unified language for both local policies and credentials. KeyNote policies and credentials, called "assertions," contain predicates that describe the trusted actions permitted to the holders of specific public keys. KeyNote, due to its intended use for delegation authority and the fact that trust negotiation uses attributes of the negotiation parties as the basis for trust, is poorly suited for trust negotiation.

Trust Builder (Seamons & Winslett, 2003) is one of the most significant proposals. It provides a set of negotiation protocols that define the ordering of messages and the type of information messages will contain, and of strategies for controlling the exact content of messages. A variety of strategies are defined to allow strangers to establish trust through the exchange of digital credentials and the use of access control policies that specify what combinations of credentials a stranger must disclose in order to gain access to each local service or credential. Trust Builder is the approach that more greatly influenced our work. For instance, we borrow from Seamons and Winslett's work (2003) the use of a tree structure to maintain the progress of a negotiation and keep track of possible alternative strategies.

Finally, the principle of separation of policy exchange from credential disclosure is also achieved by the parsimonious strategy proposed by Seamons and Winslett (2003) and by the PRUNES strategy (Yu, Ma & Winslett 2001). Both approaches are based on negotiation search tree, focusing on automatic strategies for policy exchange in order to avoid as much as possible disclosure of credentials. Yu, Ma and Seamons' (2001) work also ensures completeness of the negotiation strategy, where a negotiation strategy is said to be complete when it leads the negotiation to succeed whenever possible. According with the above definition, our approach can be considered complete as well as the one proposed in the referred work. Moreover, the authors refer to a security agent in charge of automatically carrying on negotiations, without user intervention. By contrast, we present a much more flexible approach where a user can eventually drive the negotiation process to either maximize protection, or maximize the number of potential solutions for negotiation.

Mobile Commerce with Trust-$\mathcal{X}$

In this section, we discuss how the Trust-$\mathcal{X}$ negotiation system can be properly applied to mobile commerce, and show how our method can influence mobile commerce security. The section is organized as follows. We first introduce the main issues related to the development of a system supporting negotiations for mobile users. Then, we illustrate a variety of techniques to extend Trust-$\mathcal{X}$ in order to fully support mobile negotiations.

Open Issues

The area of trust negotiation for mobile systems is today a promising and challenging research area, since it is expected that the number of wireless clients accessing Internet will rapidly increase in the next few years. This will lead to an environment where the number of wireless clients accessing the Internet to perform mobile transactions will greatly exceed the number of clients accessing the Internet through networked computers. The development of a system supporting negotiations for mobile users presents significant challenges, mainly arising from the need of migrating trust negotiation concepts and their complex requirements into a mobile context. More precisely, we have identified the following major aspects that need to be taken into account when dealing with mobile negotiations:

- Mobile devices, like cell phones, PDAs, laptops and portable MP3 players, have limited storage capacity, processing power, and network bandwidth compared to typical desktop computers. Such feature may be critical in mobile trust negotiations, since a conventional trust negotiation system requires a significant processing power for keeping track of the negotiation process and a certain storage capacity for collecting credentials and policies.

- Trust negotiation systems usually rely on credentials, signed using public keys managed by public key infrastructures. However, public key infrastructures are usually onerous for mobile devices.

- Mobile network topologies are often unpredictable and dynamically change. A mobile system must thus handle interactions that may take place in a variety of different configurations.

- A single user can possess multiple mobile devices. Since a fundamental requirement of trust negotiations is to ensure ownership of the credentials exchanged among the parties, a key issue is to allow independent devices to safely share and access user credentials.

- Networks can be easily compromised; thus suitable recovery mechanisms for mobile trust negotiations need to be developed.

In what follows, we focus on some of the issues listed above. In particular, we reason about security problems related to mobile negotiations and sketch a variety of possible solutions. We do not further discuss on issues related to network availability and quality of service since they are outside the scope of this chapter. For what concerns the mobile payments techniques, we would prefer to build on current technologies and take advantage of existing infrastructure and integrate them in our Trust-$\mathcal{X}$ framework rather than redesign them. For example, we may produce strategies and techniques for supporting mobile payments with multi-application devices but for technical specifications that address specific areas of mobile payments, such as cardholder authentication, passwords, and encryption we refer to specific organizations created for such purposes. In this way we would complement, rather than duplicate efforts. The aim of the proposed approaches is, instead, to adapt Trust-$\mathcal{X}$ in order to make it possible to perform trust negotiations and mobile transactions and payments in vulnerable environments by users having limited computational resources.

Extending Trust-$\mathcal{X}$ to Support Mobile Commerce Applications

Extending trust negotiation systems for the management of mobile users requires first to provide resource-compatibility with devices that typically have constrained resources. A mechanism for storing credentials needs thus to be devised that keeps into account the limited capacity of mobile devices. End users require device ownership: although anyone can pick up a device, only its real owner must be allowed to carry out transactions involving personal credentials. A possible approach is to centralize credential storage into a single repository, allowing each user to maintain the associated profile on a secure server. This schema for credential management is sketched in Figure 10(a). Under this approach, a user can change the device from which he/she performs transactions without the need of moving the entire profile with himself/herself, and refer to it while negotiating services. Another important issue is whether it is practical for wireless clients to efficiently perform all the phases required to complete a trust negotiation, such as the storage of all required credentials, the processing steps that include costly cryptographic verifications, and the network communications with the other negotiation participants. One potential scalable solution is to offload trust negotiation from the thin client and conduct it out-of-band between the server and an agent managing the client's credentials via a higher-speed network connection. Alternatively, it is possible to adopt ad hoc strategies for negotiations in order to reduce the information to be exchanged as much as possible. Finally, another potential approach is to let the party having a consistent connection (called *negotiation driver,* for simplicity) with sufficient bandwidth to drive the process. Obviously, this approach can succeed only if the negotiation driver is a company supplying services able to prove its trustworthiness. Under this scheme, once the driver trustworthiness is ensured, the negotiation driver can keep track of the progress of the negotiation, freeing the mobile party from carrying this burden.

A possible further extension addressing the issues listed in the previous section is sketched in Figure 10(b). Such approach consists of providing the possibility of dynamically changing the server with which to perform the negotiation, while the mobile party is moving. For instance, suppose Alice is connected via a mobile phone to a Web server, purchasing clothes at an online store. Suppose she is travelling by train while performing the transaction. Then, if the transaction cannot be completed with the same server because of Alice's change of geographic position, the server can interrupt the negotiation and suggest Alice to connect to another closer server having the same capabilities, able to carry out the negotiation in an equivalent way. Or better, the server could automatically redirect the negotiation to another trusted server, after requesting the consensus of Alice for this operation. Clearly, this implies that the server with which Alice was performing the negotiation should transmit to the new one all the information related to the ongoing negotiation process in a secure way. For instance, if we assume that both the servers are Trust-$\mathcal{X}$ compliant this implies transmitting the negotiation tree built until the interruption, the determined trust sequences, if any, and the credentials Alice has sent to the server until that point. Intuitively, this approach is based on two strong assumptions: the trustworthiness of parties and the existence of a network of trusted servers that can be interchanged during negotiations. Finally, another interesting research issue is the possibility of exploiting already executed negotiation processes with a certain entity to simplify the next mobile transactions to be executed. In a scenario characterized by a mobile user and a negotiation driver, the driver can collect the information obtained by the user in previous successful negotiations to speed up next processes. Furthermore, the driver can exploit the collected data to advertise the user the services it sells, selecting the products to advertise on the basis of user profile, and on the basis of the geographical location of the user. However, this last functionality requires addressing privacy issues that arise when private information is collected by a remote party for purposes other than the transaction which it was released for. This approach indeed relies on the Web server's possibility to store remote credentials and collect user personal information. Next example shows how a mobile commerce transaction may be employed using the approach previously introduced.

Example

Alice is a frequent flyer who usually makes use of her PDA to purchase flights tickets by KTH. Suppose she is carrying on a negotiation to buy a flight ticket for her next travel to a foreign country. Suppose, moreover, that she is travelling by train. Instead of executing the whole negotiation process in such a vulnerable environment in order to complete the transaction, Alice can just delegate the negotiation driver, that is, KTH, the task of memorizing the negotiation tree and skip the negotiation of requisites already proved in previous negotiations. Furthermore, there is no need of communicating the credit card number, which represents the most sensitive information to be exchanged, if KTH already knows it and has Alice's consent of maintaining it for use. KTH, by using Trust-X, can exploit Alice's collected data to advertise to her about the services it sells. For instance it may send Alice information about the possibility of booking hotels, renting cars and so on, on the basis of Alice's profile, and on the basis of her actual geographical location, as well as Alice's next destination.

Figure 10. Examples of possible topologies for mobile trust negotiations

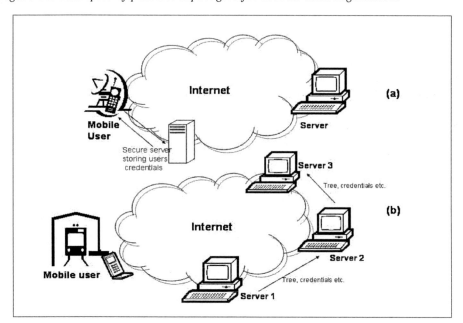

Conclusions and Future Research Directions

Automated trust negotiation between strangers promises to extend trusted interactions to a broader range of participants than it is possible with traditional security approaches based on identity and capabilities. One of the most interesting applications for trust negotiation systems is given by the possibility of performing e-commerce applications. Mobile commerce, in particular, is an important branch of e-commerce requiring additional trust establishment capabilities.

In this chapter, besides introducing the basic principles of trust negotiation, we have presented Trust-$\mathcal{X}$, a comprehensive XML-based framework for trust negotiations. We have mainly focused on disclosure policies and the various phases in which a Trust-$\mathcal{X}$ negotiation is articulated. Then, we have presented a number of possible extensions we are currently exploring for migrating the system into mobile scenarios. The work reported in this chapter is part of an on-going project aiming at fully supporting mobile commerce applications.

Additional future work includes the extension of $\mathcal{X}$-TNL along several directions, such as for instance the possibility of specifying the credential submitter. Another extension we are currently investigating is the possibility of disclosing only portions of a credential during the negotiation process. This allows us to protect the elements of a credential in a selective and differentiated way. Finally, an implementation of Trust-$\mathcal{X}$ is in progress.

References

Bertino, E., Castano, S., & Ferrari, E. (2001). On specifying security policies for Web documents with an XML-based language. *Proc. of SACMAT' 2001, ACM Symposium on Access Control Models and Technologies,* Fairfax, VA.

Bertino, E., Ferrari, E., & Squicciarini, A. (2003). X-TNL - An XML based language for trust negotiations. *Fourth IEEE International Workshop on Policies for Distributed Systems and Networks,* Como, Italy.

Bertino, E., Ferrari, E., & Squicciarini, A. (n.d.). Trust-$\mathcal{X}$ – A peer to peer framework for trust establishment. To appear in *IEEE Transactions of Knowledge and Engineering.*

Blaze, M., Feigenbaum, J., Ioannidis J., & Keromytis, A. (1999). The KeyNote trust-management system. *RFC 2704.*

Bonatti, P., & Samarati, P. (2000). Regulating access services and information release on the Web. *7th ACM Conference on Computer and Communications Security,* Athens, Greece.

Brands. (2000). *Rethinking public key infrastructure and digital credentials.* MIT Press.

Damianou, N., Dulay, N., Lupu, E., & Sloman, M. (2001). The ponder policy specification language. *International Workshop on Policies for Distributed Systems and Networks,* LNCS 1995, Bristol UK.

Dierks, T., & Allen, C. (1999). The TLS protocol version 1.0. *RFC 2246.*

Herzberg, A., Mihaeli, J., Mass, Y., Naor, D., & Ravid, Y. (2000). Access control meets public infrastructure, or: Assigning roles to strangers. *IEEE Symposium on Security and Privacy,* Oakland, CA.

Persiano, P., & Visconti, I. (2000). User privacy issues regarding certificates and the TLS protocol. *Proceedings of the ACM Conference on Computer and Communication Security,* Athens, Greece.

Seamons, K.E., Winslett, M., & Yu, T. (2001). Limiting the disclosure of access control policies during automated trust negotiation. *Network and Distributed System Security Symposium,* San Diego, CA.

Seamons, K.E., Winslett, M., & Yu, T. (2002). Requirements for policy languages for trust negotiation. *Third IEEE International Workshop on Policies for Distributed Systems and Networks,* Monterey, CA.

Stallings, W. (1999). *Cryptography and network security: Principles and practice* (2nd ed.). Prentice Hall.

Subrahmanian, V. et al. (n.d.). Hermes: Heterogeneous reasoning and mediator system. *http://www.cs.umd.edu/projects/publications*

Winsborough, W.H., & Li, N. (2002a). Protecting sensitive attributes in automated trust negotiation. *ACM Workshop on Privacy in the Electronic Society.*

Winsborough, W.H., & Li, N. (2002b). Towards practical automated trust negotiation. *Third International Workshop on Policies for Distributed Systems and Networks,* Monterey, CA.

World Wide Web Consortium. (1998). Extensible markup language (XML) 1.0. *http://www.w3c.org/TR/*

Yu, T., Ma, X., & Winslett, M. (2000). PRUNES: An efficient and complete strategy for trust negotiation over the Internet. *Proceedings of the 7th ACM Conference on Computer and Communications Security,* Athens, Greece.

Yu, T., Winslett, M., & Seamons, K.E. (2003). Supporting structured credentials and sensitive policies through interoperable strategies for automated trust negotiation. *ACM Transactions on Information and System Security, 6*(1).

Endnotes

[1]   Like for credentials, we assume that data set names are unique, and that are registered through some central organization.

[2]   Prerequisite information are encoded using the same formalism we have developed for disclosure policies.

3   With the term trust we refer to the fact that the sequence is composed by certificates whose corresponding disclosure policies are satisfied. Safety is not related, in this context, with certificates validity or their effective content.

4   Given a node $n \in \mathcal{N}$, we use the notation $\mathcal{T}(n)$ to denote the term in n; *state(n)* to denote the state of *n*; and *party(n)* to denote the owner of the term in *n*.

5   For simplicity, we focus on the most relevant policies and related terms.

Appendix

Proof of Theorem 1

We start by proving the first part of the thesis. The proof is by induction on the length l of the trust sequence.

Basics

$l = 2$, then TS = $[C_1, \{R\}]$. Let us first suppose that $|C_1| = 1$ and let c be the unique certificate in C_1. Since, by hypothesis, *TS* is a trust sequence, then the Policy Base of S must contain disclosure policy of the form: R $\leftarrow$ $\mathcal{T}$, such that: (1) $P(\mathcal{T})$ is the type of c; and (2) the $\mathcal{X}$-Profile of C contains a certificate of type P satisfying the conditions in $c(\mathcal{T})$. By Definition 4.1, *NT* contains two nodes n_1 and n_2 such that: (1) $\mathcal{T}(n_1) = $ R; (2) $\mathcal{T}(n_2) = \mathcal{T}$; (3) $state(n_1) = state(n_2) = $ DELIV; (4) $party(n_1) = S$ and $party(n_2) = C$. Additionally, $\mathcal{E}$ contains the simple arc (n_1, n_2). Thus, by Definition 4.2, $\mathcal{NT}$ contains a valid multi path $[S_1, S_2]$, such that $S_1 = \{n_1\}$, and $S_2 = \{n_2\}$, which proves the thesis. If $|S_1| > z > 1$, let $c_{11}, \ldots, c_{1z}$ be its elements. Since by hypothesis *TS* is a trust sequence, the Policy Base of S must contain a disclosure policy of the form: R $\leftarrow \mathcal{T}_{11} \ldots \mathcal{T}_{1z}$, such that $P(\mathcal{T}_{1i})$ is the type of c_{1i}, $i \in [1,z]$ and the $\mathcal{X}$-Profile of C contains a certificate of type c_{1i} satisfying the conditions in $c(\mathcal{T}_{1i})$, $i \in [1,z]$. By Definition 4.2, *NT* contains a node n_1 such that $\mathcal{T}(n_1) = R$, and a node n_{1i} such that $\mathcal{T}(n_{1i}) = \mathcal{T}_{1i}$, $i \in [1,z]$. Additionally, $state(n_1) = state(n_{1i}) = $ DELIV, $i = 1, \ldots, z$, whereas $party(n_1) = S$, $party(n_{1i}) = C$, $i = 1, \ldots, z$. Finally, $\mathcal{E}$ contains a multi edge $\{(n_1, n_{11}), \ldots, (n_1, n_{1n})\}$. Thus, by Definition 4.2, $\mathcal{NT}$ contains a valid multi path $[S_1, S_2]$, such that $S_1 = \{n_1\}$, and $S_2 = \{n_{11}, \ldots, n_{1z}\}$, which proves the thesis.

Inductive Step

Let us consider a trust sequence *TS*, such that $l = h > 2$. Suppose that the thesis holds for trust sequences of height $h' < h$ and let us prove the thesis for h. Then, TS = $[C_{1, \ldots}, C_{h-1}, \{R\}]$. By inductive hypothesis, if we consider the trust sequence *TS'* obtained from *TS* by dropping set C_1, then there exists a valid multi path $mp = [S_1, \ldots, S_p]$, in the corresponding negotiation tree. Let us thus consider set C_1. If $|C_1| = |C_2| = 1$, or $|C_2| = $

1 and $|C_l| = k > 1$, then using the same reasoning we have applied for $l = 2$ we can prove the thesis simply by concatenating to the sets of nodes in mp the nodes corresponding to the certificates in C_l, using the same strategy adopted above.

Thus, we are left to consider the case when $|C_1| = k > 1$, and $|C_2| = j > 1$. We can suppose, without loss of generality, that $j = 2$. Suppose moreover that the party of each node in S_p is C. Let $c_{11}, \ldots, c_{1k}$ be the elements in C_1 and c_{21}, c_{22} be the elements in C_2. Since, by hypothesis, TS is a trust sequence, the Policy Base of S must contain two disclosure policies of the form: $c_{2i} \leftarrow \mathcal{T}_{i1} \ldots \mathcal{T}_{in}$, $n \geq 1$, $i = 1, 2$ such that: (1) $P(\mathcal{T}_{im}) \in S_p$, $m = 1, \ldots, n$, $i = 1, 2$; and (2) the X-Profile of C contains a certificate of type $P(\mathcal{T}_{im})$ satisfying the conditions in $C(\mathcal{T}_{im})$, $m = 1, \ldots, n$, $i = 1, 2$. Let us first consider the policy $c_{21} \leftarrow \mathcal{T}_{11} \ldots \mathcal{T}_{1n}$. Suppose first that $n = 1$; that is, the right side of the policy contains only the term $\mathcal{T}_{11}$. By Definition 4.1, $\mathcal{NT}$ contains a node n_1 such that $\mathcal{T}(n_1) = c_{21}$, and a node n_2 such that $\mathcal{T}(n_2)$ is equal to the certificate type in $\mathcal{T}_{11}$. Additionally, $state(n_1) = state(n_2) = \text{DELIV}$, whereas $party(n_1) = S$, $party(n_2) = C$. Finally, $\mathcal{E}$ contains a simple edge (n_1, n_2). If $n > 1$, we can apply a similar reasoning, the only difference being that the negotiation tree will contains a multi edge instead of a simple edge, and the same reasoning can be applied to the policy $c_{22} \leftarrow \mathcal{T}_{21} \ldots \mathcal{T}_{2n}$. Thus, by Definition 4.2, $\mathcal{NT}$ contains a valid multi path mp' obtained from mp by concatenating two sets of nodes: one corresponding to the nodes added for policy $c_{21} \leftarrow \mathcal{T}_{11} \ldots \mathcal{T}_{1n}$, and the other corresponding to the nodes for policy $c_{22} \leftarrow \mathcal{T}_{21} \ldots \mathcal{T}_{2n}$, which proves the thesis.

Let us prove the second part of the thesis. Let $mp = [S_1, \ldots, S_k]$ be a valid multi path in $\mathcal{NT}$. Let $S_i \in mp$ be a generic set of $n_1 \ldots n_k$ nodes. Suppose, without loss of generality, that the party of each node in S_i is C. By Definition 4.2 the state of all the nodes in S_i is DELIV; then, there must exist in the Policy Base of C a disclosure policy: $\mathcal{T}(n_j) \leftarrow \mathcal{T}(n_{1j}) \ldots \mathcal{T}(n_{pj})$ for each node $n_j \in S_i$, and $party(n_j) = C$ for $j \in [1,k]$. Moreover, $n_{1j} \ldots n_{pj} \in S_j$ with $j > i$ and $party(n_{sj}) = S$, $s \in [1,p]$. By Definition 4.1, $Eval(\mathcal{T}(n_i), Prof_C) = \text{TRUE}$ and $Eval(\mathcal{T}(n_{si}), Prof_S) = \text{TRUE}$ for $s \in [1,p]$. Thus, for each node $n \in S_i$, there exists a certificate of type c_i such that $P(\mathcal{T}(n)) = c_i$ which satisfies the condition in $C(\mathcal{T}(n))$. Each set $S_i \in mp$ has, therefore, a corresponding set of certificates $C_i = \{c_1, \ldots, c_k\}$. The corresponding trust sequence $TS = [C_1, \ldots, C_n]$ is therefore obtained grouping all the certificates belonging to consecutive sets associated with the same party in mp into a unique set C_j until a certificate belonging to the other party is found. The resulting sequence satisfies Definition 4.3, which proves the thesis.

Chapter VII

Security Issues and Possible Countermeasures for a Mobile Agent Based M-Commerce Application

Jyh-haw Yeh, Boise State University, USA

Wen-Chen Hu, University of North Dakota, USA

Chung-wei Lee, Auburn University, USA

Abstract

With the advent of wireless and mobile networks, the Internet is rapidly evolving from a set of connected stationary machines to include mobile handheld devices. This creates new opportunities for customers to conduct business from any location at any time. However, the electronic commerce technologies currently used cannot be applied directly since most were developed based on fixed, wired networks. As a result, a new research area, mobile commerce, is now being developed to supplement existing electronic commerce capabilities. This chapter discusses the security issues related to this new field, along with possible countermeasures, and introduces a mobile agent based solution for mobile commerce.

Introduction

The Internet has been steadily growing at a rapid speed since its commercialization. The fast and convenient characteristics of the Internet attract a wide variety of users all over the world. Because of its ability to reach more potential customers, the Internet is changing the nature of business from a traditional model based on face-to-face negotiations to a more advanced model utilizing electronic commerce (e-commerce). People all over the world can sell, buy and trade goods online as long as they can access the Internet. As a result of recent advances in wireless and mobile network technology, accessing the Internet has become even more convenient. Users can now access the Internet with a handheld device from any location at any time they choose. This wireless technology evolution further broadens the scope of business from e-commerce to mobile commerce (m-commerce). Most major companies have foreseen this and devoted a significant effort to developing new m-commerce systems to facilitate this trend. However, the migration from e-commerce to m-commerce is not as easy as it first appears because all the existing e-commerce technologies were developed for wired networks, which are more reliable, more secure and faster than wireless and mobile networks. Therefore, without major revisions the current e-commerce technologies cannot be applied directly to m-commerce. This chapter addresses this issue by discussing possible solutions based on the use of mobile agent technology to overcome the underlying hardware limitations of m-commerce.

In order to fully deploy m-commerce for business, there are two levels of security requirements that must be satisfied. The lower level requirement is the need for a secure wireless infrastructure to protect each individual wireless communication and the higher level requirement is for a secure protocol with which to conduct mobile payment and business transactions, thus protecting the legitimate security concerns of the three parties involved, namely the customer, the merchant, and the bank. Wireless communication security is a serious problem for all wireless applications that must transmit data securely through an open airwave communication medium. IEEE 802.1x (IEEE, 2001) defines the standard for wireless authentication, key distribution, network monitoring, and similar issues. This standard uses EAP (Extensible Authentication Protocol) (Blunk & Vollbrecht, 1998) and its supported algorithms to authenticate exchanged messages. The algorithms supported by EAP are MD5 (Message Digest 5), TLS (Transport Layer Security) (Aboba & Simon, 1999; Dierks & Allen, 1999), TTLS (Tunneled TLS) (Funk & Blake-Wilson, 2002), LEAP (Lightweight EAP), and PEAP (Protected EAP) (Hakan, Josefsson, Zorn, Simon & Palekar, 2002). The security community has agreed that cryptography is the only solution to the problem of ensuring authenticity, privacy and integrity for communications through insecure media and many encryption algorithms have been developed over the past few decades. However, in a wireless environment with limited physical resources, most existing encryption algorithms are too computationally intensive. A lightweight encryption algorithm with an acceptable degree of security strength is a possible solution to this dilemma. Although the lower level security requirement, wireless communication security, is the topic of considerable ongoing research and is a vital preliminary to the deployment of all wireless applications, this chapter will instead focus on the higher level security requirement, mobile payment and transaction security.

A business transaction is likely to involve a secure negotiation made up of many back and forth messages. However, due to their limited bandwidth, mobile handheld devices cannot afford to receive and respond to those messages individually. To resolve this problem, the use of mobile software agent technology could provide a possible solution. The handheld device launches a smart mobile agent containing all the necessary negotiation and shopping logics to the Internet. The agent shops around and makes decisions based on the contained logics and returns only the final result to the customer via the handheld device. The handheld device verifies the result and performs the final transaction, that is, the actual purchase. In this way, the number of messages exchanged can be reduced considerably. Another advantage of using mobile agent technology is that it is not necessary for the handheld device to stay online after launching the agent. The customer can disconnect the device from the network while the smart agent traverses the Internet, visiting Web sites and gathering information.

Mobile agent technology is still in its infancy, but it has attracted a great deal of research attention because of its potential utility. The major obstacle preventing the wider deployment of mobile agent technology is, again, the related security concerns. Without sufficient protection for both the mobile agents and the foreign host platforms they visit, malicious attacks may damage either the agents or their hosts. A contaminated agent could attack a host platform by planting a virus, consuming valuable resources, extracting secret data, and so forth. On the other hand, a malicious host may alter a visiting agent's shopping logics, or even kill the whole agent, to favor itself. In this chapter, these security threats and some possible countermeasures to protect the mobile agents will be discussed.

This chapter is structured as follows:

1. **Online Business Model** describes a generic business model and lists its security and resource concerns. E-commerce and m-commerce share many of the same security concerns, since both belong to this online business model. However, to satisfy the security requirements of their different underlying infrastructures, some resource concerns in m-commerce may become more important and present greater challenges than their e-commerce counterparts.

2. **E-Commerce Approach I: SET Protocol** presents the Secure Electronic Transaction protocol to illustrate how the security concerns can be satisfied.

3. **E-Commerce Approach II: Digital Cash** presents one of the existing digital cash systems that is currently used for e-commerce.

4. **Mobile Agent Technology** discusses the basic principles of mobile agent technology.

5. **The Use of Mobile Agents for Mobile Commerce** illustrates how the mobile agent technology can be applied for mobile commerce.

6. Finally, the **Conclusion** summarizes and concludes this chapter.

Online Business Model

An online business transaction consists of two phases, shopping and purchase-payment. During the shopping phase, the customer may visit many online merchants searching for the best buy. Once a merchant has been selected, the customer may request a tamper-resistant quote from the merchant, which is a signed offer from the merchant listing the merchandise items and the offering prices. The format of a quote may look like Table 1.

The merchant's signature on the quote ensures that no other entity can modify the quote without being detected, thus guaranteeing the integrity of the quote. Once a merchant creates a quote and sends it to a customer, the merchant cannot repudiate it because no one except the merchant can generate a quote with the correct signature. Because the merchant's name is incorporated in the quote and its integrity is protected by their signature, the customer cannot maliciously present this quote to other merchants who may not want to sell the specified merchandise at the specified price. Similarly, as the customer's name is also included, a stolen quote would be useless.

After receiving a quote, the purchase-payment phase is initiated to perform the actual online purchase and payment. The customer prepares a purchase order and payment instructions based on the received quote, where

- *PO*: The purchase order includes the customer's name, the merchant's name, the merchandise items, the quantity and price of each item purchased, and the date.

- *PI*: The payment instruction consists of the customer's name, the merchant's name, the payment method such as the credit card number or the digital cash that is to be used, the total charge, and the date.

The customer initiates the purchase-payment phase by sending the prepared *PO* and *PI*, both encrypted, to the merchant. The merchant decrypts the *PO* to learn what items have been ordered, and then forwards the encrypted *PI* to the bank to ensure an authorized payment.

This online business model applies to both e-commerce and m-commerce since m-commerce is just an extension of e-commerce. However, due to the inherent physical limitations, additional challenges arise when conducting the two business phases in m-

Table 1. The format of a quote from a merchant

Merchant Name	Customer Name	Merchandise	Merchant's Signature
Quantity	Unit Price	Expiration Date	

commerce. To better understand the challenges and their possible countermeasures, it is first necessary to clarify the resource and security concerns specific to m-commerce.

The two business phases present different resource concerns. The first phase is likely to generate many message round trips between a mobile device and online merchants, which will consume a lot of network bandwidth, while the second phase requires the mobile device to have high computational power in order to perform the many encryptions needed for a secure purchase and payment transaction. In a wireless environment, both of these resources are very precious and limited; existing e-commerce approaches could not be applied directly unless their resource consumption can be reduced considerably. Later in this chapter, the mobile agent technology will be introduced for this purpose.

To address the security concerns, generally speaking, a secure communication, depending on its application, must satisfy as many as possible of the following common security goals:

- *Authenticity*: The receiving end in a communication should make sure that the sender is really who it claims to be. For mutual authentication, both ends should authenticate each other.

- *Integrity*: It should not be possible to alter transmitted data without detection.

- *Confidentiality*: Only authorized entities should be able to see protected data.

- *Non-repudiation*: The recipient should have some sort of proof to show to a third party that the sender has really committed to an action in case the sender later repudiates the commitment.

- *Anonymity*: In some cases, an entity may want to initiate an activity without revealing his/her identity.

In a business transaction, because each of the three participants plays a different role, they will have different expectations and security concerns. The following list describes the main issues for the three participants:

- **Customer***:*

    1. *Authenticity*: The customer should be capable of authenticating the other two participants.

    2. *Integrity*: It should not be possible to alter purchase orders and payment instructions without detection.

    3. *Confidentiality*: The customer definitely does not want to reveal their credit card number to the merchant, and may also not want the card issuing bank to know the contents of the purchase order.

    4. *Non-repudiation*: The customer could use the received quote as a non-repudiation proof if the merchant refuses to sell the specified goods or services as previously agreed. Also, if the customer has been charged by the merchant

before receiving the ordered goods or services, the customer should receive a payment receipt that can be presented as evidence if the merchant later refuses to deliver the order.

5. *Anonymity*: For an online business transaction, a customer may want to hide his/her identity from the merchant and/or bank. Obviously the credit card system no longer works for such cases. As with the system of paying with cash used in the real world, the use of digital cash provides a possible solution and protects anonymity in the electronic world.

• **Merchant**:

1. *Authenticity*: The merchant should be capable of authenticating the other two participants.

2. *Integrity*: It should not be possible to alter purchase orders and payment instructions without detection.

3. *Non-repudiation*: If the order has been delivered to the customer before payment, the merchant should receive a delivery receipt which can be presented as evidence if the customer later refuses to pay.

• **Bank**:

1. *Authenticity*: The bank should be capable of authenticating the other two participants.

2. *Integrity*: It should not be possible to alter purchase orders and payment instructions without detection.

With these resource and security concerns in mind, the following two sections will describe some existing e-commerce approaches to see how these concerns can be satisfied.

E-Commerce Approach I: Set Protocol

The Secure Electronic Transaction (SET) Protocol (*http://www.setco.org*) was developed in the mid 90s in response to a call by two major credit card companies, Mastercard and Visa, for the establishment of an electronic commerce standard. The protocol extends the existing credit card system and allows people to use it securely over open media. As described in the previous section, the customer prefers to hide the credit card number from the merchant, as well as to hide the goods/service order from the bank. However, these two pieces of information need to be somehow linked together to prevent the merchant from maliciously attaching the payment information to a different order. The SET protocol uses dual signatures to solve this problem.

Protocol Description

In this protocol, a public hash function H and a public key cryptosystem are set up and used by the three business participants. Each of the three participants has his/her own public and private keys. Let E_C, E_M, E_B be the encryption or signature-verification functions for the customer, the merchant, and the bank, respectively. Similarly, let D_C, D_M, D_B be the decryption or signature functions for the three participants.

During the shopping phase, the customer shops around and requests a quote from the merchant who offers the best deal. After the quote is received, the customer prepares a purchase order, PO, and a payment instruction, PI, based on the quote received, and then activates the purchase-payment phase by performing the following actions:

1.   Computes a $PIMD$, which is the message digest of an encrypted PI, that is:

$$PIMD = H(E_B(PI))$$

2.   Computes a $POMD$, which is the message digest of an encrypted PO, that is:

$$POMD = H(E_M(PO))$$

3.   Computes a $PIPOMD$, which is the message digest of the concatenated $PIMD$ and $POMD$, that is:

$$PIPOMD = H(PIMD \,||\, POMD)$$

4.   Generates a dual signature DS, which is the customer's signature on the $PIPOMD$, that is:

$$DS = D_C(PIPOMD)$$

5.   Sends the $PIMD$, $E_M(PO)$, $E_B(PI)$, and DS to the merchant.

There are thus four pieces of data sent to the merchant. However, only the clear text PO embedded in the cipher text can be retrieved by the merchant because it is encrypted by the merchant's public key. The clear text PI is encrypted by the bank's public key so that the merchant has no way to learn the credit card number inside the PI. Thus, the security goal of hiding the credit card number from the merchant is achieved. The merchant performs the following actions after receiving the message.

1.   Computes *POMD* by applying the hash function to the received $E_M(PO)$, that is:

$$POMD = H(E_M(PO))$$

2.   Verifies the dual signature *DS* by computing the following two values:

$$H(PIMD \mid\mid POMD) \text{ and } E_C(DS)$$

If the two values are equal, the merchant has verified the customer's signature, and therefore authenticates the customer. Most importantly, the merchant is convinced that both the purchase order and the payment instruction were not forged during transmission and are really from the customer. Thus, the security goals of authentication and data integrity are achieved. The two values obtained are the *PIPOMD*.

3.   Retrieves the purchase order *PO* by decrypting the received $E_M(PO)$, that is:

$$PO = D_M(E_M(PO))$$

4.   Computes $D_M(PIPOMD)$ to sign the *PIPOMD*, the value obtained at step 2.
5.   Sends the *POMD*, $E_B(PI)$, $D_M(PIPOMD)$ and *DS* to the bank.

Among the four data items sent to the bank, only the encrypted *PI* can be decrypted. The *PO* is embedded in the message digest *POMD* and therefore cannot be retrieved by the bank. Thus, the security goal of hiding the purchase order from the bank is achieved. Upon receiving the request from the merchant, the bank performs the following actions.

1.   Computes *PIMD* by applying the hash function to the received $E_B(PI)$, that is:

$$PIMD = H(E_B(PI))$$

2.   Verifies the dual signature *DS* by computing the following two values:

$$H(PIMD \mid\mid POMD) \text{ and } E_C(DS)$$

If the two values are equal, the bank has verified the customer's signature, and therefore authenticates the customer. This comparison also convinces the bank that the received *POMD*, $E_B(PI)$ and *DS* have not been modified and thus the security goal of data integrity is guaranteed. The two values obtained are the *PIPOMD*.

3.   Uses the merchant's public key to verify the merchant's signature. That is, the bank computes:

$$E_M(D_M(PIPOMD))$$

and then compares the value to the *PIPOMD* obtained in the previous step. If the two values are equal, the bank is really communicating with the merchant as it claimed. Thus, the bank authenticates the merchant.

4.   Retrieves the payment instruction *PI* by decrypting the received $E_B(PI)$, that is:

$$D_B(E_B(PI))$$

5.   Returns a digitally signed receipt to the merchant, guaranteeing payment.

After receiving the receipt from the bank, the merchant:

1.   Verifies the bank's signature on the received receipt to authenticate the bank. That is, the merchant computes and compares the following two values:

$$D_M(PIPOMD) \text{ and } PIPOMD$$

If the two values are equal, the merchant successfully authenticates the bank and knows that the received receipt is indeed from the bank.

2.   Returns the bank's receipt $D_B(PIPOMD)$, together with its own signed receipt $D_M(PIPOMD)$, to the customer.

To complete the phase, the customer authenticates both the merchant and the bank by verifying the signatures on the two receipts received.

The protocol described in this section is not exactly the same as the SET protocol. Some modifications have been made, since the original protocol does not consider all the security concerns mentioned in the previous section. For example, the original SET protocol only deals with the purchase-payment phase. For a complete online business model, the authors believe that the shopping phase is also important and should be included. Moreover, in the modified SET protocol, some extra signatures on the *PIPOMD* are needed for mutual authentication purposes.

Online E-Business Using the SET Protocol

Figure 1 shows the basic sequence of events used to conduct an online e-business transaction using the SET protocol, although the figure ignores all the cryptographic details. The double arrowheads used in Steps 1 and 2 in Figure 1 represent the many back and forth messages exchanged between the personal computer and online merchants during the shopping phase. In Step 3, the customer selects the best merchant based on the received quotes and activates the purchase-payment phase by first performing the necessary cryptographic operations on his/her personal computer. For the remaining steps in the figure, the purchase order and payment instruction and the merchandise delivery will be securely performed by passing the encrypted/signed *PI*, *PO*, and *PIPOMD* between the three business participants, as described earlier in this section.

Figure 1. The sequence of events for an online e-business transaction using the SET protocol

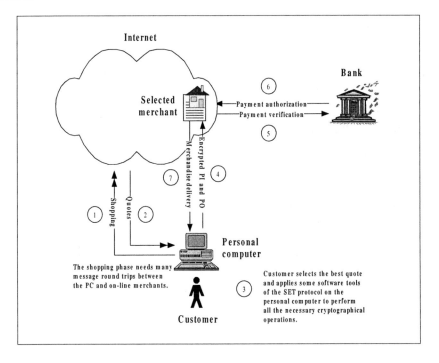

E-Commerce Approach II: Digital Cash

Based on the use of digital cash to facilitate online business, Okamoto and Ohta (1992) identified six properties a digital cash system may have:

1.   The digital cash can be sent securely through a computer network.
2.   The digital cash cannot be "double spent"; that is, it cannot be copied and reused.
3.   The anonymity of a digital cash spender (customer) should be preserved. If a business transaction uses digital cash, neither the merchant nor the bank should be able to identify the customer.
4.   Business transactions using digital cash should not have to go through a central bank.
5.   The digital cash can be transferred to others.
6.   A piece of digital cash can be divided into smaller amounts.

The system developed by Okamoto and Ohta satisfies all these requirements; other digital cash systems only satisfy some. The most difficult part of developing a digital cash system is that properties 2 and 3 above are in conflict with each other. Digital cash (a "coin") is an electronic object which is easily copied at essentially no cost. Therefore, the system must provide the business participants with some mechanism to detect a reproduced, or counterfeit, digital coin. Based on our current knowledge of the digital world, the most cost effective way to detect illegal electronic copies is by attaching a user's signature to each of the electronic coins. Any coin without a valid signature would be considered a counterfeit. However, using the existing digital signature schemes, such as DSS (FIPS, 1994) or RSA (Rivest, Shamir & Adleman, 1978), the anonymity of the coin spender cannot be preserved. In both DSS and RSA, the coin recipient must know who the coin spender is in order to identify his/her public key for signature verification.

A digital cash system developed by Brands (1994) uses a technique called "restricted blind signatures" to overcome the above problem. In this system, the customer's anonymity can be preserved if a digital coin is spent only once. However, if it is used twice, the customer can be identified by the bank. When receiving a digital coin, the merchant would first verify the validity of the coin and then request the customer to send proof that they legally possessed it. The purpose of requesting a proof is to prevent someone from stealing the coin and then trying to spend it. We will briefly describe this system below, but a more detailed treatment can be found in Brands (1994).

Initialization

The central authority and the three business participants need to perform the following steps to complete the initialization process:

- **The authority**:

  1. Picks two large prime numbers p and q, where $q = (p-1)/2$. Let g be the square of a primitive root mod p. This implies that $g^{d_1} \equiv g^{d_2} \pmod{p} \Leftrightarrow d_1 \equiv d_2 \pmod{q}$

  2. Chooses two secret random exponents d_1 and d_2. Let $g_1 = g^{d_1} \pmod{p}$; $g_2 = g^{d_2} \pmod{p}$ and then discards the two random exponents.

  3. Makes the three numbers g, g_1 and g_2 public.

  4. Chooses two public hash functions H_1 and H_2. The first hash function H_1 takes a tuple of 5 integers as input and outputs an integer mod q. The second hash function H_2 takes a tuple of 4 integers as input and outputs an integer mod q.

- **The bank**:

  1. Chooses its own secret identity number x.

  2. Computes three numbers h, h_1 and h_2 and makes them public, where $h \equiv g^x \pmod{p}$; $h_1 \equiv g_1{}^x \pmod{p}$; $h_2 \equiv g_2{}^x \pmod{p}$

- **The coin spender**:

  1. Chooses their own secret identity number u.

  2. Computes an account number C, where $C \equiv g_1{}^u \pmod{p}$

  3. Sends the number C to the bank, which stores C along with the coin spender's personal information such as name, address, and so forth.

  4. The bank sends back a value to the coin spender, where $z' \equiv (Cg_2)^x \pmod{p}$

- **The Merchant**:

  The merchant chooses an identity number m and registers it with the bank.

Creating a Coin

The coin spender requests digital coins through the bank by presenting its account identity C to the bank. A coin is a tuple of six numbers (D, E, z, a, b, r) where the six numbers are constructed as follows:

1. After receiving the request from the coin spender, the bank picks a different random number v for each coin, and then computes $g_v \equiv g^v \pmod{p}$; $\alpha \equiv (Cg_2)^v \pmod{p}$. The bank sends both and to the coin spender. Note that each coin has a different pair of (g_v, α).

2. The coin spender picks a random secret tuple of five integers for each coin requested: (s, x_1, x_2, y_1, y_2).

3.   The coin spender constructs the first five numbers of the tuple representing a coin as below.

$$D \equiv (Cg_2)^s \pmod{p}; E \equiv g_1^{x_1} g_2^{x_2} \pmod{p}; z \equiv z'^S \pmod{p};$$
$$a \equiv g_v^{y_1} g_v^{y_2} \pmod{p}; b \equiv \alpha^{sy_1} D^{y_2} \pmod{p}$$

$D = 1$ is prohibited. There are two possible cases for D to be 1. The first is if $s = 0$, then $D = 1$. Thus, the coin spender should not pick 0 for the random number s. The second is if $Cg_2 \equiv 1 \pmod{p}$, then $D = 1$. However, this case is highly unlikely to occur since it means that the coin spender has solved a difficult discrete logarithm problem by a lucky choice of u.

4.   In order to construct the last (6th) number of the coin, the coin spender computes a value e and sends it to the bank, where:

$$e \equiv y_1^{-1} H_1(D, E, z, a, b) \pmod{q}$$

5.   Upon receiving e, the bank computes $e' \equiv (ex + v) \pmod{q}$ and sends it back to the coin spender.

6.   The coin spender constructs r by computing $r \equiv (y_1 e' + y_2) \pmod{q}$

After this step, the coin construction is complete and the coin spender now owns the coin by knowing the magic six numbers. Finally, the bank deducts the amount of the coin from the spender's bank account to complete their withdrawal.

Spending the Coin

When the coin spender would like to spend a coin (D, E, z, a, b, r), he/she sends the tuple of six numbers to the merchant. The following procedure is then performed:

1.   The merchant computes whether:

$$g^r \equiv ah^{H_1(D, E, z, a, b)} \pmod{p}; D^r \equiv z^{H_1(D, E, z, a, b)} b \pmod{p}$$

If both of the above hold, the merchant knows that the coin with the six numbers is constructed through the bank, and therefore is valid. However, to avoid double spending, more effort is necessary.

2.   The merchant computes and sends a value $k = H_2(D, E, m, t)$ to the coin spender, where t is a timestamp of the transaction. Different transactions will thus have different values of k.

3.   The coin spender computes and sends two numbers:

$$r_1 \equiv (kus + x_1) \pmod{q}; \; r_2 \equiv (ks + x_2) \pmod{q}$$

to the merchant.

4.   The merchant computes whether

$$g_1^{y_1} g_2^{y_2} \equiv D^k E \pmod{p}$$

If the above checking procedure withstands this scrutiny, the coin is valid and the merchant accepts the coin. Note that a correct pair of (r_1, r_2) is a proof showing that the coin spender legally possesses the coin and has not stolen it from someone else.

Depositing the Coin in the Merchant's Bank Account

The merchant cashes the "coin" by depositing it to the bank. The merchant sends the coin (D, E, z, a, b, r), along with the triple (r_1, r_2, k), to the bank. The bank then performs the following two steps:

1.   If the coin has been previously deposited, a fraud control procedure, discussed in the next section, will take over to deal with the fraudulent case. Otherwise, step 2 will be performed.

2.   The bank checks whether:

$$g^r \equiv ah^{H_1(D, E, z, a, b)} \pmod{p}; \; D^r \equiv z^{H_1(D, E, z, a, b)} b \pmod{p}; \; g_1^{y_1} g_2^{y_2} \equiv D^k E \pmod{p}$$

If all three of the above are true, the coin is valid and the merchant's bank account is credited.

Double Spending

This subsection describes several possible fraudulent double spending cases and how the previously described digital cash system handles them.

1.   The coin spender tries to spend the coin twice with two different merchants, M_1 and M_2. M_1 submits the coin with the triple (r_1, r_2, k) to the bank, but M_2 submits the coin along with a different triple (r_1', r_2', k'). The bank will detect the double deposits, and

then initiate their fraud control procedure. The procedure will then be able to discover the malicious spender's secret identity, u, since:

$$r_1 - r_1' \equiv us(k - k') \pmod{q}; \ r_2 - r_2' \equiv s(k - k') \pmod{q}$$

$$\Rightarrow u \equiv \frac{r_1 - r_1'}{r_2 - r_2'} \pmod{q}$$

The bank can then identify the coin spender by computing the spender's public identity $C \equiv g^u \pmod{p}$.

2. The merchant tries to deposit the coin twice, once with the legitimate triple (r_1, r_2, k) and once with a forged triple (r_1', r_2', k'). Making up a valid forged triple is extremely difficult for the merchant since the merchant does not know the secret numbers u, s, x_1, and x_2, but must produce and such that:

$$g_1^{r_1'} g_2^{r_2'} \equiv D^{k'} E \pmod{p}$$

3. A malicious merchant *Devil* tries to deposit the coin to the bank, but also tries to use it to pay another merchant, *Angel*. *Angel* computes k', which has almost a zero chance of being equal to the original k. *Devil* doesn't know u, x_1, x_2 and s, but he must produce r_1' and r_2' such that:

$$g_1^{r_1'} g_2^{r_2'} \equiv D^{k'} E \pmod{p}$$

This is again a difficult discrete logarithm problem. Note that *Devil* cannot simply use the already known r_1 and r_2, since the merchant would detect that

$$g_1^{r_1} g_2^{r_2} \neq D^{k'} E \pmod{p}.$$

Anonymity

To see how the above scheme preserves the anonymity of the coin spender, consider the following two cases:

1. Can the merchant by itself identify the coin spender? The answer is "no," since the coin spender need not provide any of his/her identities, neither u nor C, during the entire transaction with the merchant.
2. Is it possible for the merchant and the bank, acting together, to derive the spender's identity? Before answering this question, we would like to assume that banks are usually trustworthy, and thus this case is most likely not an issue. However, in

certain rare situations, if the bank is malicious and tries to illegally identify the coin spender, the scheme described in this section also provides protection against it. The bank and the merchant together know about both the coin (D, E, z, a, b, r) and the triple (r_1, r_2, k). Since s, x_1, x_2, y_1, and y_2 are secret numbers and unknown to both the bank and merchant, the first five numbers D, E, z, a, b of the coin will just look like some random powers of $g \pmod p$. Therefore, the spender's identity C cannot be derived from those numbers. Note that when $e \equiv y_1^{-1} H_1(D, E, z, a, b) \pmod q$ is sent to the bank from the spender, the bank might calculate the value of H_1 and thus derive y_1. However, the bank has not actually seen the coin at the time of receiving the number e from the spender, and so cannot calculate the value of H_1. The bank could try to keep a list of all values of e it has received from the spenders and a list of all values of H_1 for all deposited coins, and then derive y_1 by trying all possible combinations of these two lists. Obviously, this approach requires a highly expensive and time-consuming exponential processing operation. For systems with millions of coins, this level of exhaustive matching is not practical.

Online E-Business Using Digital Cash

Figure 2 gives a basic model showing the sequence of events for conducting an online e-business transaction using a digital cash system. The shopping phase in this model, indicated by the double arrows in Steps 1 and 2 in Figure 2, is the same shopping scenario as that used in the SET protocol in Figure 1 and requires many back and forth message

Figure 2. The sequence of events for an online e-business transaction using a digital cash system

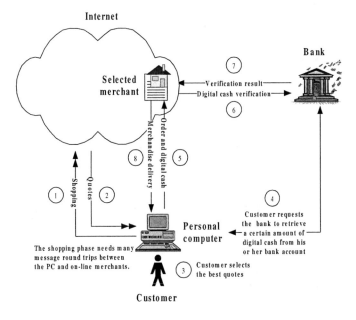

round trips between the personal computer and online merchants. However, these two models differ in their purchase-payment phases. Instead of providing the credit card number to the merchant, the personal computer in this model, on behalf of the customer, will withdraw an appropriate amount of digital cash from the bank and use the cash to make the purchase and payment. After receiving the digital cash from the customer, the merchant only forwards the received cash, without attaching any information about the customer, to the bank for verification. The bank is capable of verifying and authorizing the digital cash only by checking its own "blind signatures" on the cash, without the necessity of knowing the customer's identity. Thus, the anonymity of the customer can be preserved.

E-Commerce Approaches' Limitations

To conduct a business transaction using the existing e-commerce approaches, as described in the previous two sections, requires many message round trips and multiple cryptographic operations. If the underlying infrastructure is based on the use of wireless and mobile networks with limited resources, these approaches cannot be applied unless the resource consumption can be reduced significantly. The next two sections provide a possible solution that would reduce the necessary level of resource consumption for m-commerce by utilizing a new option, mobile agent technology.

Mobile Agent Technology

Mobile agent technology advances the distributed computing paradigm one step further to offer two extra properties: client customization and autonomy. End users are now able to virtually install new software in targeted foreign hosts by creating and launching a personalized mobile agent onto the Internet, thereby automatically accomplishing the assigned mission without the need for interactive guidance from the user. A mobile agent acts as a smart software agent that can be executed in foreign hosts on behalf of its owner. It can make decisions autonomously, based on the decision logics it contains. Once it has been launched, it is independent from its owner. During its life, it may visit many foreign hosts, communicate with other agents, and finally return to its owner with the results.

Several agent systems have been developed by both university and industrial research groups. Dartmouth College developed a mobile agent system, D'Agents (Gray, Kotz, Cybenko & Rus, 1998), which uses PKI for authentication, and applies the RSA algorithm to generate a public and private key pair. After a foreign host authenticates a visiting agent, the host assigns a set of access rights to the agent and sets up an appropriate execution environment. The resource access control within the host that interacts with the visiting agent is controlled by a stationary resource management agent who checks an access list each time an access request arrives. Ajanta is a Java-based mobile agent system developed at the University of Minnesota (Karnik & Tripathis, 1999). Here, an authentication server distributes a ticket to each of the registered clients. An agent acting on behalf of a client is authenticated by its possession of an appropriate ticket. Resource accesses are controlled by a security manager based on an access control list. Java Aglets (Lange & Oshima, 1998) are another Java-based mobile agent system developed at IBM's Tokyo Research Laboratory. The IBM Aglets Workbench consists of a development kit for aglets and a host platform for aglet execution. Aglets may visit various hosts that are defined as a context in the IBM Aglets. The context owner must take steps to secure these hosts against malicious aglets. Other mobile agent systems include Ara (Peine & Stolpmann, 1997), Mole (Straser, Baumann & Hohl, 1996), and Telescript (White, 1994), the first two of which were developed as university projects and the third as a commercial product.

Sidestepping the lengthy standardization process needed for a new Internet application protocol, the customization feature of the mobile agent technology allows users to install new software into networks by simply launching appropriate agents. This great benefit of using mobile agents for applications is well understood. However, there is a major obstacle for widely deploying mobile agent technology. Until the security concerns can be resolved, the technology will not be able to reach its full potential. The concerns can be divided into four categories, as follows:

1. *Attacks on hosts by agents:* This type of attack was identified as soon as the mobile agent paradigm was proposed. Executing a program without knowing its real origin and purpose is extremely dangerous. Malicious codes can damage a computer in various ways, such as reading secret data without permission, exhausting resources by performing excessive amounts of computation or sending a huge number of messages, or changing the computer settings to make it behave abnormally. Trojan horses, viruses, and worms are well-known examples of malicious programs. In the mobile agent era, it is expected that attackers will have greater opportunities to implant such malicious codes. Fortunately, the countermeasures needed to resist this type of attack are relatively straightforward, being similar to the traditional protection techniques already employed in trusted systems. These techniques can be used to provide analogous protection to hosts in the mobile agent paradigm.

2. *Attacks on agents by rival agents:* An agent can launch an attack on a rival agent if the hosting environment does not provide sufficient protection. An agent can be malicious, eavesdropping on conversations between other agents and the host, launching a denial-of-service attack by sending messages to other agents repeatedly, or sending incorrect responses to requests it has received from other agents. A possible countermeasure is to allow the host to protect visiting agents against each other. Whenever an agent tries to access or communicate with a target agent, the host would consider the target agent as part of its own resources and provide the same level of protection as it does for its other resources.

3. *Attacks on agents by hosts:* A host can attack a visiting agent by changing the contained decision logic, spying on its accumulated data, or even killing the entire agent. In the mobile agent paradigm, there is an assumption that the host will provide appropriate resources for executing the mobile codes contained in a

visiting agent. In other words, in order to execute the mobile codes, the host must have complete access rights and thus control of the agent. This leads to a serious vulnerability if the host itself is malicious. The possible countermeasures are trusted hardware (Chess, Grosof, Harrison, Levine, Parris & Tsudik, 1995), encrypted functions (Sander & Tschudin, 1998), time-limited blackbox protection (Hohl, 1998a), or a trusted virtual marketplace (Chavez & Maes, 1996; Collins, Youngdahl, Jamison, Mobasher & Gini, 1998; Tsvetovatyy & Gini, 1996). Trusted hardware consists of tamper-resistant hardware attached to each host, which can be used as a communication bridge between the host and the agent so that a malicious host is unable to access the agent directly. Sander and Tschudin (1998) proposed the concept of encrypted functions. A function f is encrypted by users as $E(f)$, which is then executed by the host, without the host having access to f. This idea is a promising way to protect agents from malicious hosts. However, the actual implementation of this approach is not yet very clear. Time-limited blackbox protection is completely based on software. The agent code is obfuscated so that it is hard to analyze within a limited time period. However, the obfuscated code can be studied off-line by attackers. This off-line study may provide some hints that allow a faster analysis of future obfuscated mobile codes from the same source. The reason for protecting agents from hosts is because the hosts themselves may not be trustworthy. The trusted virtual marketplace approach is an attempt to provide a set of reliable hosts operated by trusted authorities. The marketplace not only guarantees the trustworthiness of all its hosts, but also needs to provide a good security mechanism to prevent attacks from other agents or outsiders. Within the marketplace, all agents can sell, buy, or trade goods without the fear of being attacked.

4.   *Attacks on the agent system by other entities:* An agent system includes both mobile agents and host platforms. Other entities may attack the system by taking actions that disrupt, harm, or subvert the agent system. The mechanisms used to protect the hosts can be extended to protect the whole agent system by considering the visiting agents as part of the hosts' resources.

Mobile agents comprise a broad research area with two major categories: how to make mobile agent systems more secure and how to apply mobile agent technology to applications. This section described these security issues and their possible countermeasures and the next section will present ways to use mobile agents for m-commerce, illustrating how mobile agent technology is particularly suited to this application.

Use of Mobile Agents for Mobile Commerce

A typical scenario applying mobile software agents for m-commerce would operate as follows. The mobile device launches a smart mobile agent containing all the necessary negotiation and shopping logics to the Internet. The agent shops around and makes decisions based on the contained logics and finally returns the best quote to the mobile device. As a result, during the shopping phase, once the agent has been launched only one message must be received and responded to by the mobile device. Another advantage of using mobile agent technology for m-commerce is the agent's real-time interaction capability. For many time-critical applications, the mobile agent can make decisions on the spot, without interactively asking for its owner's confirmation. Applications such as auctions or stock market transactions are typical time critical examples.

After the agent brings back a quote, the mobile device verifies the quote and performs the final purchase transaction. As discussed earlier in this chapter, the purchase-payment phase requires the business transaction initiator to perform a number of cryptographic operations. As an initiator, the mobile device usually lacks the computational power needed for these expensive operations. This will continue to pose a problem until lightweight encryption algorithms become available or until the hardware technology advances to provide sufficient computational power. However, an interim solution may be possible if each mobile access point is connected to a local auxiliary encryption server. The mobile device could make a request to the server for encryption service before triggering the final purchase-payment phase. However, this approach is likely to increase the complexity of the protocol since it involves another entity. This server must also be trustworthy to avoid compromising the confidentiality of the customer.

Online M-Business Using Mobile Agents

Figure 3 gives the sequence of events for an online mobile business transaction using mobile agent technology incorporating an encryption server.

In the figure, the shopping phase begins at Step 1 and ends at Step 2, in which the mobile agent shops around on the Internet for the best buy and brings back a quote from the selected merchant. The single arrowheads in Steps 1 and 2 in this figure indicate there is only one message round trip between the mobile device and online merchants during the shopping phase. To illustrate how a typical purchasing agent operates, we used an agent similar to the one used by Hohl (1998b). This agent consists of a code block and a data block as follows:

```
// CODE BLOCK
public void startAgent(){
1   if (merchantlist == null){
2       merchantlist = getTrader().getProviderOf("BuyFlowers");
3       go(merchantlist[1]);
4        break;
5   }
6   if (merchantlist[merchantlistindex].askprice(flowers) < bestprice){
7       bestprice = merchantlist[merchantlistindex].askprice(flowers);
```

Figure 3. The sequence of events for an online mobile business using mobile agents and an encryption server

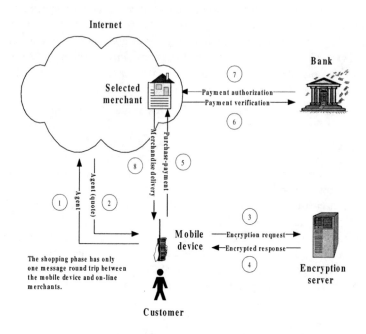

```
8    bestmerchant = merchantlist[merchantlistindex];
9    }
10   if (merchantlistindex >= (merchantlist.length - 1)){
11       requestquote(bestmerchant, flowers);
12         go(home);
13   }
14   go(merchantlist[++merchantlistindex]);
15 }


// DATA BLOCK
address home = "PDA, sweet PDA";
float maximumprice = 20.00$;
good flowers = 10 red roses;
address merchantlist[] = empty list;
int merchantlistindex = 0;
float bestprice = 20.00$;
address bestmerchant = empty;
```

The purchasing agent visits a list of pre-selected online merchants to search for the lowest price of a bunch of flowers. This "lowest price" shopping strategy is encoded in the code block from line 6 to line 8. The data block specifies the agent owner's budget ($20), the merchandise to be purchased (10 red roses), the accumulated values of the agent's itinerary, and some other bookkeeping variables. Beginning at "home," the agent requests a list of online merchants to visit on line 2. Then the agent migrates to each of the merchants in the list. While visiting a merchant, the agent compares the merchant's offering price to the currently best known price, and then updates the "bestprice" and the "bestmerchant" variables if necessary. After all the listed merchants have been visited, the variable "bestmerchant" will contain the merchant who offered the best quote. Finally, line 11 in the agent's source code requests the best merchant to send an official signed quote to the agent or directly to the agent's home.

After receiving the official quote from the merchant selected, in order to activate the purchase-payment phase, the mobile device will request the encryption server to perform all the necessary cryptographic operations, as shown in Steps 3 and 4 in Figure 3. The necessary cryptographic operations were discussed in the sections "E-Commerce Approach I" and "E-Commerce Approach II". Finally, Steps 5 to 8 in Figure 3 perform the actual purchase and payment transaction by sending messages among the three business participants.

Conclusion

As wireless communication technology has advanced, new avenues of mobile commerce have become available. However, this opportunity to reach more customers through wireless channels and mobile devices has led to a higher risk for theft and fraud. Because of the portable features introduced for user convenience, mobile devices usually have a limited display size, limited input capability, limited computation power, limited power usage, and limited data transfer rate. The insecure broadcast medium and limited physical resources of mobile devices have made the development of security mechanisms even more challenging.

This chapter has discussed the common resource and security concerns for involved in conducting an online business. In spite of their different underlying communication infrastructures, both e-commerce and m-commerce face many of the same security concerns and thus share the same security requirements. To see how these security requirements are satisfied in e-commerce, this chapter described two existing approaches, SET protocol and digital cash. However, until the intensive resource consumption can be reduced, these existing approaches cannot be used directly for m-commerce. Fortunately, by utilizing the emerging mobile agent technology, the application of existing e-commerce methods for m-commerce becomes possible, especially for those methods that require many message round trips. This chapter also illustrated how to apply the mobile agent technology for m-commerce using an example.

References

Aboba, B., & Simon, D. (1999). PPP EAP TLS Authentication Protocol. *IETF RFC 2716*.

Blunk, L., & Vollbrecht, J. (1998). PPP Extensible Authentication Protocol (EAP). *IETF RFC 2284*.

Brands, S. (1994). Untraceable off-line cash in wallets with observers. *Advances in Cryptology - CRYPTO'93*. Springer-Verlag.

Chavez, A., & Maes, P. (1996). Kasbah: An agent marketplace for buying and selling goods. *Proceedings of the First International Conference on the Practical Application of Intelligent Agents and Multi-Agent Technology (PAAM'96)*.

Chess, D., Grosof, B., Harrison, C., Levine, D., Parris, C., & Tsudik, G. (1995). Internet agents for mobile computing. Technical Report, RC 20010. IBM T.J. Watson Research Center.

Collins, J., Youngdahl, B., Jamison, S., Mobasher, B., & Gini, M. (1998). A market architecture for multi-agent contracting. *Proceedings of the Second International Conference on Autonomous Agents*.

Dierks, T., & Allen, C. (1999). The TLS Protocol Version 1.0. *IETF RFC 2246*.

FIPS. (1994). Digital Signature Standard (DSS). *Federal Information Processing Standards Publication 186*.

Funk, P., & Blake-Wilson, S. (2002). EAP Tunneled TLS Authentication Protocol (EAP-TTLS). *IETF draft-ietf-pppext-eap-ttls-02.txt*

Gray, R., Kotz, D., Cybenko, G., & Rus, D. (1998). D'Agents: Security in a multiple-language, mobile-agent system. In G. Vigna (Eds.), *Mobile agents and security*. Springer-Verlag.

Hakan, A., Josefsson, S., Zorn, G., Simon, D., & Palekar, A. (2002). Protected EAP Protocol (PEAP). *IETF draft-josefsson-pppext-eap-tls-eap-05.txt*

Hohl, F. (1998a). Time limited blackbox security: Protecting mobile agents from malicious hosts. *Mobile agent security*. Springer-Verlag.

Hohl, F. (1998b). A model of attacks of malicious hosts against mobile agents. *Secure Internet mobile computation: Fourth Workshop on Mobile Object Systems (MOS'98)*.

IEEE Standard for Local and Metropolitan Area Networks - Port-Based Network Access Control. (2001). *IEEE Std 802.1x-2001*.

Karnik, N., & Tripathis, A. (1999). Security in the Ajanta mobile agent system. Technical Report. Department of Computer Science, University of Minnesota.

Lange, D., & Oshima, M. (1998). *Programming and deploying JAVA mobile agents with aglets*. Addison-Wesley.

Okamoto, T., & Ohta, K. (1992). Universal electronic cash. *Advances in Cryptology - CRYPTO'91*. Springer-Verlag.

Peine, H., & Stolpmann, T. (1997). The architecture of the Ara platform for mobile agents. In Rothermel & Popescu-Zeletin (Eds.), *Mobile agents: 1st International Workshop MA'97*. Springer-Verlag.

Rivest, R., Shamir, A., & Adleman, L. (1978). A method for obtaining digital signatures and public-key cryptosystems. *Communications of the ACM, 21*(2).

Sander, T., & Tschudin, C. (1998). Protecting mobile agents against malicious hosts. *Mobile agent security*. Springer-Verlag.

SET Secure Electronic Transaction Specification. *http://www.setco.org*

Straser, M., Baumann, J., & Hohl, F. (1996). A Java based mobile agent system. In M. Muhlauser (Ed.), *Special issues in object-oriented programming: Workshop Reader of the 10th European Conference on Object-Oriented Programming ECOOP'96*.

Tsvetovatyy, M., & Gini, M. (1996). Toward a virtual marketplace: Architectures and strategies. *Proceedings of the First International Conference on the Practical Application of Intelligent Agents and Multi-Agent Technology (PAAM'96)*.

White, J. (1994). *The foundation for the electronic marketplace*. Technical Report. General Magic, Inc.

Chapter VIII

Secure Multicast for Mobile Commerce Applications:
Issues and Challenges

Mohamed Eltoweissy, Virginia Tech, USA

Sushil Jajodia, George Mason University, USA

Ravi Mukkamala, Old Dominion University, USA

Abstract

With the rapid growth in mobile commerce (m-commerce) applications, the need for providing suitable infrastructure to support these applications has become critical. Secure multicast is a key element of this infrastructure, in particular, to support group m-commerce applications such as mobile auctions, product recommendation systems, and financial services. Despite considerable attention to m-commerce security, most existing security solutions focus on unicast communications. On the other hand, numerous solutions for secure multicast exist that are not specifically designed with m-commerce as a target environment. Clearly, to address secure multicast in m-commerce, we must start by forming a comprehensive picture of the different facets of the problem and its solutions. In this chapter, we identify system parameters and subsequent security requirements for secure multicast in m-commerce. Attacks on m-

commerce environments may undermine satisfying these security requirements resulting, at most times, in major losses. We present a taxonomy of common attacks and identify core services needed to mitigate these attacks and provide efficient solutions for secure multicast in m-commerce. Among these services, authentication and key management play a major role. Given the varying requirements of m-commerce applications and the large number of current key management schemes, we provide a taxonomy and a set of performance metrics to aid m-commerce system designers in the evaluation and selection of key management schemes.

Introduction

The exponential growth of the Internet, wireless communications, and electronic commerce, coupled with the recent advances in mobile Web services and pervasive computing, are transforming mobile commerce (m-commerce) from an idea to reality. However, for m-commerce to realize its potential, there is a critical need for providing suitable service environments where numerous mobile, context-aware, smart services will interact among themselves, and consumers and suppliers to accomplish commercial transactions. Secure group communications is, therefore, one of the key elements of this service environment. M-commerce applications such as mobile auctions, product recommendation systems, and financial services require secure and reliable group communications services (Varshney & Vetter, 2002). In addition to being secure, group communications services underlying such applications also need to be efficient in terms of the computing and communications overhead that they impose on the mobile devices. While real-time response is of concern in some applications (e.g., stock trading transactions), dynamic joins/leaves of group members is of concern in other applications (e.g., online video games). Unlike e-commerce applications that run on fixed networking infrastructures with fairly high reliability and bandwidths, m-commerce applications have to depend (at least partly) on wireless infrastructure. Typically, wireless infrastructure has low bandwidths, is power constrained, and is often not so dependable. These requirements, as well as others to be discussed shortly in this chapter, call for secure multicast communications services supporting m-commerce applications.

In order to further illustrate the need for secure multicast communications in m-commerce, let us consider two scenarios, one involving mobile auctions and the other a collaborative investigation team.

- *Mobile auctions*: Consider an auctioning system where both sellers and buyers can participate in an auction involving both stationary and mobile users. For example, an antique collector on travel may want to be alerted about online auctions even when on travel. Since some of these auctions may have only short durations for the sale of the items, it is important that the mobile user be able to participate in the process while on the move. For example, let us assume that a firm XYZ specializes in online antique auctions. All potential customers must subscribe to this firm's services. Whenever a seller (not necessarily a subscriber) intends to auction an item, he/she informs the XYZ firm, providing a minimum price. The firm sends this information to all its subscribers through a secure multicast. While the users on the Internet with fixed IP addresses can be reached via the IP Multicast protocols, the coverage of mobile subscribers calls for a mobile multicast protocol. One of the challenges in achieving this coverage is the ability to locate the mobile users and efficiently multicast the messages to them. Obviously, they would be geographically distributed in different regions. Another challenge is timely delivery. Since most auctions are time-sensitive, it is important that all subscribers receive the information in a timely manner, and their responses (or bids) also reach the destination in a timely manner. In addition, it may be important to guarantee delivery to all subscribers. In other words, each auction message should reach its subscribers (mobile or stationary) with a very high probability. If XYZ firm cannot offer such guarantees, then it will soon lose its clients. Similarly, it is most important that the messages received by the subscribers be genuine. This can be enforced by some security authentication measures. In summary, this scenario illustrates the need for a secure multicast protocol that is reliable, real-time, secure, and scalable. It should handle both mobile users and static Internet users.

- *Collaborative investigation team*: Let us now consider a team of experts investigating an accident at a production plant. The accident resulted in injuries, loss of equipment, and loss of production. It is the team's responsibility to determine the fault, rectify or replace machinery, and restart production as soon as possible. Such investigation involves personnel from several agencies including the production mangers, the plant managers, the machinery manufacturers, the labor union representatives, the injured personnel, the physicians (if seriously injured), the insurance agents, and so forth. Clearly, it is impossible to assemble them all in one place as they may be geographically distributed. However, if we assume that each of them has access to a laptop with wireless connection, then a mobile multicast session can be set up among the team members. Since the investigation may involve access to some confidential documents, it is important that the multicast session be secure. In addition, the membership within a session may be dynamic. For example, as the chief investigator begins investigation, he/she may find the need to bring in the machine manufacturer's design engineer to discuss some details about the machine's safety features. However, once this is done, the designer can be let go. So there are frequent joins and leaves into the multicast session. The mobility is essential since the needed persons may be at any place at the time they are required. For example, the maintenance engineer involved may be at a different plant location at the time of investigation. The physician who attended the injured may be in a hospital. The insurance agent may be driving on the way to investigate yet another claim. The design engineer may be located in another country (in a different time zone). While some of the personnel may participate in the group interaction using mobile phones, in general they need access to laptops where the discussions or documentary evidence are being shown to the members in a session. It is also essential to authenticate each participant in the session and record his or her comments in a way to ensure non-repudiation. The session needs to be encrypted so only the authorized participants can know the conversations, due to the confidential nature of the contents. Clearly, this calls for a reliable secure multicast service in a mobile environment.

In the rest of the chapter, we discuss the primary issues underlying secure m-commerce environments. Based on these issues, we then identify a set of m-commerce multicast security requirements. Under trusted system conditions, these requirements will be satisfied. However, attacks on m-commerce environments may disrupt the fulfillment of these requirements, resulting, at most times, in major losses. We investigated different attacks and in this chapter, we present a taxonomy of common attacks that impede satisfying the security requirements. Core services needed for efficient secure multicast in m-commerce are presented next. Among these services, multicast protocols, authentication and key management play a major role and are therefore explained in more detail.

Dimensions of Secure Mobile Commerce

Security in mobile networks is particularly difficult to achieve. Many characteristics are at play. These include the vulnerability of the broadcast links, the limited physical protection of the nodes, the transient and sporadic nature of connectivity, the dynamically changing topology, the absence of a certification authority, the lack of centralized monitoring or management point, and the heterogeneity of devices and networks. This list is by no means comprehensive. In the following discussion, we look at some of these issues. (In this chapter, we refer to mobile and wireless interchangeably to mean that the mobile devices we consider are employing wireless communication and that the wireless communication is primarily used by the mobile devices.)

Wireless Security Issues

Maintaining security is one of the biggest concerns in wireless systems. But unless security is ensured, it cannot be used for any m-commerce applications. Today, encryption is the primary mechanism through which security is guaranteed by the wireless and mobile systems. Encryption is offered using symmetric and asymmetric keys. Under the symmetric schemes, both the sender and the receiver share the same secret key. Typically, the data are encrypted at the sender end and decrypted at the receiver end. The most widely used algorithm for encryption is DES or Data Encryption Standard. Most secure applications use this algorithm (Kornak & Distefano, 2002). The 2G wireless standard GSM encrypts all data between the mobile phone and the base-station using an A5 algorithm (Dornan, 2001).

Under the asymmetric schemes, there are two keys—a private key held by the owner and a public key known to all. Whenever data (or voice) need to be sent from a source to a receiver, the source encrypts using the public key of the receiver and the receiver uses its private key to decrypt it. The most commonly used asymmetric algorithm is RSA (Schneier, 1996). Generally, encryption using asymmetric algorithms is more computation-intensive and complex. For this reason, GSM uses asymmetric key algorithm for exchanging the secret keys and the symmetric A5 algorithm for actual data encryption (Dornan, 2001).

Another problem that is encountered in wireless systems is the end-to-end security. While the wired Internet counterpart covers the entire end-to-end connection in offering security (e.g., via SSL), the wireless systems cover only part of it. For example, the A5 protocol used by GSM only covers the air part of an end-to-end connection. In this case, the application has to use its own encryption prior to sending data on the air. Similarly, the WAP (wireless application protocol) security covers only the mobile part of the data link (up to the WAP gateway). Once again, the application may have to explicitly encrypt data to obtain a truly end-to-end secure service (Malloy, Varshney & Snow, 2002).

Another mechanism for security is using some hardware devices for authentication. For example, SIM or Subscriber Identity Module, is the central element of the security mechanism in m-commerce and is included in protocols such as GSM, GPRS, or UMTS. It is typically implemented as a smart card that serves as repository for all the subscriber's vital information. It includes an individual authentication key and a PIN code that the user has to enter in order to unlock the SIM. The same authentication key (symmetric key) is used in the user's home location registry (HLR) (Sadeh, 2002). WAP suggested another card, the WIM or wireless identity module, that is issued by a bank, credit card company, or a third party. In fact, a dual slot handset solution has also been suggested (Sadeh, 2002).

The other security concerns in these systems are viruses, cloning and theft. Since data are downloaded onto the wireless devices, the threats of viruses always exist. They can be thwarted by the same means as on PCs. Cloning is when some device clones as another device, thus hiding its own identity. Using mechanisms such as SIM cards, this could be mitigated. Using measures such as biometrics to verify the user's identity can prevent theft of the wireless devices and then its misuse. This way, even if a mobile device is stolen, the miscreants still cannot use it.

Wireless Network Issues

When dealing with wireless networks for m-commerce, we need to keep in mind the following limitations of this technology (Varshney, 2003).

- *Coverage area.* Wireless coverage is not pervasive. In addition, there is no guarantee that the signal can penetrate through all its obstacles such as buildings and tunnels. Thus, mobile applications should be prepared for interruptions in service, as the user is moving.

- *Bandwidth.* The bandwidth offered by a connection depends on the allocated bandwidth for the channel as well as the wireless protocol. As of today, these are much lower than the conventional wired networks.

- *Latency.* This is the time between a user sending a message to the time it reaches its destination. In addition to the bandwidth, factors such as the propagation delay, the protocol overhead, and the traffic on the network affect the latency.

- *Reliability.* This is a major concern in wireless networks. Dropped bits or frames and corrupted frames are common in wireless networks. This may often result in dropped connections.

- *Cost.* This is yet another criterion. While the connection charges are coming down, they are still high compared to the wired counterpart.

Node Issues

In m-commerce applications, since several remote entities participate in a transaction, nodes must assume some degree of trust in other nodes in accomplishing their tasks. For example, nodes are expected to cooperate to route messages from source to destination. Similarly, implementation of reliable multicast (as explained later) requires the cooperation of several nodes.

In addition to this cooperative behavior, to preserve resources such as power and bandwidth, mobile nodes are expected to have some autonomous decision authority. For example a node may decide not to participate in carrying out a transaction because of its depleting battery. Alternately, a multicast coordinator may tune the quality of service provided based on the available nodes.

Communication Technology Issues

Bandwidth is a primary criterion in the success of successful implementation of a wide variety of m-commerce applications. Today, cell phone technology uses either 2G (second generation) or 2 ½ G technology. 2G phones convert all speech into digital form. The most popular of the 2G technologies is GSM, or Global System for Mobile Communications. Typically, the data rate in these systems is about 10-30 Kbps. The next generation, the 2 ½ G, refers to both WAP (Wireless Application Protocol) and higher data speeds matching those of fast modems (Dornan, 2001). The third generation wireless (3G) technology is expected to provide higher data transfer rates of up to 2 Mbps. It is also expected to provide a variety of advanced services including video conferencing. Finally, the 4G is expected to provide data rates of up to 100 Mbps (Dornan, 2001).

M-Commerce Multicast
Security Requirements

There are a wide variety of security requirements affecting multicast group communications in m-commerce. The precise set of requirements is determined by the specifics of an m-commerce service. However, a common set of requirements can be given that many m-commerce applications share. Following is a set of such key requirements.

- *Confidentiality*: The sender of a message (data or information) should be able to determine the set of receivers that have a right to read the data content. In multicast communications, due to changes in group membership, we consider two types of confidentiality—backward and forward confidentiality. Forward confidentiality means that a departing member cannot read messages multicast after its departure. Enforcement of this rule requires that no arbitrary number of departing members can collude to read future traffic. Likewise, backward confidentiality means that new members will not be able to read multicast messages prior to its join. This requires that no arbitrary number of new members can collude to read past traffic.

- *Authenticity*: It should be possible for the communicating partners to be able to unambiguously identify each other. There are three potential authentication requirements in multicast communications: group, sender, and source authentication (Varshney, 2002). Group authentication ensures that the data have originated from some member of the group, be it a sender or a receiver. Sender authentication ensures that the data have originated from only the designated senders. Finally, source authentication requires that the individual sender of the multicast data be authenticated.

- *Integrity*: Maintaining integrity of multicasted data means that data content remains unchanged during transmission. The successful execution of m-commerce transactions among group participants generally requires the assurance that session traffic be protected and hence are not altered during transmission.

- *Availability*: This means that eligible participants with appropriate privileges should receive services as contracted. In m-commerce transactions, it is important to ensure the availability and continuity of secure services given an environment characterized by transient broadcast communications that may involve many entities with heterogeneous resources. Unlike wired services, unavailability of services is much more likely, if not properly handled.

- *Access Control*: We need to ensure that only those with appropriate credentials are permitted access to the group session. Access control is needed to control, to grant and revoke privileges and also to keep track on the amount of usages of each member (e.g., for accounting purposes) (Canetti et al., 1999).

Other security requirements for m-commerce applications include *multilevel security, non-repudiation,* and *interoperability.* The security architecture deployed should be able to provide different levels of security services based on system policy, context information, environmental situations, temporal circumstances, available resources, and so forth (Eltoweissy & Bansemer, 2003). Also, due to the heterogeneity in the operating environments (e.g., a transaction across a wire-line, wireless, and ad hoc networks), it is necessary to support multiple interoperable security services. Finally, non-repudiation is essential so that the authenticated exchange can afterwards be unambiguously proved to have happened (Grahn, Pulkkis & Guillard, 2002).

Security Attacks in M-Commerce Environments

In this section, we analyze attacks against satisfying the multicast security requirements outlined in the previous section. We classify attacks according to their violation of the main security requirements of confidentiality, integrity, authenticity and availability.

Attacks Against Confidentiality

This category consists of attacks that attempt to threaten the confidentiality of data being sent in an m-commerce multicast message. Three types of attacks appear to be commonplace.

- *Traffic analysis*: Using a wireless card in promiscuous mode and software to count the number and size of packets being transmitted, an attacker can determine that there is activity on the network, the location of wireless access points, and the type of protocol being used in the transmission. Thus, while the attacker may not know the exact content of messages being exchanged between parties, it can detect the degree of activity and make some inferences.

- *Eavesdropping*: Both passive and active eavesdropping may have damaging effects on m-commerce. Assuming that a session is not encrypted, which seems to be the case with at least half of the wireless traffic (Welch & Lathrop, 2003), an attacker that passively monitors traffic can read the data transmitted in the session and also can gather information indirectly by examining the source of a packet, its destination, size, number, and time of transmission. In addition to passive listening, attackers in active eavesdropping inject messages to help them determine the contents of messages. Access to transmission and (partially) known plaintext, such as a destination IP address, are sufficient for this attack.

- *Man-in-the-middle (violation of privacy)*: Without encryption or authentication in use, an attacker can read data from an ongoing session violating confidentiality or modify packets, thus violating the integrity of data. The attacker establishes a rogue intermediary, like an access point or an end-node router, the target unwittingly associates to the rogue that acts as a proxy to the actual network.

Attacks Against Integrity and Authenticity

Launching these attacks generally requires successful system intrusion and the use of one or more of the confidentiality attacks described above. Three primary types of this category are identified below.

- *Session hijacking*: Here, the attacker takes away an authorized and authenticated session from its legitimate owner. The target knows that it no longer has access to the session but may not know that the session has been taken over by an attacker who is masquerading as the target.

- *Replay*: An attacker captures the authentication of a session to gain access to the network sometime after the original session. Since the session was valid, the attacker may interact with the network using the credentials and authorizations of the target.

- *Man-in-the-middle (code and data injection or modification)*: This is similar to the man-in-the-middle attack on confidentiality above.

Attacks Against Availability

These are also known as denial-of-service (DoS) attacks (Mirkovic, Martin & Reiher, 2002; Welch & Lathrop, 2002; Wood & Stankovic, 2002). DoS attacks can be classified into the following three categories.

- *Disabling of service*: An attacker, with access to transmission, can inject malicious code by exploiting a flow in the design or implementation of an application. Even without access to transmission, an attacker can use a jamming device to corrupt the communication signals. In addition, physical tampering with network nodes is made easy with the large-scale deployment of small inexpensive devices characteristic to many mobile network.

- *Exhaustion*: With access to transmission, an attacker can deplete the battery of a device or deny access to processing by engaging the device in expensive computations, storage of state information, or high traffic load.

- *Cycle-stealing (or service degradation)*: Here, an attacker's intent is to consume some portion of the system resources. Since the attacks do not lead to total service disabling, they could remain undetected for a significant period of time (Mirkovic, Martin & Reiher, 2002).

It is to be emphasized that the combination of the challenges outlined in the second and third sections make m-commerce environments inherently weaker than their wired counterparts. The problem is indeed exacerbated with the use of group communications. For example, due to hardware limitations and the involvement of many mobile parties that may join or leave the group arbitrarily, access control can no longer depend on access control lists (ACLs); instead, it will require distributed solutions with highly dynamic and distributed trust functions. This will increase the complexity of the solution and the exposure to attack. Uncontrolled, or loosely controlled, group access allows any host in the global network to send multicast data to a group, which may cause congestion, or even worse, denial of service. Also, due to the limited communication range of most mobile devices, it is possible to have long chains of multihop routes from sender to receiver(s). The resulting length of the communication path increases the probability of attacks such as the man-in-the-middle attack. Moreover, given the collaborative nature of nodes assumed in mobile ad hoc networks, a compromised node could paralyze the entire network by disseminating false routing information. Thus, security multicasting is much more important in m-commerce.

Core Services for Efficient Secure Multicast in M-Commerce

Now that we are motivated by the need for secure multicasting in m-commerce, we look at the services needed to support efficient secure multicasting. Especially, establishing security among dynamic groups is more complex. For example, managing the dynamic nature of multicast groups during the lifetime of the group involves a variety of activities including the creation of a group; the sending, routing and reception of group communications; the modification of group membership; and finally the deletion of a group. A set of core services needed for such management is described below.

Cryptography

The requirements of secure multicast can be satisfied only with the use of cryptographic techniques. Thus, besides data traffic, group members also exchange keying material. The keying material comprises the keys used to encrypt/decrypt the data traffic and the keys, if any, used to encrypt/decrypt the keys used for the data traffic when the latter need to be updated (Bruschi & Rosti, 2000).

Denying Access to Physical Layer

This is an essential service to ameliorate the problem of denial of service due to jamming. It also may provide lightweight methods to help strengthen confidentiality and aid in group-authentication (Jones et al., 2003). It can be achieved by possibly a combination of several techniques. Following are a few techniques to achieve this objective.

- *Frequency hopping*: This technique can provide the needed service to wireless networks. Given that a perpetrator can use known techniques to discover a hopping sequence by monitoring transmissions, security can only be provided if the design modifies the hopping sequence in less time than is required to discover the sequence. Parameters in the specification of frequency hopping determine the time required to discover the sequence:

  - *Hopping Set*: The set of frequencies available for hopping,

  - *Dwell Time*: The time interval per hop, and

  - *Hopping Pattern*: The sequence in which frequencies in the hopping set are visited.

  A dynamic combination of these parameters can improve security at little expense of memory, computation and power. As frequency hopping requires events to happen simultaneously for both senders and receivers, all must maintain a synchronized clock.

- *Resistance to physical tampering*: Form factor and low cost of the majority of mobile wireless devices lead to considering only minimal tamper resistance and protection. Indeed, rudimentary tamper protection can be obtained by blanking out memory if the device is pried open. However, the protection offered by this solution is far from adequate. Researchers in Jones et al. (2003) propose a lightweight solution to the tampering problem that does not rely on the use of sophisticated tamper-resistant hardware. Their solution depends on the concept of neighborhood awareness.

Authentication

The two popular techniques for authentication are digital signatures and message authentication codes. Among these, digital signatures form the basis of authentication protocols in secure multicast. Here, a sender produces a digital signature based on the message contents and its own private key. They are used to allow receivers to verify the credentials of the entity sending the message.

A message authentication code (MAC) is an authentication tag (also called a checksum) derived by applying an authentication scheme, together with a secret key, to a message. Unlike digital signatures, MACs are computed and verified with the same key, so that they can only be verified by the intended recipient. There are four types of MACs: (1) unconditionally secure, (2) hash function-based, (3) stream cipher-based, or (4) block cipher-based (Di Pietro & Mancini, 2003). Depending on the type of security and the overhead that can be afforded, a specific technique may be chosen.

Group Membership Control

This is the most basic component of a secure multicast protocol. It allows only the authorized hosts to join the multicast group, guarding against unilateral subscriptions by arbitrary hosts. A group membership control protocol is employed in order to validate group members before giving them access to group communications. As previously mentioned, there is a need for group membership control protocols based on distributed trust and group decisions.

Key Management

Key management is at the heart of a secure multicast. Key management is usually defined by the key agreement mechanism when the multicast session is initiated and during the successive key exchanges throughout the session when there are changes in group membership. Effective key management schemes must ensure that none of the keys are compromised during initial key distribution or during re-keying. Ideally, the key management protocol must be such that hosts can join and leave the multicast group without affecting the other members of the group. In practice, addition and removal of hosts must take place affecting as few members of the group as possible.

The dynamics of mobile commerce complicates key management. For example, mobility support necessitates not only supporting member joins and leaves but also member transfers between networks while remaining in the session. Also, the cooperative operation inherent in mobile ad hoc networks requires a key management solution to consider the level of trust to impart to the nodes in the network and the performance implications should a member node leave the network.

Reliable and Efficient Routing

Routing protocols play an integral role in support of multicast communications for m-commerce. No single routing protocol can be expected to handle all the different types of multicast group requirements. Some groups may have short delay tolerances between communicating members. Others may tolerate delay but require that data be received at a constant rate. Some groups, by virtue of their size, may impose considerable overhead on participating routers if the supporting routing protocol exhibits poor scaling properties such as significant state requirements. An overview of multicast routing protocols (MRP) is presented in the next section. (A detailed study of multicast routing protocols is beyond the scope of this chapter.)

Multicast Routing

During the lifetime of a multicast group, a variety of activities occur, including the creation of a group, the sending, routing and reception of group communications, the modification of group membership, and, finally, the deletion of a group. MRPs have an effect on all entities involved in multicast communications. This impact can be manifested in terms of increased bandwidth consumption, memory consumption, or processing overhead. In addition to these costs, the MRPs will affect multicast performance through the imposition of various latencies such as delays in joining or leaving a group and delays in communications between members.

The extent of these impacts is dependent upon the attributes of the MRP. Key attributes of MRPs are the type of delivery tree created, the joining process, and unicast routing algorithm dependence. Today's MRPs employ two main types of trees: shortest path trees (SPTs) and shared trees (SPTs). SPTs result in a tree that describes the shortest path from a particular source to all recipients on the tree. SPTs are built for each sender in a multicast group and are distinguished within routers by the tuple (source, group) where source is the unicast IP address of the sender and group is the multicast address of the group. Examples of protocols employing SPTs include Distance Vector Multicast Routing Protocol (DVMRP) (Thaler, Estrin & Meyer, 1998), Multicast Open Shortest Path First (MOSPF) (Moy, 1994), and Protocol Independent Multicast - Dense Mode (PIM-DM) (Deering, Estrin & Farinacci, 1999). Shared trees, as the name implies, result in a single tree being used regardless of the source of the data; thus, only one tree is built for an entire multicast group. Examples of shared tree protocols include Core based Tress (CBT) (Ballardie, 1995) and Simple Multicast (SM) (Perlman et al., 1999). Because SPTs are optimal distribution trees they will impose lower delays in data delivery. Shared trees will impose greater delays but this delay can be minimized through the use of various heuristics for computing near-optimal shared trees (Kompella & Pasquale, 1993). Some MRPs support a hybrid approach through the utilization of shared trees and, when dictated by traffic (e.g., high bandwidth consuming senders), source-based trees. Examples include Protocol Independent Multicast –Sparse Mode (PIM-SM) (Estrin, Farinacci & Helmy, 1998).

Joining a multicast group can be implicit or explicit. As implied by the name, explicit join requires a recipient to explicitly request to receive data for the multicast group. MOSPF, CBT, and SM use explicit join. On the other hand, some routing protocols utilize data driven methods to establish group membership. All hosts receive data implicitly (implicit join) unless their associated multicast router removes itself from the delivery tree via a mechanism such as prune message. The protocols are termed data driven because the process of forwarding data to all sub-networks creates the underlying delivery tree for the multicast group. DVMRP and PIM-SM use implicit join. The advantage of explicit joins is that recipients only receive data they request and thus bandwidth overhead is reduced. Conversely, data driven or implicit join protocols require data to be periodically forwarded throughout an internetwork, potentially to networks with no group members. Because of the additional bandwidth consumed by data driven protocols to create and maintain the distribution tree, protocols that utilize explicit joins are inherently more scalable. Moreover, MRPs that are data-driven rely on multicast data delivery (via

Table 1. Summary of multicast routing protocols attributes

Routing Protocol	Tree type	Scalability	Delivery Tree Building Process	Intra/ Inter Domain	Join Type	Routing Algorithm Dependence
DVMRP	shortest path	O(S X G)	data driven	intra	implicit	dependent
MOSPF	shortest path	O(S X G)	underlying routing database	intra	explicit	dependent
PIM-DM	shortest path	O(S X G)	data driven	intra	both	independent
PIM-SM	hybrid	O(G) - O(S X G)	RP-centered shared trees	intra	implicit	independent
CBT	shared	O(G)	Core-based shared trees	intra	explicit	loose coupling
SM	shared	$O(G)$	Core-based shared trees	inter	explicit	independent

flooding to all links) to build and maintain distribution trees. Conversely, the process of explicitly joining a group creates the necessary state in routers to begin the distribution of data to the joining member. Depending upon the periodicity of flooding mechanisms, an MRP that employs explicit joins can be expected to exhibit lower join and leave latencies.

MRPs have varying degrees of dependency on underlying unicast routing protocols. Some MRPs are completely dependent upon a particular unicast routing protocols. Others operate independently from the underlying unicast routing protocols and thus offer more flexibility. DVMRP and MOSPF are both completely dependent upon specific unicast routing protocols being present. Both PIM-DM and PIM-SM were purposely designed to maintain complete independence from unicast routing protocols. On the other hand, CBT, while not reliant on a specific routing protocol, is loosely coupled to underlying routing protocols.

SPTs offer the best method to minimize delay at the price of reduced scalability. Conversely, the shared trees utilized by PIM-SM and CBT result in lower overall costs in both bandwidth consumed and state information required with greater relative latency. The bandwidth available, the number of groups and senders on the internetwork, and the timeliness requirements will all affect the choice of the multicast routing algorithm. Table 1 summarizes our discussion on the attributes of multicast routing protocols.

It is to be noted that this survey of MRP and their attributes is not intended to be a complete characterization of all MRPs. There are many other protocols in varying stages of development (Moy, 1994). However, many of the newer protocols are actually evolutionary advances of the core MRPs listed above. Protocols such as Ordered Core Based Trees (OCBT) (Shields, 1996) were designed as a result of flaws in current protocols such as the formation of loops. Other protocols such as HIP (Shields, 1998), KHIP (Shields & Garcia-Luna-Aceves, 1999), and Boarder Gateway Multicast Routing Protocol (BGMP) (Kumar, Radoslavov & Thaler, 1998) were designed to extend the underlying MRP to allow inter-domain multicasting capabilities. More recently, application level multicast is emerging as a viable alternative to network level multicast, especially for peer-to-peer and mobile ad hoc networks (Banerjee, Bhattacharjee &

Kommareddy, 2002; Gui & Mohapatra, 2003; Moharram, Mukkamala & Eltoweissy, 2004; Ratnasamy et al., 2001). Additional characteristics to consider in such networks are transient communications, weak infrastructure, and routing node autonomy. All issues discussed previously become more amplified under these more restrictive characteristics (Moharrum, Mukkamala & Eltoweissy, 2004).

Multicast Authentication

In multicasting, whenever a group member receives a message, it would like to ensure the authenticity of the message. This is referred to as source authentication. Typically, digital signatures are used for this purpose. For example, if the source uses its private key to digitally sign a message, then the receivers could use the public key of the sender to verify the message authenticity. This is an essential function in m-commerce also.

While it is not difficult to design an authentication protocol, it is certainly a challenge to design one that is efficient. In particular, a multicast authentication protocol should satisfy the following properties (Perrig, 2001):

- Efficient generation and verification of signatures

- Real-time authentication

- Individual message authentication by the receiver

- Robustness to packet loss

- Scalability

- Small size of authentication information

Among the several existing mulicast authentication protocols, BiBa (Perrig, 2001) and TESLA (Perrig et al., 2002) seem to be most efficient and scalable in terms of the above properties.

In BiBa (Bins and Balls signature) (Perrig, 2001), a sender precomputes values that it uses to generate BiBa signatures. The values are generated randomly in such a way that the receivers can instantly authenticate them using the public key of the sender. Each such value is referred to as a SEAL (or self authentication values). Here, the signer first computes the hash value h of the message to be multicasted. The signer then computes the hash function Gh to all the SEALs it currently has generated. It now finds two seals that have the same hash value (using G_h). Such a pair of SEALs forms the signature. When a receiver receives the message along with the SEAL pair, it regenerates the hash h, and verifies to see that the hash G_h when applied on the pair of SEALs gives the same value. Thus the verification process only involves the computation of three hash function computations. The security aspects of the scheme are discussed in Perrig (2001).

TELSA (Timed Efficient Stream Loss-tolerant Authentication) is another broadcast authentication protocol (Perrig et al., 2002). It requires that all the receivers in the group be loosely time synchronized (i.e., the time difference is at most D) with the sender. Like BiBa, it needs an efficient mechanism to authenticate keys at the receiver. In addition, it requires either the sender or the receiver to buffer some messages. The protocol mainly depends on the sender's ability to split time into time intervals, to generate sequence of SEALs (as in BiBa), and to assign them to the time intervals. For a message sent during a time interval, the sender uses the corresponding signature to generate a message authentication code (MAC). This is appended to the message. When a receiver receives a message with the MAC, it verifies its authenticity with the corresponding signature that it knows a priori. Messages with verified MACs are accepted.

Multicast Key Management

A considerable number of key management protocols have been proposed in the literature (Benerjee & Bhattacharjee, 2001; Di Pietro, Mancini & Jajodia, 2002; Doneti, Mukherjee & Samal, 200; Eltoweissy & Bansemer, 2003; Harney & Muckenhirn, 1997; Hubaux, Buttyan & Capkin, 2001; Kruus, 1998; Law, Etalle & Hartel, 2002; Mittra, 1997; Rafaeli, 2000; Selcuk, McCubbin & Sidhu, 2000; Setia, Zhu & Jajodia, 2002; Wallner, Harder & Agee, 1999; Wong, Gouda & Lam, 2000). Existing literature describes different ways to classify multicast key management solutions (Bruschi & Rosti, 2000; Dondeti, Mukherjee & Samal, 2000; Eskicioglu, 2002; Rafaeli, 2000). In Dondeti, Mukherjee, and Samal (2000), protocols are classified as either scalable or non-scalable, while in Bruschi and Rosti (2000), protocols are classified according to the stricture used for key distribution into flat, tree-based, clustered, and others. A third classification in Rafaeli (2000) is based on the authority that controls the key management; host-based, sub-group-based, and centralized are the three values used in this classification. Finally, Eskicioglu (2002) uses a two-dimension classification based on the control authority and scalability. In our opinion, scalability is better used as a performance metric rather than a solution classification one. Also, we distinguish between the data group and the control group. The data group comprises all the members interested in receiving data traffic targeted to the group, while the control group is comprised of all the entities involved in the (re-)keying operations such as key generation, distribution, and agreement. We propose a new two-dimension classification based on the characteristics of the control group and the structure used for key distribution. For simplicity, in this chapter, we use the type of entities involved in the control group as the characteristic representing the control group.

In general, there are two types of approaches to building key management structures. One involves maintaining a structure of keys (key-based structure), while the other maintains a structure of nodes (node-based structure). Using either approach, three main structures exist; one structure involves maintenance of a flat organization (Harney & Muckenhirn, 1997), another structure calls for maintaining a hierarchical organization (Wong, Gouda & Lam, 2000), while a third one uses clusters (Mittra, 1997). Yet, a fourth alternative may use a hybrid approach (Eltoweissy & Bansemer, 2003).

The other dimension of our classification is the control group. Accordingly, key management solutions may be divided into two classes:

- *Centralized schemes*: a single group controller responsible for the generation, distribution, and replacement of all group keys. The central group controller does not have to rely on any auxiliary entity to perform key management functions. Moreover, it may achieve a more reliable and synchronized key distribution. With only one control entity, however, the controller is a critical point of failure. Also, mobility and scalability requirements cannot be met with a centralized server especially for large groups.

- *Distributed schemes*: further divided into server-based and node-based schemes.

- *Server-based*: the management of the group is divided among a set of servers. The most common example of this group is Iolus, where the multicast group is divided into sub-groups with each sub-group having its own controller (Mittra, 1997). Other examples include key management servers that do not belong to the group and are there to support mobility services for key management (Rafaeli, 2000). The distributed server approach ameliorates the problem of a single point of failure. However, trust issues arise where the group owner must trust all controllers instead of just one.

- *Distributed node-based*: no explicit group controller and the key management functions are distributed among the members (Di Pietro, Mancini & Jajodia, 2002; Doneti, Mukherjee & Samal, 2000; Law, Etalle & Hartel, 2002). Each member is trusted to contribute its share to generate the group keys. For some large-scale mobile or ah hoc networks, this approach may provide the needed solution to cope with the issues of mobility and lack of infrastructure. Synchronization and trust issues complicate the use of this approach.

Overview of Multicast Key Management Schemes

There are many different schemes for key management in secure multicast communications. These schemes range from a centralized, straightforward approach to a totally distributed management solution that calls for each member to contribute to the construction of the group key. Each system of key management has its benefits; from low overhead on the system resources in the more simplistic approaches to producing a cryptographic key that may never be broken by an intruder in the more complex methods. Following is a summary of some current key management schemes.

Group Key Management Protocol

The most straightforward method of key distribution is to use a centralized group key controller, as in the Group Key Management Protocol (GKMP) (Harney & Muckenhirn, 1997). The centralized controller in this protocol has command of all the group key management. GKMP requires that every time a member leaves the group, a new group key is generated and distributed to the group members. This requires that the new group key be encrypted with each member's personal key encryption key. This distribution cost is linear to the group size. This approach also requires the centralized controller to store keys that total the number of group members plus one. The most considerable drawback of GKMP is that failure of the centralized controller is fatal to the whole system.

Iolus

The Iolus key management scheme uses a secure distribution tree to link users to a single group (Mittra, 1997). In practice, the multicast group is divided into subgroups. At the top level, there is a group security controller (GSC), which controls the subgroup controllers known as group security intermediaries (GSIs). Both the GSCs and GSIs can be called by a common name, group security agents (GSAs).

In Iolus, each subgroup has its own security keys, managed by the GSI for that subgroup. The GSI acts as a mediator between its subgroup and the other subgroups, generates the key, and takes care of registrations to the upper level hierarchies of the system. This calls for the GSI to deliver messages from and to the other subgroups.

Complementary Key Scheme

The complementary key scheme (CKS) optimizes the key management bandwidth usage at the cost of key storage space. CKS has a root controller that shares a separate key encryption key with each member. The root generates the group key for multicast communication and distributes it separately to each member, encrypted with that member's separate key encryption key.

This scheme is called complementary because the root generates something known as a complementary variable for each member and sends this variable to all the members of the group. The root will not send a member its own variable, just the complementary variable of all other members. This means that each member has to store variables that total the number of members of the group plus one; the key encryption key, the group key, and all other members' complementary variables. As the group grows, so does the number of variables each member must store.

Hierarchical Tree Schemes

Hierarchical tree schemes assign several keys per user, and result in a balance between storage space, number of message transmissions, and key encryptions (Wong, Gouda & Lam, 2000). The keys are organized in a k-ary tree so that internal nodes of the tree hold a key and some keys are common to several users in a manner similar to Iolus (Mittra, 1997). Thus, each member knows a subset of all keys including a personal key encryption key. The keys are structured so that each user knows the keys along the path from itself to the root, but no other keys.

The general logical key hierarchy (LKH) scheme for group key management uses a central key server to store and distribute group keys (Wong, Gouda & Lam, 2000). LKH uses a tree structure for key management. A symmetric key corresponds to each node in the tree. Each node knows only the corresponding keys up to the central node. This is called the key path and is simply a set of keys a particular node has knowledge of. By using key paths, re-keying can be minimized when a new node leaves or joins the group. Only nodes that know about keys on the new node's key path need to be changed.

Distributed Framework for Scalable Secure Many-to-Many Communications

Distributed Framework for Scalable Secure Many-to-Many Communications (DISEC) (Kruus, 1998) is a totally distributed multicast key management scheme that does not make use of a centralized controller. It is best suited for many-to-many communication where most of the group members are multicast sources. The main idea in DISEC is to distribute the key management tasks and overhead evenly between group members as opposed to mechanisms where the controller does most of the work.

Pre-Deployed Keying

Pre-deploying keying is the process of distributing keys to the nodes of the network before deployment. This process can be used on networks where computing resources are limited, such as wireless ad-hoc and sensor networks. Pre-deployed keys can be used in network-wide and single node settings. Network-wide pre-deploy keying involves giving a single key to each group in the entire network. Using a network-wide key minimizes the amount of storage used on the node. If the network key was to be compromised all communications that flow through the network could be viewed. Node-specific pre-deployed keying involves giving a key to each unique node combination on the network. Using node-specific pre-deployed keying involves more resources, which may be unacceptable in the typical wireless node platform. The node combination key offers more protection than the network key model. If a combination key is compromised, only the communication between the two nodes that share that key could be viewed.

Evaluation of Key Management Schemes

Quite a number of schemes have been proposed and/or developed for key management for secure group communications. However, the effectiveness of any proposed scheme and its suitability for m-commerce applications must be measured against objective criteria, which can then be used as the basis for comparing it with other schemes or implementations. In general, multicast key management can be evaluated based on a set of metric groups shown in Table 2. In addition to these metrics, resilience to intermittent communications due to mobility is also an important selection criterion.

While a number of performance evaluation studies exist (Moyer, Rao & Rohatgi, 1999; Setia, Zhu & Jajodia, 2002; Zhang et al., 2002), in this chapter a study by Setia, Zhu and

Jajodia has been chosen for discussion as representative of the processes and methodology widely used for comparative performance evaluations (Setia, Zhu & Jajodia, 2002). The study proposes and examines a group key management technique that addresses the problem of reliable and timely delivery of updated keys to group members. The proposed protocol is called WKA-BKR, which is based on two principle ideas, weighted key assignment and batched key retransmission, which, according to the authors, reduce the bandwidth overhead of reliable key delivery protocol by exploiting the special properties of logical key hierarchies and the group rekey transport payload. In the performance evaluation, certain aspects of WKA-BKR are compared with two other group key management techniques, multi-send protocol, and proactive forward error correction-based (FEC-based) rekey transport.

In the performance evaluation of WKA-BKR, multi-send, and proactive FEC-based rekey transport protocols, two metrics were chosen:

- *Average bandwidth overhead.* Because of inherent differences in the three protocols, this is defined a little differently for each of them.
  - *WKA-BKR*: bandwidth overhead is the ratio of the total number of keys transmitted by the key server during the rekey event to the total number of encrypted keys.
  - *Multi-send*: bandwidth overhead is the ratio of the total number of packets multicast during the rekey, including all replicated and retransmitted packets, to the total number of packets in the rekey payload.

Table 2. Evaluation metrics for key management schemes

Metric Group	Measurement
Time complexity	Measured in terns of the time needed for a group to be initialized with a group key before normal multicast commences and the time needed for a new key to be distributed upon a member's join or leave.
Computation complexity	Measured in terms of the total number of key encryptions during data transmission and the number of key encryptions at sender.
Communication complexity	Measured in terms of the number of messages needed for re-keying times their size in bits.
Storage complexity	Measured in terms of the amount of storage required to store the keys in the multicast group; the keys managed by sender, keys at a member, and the keys at sub-group controller.
Collusion	Measured in terms of the minimum number of departing members that can collude to read future traffic. Likewise, the minimum number of new members that can collude to read past traffic.
Scalability	Measured in terms of the degree of dependency of the data transmission and encryption on the size of the group, and the effect of removing a member on the other members of the group.
Trust	Measured in terms of the (quantified) reputation level of an entity involved in key management and the number of entities at each reputation level that must participate in the key management function.

- *Proactive FEC*: bandwidth overhead is the ratio of the total number of packets multicast during the rekey, including all the parity packets, to the total number of packets in the rekey payload.

- *Rekeying latency.* This is defined in Setia, Zhu, and Jajodia (2002) as, "the number of multicast rounds taken by a protocol for successfully delivering the keys in the rekey payload to all the members of the group."

Evaluation results indicated a substantial difference in bandwidth overhead between the three key management techniques, especially as the percentage of high-loss receivers increased. WKA-BKR out performs the FEC-based protocol by some 26%, while both of these were significantly more efficient than the multi-send protocol. A graphic comparison of bandwidth overhead may be seen in Figure 1.

In terms of the second performance metric, an examination was made of the distribution of the number of members who had not yet received all their keys at the beginning of an arbitrarily chosen round. As seen in Figure 2, FEC is marginally better than WKA-BKR, but both of these again far outperform multi-send.

Conclusions of this study include (1) WKA-BKR has a substantially lower bandwidth overhead than the other protocols tested; (2) FEC-based protocols have slightly lower latency than WKA-BKR; both have substantially lower latency than multi-send; and (3) WKA-BKR outperforms the other tested protocols over a wide range of group sizes and also tends to be less sensitive to network loss conditions.

Figure 1. Key server bandwidth overhead

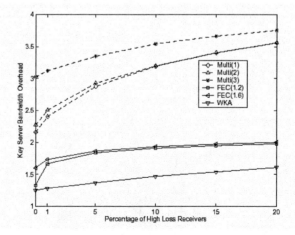

Figure 2. Latency of key delivery

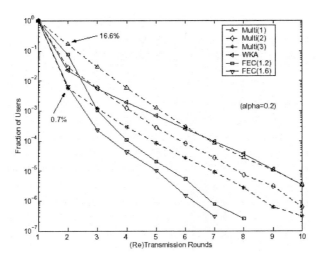

Example Revisited

Let us now revisit the mobile auctioning system introduced in the first section. A typical scenario depicting this system is shown in Figure 3. Here, a central auctioning system is connected to the Internet through a reliable, high-bandwidth line. To accommodate the mobile users geographically distributed throughout the country, the central agency has established several agents. The agents are connected to the central agency through a high-bandwidth connection via the Internet. Thus, the agents and the central agency can exchange information reliably and at high data rates.

The subscribers may be either mobile or connected through a wired connection to the agents or to the central agency. Whenever an auctioning has to take place for an item, the central agency multicasts via the wired network to its agents. In turn, each agent shall multicast the message in its region. Since the auctioning information is being pushed to the subscribers via multicast, the cellular operators (e.g., Verizon, Sprint, Suncom) also play a role in the scenario.

The multicast message, containing encrypted data from the auctioning system, is received by the subscribers via wireless or wired network. The auctioning system software installed on each (m-commerce aware) device (e.g., cell phone, laptop, workstation) receives the message, decrypts it and presents to its user. The software also checks for the authenticity of the sender (i.e., certified by the auctioning system) and the integrity of the message (e.g., digital signature). All these aspects require careful consideration of the encryption scheme, the length of the keys, the cost of encryption (to send) and decryption (to receive) at the mobile device.

Figure 3. Scenario illustrating mobile auctioning system

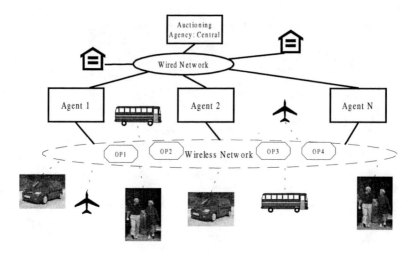

All the issues of group key management that we had discussed in the earlier sections are applicable here since users may subscribe as well as unsubscribe. The agents along with the central agency could implement the administrative functions of group management and key changes when users join and leave. The efficiency of this system greatly depends on the dynamics of the membership. If users are allowed to join and leave at the beginning of a month, then batch group management techniques may be used to reduce the overhead.

The reliability issue of the wireless network may also need to be addressed here. Multicasting itself assumes a reliable underlying communication network system. In the case of wireless systems, this may be achieved through mechanisms such as repeated transmissions with duplicate filtering at the end-user software.

In summary, this mobile auctioning system encompasses all aspects of multicasting that we discussed so far in the context of m-commerce.

Conclusion

We aimed at motivating research and providing a comprehensive picture of the salient issues in secure multicast communications for mobile commerce. Mobile commerce applications such as mobile auctions and collaborative investigation services need secure multicast support. Most existing security solutions for m-commerce applications, however, assume unicast communications. On the other hand, numerous solutions for secure multicast exist that are not specifically designed for m-commerce. In this chapter, we identified and discussed different facets of the multicast security problem in m-commerce. In particular, we identified system parameters and subsequent security requirements. We presented a taxonomy of common attacks and identified core services needed to mitigate these attacks. Key management services play a basic role in securing multicast communications. Given the varying requirements of m-commerce applications and the large number of current key management schemes, we provided a taxonomy and a set of performance metrics to aid in the evaluation and selection of key management schemes.

Numerous generic schemes exist for authentication and key management in multicast communications that can be applied to m-commerce environments. However, schemes that consider application semantics, such as transaction semantics, and communication semantics, such as ad hoc routing semantics, are still an open research issue. Other open research issues related to multicast security in m-commerce include trust relations, multi-level access control and membership verification, and denial of service attacks.

References

Ballardie, A. (1995). A new approach to multicast communication in a datagram internetwork. PhD Dissertation. University of London.

Banerjee, S., Bhattacharjee, B., & Kommareddy. C. (2002). Scalable application layer multicast. *Proceedings of ACM Sigcomm 2002*, Pittsburgh, Pennsylvania.

Benerjee, S., & Bhattacharjee, B. (2001). Scalable secure group communication over IP multicast. *International Conference on Network Protocols, ICNP.*

Bruschi, D., & Rosti, E. (2000). Secure multicast in wireless networks of mobile hosts: Protocols and issues. Technical Report. Department of Information Science, University of Milano, Italy.

Canetti, R., Garay, J., Itkis, G., Micciancio, D., & Naor, M. (1999). Multicast security: A taxonomy and efficient constructions. *INFOCOMM.*

Deering, S., Estrin, D., & Farinacci, D., (1999). Protocol independent multicast version 2 dense mode specification. *Draft-ietf-pim-v2-dm-03.txt.*

Di Pietro, R., & Mancini, L. (2003). Security and privacy issues of handheld and wearable devices. *Communications of the ACM, 46*(9).

Di Pietro, R., Mancini, L., & Jajodia, S. (2002). Efficient and secure keys management for wireless mobile communications. *POMC '02, ACM.*

Dondeti, L., Mukherjee, S., & Samal, A. (2000a). DISEC: A distributed framework for scalable secure many-to-many communication. *Proceeding of the Fifth IEEE Symposium of Computers and Communications.*

Dondeti, L., Mukherjee, S., & Samal, A. (2000b). Survey and comparison of secure group communication protocols. Technical Report. University of Nebraska-Lincoln.

Dornan, A. (2001). *The essential guide to wireless communications applications.* New Jersey: Prentice-Hall.

Eltoweissy, M., & Bansemer, J. (2003). A framework for key management in secure group environments. *Journal of Internet Technology.*

Eltoweissy, M., Heydari, H., Morales, L., & Sudborough, H. (2004). Combinatorial optimization of key management in secure group communications. *Journal of System and Network Management.* Kluwer Academic Publishing.

Eskicioglu, A. (2002). Multimedia security in group communications: Recent progress in wired and wireless networks. Technical Report. Department of Computer and Information Science, CUNY.

Estrin, D., Farinacci, A., & Helmy, A. (1998). Protocol independent multicast-sparse mode (PIM-SM): Protocol specification. *RFC 2362.*

Grahn, K., Pulkkis, G., & Guillard, J.S. (2002). Security of mobile and wireless networks. *Information Science.*

Gui, C., & Mohapatra, P. (2003). Efficient overlay multicast for mobile ad hoc networks. *Proc. of IEEE WCNC.*

Harney, H., & Muckenhirn, C. (1997). Group key management protocol (GKMP) specifications. *RFC2093.*

Hubaux, J.P., Buttyan, L., & Capkin, S. (2001). The quest for security in mobile ad hoc networks. *Proceedings of the ACM Symposium on Mobile Ad Hoc Networks and Computing.*

Jones, K., Wadaa, A., Olariu, S., Wilson, L., & Eltoweissy, M. (2003). A scalable solution for securing wireless sensor networks. *Proceedings of the New Security Paradigms Workshop.*

Kompella, V., & Pasquale, J. (1993). Multicast routing for multimedia communication. *IEEE/ACM Transactions on Networking.*

Kornak, A., & Distefano, J. (2002). *Guide to wireless enterprise application architecture.* John Wiley & Sons, Inc.

Kruus, P. (1998). A survey of multicast security issues and architectures. *Proceedings of the 21st National Information Systems Security Conference,* Arlington, VA.

Kumar, S., Radoslavov, P., & Thaler, D. (1998). The MASC/BGMP architecture for inter-domain multicast routing. *Proceedings of ACM SIGCOMM98,* Vancouver, Canada.

Law, Y.W., Etalle, S., & Hartel, P. (2002). *Key management with group-wise pre-deployed keying and secret sharing pre-deployed keying.* University of Twente.

Malloy, D., Varshney, U., & Snow, A.P. (2002). Supporting mobile commerce applications using dependable wireless networks. *ACM/Kluwer Journal on Mobile Networks and Applications, 7,* 225-234.

Maufer, T. (1998). *Deploying IP multicast in the enterprise.* Prentice Hall.

Mirkovic, J., Martin, J., & Reiher, P. (2002). A taxonomy of DDoS attacks and DDoS defense mechanisms. Technical Report #020018. Computer Science Department, University of California, Los Angeles.

Mittra, S. (1997). Iolus: A framework for scalable secure multicast. *ACM SIGCOMM '97*, Cannes, France.

Moharram, M., Mukkamala, R., & Eltoweissy, M. (2004). CKDS: An efficient combinatorial key management scheme for wireless ad hoc networks. *IEEE Workshop on Energy-Efficient Wireless Communications and Networking (EWCN'04)*.

Moy, J. (1994). Multicast extensions to OSPF. *RFC 1584*.

Moyer, M., Rao, J., & Rohatgi, P. (1999). A survey of security issues in multicast communications. *IEEE Network*.

Perlman, R., Lee, C.Y., Ballardie, A., Crowcroft, J., Wang, Z., Maufer, T., Diot, C., Thoo, J., & Green, M. (1999). Simple multicast: A design for simple, low-overhead multicast. *Draft-perlman-simple-multicast-02.txt*.

Perrig, A. (2001). The biba one-time signature and broadcast authentication protocol. *ACM Conference on Computer and Communications Security* (pp. 28-37).

Perrig, A., Canetti, R., Song, D., & Tygar, D. (2002). Efficient authentication and signing of multicast streams over lossy channels. *IEEE Security and Privacy*.

Rafaeli, S. (2000). A decentralized architecture for group key management. MS Thesis. Computing Department, Lancaster University, UK.

Ratnasamy, S., Handley, M., Karp, R., & Shenker, S. (2001). Application-level multicast using content-addressable networks. *Proceedings of Third International Workshop on Networked Group Communication (NGC '01)*, London, England.

Sadeh, N. (2002). *M-commerce: Technologies, services, and business models*. John Wiley & Sons, Inc.

Schneier, B. (1996). *Applied cryptography*. John Wiley & Sons, Inc.

Selcuk, A., McCubbin, C., & Sidhu, D. (2000). Probabilistic optimization of LKH-based multicast key distribution schemes. *IETF Internet Draft*.

Setia, S., Zhu S., & Jajodia, S. (2002). A comparative performance analysis of reliable group rekey transport protocols for secure multicast. *Performance Evaluation Journal*.

Shields, C. (1996). Ordered core based trees. Masters Thesis. University of California, Santa Cruz.

Shields, C. (1998). The HIP protocol for hierarchical multicast routing. *Proceedings Seventeenth Annual ACM SIGACT-SIGOPS Symposium on Principles of Distributed Computing (PODC 98)*, Puerto Vallarta, Mexico.

Shields, C. & Garcia-Luna-Aceves, J.J. (1999). KHIP - A scalable protocol for secure multicast routing. *Proceedings of ACM SIGCOMM99*, Cambridge, Massachusetts.

Thaler, D., Estrin, D., & Meyer, D. (1998). Border gateway multicast protocol (BGMP): Protocol specification. *Draft-ietf-idmr-gum-03.txt*. Work in progress.

Varshney, U. (2002). Multicast over wireless networks. *Communications of the ACM, 45* (12), 31-37.

Varshney, U. (2003). Location management for mobile commerce applications in wireless Internet environment. *ACM Trans. Internet Technology, 3*(3), 236-255.

Varshney, U., & Vetter, R. (2002). Mobile commerce: Framework, applications, and networking support. *ACM/Kluwer Journal on Mobile Networks and Applications (MONET), 7,* 185-198.

Waitzman, D., Partridge, C., & Deering, S.E. (1998). Distance vector multicast routing protocol. *RFC 1075.*

Wallner, D., Harder, E., & Agee, R. (1999). *Key management for multicast: Issues and architectures.* National Security Agency.

Welch, D., & Lathrop, S. (2003). A survey of 802.11a wireless security threats and security mechanisms. Technical Report ITOC-TR-2003-101. Department of Electrical Engineering and Computer Science, US Military Academy.

Wong, C., Gouda, M., & Lam, S. (2000). Secure group communications using key graphs. *IEEE/ACM Transactions on Networking, 8*(1).

Wood, A., & Stankovic, J. (2002, October). Denial of service in sensor networks. *IEEE Computer.*

Zhang, C., DeCleene, B., Kurose, J., & Towsley, D. (2002). Comparison of inter-area rekeying algorithms for secure wireless group communications. Technical Report. UMass.

Section III

Mobile Commerce Payment Methods

Chapter IX

M-Payment Solutions and M-Commerce Fraud Management

Seema Nambiar, Virginia Tech, USA

Chang-Tien Lu, Virginia Tech, USA

Abstract

Mobile security and payment are central to m-commerce. The shift from physical to virtual payments has brought enormous benefits to consumers and merchants. For consumers it means ease of use. For mobile operators, mobile payment presents a unique opportunity to consolidate their central role in the m-commerce value chain. Financial organizations view mobile payment and mobile banking as a way of providing added convenience to their customers along with an opportunity to reduce their operating costs. The chapter starts by giving a general introduction to m-payment by providing an overview of the m-payment value chain, lifecycle and characteristics. In the second section, we will review competing mobile payment solutions that are found in the marketplace. The third section will review different types of mobile frauds in the m-commerce environment and solutions to prevent such frauds.

Introduction

Mobile commerce (m-commerce) grows dramatically. The global m-commerce market is expected to be worth a staggering US$200 billion by 2004 (Durlacher Research, n.d.; More Magic Software, 2000). M-commerce can be defined as any electronic transaction or information interaction conducted using a mobile device and mobile networks, for example, wireless or switched public network, which leads to transfer of real or perceived value in exchange for information, services or goods (MobileInfo.com). M-commerce involves m-payment, which is defined as the process of two parties exchanging financial value using a mobile device in return for goods or services. A mobile device is a wireless communication tool, including mobile phones, PDAs, wireless tablets, and mobile computers (Mobile Payment Forum, 2002).

Due to the widespread use of mobile phones today, a number of payment schemes have emerged which allow the payment of services/goods from these mobile devices. In the following sections an overall view of the m-payment value chain, the m-payment life cycle and the m-payment characteristics is given. Also the operational issues are analyzed, which are critical to the adoption level of a payment system. The operational issues or characteristics will help in the unambiguous identification of the payment solutions.

M-Payment Value Chain

Many different actors can be involved in mobile payment process (McKitterick & Dowling, n.d.; Mobile Payment Forum, 2002). For example, there is a consumer who owns the mobile device and is willing to pay for a service or product. The consumer initializes the mobile purchase, registers with the payment provider and authorizes the payment. A content provider or merchant sells product to the customer. In the mobile payment context, content can range from news to directory services, shopping and ticketing services, entertainment services, and financial services. The provider or merchant forwards the purchase requests to a payment service provider, relays authorization requests back to the customer and is responsible for the delivery of the content. Another actor in the payment procedure is the payment service provider, who is responsible for controlling the flow of transaction between mobile consumers, content providers and trusted third party (TTP) as well as for enabling and routing the payment message initiated from the mobile device to be cleared by the TTP. Payment service provider could be a mobile operator, a bank, a credit card company or an independent payment vendor. Another group of stakeholders is the trusted third party, which might involve network operators, banks and credit card companies. The main role of the TTP is to perform the authentication and the authorization of transaction parties and the payment settlement.

Finally there are mobile operators who are more concerned with the standardization and interoperability issues. They may also operate mobile payment procedure themselves and provide payment services for customers and merchants. One thing that needs to be considered is who receives the customer data. Customers rarely wish to divulge any information, whereas the same customer information might be important for merchants or content providers for their business. Payment procedures need to ensure that none of the players receive the data, for example, when customers use a prepaid payment solution to buy goods but also need to require divulging customer information to any of the players considered.

M-Payment Lifecycle

Payment transaction process in a mobile environment is very similar to typical payment card transaction. The only difference is that the transport of payment detail involves wireless service provider. WAP/HTML based browser protocol might be used or payment details might be transported using technologies such as blue tooth and infrared (Mobile Payment Forum, 2002).

Mobile payment lifecycle shown in Figure 1 includes several main steps (Telecom Media Networks, 2002):

1.   *Registration*: Customer opens an account with payment service provider for payment service through a particular payment method.

2.   *Transaction*: Four steps are identified in an m-payment transaction.

   (a) Customer indicates the desire to purchase a content using a mobile phone button or by sending an SMS (short message service).

   (b) Content provider forwards the request to the payment service provider.

   (c) Payment service provider then requests the trusted third party for authentication and authorization.

Figure 1. M-payment life cycle

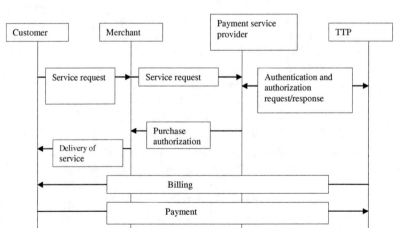

(d) Payment service provider informs content provider about the status of the authentication and authorization. If customer is successfully authenticated and authorized, content provider will deliver the purchased content.

3.   *Payment settlement*: Payment settlement can take place during real-time, prepaid or postpaid mode (Xiaolin & Chen, 2003). A real-time payment method involves the exchange of some form of electronic currency, for example, payment settlement directly through a bank account. In a prepaid type of settlement customers pay in advance using smart cards or electronic wallets. In the post-pay mode, the payment service provider sends billing information to the trusted third party, which sends the bill to customers, receives the money back, and then sends the revenue to payment service provider.

Operational Issues in M-Commerce Payment

Payment schemes can be classified as account based and token based. In the account-based scheme, consumers are billed on their account. This scheme is not suitable for small value transactions. In the token-based scheme, a token is a medium of payment transaction representing some monetary value and requires the support of the payment provider or TTP. Customers have to convert the actual currency to tokens. There are three different billing methods. One is real time, in which some form of electronic currency is exchanged during the transaction. The payment settlement can also be prepaid where customers pay in advance to have a successful transaction. Another method is the postpaid method in which customers pay after they receive the service/good.

Customers will choose a new payment method only if it allows them to pay in an accustomed method. The different payment settlement methods offered by the provider will hence play a crucial role. Based on payment settlement methods, the payment solutions can also be categorized as smart and prepaid cards solution, electronic cash or digital wallets solution, direct debiting and off-line-procedure solution, and credit cards and payments via the phone bill solution. In the payment using smart card or prepaid card solution, customers buy a smart card or prepaid card where the money-value is stored and then pay off for goods or services purchased. Customers can also upload a digital wallet with electronic coins on a prepaid basis. The smart cards, prepaid cards and digital wallets are thus used for prepaid payment solution. Another form of payment settlement is direct debit from the bank, which is a real-time payment method, since the purchase amount will be deducted as soon as the customer authorizes the payment. Payment method can also be using the phone bill or the credit card, where the customer pays for the good or services purchased at a later time. Payment by phone bill is one of the simplest methods of payment in which a special merchant-specific phone number is called from the mobile phone, which causes a predefined amount to be billed to callers' telephone bill. These types of payment schemes are applicable only to a single payment amount, providing limited security, and requiring users and merchants to share the same mobile operator (Pierce, 2000).

Smart cards can be used for all the three types of payment methods, for example, credit, debit and stored value as well as in authentication, authorization and transaction processing (Shelfer & Procaccino, 2002). A smart card thus enables the storage and communication of personal information such as value of goods and identity. A smart card can be either a memory card or processing enabled card. Memory cards are one type of prepaid cards, which transfer electronic equivalent of cash to the merchant electronic register. Processor cards, on the other hand, can be used as a debit card, credit card or a stored value card. A major drawback is the large costs associated with replacement of the existing infrastructure. In addition, the model lacks technical interoperability among existing smart card architectures.

The adoption of various payment frequencies in payment process is also a critical factor to make m-commerce payment succeed. It can be paid per view where consumers pay for each view, or increment, of the desired content; for example, downloading Mp3 files, video file or ring tones. It can also be paid per unit, where consumers pay once for each unit successfully completed with the content provider. A consumer would spend a certain number of units during each session, which is subsequently billed to the customer; for example, customer participating in an online game. The third type is a flat rate payment where consumers pay a recurring amount to access content on an unlimited basis for a certain period of time; for example, customer being charged to have access to an online magazine (McKitterick & Dowling, n.d.). The success of a payment solution will also depend on whether it can pay for a wide range of products and services. The payment can be a micro-payment, which refers to a payment of approximately $10 or less. In a micropayment system the number of transactions between each payer and the merchant is large as compared to the amount of each individual transaction. As a result transaction-processing cost grows for such systems. This kind of setting is addressed by a subscription scheme where a bulk amount is paid for which the use of a service is bought for a certain period of time. Traditional account based systems are not suitable for these kinds of transactions and hence the need for third-party payment processors arises which accumulate the transactions that can be paid for at a later time. The payment can also be macro-payments, which refers to larger value payments such as online shopping. It is also important to consider the technical infrastructure required by the customers to participate in a payment system (Krueger, 2001; Mobey Forum Mobile Financial Services Ltd, 2001). Some solutions do not require any changes to the hardware or software, which will then have a trade-off on the security aspect of payment. Some solutions require a sophisticated technology, which may be very secure but may not have taken the user's convenience into consideration. Most current payment solutions are SMS or WAP (Wireless Application Protocol) based. Some of the solutions use dual chip. In addition to SIM (Secure Identification Module), a second chip, such as WIM (Wireless Identity Module), standard smart cards and memory flash cards, is integrated into mobile device to provide the security functionality. The dual slot technology can also be used for payment services. This technology uses a regular SIM-card to identify the mobile device and also provide a second card slot for a credit or debit card integrated within a mobile phone. Payment solutions relying on an external chip card reader, which is connected to the mobile terminal using Bluetooth, infrared technologies or a cable, also come under the dual slot category.

In addition, software based payment solutions have been considered. A software agent based wireless e-commerce environment has been proposed (Maamar et al., 2001), called Electronic Commerce through Wireless Devices (E-CWE). The environment associates users with user-agents, embodies user-agents with personalization and mobility mecha-nisms, and relates providers to provider-agents. Initially a J2ME application has to be downloaded which provides the interface to credit card information, including merchant and payment data. Then credit information is posted via HTTPS connection to the payment service provider. All business logic is fetched from the Web server and usually no new software or hardware is required on the device.

Mobile Payment Systems or Solutions

This section will portray current mobile payment solutions and compare them from user perspective of cost, security and convenience. The Electronic Payment Systems Obser-vatory (ePSO) identified over 30 different mobile payment solutions, each with its own particular set of technologies (ePSO, n.d.). Mobile operators provide many solutions: some by financial players and others involving alliances between operators and financial organizations. Most of the solutions involve a relatively similar process.

Existing mobile solutions are categorized based on the payment settlement methods that are prepaid (using smart cards or digital wallet), instant paid (direct debiting or off-line payments), and post paid (credit card or telephone bill). The three payment settlement options may vary in their requirements, process of payment and technologies used. The only requirement to a prepaid type of payment solution is a PIN for authorizing a transaction and a smart card value or stored value card for making payment. The technological requirements range between just a mobile phone to a smart card with a dual slot phone and smart card reader. The payment procedure starts with customers selecting a product or service and the mode of payment. Next, customers authorize the transaction using PIN number and then the payment amount is deducted from the stored value card.

Payment solutions based on payment direct from credit or bank accounts require an agreement between customer and payment provider that authorizes the payment pro-vider to divulge the customer information to merchant and charge the customer. Customers have to divulge their credit card information or bank account number to payment service providers. The transaction also requires a PIN or a password. The technologies in use today for this type of solutions are a dual slot phone with a smart reader, dual chip phones (SIM+WIM), and payment provider calling back the customer's mobile phone. In general the solutions in this category follow the same high-level process. Customers select a product or service and the payment mode and authorize the transaction by entering a PIN or password. The payment provider forwards the card/bank information to the merchant. The payment amount is deducted from bank account or credited to customers' account and paid to the merchant.

The solutions based on charging the customer through phone bill require an agreement between customer and payment provider to charge the customer's phone bill. Such solutions require infrared or bluetooth technologies for establishing connection to the point of sale. In some cases a premium rate is enough. If the mobile phone uses a bluetooth/infrared technology, the point of sale contacts the mobile phone using the technology. Customers will then choose the product or service and authorize the payment with a button click on the mobile phone. Subsequently, the amount is charged to the phone bill. If the mobile phone uses just a premium rate to select a product or service, the mobile network calls the point of sale to authorize the sale and subsequently the amount is charged to the phone bill.

The following section portrays some current payment solutions such as Paybox, iPIN, m-PayBill, m-Pay and Jalda. A general analysis of the payment solutions based on customer requirements of cost, security and convenience is also provided.

Payment Solutions

Paybox

One of the most widespread mobile phone payment applications is Paybox (Paybox.net, 2002), which was launched in Germany in May 2000. Later it was launched in Austria, Spain, Sweden and the UK. This service enables customers to purchase goods and services and make bank transactions via mobile phone. The value of purchases or credit transfers is debited from customers' bank account. The infrastructures needed to use Paybox are a mobile phone, a bank account and a paybox registration. A typical real-world mobile transaction using Paybox is given in Figure 2. Customers send their phone number to a merchant. The merchant communicates this phone number and the price. The Paybox system calls the customer and asks for payment authorization. Payers authorize by their PIN. Paybox informs the trusted third party to settle the payment.

Paybox is very simple and easy to use because of the very limited infrastructures needed and only costs a small annual fee for customers. M-payment is independent. For example,

Figure 2. Paybox transaction

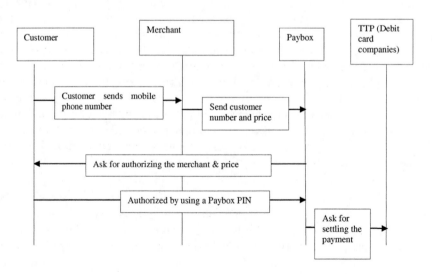

it allows services to customers of any bank or mobile operator. A key advantage of the independent payers is that they enable every mobile user to use the service upon registration, regardless of their mobile service provider. This independency of Paybox is also helpful to merchants since teaming up with such a payer is more efficient than teaming up with three or more separate mobile operators. Paybox also promises to provide a fraud protected cost effective system. The disadvantages are that the operation of Paybox is expensive since the system has to make voice calls using integrated voice recognition system (IVR) to the customer, which could range over various durations. In addition, there is no data privacy and customer and merchant have no proof of transaction, which might be a possible cause of fraud. The high latency also restricts it to high value transactions (Fischer, 2002). Most of all the transaction can be done only using a GSM enabled phone.

An annual fee is charged to customers, but there is no transaction fee involved. Paybox can be used with any mobile phone. Hence infrastructure costs are low. Peer to peer transactions come with an extra cost. Customers need to know only the PIN number to participate and the IVR system will then guide them through the rest of the payment process. Processing of transactions is fast. Paybox is suitable for macro as well as small payments. Paybox can also be used for peer-to-peer transactions where customers can send and receive money to other participants. Paybox owns customers' data and does not give the personal data to any other parties involved in the process. However, one drawback is that both customers and merchants do not have any proof of the transaction. Some fraud prevention techniques are promised by Paybox (Paybox.net, 2001), including address checking and correction using fuzzy logic tools, using checksums for credit card numbers and bank account numbers, checks on the demographic data, credit history checks, and address verification by sending the final PIN.

iPIN

iPIN is a privately held corporation based in Belmont, CA (USA) (ePSO, n.d.; Cap, Gemini, Ernst & Young, 2002). iPIN's Enterprise Payment Platform (EPP) is a leading end-to-end electronic and mobile commerce payment technology. It allows virtual point of sale and peer-to-peer payments over fixed as well as wireless networks. Seven software components have been identified in iPIN (Cap, Gemini, Ernst &Young, 2002). The main component of the iPIN payment system is the commerce router, which manages transactions throughout the payment lifecycle. It serves the user-interface pages and manages all end-user customer account activity. The repository is used for managing configurations and merchant information. Billing engine does the transaction fee calculation and facilitates account settlement. The merchant POS controller connects to the merchant's point of sale. The payment gateway connects to financial providers such as banks and credit card companies. The business intelligent module of iPIN keeps track of the success and returns on investments. The usage of the iPIN multiple payment instruments enables a customer to choose prepaid, debit or credit solution.

A typical transaction using the iPIN payment system is shown in Figure 3. Customers initiate purchase requests to merchant. The merchant sends an authorization request to

Figure 3. Transaction in an iPIN payment solution

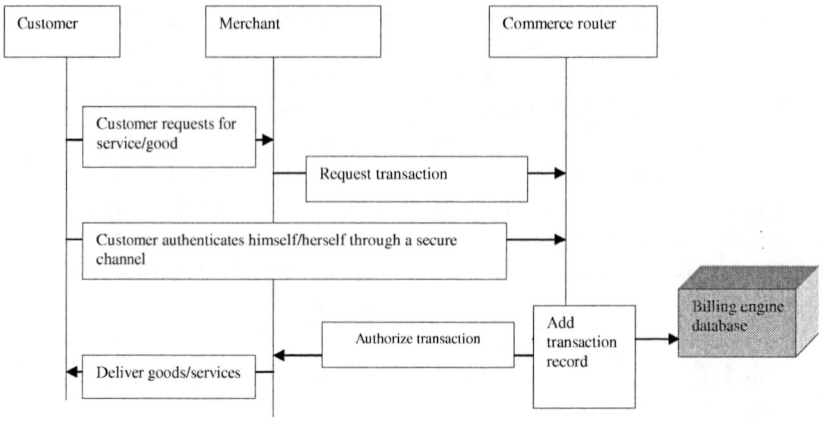

the issuer's commerce router. Customers are redirected to the commerce router for authenticating themselves after a secure session is established with the commerce router. After successful authentication is complete, the commerce router authorizes the transaction. Then the router establishes a transaction record in the database and sends the authorization response to the merchant. The merchant then sends a clearing message to the commerce router, confirming the transaction.

iPIN offers users a secure and efficient way to purchase virtual goods and services with a variety of connected devices including Web, WAP, SMS and IVR. Throughout the purchase process, the enterprise houses the user's personal profile and guarantees payment to merchants without actually transferring customers' private financial information. Fees are based on transactions. There is no setup fee for the customer. The only effort by consumers is to open or activate an account. Users are afforded several payment options including micro payment, and can choose to associate these charges to a prepaid account, monthly bill, and bankcard or loyalty program. Available via a mobile handset, self-care tools let users access detailed transaction histories, set account preferences such as spending limits and preferred account details, and receive answers to frequently asked questions. iPIN provides for interoperability between a group of individual payment networks, allowing merchants from one network to sell to users from other networks, while giving users access to a larger group of merchants and products.

Vodafone m-PayBill

m-PayBill supports virtual POS for micro and small payments (ePSO, n.d.; Vodafone M-Pay bill, n.d.). The bill is charged to customers' phone bill or from the prepaid airtime. The requirements for this payment solution are a WAP phone or a Web browser to settle the payment. Figure 4 shows a typical micro payment transaction using Vodafone. The Vodafone customers register for m-PayBill online by entering their mobile phone number,

Figure 4. Transactions in Vodafone-mPayBill solution

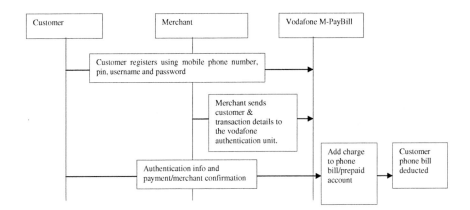

choosing a username, a password, and a four-digit PIN. When using a WAP phone the user is asked to enter the PIN for identification. Purchase amount is then charged to the phone bill or deducted from prepaid airtime.

m-PayBill membership is free; there are no basic or transaction fees. No extra infrastructure needed to perform the transaction except for a WAP phone. m-PayBill provides interoperability by having service providers outside of European Union plus Norway, Iceland and Liechtenstein. The personal information is transferred to the service providers in other countries for purchases outside the European Union. The security of the information will then depend on the privacy policy of that country. Payment information is maintained on the server and does not change hands, thus preventing any chances of fraud. The process is basically easy to understand and provides faster transactions. Customers who already registered with the Vodafone network operator need not register again to use the procedure. Payment solution, however, is only applicable to micro-payments.

m-Pay

m-Pay is a mobile payment solution developed in corporation between PBS, Orange and Gem plus (PBS ,n.d.). It is a server-based credit/debit card payment solution via mobile phone for goods ordered via telephone sales and on the Internet through the PC or a WAP mobile phone. To use this application the user sends a written application to Orange asking to link the payment data to the GSM data in a payment server. Activating the payment function on the mobile phone requires an individually allocated PIN-code, which is connected to the SIM-card in the mobile phone. A typical transaction using m-Pay is given in Figure 5.

Figure 5. Payment transaction in an m-Pay solution

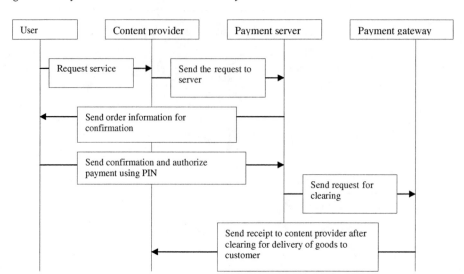

Customers request a service or product from the content provider. This request in the form of an SMS message is sent to payment server, which takes care of authorizing the payment request. Payment server sends the order information to customers for confirmation, which customers do by using a personal identification number presented in the SIM card. The server will then translate the mobile phone number into a valid card number and conduct a debit/credit card transaction. This confirmation is sent to the payment gateway for clearing, after which a receipt is generated by the gateway and sent to the content provider.

Customers must first register with Orange to use m-Pay. The registration is free but a new "Orange" SIM card required and payment confirmation service provided comes with a cost. An advantage with regards to cost is that customers need not buy new handsets to use the solution. None of the sensitive information is put on air. A payment receipt will be sent, whereupon customers receive notification in the form of an SMS message. The payment is carried out by exchange of e-payment certificates. The PBS payment server verifies any transaction from the SIM card, which ensures that the merchant is approved to trade and also that the card has not been reported stolen or stopped from further transactions. To use this payment application, users have to download a script over the air to activate the dormant payment application in their SIM card. The payment transaction will take less than 10 seconds. After the PIN code has been accepted by the SIM application, customers are able to buy airtime and the amount will automatically be drawn from their credit/debit card account.

Jalda

Jalda is an account-based system wherein both consumers and retailers are connected to a special account managed by a payment provider, who usually acts as the certificate authority (Dahlström, 2001; ePSO, n.d.). For payments using mobile phones, the certificate is stored centrally with the payment provider. Users authorize a transaction through a PIN-code. It can also be used for Internet transactions, in which case the certificate is stored in the hard drive. Jalda is a session-based Internet payment method that enables payment by the second, item, quantity, mouse click, search, character, page, or practically any other parameters. Jalda consists of two parts: an application program interface (API) and a payment server that administers user data and keeps track of transactions. The Jalda actors are consumers who use Jalda API applications to purchase via the mobile phone and the content provider who uses the Jalda API to charge consumers for service.

The system enables customers to be charged by whatever parameter the content provider desires. The content provider deducts a small transaction fee from the customer phone bills. The infrastructure required is a WAP phone. Security of payments is guaranteed by using strong authentication and non-repudiation protocols. Self-administration interface enables users to control their account. A payment receipt is sent to users, which may be stored in the WAP phone. Jalda is an account-based payment method, enabling both prepaid and credit-based payments. The accounts are managed and held by the payment provider and the payment provider usually acts as the certificate authority. Jalda can also be used for normal payments as well as micro-payments. The Jalda micropayment protocol is based on a concept of a payment session that is initiated by the payer by accepting and electronically signing a session contract with the merchant. The payment provider will then verify the contract for the vendor. After successful verification the vendor can then start keeping track of the service used by sending periodic indications when the consumer is consuming the service.

Jalda supports interoperability but does not enforce it as a global standard. Hence two payment providers need to make an agreement before the respective users can purchase goods from the other payment provider's merchants.

Other Solutions

Nokia launched a dual chip solution called EMPS (Electronic Mobile Payment Services). One chip was a usual SIM (subscriber identity module) card and the other was a WIM (WAP Identity module) for making mobile payments. Parkit is used in some cities of Finland to pay for parking. In this solution a service number of the parking area is called after which parking is registered and customers end the parking by calling again to a nationwide "ending number". The parking fee will be included on customers' telephone bill, credit card bill or a separate bill.

Table 1.The categorization of payment solutions

Payment Solutions	Instant Paid	Prepaid	Postpaid
Paybox	X		
IPIN	X	X	X
m-PayBill		X	X
m-Pay	X		X
Jalda		X	X

Table 2. Summary of the payment solutions

Payment Model	COST	CONVENIENCE	SECURITY
Paybox	An annual fee is charged to customer, but no transaction fee is involved. Peer-to-peer transaction comes with extra cost. Infrastructure costs are low.	Useful for macro, micro and peer-to-peer transactions. Customer is required to know only the PIN number to participate.	Customer personal data is kept in the Paybox server and not exchanged with other participants. Fraud prevention techniques are employed.
iPIN	No setup fee. Fees are based on transactions. Infrastructure costs are low.	Several payment options including micro-payments are offered. Interoperability between groups of individual payment networks is provided.	Enterprise houses users' personal data and guarantees privacy.
Vodafone m-PayBill	Membership is free. No basic or transaction fees. Infrastructure cost does not exist except that the customer might require a WAP enabled phone.	Only applicable to micro-payments. Payment process is more customer friendly. Customer who registered with Vodafone operator can automatically use the solution.	Interoperability between various countries is provided, but requires transfer of personal information. The privacy of the data will depend on the countries' privacy policy.
m-Pay	Registration is free. A new Orange SIM card is needed, which comes with a cost. Payment confirmation is also provided with a cost.	Customers need to download a script to activate applications on SIM card. Payment transaction is fast.	Payment is carried out by exchange of certificates. Customer receives payment confirmation in the form of SMS. Server verifies every transaction from SIM card.
Jalda	Content provider charges a small transaction fee from customers' phone bills. The customer might require a WAP enabled phone.	It can be used for normal as well as micro-payments, and supports interoperability but has not been enforced as a global standard.	Usage of strong authentication and non-repudiation protocols guaranteed. Payment receipt is sent to user.

General Analysis of the Payment Solutions

Payment solutions can be categorized on the basis of the payment settlement methods, which are instant-paid, postpaid, prepaid or a combination of these. In the prepaid solution, customers buy a smart card where the amount equivalent is stored and then pay of this for goods or services desired. Subscription of services can also be considered as prepaid type of payment. The prepaid type of solutions allows privacy to users since at no point of the process is required to disclose any personal data. The instant paid solution is that payment settlement is done as soon as users confirm the payment as in direct debiting systems. In the postpaid solution customers pay for goods or services later. Payment by credit card and phone bill is an example. Table 1 shows this categorization for Paybox, iPIN, m-PayBill, m-Pay and Jalda.

The key to the acceptance of a mobile payment procedure is in the hands of customers. The determinants affecting the adoption of a payment solution are cost, security and convenience. Cost includes direct transaction cost, fixed cost of usage and cost for technical infrastructure on the part of the customer. *Security* is evaluated by confidentiality of data and confirmation of the payment. *Convenience* means ease, comfort, fast processing and number of accepting merchants and interoperability. Table 2 gives a summary of the payment solutions based on the customer requirements.

Fraud Management Systems in M-Commerce

Fraud is defined as access or usage of the network with the intent of not paying for the service accessed. It can be either external or internal to the operator's network, and often involves both. Telecommunication fraud is estimated at 22 billion US dollars (USD) per year and growing annually at 2 billion USD (18 billion to fixed line fraud and 4 billion attributed to cellular). The convergence of voice and data communications, which has been driven by the tremendous uptake of the Internet and mobile phone ownership, has made fraud a high priority item on the agenda of most telecommunication operators. The advent of e-commerce activity further compounds the problem as industry analysts predict phenomenal growth in e-commerce over the next 3 years, with 40% of all e-commerce transactions expected to occur using mobile devices such as phones and personal assistants.

Many mobile payment solutions failed since they were unable to accumulate critical user mass. Merchants and consumers expressed their distrust in the electronic payment systems (Dahleberg & Tuunainen, 2001). The possible modes of fraud that will be experienced within m-commerce payment activity will encompass frauds related to security breaches in the underlying payment model, as well as in the underlying carrier network. A number of technologies are being used to prevent and detect these kinds of frauds. The frauds that can occur in the m-commerce environment have thus been categorized as mobile phone fraud, mobile network fraud and fraud specific to the m-commerce transaction process.

Mobile Phone Fraud

Criminals and hackers have devoted time and money to develop and refine their techniques, applying them to mobile phones as well. Not only is mobile phone fraud profitable, the stolen handsets have also provided anonymity to callers engaged in criminal activities. The various types of mobile phone fraud may be classified into two categories: subscription fraud and cloning fraud. Subscription fraud occurs from obtaining a subscription to a service, often with false identity details and no intention of paying. Cases of bad debt are also included in this category. In subscription fraud, all the calls for an account are fraudulent so there is no fraud-free period. Rules that are good for one time period may not be relevant for future time periods because calling behavior changes over time.

A signature-based system has been proposed in Cahill, Lambert et al. (2000). This system is event-driven rather than time driven so that fraud can be detected as it is happening and not at fixed intervals of time. It is based on the concept of account signatures, which may describe call durations, times between calls, days of week and times of day, terminating numbers, and payment methods for the particular account. All fraud records for particular kind of fraud are put into a fraud signature. For detecting a possible fraud, the call is scored by comparing its probability under the account signature to its probability under a fraud signature. Calls that are unexpected under the account signature and expected under the fraud signature receive higher scores and will be considered as more suspicious.

Cloning is the complete duplication of a legitimate mobile identification, namely, the MIN/ESN pair. Cloned phones can be identified with a technology called call pattern analysis. When a subscriber's phone deviates from its normal activity, it triggers an alarm at the service provider's fraud management system. It is put into queue where a fraud analyst ascertains whether the customer has been victimized and then remedies the situation by dropping the connection.

Location awareness of the mobile phone can be used to detect clones within a local system and to detect roamer clones (Patel, 1997). The success of these techniques is based on the assumption that the legitimate phones will stay powered up most of the time. Clones, by definition, will exist at a different location from the legitimate mobile phone. Clone detection within a user's current system can be recognized by "too many locations" and "impossible locations". A phone cannot be making a call from one cell site, and sending a registration message from another. In the cases of too many locations, fraud can be detected when getting registration messages from two different locations at almost the same time or getting two registration messages in an interval shorter than the re-registration period. Impossible location or velocity violation occurs when after a registration message at a location, another registration attempts from a location that is impossible to reach in the time elapsed. For the roaming, fraud is detected by monitoring handsets locations at the Home Location Register (HLR) and registration messages from Mobile Switching Center at Visitor Location Register (MSC/VLR) when mobiles enter a new system.

Mobile Network Fraud

A mobile wireless network is vulnerable due to its features of open medium, dynamic changing network topology, cooperative algorithms, lack of centralized monitoring and management point, and lack of a clear line of defense. There are many techniques to prevent mobile network intrusion such as secure MAC, secure routing and encryption. Intrusion detection approaches can be broadly classified into two categories based on model of intrusions: misuse and anomaly detection. Misuse detection refers to attempting to recognize the attacks of previously observed intrusions in the form of a pattern or signature, and monitor the occurrence of these patterns; for example, frequent changes of directory or attempts to read a password file. Anomaly detection refers to establishing a historical normal profile for each user, and then using sufficiently large deviation from the profile to indicate possible intrusions.

Anomaly detection is a critical component of the overall intrusion detection and response mechanism. Trace analysis and anomaly detection should be done locally in each node and possibly through cooperation with all nodes in the network. In the anomaly detection model (Zhang & Lee, 2003), the attack model consists of attack on routing protocols wherein attacks behave by acting on routing protocols, or it may be a traffic pattern distortion. The audit data of the model are comprised of the local routing information and position locator of the mobile node. Classifiers are used as intrusion detectors and features are selected from the audit data. There are five steps to detect a possible intrusion in the network: selecting audit data, performing appropriate data transformation, computing classifier using training data, applying the classifier to test data, and post-processing alarms to produce intrusion reports.

A technique called Trace modulation has been used in Nobile, Satyanarayanan, and Nguyen, 1997), where the end-to-end characteristics of a wireless network are recreated. Trace modulation is transparent to applications and accounts for all network traffic sent or received by the system under test. These techniques can be used to detect possible bugs in the mobile network system

M-Commerce Payment Specific Fraud

Various types of frauds may arise due to security breaches in the payment model. With the mobile Internet, a fraudster can pick sensitive information out of the air. The vulnerabilities may include infection of the mobile device by a virus, use of PINs and passwords, which are easily guessable, possibility of messages getting lost, spoofing on cardholder or the payment provider and message replay. The requirements for protecting m-commerce transactions are similar to those for protecting fixed-line transactions. Sensitive data, for example, must be secured during transmission. The following sections state various frauds that may occur during the payment life cycle and the availability of the prevention and management schemes.

Fraud Prevention During Payment Authentication

Just as with the fixed line Internet, authenticating a user's identity may be the hurdle at which demand for m-commerce services could fall. Authentication is a process of associating a particular individual with an identity. Two different techniques have been used for authorization. One is a knowledge-based approach in which individuals use the "personal knowledge" about something, like a password or a PIN to identify themselves. The other is a token based approach in which the identification is done based on something a person has, like a driver's license number and credit card number. Both these approaches are susceptible to fraud due to lost or stolen tokens and also due to personal identifications that are used by fraudsters (Miller, 1994). A distributed scheme that solves the problem of uncovering the PIN has been proposed by Tang, Terziyan, and Veijalainen (2003). The authors suggest that instead of storing the entire PIN digits in the SIM of the mobile device, a part of the PIN is stored in the remote machine in the network. The PIN verification then involves both the mobile device and the remote machine, each verifying their respective parts of the PIN.

The increased use of wireless devices in m-commerce makes the need for identity verification even more important yet difficult to ensure; hence the need of biometrics in this field becomes more important. A biometric identification process for smart cards has been proposed by Jain, Hong, and Pankanti (2000). A biometric system has been defined as a system that makes personal identification based on some physical or behavioral characteristics of the person. In the enrollment phase a characteristic feature of the individual is scanned and converted to a digital representation. This digital form is then processed to a compact but expressive form called a template, which is stored in the smart card. During the recognition phase the biometric reader captures the characteristic and converts it into a digital form. The generated template is compared with the one stored in the smart card to establish the identity of the individual. In voice biometric systems mobile phone speakers are identified and verified based on their voice. The significant difference between a regular biometric system and the voice biometric system is that the regular one processes an image for identification whereas the voice biometric system processes acoustic information. This difference in processing results in a major difference in their acceptance since the regular biometric system requires extra infrastructure like image scanner whereas the voice biometric system can be deployed in the existing telecom systems using specialized applications (Markowitz, 2000). Radio frequency fingerprinting has been used to identify mobile phones. The Supervisory Audio Tones (SAT) tone frequency, SAT tone deviation, maximum deviation, frequency error, supervisory frequency, and supervisory tone deviation are used to fingerprint or individualize a mobile phone (Boucher, 2001).

It is being observed that the mobile phone is vulnerable to malicious software like viruses, which might be capable of creating unauthorized copies of the PIN or password when the user creates an authentication response to the payment provider. Therefore the various possibilities of virus infection in mobile phones should also be addressed. Two kinds of applications infected by virus can be downloaded. One is the signed application, which is authenticated by checking the signature using the public key stored in the mobile phone. The other is an unsigned application, which is basically un-trusted, and is the basic cause of identity fraud. To prevent such a fraud it would be appropriate to limit the access of the application to a sensitive resource on the mobile device by systematic denial or by sending a prompt to the user for validation.

Fraud During Payment Transaction and Settlement

A fraudulent transaction requires the fraudster to be in possession of the customer signature, such as PIN or password, and also to be able to send the response message to the payment provider. A possible way to prevent such a fraud is to send an authentication request number from authentication server to customer together with the authentication request, which should be unique for the transaction and should only be used for the message exchange with the cardholder.

The authentication gateway in a mobile commerce environment injects messages into the mobile network through a Short Message Switching Center for SMS as the transport or Unstructured Supplementary Services Data Center (USSDC) when using USSD as the transport. The messages pass through the Signaling System 7 (SS7) based network associated with the mobile network. This is the signaling network used for control of the mobile network. It is possible that SMS messages can be read or manipulated if the SMS switching center is accessible to the user. The capture of the messages is a source of mass fraud attacks. Hence mobile operators involved in the payment process should be encouraged to review their procedures for protecting all the vulnerable parts of their network, including the BSSs, SS7 networks and the SMSC/USSDC and their interfaces.

To decrease the probability of fraud, prepaid solutions were introduced which allow users to access specific services for which they pay in advance. In GSM mobile networks the prepaid solutions are intelligent network, which allows automatic call termination when the prepaid value reaches zero. Fraud prevention during payment settlement generally involves supporting the non-repudiation property of mobile networking. Zhou and Lam proposed an efficient technique for non-repudiation of billing using digital signatures and hashing mechanisms (Zhou & Lam, 1998). In this scheme a mobile user needs to submit a digital signature when requesting a call along with a chained hash value. After this, a series of hashed values are released at predefined intervals, which allows at most the last unit of service in dispute. The problem of uncollectible debt in telecommunication services is addressed by using a goal-directed Bayesian network for classification, which distinguishes customers who are likely to have bad debt (Maamar et al., 2001). Digital data can be copied and a user can spend a valid electronic coin several times. Requiring the vendors to contact the financial institution during every sale, in order to determine whether the dollar spent is still good, can prevent double spending. Double spending can also be prevented using tamper resistant smart cards, which contain a small database of all transactions. Double spending can also be detected, in which case a double spender is identified when the cash is settled in the bank. In another detection mechanism tamper resistant device, "Observer" is used to prevent double spending physically. This allows the owner to spend the coin once in an anonymous manner, but the identity of the owner would be revealed if he or she tries to use it again (Chaum & Pedersen, 1992). The detection schemes thus do not prevent but deter double spending and also do not require any specific hardware.

Research Issues and Conclusions

Research Issues

Without a wide popularity and usage, any given payment solution will not survive, regardless of its different attractive features. The disappearance of some innovative electronic payment procedures like eCash serves as an example of this fact. A mobile payment procedure today should not only consider the option of low to medium macro-payments, but also include at least the potential for further development in the direction of cost-effective micro payments.

Apart from the widespread acceptance of the solution by customers, another issue that remains to be solved is an issue of different mobile payment service providers. Because of their existing customer base, technical expertise and familiarity with billing, mobile telephone operators are natural candidates of the service providers. However, risk management and the need to ensure the cooperation of different providers for interoperability in an efficient m-payment system may complicate the issue. Future payment models may be the bank-dominated models where the mobile phones will provide just another way for customers to access their bank account. The PKI security standard, which is now widespread in the e-commerce scenario, can be applied to the m-commerce scenario as well. Integrating PKI into a single SIM handset needs further study. Finally, EMV, a standard for debit and credit bankcards, deserves consideration.

Conclusions

Mobile security and payment are central to m-commerce. Today, a number of competing mobile payment solutions have already found their way into the marketplace. In this chapter we surveyed several payment solutions and listed some fraud management schemes, which are central to a successful payment solution.

An important point which influences the establishment of the mobile payment procedure is the technical infrastructure needed on the customer side. A sophisticated technology may fail if the customer is not able to handle it with ease. On the other hand, simple procedures based on simple message exchange via short messaging services (SMS) may prove profitable. Thus, at present and in the future the important payment solutions will be SMS-based, which can easily be charged to the mobile phone bill of customers. Some other procedures may integrate two or more solutions. An important observation is that m-payments are still in their infancy. The m-payment solutions are still being developed with standards defined on individual business segments, which is a major reason for market fragmentation in this area even though the mobile marketplace is global. Other interesting areas related to m-commerce payment not mentioned in this chapter are issues of standardization and interoperability. These issues will have to be resolved for these solutions to reach their full potential, especially in places like Europe, where there are a large number of mobile operators and users who tend to roam into different areas.

Mobile commerce can only be conducted if all parties believe that there is adequate security. The majority of users of mobile commerce technologies are concerned about security. A sound security policy includes identifying security risks, implementing effective security measures, and educating users on the importance of security procedures. Fraud management systems are becoming increasingly important for wireless carriers. The challenge is to monitor and profile the activity of the users and to be alert to the changing nature of fraud.

References

Boucher, N.J. (2001). *The cellular radio handbook: A reference for cellular system operation* (4th ed.). New York: A Wiley-Interscience Publication, John Wiley & Sons Inc.

Cahill, M.H., Lambert, D., Pinheiro, J.C., & Sun, D.X. (2000). Detecting fraud in real world. In J. Abello, P. Pardalos & M. Resende (Eds.), *Handbook of massive datasets.* New York: Kluwer Press.

Chaum, D., & Pedersen, T. (1992). Wallet databases with observers. In E. Brickell (Ed.), *Proceedings of Crypto 92* (vol. 0740 of LNCS, pp. 89-105).

Dahleberg, T., & Tuunainen, V. (2001). Mobile payments: The trust perspective. Workshop Sollentuna September 2001. Retrieved September 14, 2003, from *http://web.hhs.se/cic/seamless/Portal/Documents/Sollentuna/Abstract_Dahlberg_Tuunainen.doc*

Dahlström, E. (2001). The Jalda payment method. *ePSO-Newsletter, 5*(5). Retrieved September 13, 2003, from *http://epso.jrc.es/newsletter/vol05/5.html*

Fischer, I.M. (2002). Towards a generalized payment model for Internet services. Masters thesis. Technical University of Vienna.

Jain, A., Hong, L., & Pankanti, S. (2000). Biometric identification. *Communications of the ACM, 43*(2). Retrieved September 14, 2003, from the ACM Digital Library.

Krueger, M. (2001). The future of m-payments - business options and policy issues. Electronic Payment Systems Observatory (ePSO) Institute for Prospective Technological Studies. Retrieved September 2003, from *http://www.e-pso.info/epso/index.html*

Maamar, Z., Yahyaoui, H., Mansoor, W., & Heuvel, W. (2001). Software agents and wireless e-commerce. *ACM SIGecom Exchanges, 2*(3). Retrieved September 14, 2003, from the ACM Digital Library.

Markowitz, A.J. (2000). Voice biometrics. *Communications of the ACM, 43*(9). Retrieved September 14, 2003, from the ACM Digital Library.

McKitterick, D., & Dowling J. (*2003*). State of the art review of mobile payment technology. Retrieved September 14, 2003, from Trinity College Of Dublin, Department of Computer Science Web site: *http://www.cs.tcd.ie/publications/tech-reports/reports.03/TCD-CS-2003-24.pdf*

Miller, B. (1994). Vital signs of identity [biometrics]. *IEEE Spectrum Magazine, 31*(2), 22-30. Retrieved September 14, 2003, from the IEEE Xplore Online Delivery System.

Mobey Forum Mobile Financial Services Ltd. (2001). The preferred payment Architecture Technical Documentation. Retrieved September 2003, from *http://ipsi.fraunhofer.de/ mobile/teaching/m-commerce_ws0203/payment/MobeyTechnical.pdf*

Mobile Commerce Report. Retrieved September 9, 2003, from *http://www.durlacher.com/ downloads/mcomreport.pdf*

MobileInfo.com: M-Commerce. Retrieved September 9, 2003, from *http:// www.mobileinfo.com/Mcommerce/index.htm*

Mobile Payment Forum. (2002). Enabling secure, interoperable, and user-friendly mobile payments. Retrieved September 9, 2003, from *http://www.mobilepaymentforum.org/ pdfs/mpf_whitepaper.pdf*

Mobile Payments in M-Commerce, White paper. (2002). Retrieved September 2003, from Cap, Gemini, Ernst and Young Web site: *http://www.cgey.com/tmn/pdf/ MobilePaymentsinMCommrce.pdf*

More Magic Software (2000, November 24). Payment transaction platform. Retrieved September 9, 2003, from *http://www.moremagic.com/whitepapers/technical_ wp_twp021c.html*

Nobile, B.D., Satyanarayanan, M., & Nguyen, G.T. (1997). Trace-based mobile network emulation. *Proceedings of the ACM SIGCOMM '97 Conference on Applications, Technologies, Architectures, and Protocols for Computer Communication.* Retrieved September 14, 2003, from the ACM Digital Library.

Patel, S. (1997). Location, identity and wireless fraud detection. *IEEE International Conference on Personal Wireless Communications, 17-19 Dec.* (pp. 515-521). Retrieved September 14, 2003, from the IEEE Xplore Online Delivery System.

Paybox: ePSO Inventory Database (n.d.). Retrieved September 13, 2003, from *http:// www.e-pso.info/epso/index.html*

Paybox.net. (2001). Paybox security, Whitepaper, business and technical information regarding the security at paybox. Retrieved September 2003, from *http://www. paybox.net/publicrelations/public_relations_whitepapers.html*

Paybox.net. (2002). Mobile commerce delivery made simple: Whitepaper. Retrieved September 13, 2003, from *http://www.paybox.net/publicrelations/public_ rela- tions_ whitepapers.html*

Payment Technology. Retrieved September 13, 2003, from Trinity College Of Dublin, Department of Computer Science Web site: *http://www.cs.tcd.ie/publications/ tech-reports/reports.03/TCD-CS-2003-24.pdf*

PBS. (n.d.). *Mobile payment.* Retrieved September 14, 2003, from *http://www.pbs.dk/ english/produkter/mbetaling.htm*

Pierce, M. (2000). *Multi-party electronic payments for mobile communications.* Doctoral dissertation. University of Dublin.

Shelfer, K.M., & Procaccino, J.D. (2002). Smart card evolution. *Communications of the ACM, 45*(7). Retrieved September 14, 2003, from the ACM Digital Library.

Tang, J., Terziyan, V., & Veijalainen, J. (2003). Distributed PIN verification scheme for improving security of mobile devices. *Mobile Networks and Applications, 8*(2). Retrieved September 14, 2003, from the ACM Digital Library.

Telecom Media Networks. (2000, September). Mobile payments-commerce. Retrieved September 13, 2003, from *http://www.cgey.com/tmn/pdf/MobilePaymentsin MCommrce.pdf*

Vodafone M-Pay Bill. (n.d.). What is Vodafone m-pay bill? Retrieved September 2003, from *http://mpay-bill.vodafone.co.uk/w_mpay.html*

Xiaolin, Z., & Chen, D. (2003). Study of mobile payment systems. *IEEE International Conference on E-commerce* (pp. 24-27). Retrieved September 14, 2003, from the IEEE Xplore Online Delivery System.

Zhang, Y., & Lee, W. (2003). Intrusion detection techniques for mobile wireless networks. *Wireless Networks, 9*(5). Retrieved September 14, 2003, from the ACM Digital Library.

Zhou, J., & Lam, K. (1998). Undeniable billing in mobile communication. *Proceedings of the 4th Annual ACM/IEEE International Conference on Mobile Computing and Networking* (pp. 284-290). Retrieved September 14, 2003, from the ACM Digital Library.

Chapter X

Multi-Party Micro-Payment for Mobile Commerce

Jianming Zhu, Xidian University, China

Jianfeng Ma, Xidian University, China

Abstract

This chapter introduces a new micro-payment scheme that is able to apply to multi-party for mobile commerce, which allows a mobile user to pay every party involved in providing services. The micro-payment, which refers to low-value financial transactions ranging from several cents to a few dollars, is an important technique in m-commerce. Our scheme is based on the hash function and without any additional communication and expensive public key cryptography in order to achieve good efficiency and low transaction costs. In the scheme, the mobile user releases an ongoing stream of low-valued micro-payment tokens into the network in exchange for the requested services. The scheme that is put forward satisfies the requirements for security, anonymity, efficiency and lightweight.

Introduction

The remarkable development of the Internet has brought with it the need to perform commercial transactions over the network, thereby enabling electronic commerce (e-commerce). A key requirement of e-commerce transactions is the technique to allow payment to be made for any purchased item. When such a payment is effected electronically, by exchanging monetary value across a computer network, it becomes an electronic payment. Many electronic payment schemes have been proposed, and a lot of them assume the use of nowadays well-established credit card business environment. The most well-agreed and dominant electronic payment protocol is the SET (Secure Electronic Transaction) protocol (MasterCard & Visa, 1997), produced by Visa and MasterCard to be their standard for processing credit card transactions over networks like the Internet. However, electronic payment research has been largely concerned with the problem of making payment to a single vendor across the Internet. Some of them are completely unsuitable for frequent multi-party payment systems.

Recently, mobile communication is one of the fastest growing sectors of the IT industry and the emergence of wireless and mobile network has made it possible for the admission of electronic commerce to a new application and research subject: m-commerce, which is defined as the exchanging or buying and selling of commodities, services, or information on the Internet through wireless network by mobile handheld devices. M-commerce introduces the mobile networks to e-commerce – the mobile handsets provide the users with the possibility to perform an e-commerce transaction whenever they want, wherever they are. The mobile handsets also offer the content providers an already existing infrastructure that enables the identification of the users. While some of the existing e-commerce services could properly be used on mobile devices, many of them are simply not suitable due to technical and physical restrictions.

Wireless network is susceptible to security attacks because in an open network, information can be intercepted and tampered with easily. Wireless communication suffers from threats inherited from wired networks and those that are specific in the wireless environment. On the other hand, because of its limited resource and higher channel error rate than that of wired networks, those security schemes in wired network could not be used directly in wireless environment. Hence, how to build a secure and efficient environment for mobile electronic payment is a key issue in m-commerce development.

Micro-Payment

With the rapid development of the Internet, more and more computer users rely on computer networks for information ranging from daily news and journal papers to movies and so on. Most of the information items on the Internet have low value, ranging from cents to several dollars.

A micro-payment system is a special kind of electronic payment system, which is used to purchase information goods over the computer network. The important factors in such a payment system are small amount of payment value (e.g., less than one dollar or a few cents) and high frequency of transactions on the electronic commerce network. In network business transactions, a customer uses a WWW browser to buy data, software, games, music, news, or other services, and transfers this information or services online through electronic communication networks. For a small amount of payment, the systems

Figure 1. Basic model of micro-payment

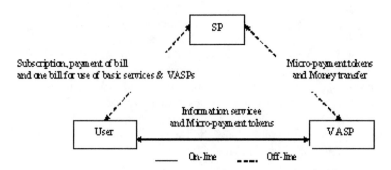

do not require high transaction security but have to reduce the cost of transaction. However, some security requirements are essential, such as the authentication of the customer and the merchant, and the protection of the integrity of transaction processes. In general, a practical system has three main properties in transaction: (1) customers get information goods in real time, (2) the prices of information goods are low, and (3) the transactions occur frequently. In mobile commerce, customers buy information or services online through wireless network with mobile devices.

Basically, a micro-payment system is composed of three entities, that is, users, service providers (SPs), and value added service providers (VASPs). Figure 1 shows a basic model of micro-payment system.

The role players in the mobile micro-payment shown in Figure 1 comprise mobile users, SPs and VASPs. Here, a SP plays the role of the broker in general micro-payment environments. It bills the user for both basic and value-added services, and then redeems the relevant payment to the VASP. Considering the lightweight nature of most transactions to be carried out through mobile communications, the VASP-SP interface will be usually off-line.

Multi-Party Micro-Payment

In mobile environments, mobile users will have constant connectivity through a number of mobile access networks using a variety of mobile communication protocols. There will be a large number of independent public and private mobile network operators, perhaps many thousands within a single city. The size of the different access networks will range from wireless in-building networks, to local area wireless networks for pedestrians, to wide area city and suburban cellular networks, and to global satellite broadcast networks, as depicted in Figure 2 (Peirce, 2000).

In this environment users will always be in the range of one or more mobile networks and will be able to select one that meets their requirements best at the time. Roaming between independent networks will occur daily, even for those mobile users who never venture out of their home city. The mobile infrastructure for such a mobile communication

Figure 2. Envisioned multi-party electronic payments in mobile environment

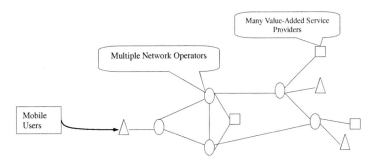

environment will be developed from the evolution of existing wide-area cellular communication together with the emergence of low-cost local area wireless techniques.

While there will be a large number of different network operators, both mobile and fixed, there will be an even greater number of independent VASPs. These will provide additional services other than transport of user traffic. For example, a VASP might provide information services such as weather forecasts, street maps, stock quotes, and news. Services such as voicemail, online banking, and market trading will also be provided. Some VASPs will allow the purchase of material goods such as concert tickets, drinks from a local vending machine, or the payment for a car wash. Indeed VASPs will ultimately provide any services that can be paid for. Like network operators, these VASPs are willing to dynamically set charges on a per-call basis, but unwilling to be constrained by NO-pricing models. It should be possible for any entities with a network connection to provide services to users willing to pay for them.

A typical scenario in which multi-party payments are required is now described. A mobile visitor might drive into a new city. As he arrives at the city outskirts, through one of the wide-area mobile networks he can obtain a city traffic report and directions to his hotel. Later, having checked into his room, he uses the hotel local area wireless network to call an acquaintance, informing her of his arrival. They make arrangements to meet in a cafe in a nearby shopping center. Arriving early at the cafe, our visitor uses the local pedestrian network covering the shopping center to make a long distance call, which is routed through two independent networks, to a remote VASP that provides voicemail services for him. So, we should design a multi-party electronic payment scheme that allows all parties involved in a transaction to be paid in real-time.

Related Works

Many electronic payment systems have been developed. In general, electronic payment systems are classified into macro-payments and micro-payments by the amount of payment value. Different payment systems handle different security requirements placed upon each as the systems are varied. Although several different micro-payment schemes exist, not all of them are suitable for all m-commerce uses. The purpose of this section is to review existing payment techniques and the underlying cryptographic algorithms on which they are built, in order to take their suitability for use in a multi-party payment environment.

Macro-Payment

Such electronic payment systems, designed to securely allow payments ranging in value from approximately one dollar to several thousand dollars to be made, are known as macro-payment systems. Payments larger than this are usually using traditional bank transfers over private banking networks. For macro-payment systems, systems are classified into three types of models based on how the payments are implemented, which are credit card based, digital cash, and electronic check (Hwang et al., 2001). Such systems typically use complex encryption techniques and require communications with an authorization server to request and confirm payment. In the following, a brief discussion of payment systems based on these models is presented.

Credit card-based payment systems, such as SET (Secure Electronic Transaction) (MasterCard & Visa, 1997) and iKP (Hauser et al., 1996), are both online and postpaid payment with credit card. Specially, iKP can be implemented on different security levels. According to the security requirements, users can choose a suitable level to implement. Hence, iKP can be used in micro-payment, too.

There are many payment systems based upon cash-like payment, such as ECash (Wayner, 1994) and Conditional Access for Europe (CAFÉ) (Boly et al., 1994). A check is a signed order to pay an identified payee using funds from the payer's bank account. In an electronic check scheme the check is usually generated and digitally signed by the payer before being transmitted across the network to the payee for verification. The payee endorses the check by applying a further digital signature before sending it to his network bank. In this field, Financial Services Technology Consortium (FSTC) (Doggest, 1995) and Netcheque (Neumann & Medvinsky, 1995) are famous electronic check models.

The foregoing payment systems cause computation and communication overhead cost to perform the protocol. Nevertheless they provide high-level security. However, these techniques are not suitable for micro-payment, because the cost for each transaction may be higher than the value of payment.

Micro-Payment

A micro-payment scheme is an electronic payment system designed to allow efficient and frequent payments of small amount, as small as a tenth of a cent. In order to be efficient, and keep the transaction cost very low, micro-payments minimize the communication and computation employed. Micro-payment schemes aim to allow offline payment verification to utilize lightweight cryptographic primitives. The security requirements are relaxed, in order to increase efficiency, which is acceptable due to the small amount involved.

The cost of fraud is more expensive than the possible value to be gained by cheating. The majority of micro-payment schemes were designed to pay for information goods on the Internet. A network user might pay to consult an online database, read some financial Web pages, listen to a song, or play an online game, and it has great potential to pay not only for information but for voice and data transport services, and the quality of service provided. Ultimately, it should be possible to pay the multiple parties involved in providing all aspects of a service as that service is consumed.

Two types of models classified for the micro-payment systems are the notational model and the token model (Ferreira & Dahab, 1998). In the notational model payment systems, users transfer the payment message enabling the value of the payment and the payment orders. Some of such systems are Millicent (Manasse, 1995), Micro-iKP (Bellare et al., 1995), NetBill (Sirbu & Tygar, 1995), and SVP (Stern & Vaudenay, 1997). In the token model payment systems, transaction mainly exchanges tokens. The token represents coins or bank notes. The PayWord and MicroMint (Rivest & Shamir, 1996) are payment systems of such type.

In our recent study (Zhu & Ma, 2002), we present a simple and efficient micro-payment scheme for electronic commerce. In our scheme, we adopt the signcryption arithmetic and avoid the public key infrastructure. In each transaction, this scheme needs only one round communication. Our scheme is simple, safe, efficient and economical.

These micro-payment systems are efficient for repeated small payments. In order to achieve good efficiency and low transaction costs, a practical micro-payment system is needed without any additional communication and expensive public key cryptography. After investigating the various existing micro-payments schemes, we have classified micro-payments into four categories based on the employed cryptographic constructs and the communication overhead—hash chains, hash collisions and sequences, secret sharing, and probability. The fact has indicated that hash chains are best suited to a scenario with computational lightweight user devices with small storage and limited bandwidth, and vendors who have to process a large number of payments per second (Peirce, 2000). These properties are apt to mobile circumstances. Hence, we focus on micro-payments mechanisms based on hash chains.

Firstly, we introduce the notion about hash chain, and then review the key concepts of several micro-payment systems below and present evaluation for them.

Hash Chains

Digital signature is used to authenticate a payment, but for the micro-payment schemes it has to be done inexpensively. Methods using hash function are discussed here.

Hash Function and Hash Chain

A one-way function is a function easy to compute but computationally infeasible to invert. Lamport (Lamport, 1981) proposed the use of repeated evaluations of one-way function, to generate a chain of values. A hash function is a one-way function that takes a variable length input, the pre-image, and produces a fixed length output, the hash value. A collision-resistant hash function is a hash function computationally difficult to find two different pre-images that map to the same hash value. In this chapter, the term hash function is used to refer to a collision-resistant one-way hash function unless otherwise stated. A hash chain of length n is constructed by applying a hash function n times to a random value labeled x_n. The value x_n is called the root value of the hash chain. We define a hash chain derived using a hash function h recursively as:

$$h^n(y) = h(h^{n-1}(y)), h^0(y) = x_n$$

where $h^n(y)$ is the result of applying a hash function repeatedly n times to an original value y. The final hash value, or anchor, of the hash chain after applying the hash function n times is $x_0 = h^n(x_n)$. The hashes are numbered in increasing order from the chain anchor x_0, so that $h(x_1) = x_0$, and $h(x_2) = x_1$.

Each hash value in the chain can provide a single user authentication. The user releases x_1 for the first authentication, x_2 for the second and so on. The server only has to apply a single hash function to verify that the received value hashes to the previous value. The user only needs to store x_n, from which the rest of chain can be re-computed. As show in Peirce (2000), hashing is highly efficient, approximately four orders of magnitude faster than generating a public key signature. The final hash x_0 of a chain may need to be securely swapped across a network. A public key digital signature can be applied to x_0, to produce a signed commitment to the hash chain, showing it to be genuine. Since the hash function is one-way, only the user could have generated this value, and knowledge of it can the constitute proof of payment.

Hash values from a user-generated hash chain can be used as authenticated payment tokens. The first micro-payment schemes that independently proposed this idea were Pederson's phone ticks (Pederson, 1996), PayWord (Rivest & Shamir, 1996), and iKP micro-payments (Hauser et al., 1996). In the first payment to a new vendor, the user signs a commitment to that vendor with a new hash chain. By including the vendor identity in the commitment, the vendor is linked to the chain, preventing it being redeemed by other vendors. For each micro-payment, the user releases the next payment hash, the pre-image of the current value, to the vendor. Since the hash function is one-way, only the user can generate this value, and knowledge of it can constitute the proof of payment. In essence, the hash chain links the correctness of the current payment to the validity of previous payments. Each hash value is worth the same amount, which can be specified in the commitment. A payment of m units is made by releasing the single hash value that is the mth pre-image of the current hash in the chain. The vendor only needs to apply m times hash to verify it.

By using a hash chain, the computational cost of a payment is now a single hashing operation for the vendor, after the initial single verification of the digital signature for a new chain. Where a user spends n hashes from a chain to make z payments at the vendor, the average cost per payment is (n hashes + 1 signature)/z. Thus, in the worst case, where a user only ever makes a single purchase from a vendor, the cost is similar to that in the public key schemes. Therefore, as with the majority of micro-payment systems, the scheme is optimized for repeated payments to the same vendor.

Hash Collisions and Hash Sequences

A hash function collision occurs when two entries have the same hash value. Two values x_1, x_2 form a two-way hash function collision if they both hash to the same value y_1:

$$h(x_1) = h(x_2) = y_1$$

This property can be used to define an electronic coin as a k-way hash function collision, as shown in Figure 3. An issuer, who invests a large amount of computation to search for hash function collisions, creates the coin. It is efficient to verify that the coin is valid, by checking that each pre-image is unique and that they all hash to the same value. The collision is being used to authenticate the coin instead of the digital signature. The longer the length of the hash function output, the more difficult it is to find collisions.

The definition of a coin can be modified so that the broker who prevents stolen coins being spent can issue user-specific coins. The user identity U is hashed with a second hash function h2 to produce a group of numbers, each labeled di. A coin is now a set of k pre-images $\{x_1, x_2, ..., x_k\}$ whose hash values $\{y_1, y_2, ..., y_k\}$ form a sequence where the difference between each hash value links them to a specific user identity U:

$$h2(U) = \{d_1, d_2, ..., d_{k-1}\}$$
$$y_{i+1} = y_i + d_i \ (\text{mod } 2^U) \text{ for } i = 1, 2, ..., k-1$$

Figure 3. Electronic coin as k-way hash function collision

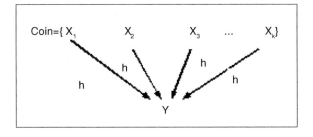

Effectively, the hash values combine to form a hash of the user identity. Coin verification will require one additional hash computation per purchase.

PayWord Scheme

"PayWord" is a credit-based scheme, based on chains of "payword" (hash value), which aims to reduce the number of public key operations required per payment by using faster hash functions. In this scheme (Rivest & Shamir, 1996), the role players are brokers (B), users (U), and vendors (V). Brokers authorize users to make micro-payments to vendors, and redeem the payments collected by the vendors. While user-vendor relationships are temporary, broker-user and broker-vendor relationships are long-term. This scheme uses public-key cryptography. The user establishes an account with a broker, who issues the user a digitally-signed PayWord Certificate.

PayWord Evaluation

PayWord is an off-line system. The customer only needs to contact the broker at the beginning of each certificate lifetime in order to obtain a new-signed certificate. The system aims to minimize the number of public key operations required per payment using hash operations instead whenever possible. It is credit-based scheme where a user's account is not be made against an account with insufficient funds. The paywords in the specific system and the paywords in the chain have no value to another vendor. Since PayWord requires using each hash chain for each vendor, the user has to maintain all indices after dealing with all vendors. On the user's side, he or she must compute expensive public key operations as many as the number of vendors that he/she wants to transact with. Therefore, it is not suitable for multi-vendor.

NetPay Scheme

NetPay (Dai & Lo, 1999), a secure, cheap, widely available, and debit-based protocol of a micro-payment system, differs from previous protocols in the following aspects: NetPay uses touchstones signed by the broker and indices signed by vendors transmitted from vendor to vendor. The signed touchstone is used by vendor to verify the electronic currency-paywords, while the signed index is used to prevent double spending from customers and to be disputed between vendors. There are no customer trusts required.

In NetPay Scheme, consider a trading community consisting of the customer (C), the vendor (V), and the broker (B). Assume that the broker is honest and is trusted by both the customer and the vendor. The vendor and the customer open accounts and deposit funds with the broker. The payment only involves C and V, and B is responsible for the registration of the customer and for crediting the vendor's account and debiting the customer's account.

NetPay Evaluation

NetPay is a basic off-line protocol suitable for micro-payments in distributed systems on the WWW. Since only the broker knows the mapping between the pseudonyms (IDc) and the true identity of a customer, the protocol protects the customer's privacy. The protocol prevents customers from double spending and any internal and external adversaries from forging, so it satisfies the requirements of security that a micro-payment system should have. The protocol is "cheap" since it just involves a small number of public-key operations per purchase. NetPay can easily handle more transactions than other schemes. In extended NetPay system, a coin can be divided in small denominations; that is, it has divisibility. NetPay is extremely powerful for a customer performing many purchases from a vendor, and then changing to another vendor. Unfortunately, this scheme is too open to control. A malicious entity can request a chain transfer on behalf of a user at any time, as no proof of user presence is required. Among competing vendors, this provides an easy denial-of-service attack. A user and a vendor may collude to cheat other vendors and allow infinite double spending with post-fact detection.

Millicent Scheme

A number of micro-payment schemes eliminate the use of computationally expensive asymmetric cryptography and instead rely on shared secret keys between the parties. Shared secret keys can be used to provide authentication and integrity by the use of a message authentication code (MAC). A keyed hash, where the secret key K is appended to the message M and a hash function applied to the combined value, will act as a simple MAC. Using a one-time pad, instead of full encryption, can also provide secrecy. To generate a onetime pad, a random number N is chosen, hashed with the secret, and XORed with the message to hide it:

$$H(N, K) \oplus M$$

N is also sent with the XORed message, but the secret K is required to recover M. While symmetric keys are more efficient, there is the problem of how initially to swap the secret value for a new relationship.

Public key cryptography or out-of-band communication is used to solve this key distribution problem. In a large system, the number of shared secrets that each entity must securely keep can become unwieldy. In addition, each key needs to be refreshed periodically to prevent cryptanalysis and to limit the timeframe of a brute force attack.

Millicent scheme (Manasse, 1995), which was one of the first micro-payment systems to be proposed, uses a broker to aggregate user micro-payments made to many vendors. There are vendor-broker and user-vendor shared secrets. A vendor issues value to users in the form of an authenticated message, called scrip, which specifies the value a user has at that specific vendor, rather like a temporary account.

Millicent Evaluation

Millicent employs no public-key cryptography and is optimized for repeated micro-payments to the same vendor. Its distributed approach allows a payment to be validated, and double spending to be prevented without the overhead of contacting the broker online during purchase. Key drawbacks with Millicent include: the broker must be online whenever the customer wishes to interact with the new vendor; the customer must nearly always be able to connect to the broker in order to make sure of the ability to perform payments; the vendor scrip is vendor-specific and has no value to another vendor; and transactions are very complicated when the customer and the vendor have different brokers.

Conclusion

There is a growing need for an effective, efficient micro-payment technology for high-volume, low-value e-commerce products and services. Current macro-payment schemes cannot be used to such a domain. Most existing micro-payment techniques proposed or prototyped to date suffer from problems with security, lack of anonymity and performance. On the other hand, rapid development in mobile communication has given rise to a large number of independent network operators, spanning many different geographic areas and countries. When these operators use a common mobile standard, it is possible to allow subscribers to roam from the home network to a visited location, choosing among the new operators available. So, micro-payment schemes should be used in multi-party environments and satisfy the requirements for security, anonymity, efficiency and lightweight.

Multi-Party Micro-Payment Scheme for Mobile Commerce

In order to be efficient, and to keep the transaction cost very low, micro-payment minimizes the communication and computation. Micro-payment schemes aim to allow offline payment verification to use lightweight cryptographic primitives. The security requirements are relaxed, in order to increase efficiency, which is acceptable due to the small amount involved. The cost of fraud is made more expensive than the possible value to be gained by cheating.

On the other hand, in a mobile communication system, there are some things to consider when micro-payment protocols are being designed. First, the low computing power of mobile devices should be considered, which means a protocol requiring heavy computation on the mobile nodes is not adequate. Secondly, wireless mobile communication networks have a lower bandwidth and a higher channel error rate than wired networks. So, the micro-payment protocols should be designed to minimize the message sizes and the number of messages exchanged and to have some fault-tolerance.

In fact, micro-payment research has been mainly confined to the Internet scenario of paying for information goods from a Web server over HTTP. User payments to a single vendor have been the only environment considered. As we have already said, we see a tremendous potential for multi-party micro-payments, where a user pays multiple parties at the same time, not only for information goods, but also for transport services, quality-of-service, and bandwidth reservations. In this section, we present a multi-party micro-payment scheme for mobile commerce based on Peirce (2000).

System Model

Any network communications that extend beyond the local administrative domain will involve entities belonging to different foreign networks. Ultimately, each entity through which the network traffic passes, or which provides part of the service, will be remunerated for their participation.

In the billing model, every customer registers with different merchants and obtains services (or goods) from the merchants. The transaction cost is low in this model. However, it is very inconvenient to the customers. If a customer wants to purchase goods from 100 different merchants, he or she has to open accounts with these merchants and remember 100 different encryption (decryption) keys. This is a very tedious task for the customers.

For the credit card model, the customer sends his or her credit card number to the merchant through some secure channel between them. But the high credit card transaction cost makes this model unsuitable for the micro-payments.

The electronic check model is also a candidate. The electronic check model depends on a hierarchical banking infrastructure to transfer funds along a path inside the hierarchical structure. If the system is based on the public key cryptosystem, the banks have to provide online key revocation servers for their customers whose secret keys are compromised. These servers must be available to all merchants at any time. Any unavailability of these servers will cause the compromised secret keys. If the electronic check system is based on the private key cryptosystem, a hierarchical accounting structure has to be established so that funds can be transferred. Incorporating such an accounting infrastructure into the existing banking system will be expensive. Moreover, a fund transfer operation involves at least three accounting servers if the customer and the merchant do not share a common accounting server. Furthermore, the merchant has to clear the check online before he or she honors the customer's purchasing request. This means that the computer systems and the communication channels along the check clearing path must be reliable all times, which is not the case in wireless environment.

The electronic currency is not considered since the electronic check model is just a simplified (or special) electronic currency model.

Based on the above observations, we consider the debit model as the model for our micro-payment protocol. The money debit model is an online system. The customer's bank debits the customer's account, transfers the funds to the merchant's bank; the merchant's bank credits the merchant's account. This is the scenario of the debit model. It is not realistic for us to assume that every bank will provide online transfer service to its

Figure 4. Multi-party payment model

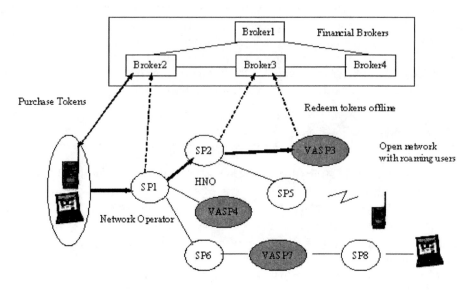

customers at the present time. Instead, a trusted electronic payment service provider is established to handle all fund transfers between the customers and the merchants. We call it the broker.

A high level model of the system, its players and their interactions are shown in Figure 4 (Peirce, 2000). A user attaches to the network through an access network operator (NO), either over a mobile wireless link or from a fixed terminal. The user makes calls or sends packets through the access NO, for which he pays in real time. The connection may pass through one or more other network operators before reaching the destination user or VASP. A service provider (SP) is any entity who provides a service during that connection and includes both NOs and VASPs. The user releases a stream of micro-payment tokens into the network to pay all the SPs as the call proceeds. Tokens are based on hash chain constructions. Payment tokens are purchased by the user from one of several online brokers. The tokens are spent through their home network operator (HNO), who prevents being cheated by the user or the other SPs. When the mobile user roamed to the foreign network, foreign network operator can authenticate to the user by running the current authentication protocol and can play a role of HNO in a payment process.

In this chapter, we adopt following notations for describing the proposed scheme.

$\{X\}_K$ X encrypted with key K

$\{X\}sig_A$ X digitally signed by A

$h(.)$ a cryptographically strong hash function

Protocol Goals

In this section, we provide the requirements of the multi-party payment solution. Here are the 7 goals for the protocol (Peirce, 2000).

- *Real-time payment anywhere.* A mobile user should be able to pay all parties involved in providing service in real time, regardless of his or her current location and without the need for authentication.

- *Off-line payment verification.* Any entity accepting payment should be able to efficiently verify its validity off-line, without the need to contact a third party. Each payee should be guaranteed to be able to redeem a valid token with a broker.

- *Remove user trust and accountability.* Since mobile users are the greatest number of entities within the system they should be trusted the least.

- *No user signatures and certificates.* The use of signatures implies the existence of a PKI with at least one certificate per signer. With millions of users, maintaining such a PKI is a huge task, especially considering that certificates will need to be revoked and the validity of a certificate needs to be checked by each party wishing to verify a user's digital signature.

- *Prevent inter-service provider fraud.* With a great number of NOs and VASPs, the possibility of any frauds among these entities needs to be removed.

- *Fault-tolerant.* The protocol should be fault-tolerant because wireless mobile communication networks have a higher channel error rate than wired networks.

- *Anonymity.* The customer anonymity should be protected. A fundamental property of physical cash is that the relationship between customers and their purchases is untraceable. This means that the payment systems do not allow payments to be traced without compromising the security of the system.

In summary, we wish to remove unnecessary trust from the system, reduce the online communications overhead of contacting a home location, eliminate fraud due to falsification, provide fair dynamic charging, and allow real-time payment anywhere by anyone who holds valid payment tokens.

Payment Chain Purchase

A mobile user purchases prepaid tokens, through their mobile terminals, from a third party broker, using an existing macro-payment system. The mobile user initially creates the tokens by repeatedly applying a one-way hash function h to a root value P_N to generate a payment hash chain. The chain has no monetary value until committed by a broker. To obtain this commitment, the mobile user makes a macro-payment to the broker, sending along the final hash P_0, the chain length N, the desired total value of the chain, and the identity of the HNO through whom it must be spent, all encrypted with the broker's public key. It is assumed that the user has securely obtained and verified the broker's public key certificate beforehand.

The broker commits the hash chain by digitally signing the payment chain commitment:

$$Comm_P = \{P_0, \; Length, \; Chain\_value, \; HNO, \; Expiry\} Sig_{Broker}$$

The commitment shows that each payment hash value from the chain represents pre-paid value, redeemable at the broker. The value of a single payment hash is later fixed, on a per call basis, by the HNO. This allows the same hash value to be used to pay all parties. The user is given $Comm_P$, which is stored with the secret P_N.

A short expiry field is included in the commitment to limit the state that must be remembered by the broker to prevent double redeeming. Redemption must take place before expiry, after which the user's refunds unspent value can be given. Similarly, if a payment chain is accidentally deleted, the unspent value may be reclaimed, provided the broker has a record of the chain owner.

The HNO will prevent more than the total value of the chain being spent. Failure to do so will be detected by the broker when the hashes are redeemed. The chain length is included in the commitment so that the HNO does not set the hash value to require more hashes than that used in the chain to spend the total value.

Pricing Contract

To get some services from a VASP, the user sends the request details, such as destination, service type, Quality of Service (QoS) requirements, and the payment chain commitment to the HNO. A signed pricing contract is then generated by the SPs involved in the visit. Its purpose is to allow verifiable dynamic tariffs; fix the starting hash in the payment chain; decide the value per payment hash for the visit; create a record of the visit; and link a single payment commitment to multiple SPs for the visit. The fields in the pricing contract consist of:

$$PricingContract = \{TID, SP, Charge, Comm_P, P_{start}, Start, P\_value, Comm_E, R\_Broker\} sig_{SP}$$

- *TID*. Transaction identifier for the contract, partly generated by each SP. Each SP's part of the TID acts as a nonce guaranteeing freshness of the contract and preventing an old or partial contract being replayed to them.

- *SPs*. The identity of each NO and VASP involved in the visit. When combined with the transaction ID, a unique identifier for the contract is obtained.

- *Charge*. Charging mechanism and individual tariff rate for each SP. The charging mechanism might be based on visit duration, volume of data, or both.

- $Comm_P$. Payment chain commitment, spendable through the HNO.

- P_{Start}. Starting payment hash from the payment chain for the visit. This is the next unspent hash value.

- $Start$. Position of P_{Start} in the payment chain.

- P_value. The value per payment hash for the duration of the visit; it can be fixed in the broker commitment.

- $Comm_E$. An endorsement chain commitment that is a hash chain created and signed by the HNO for each visit. This is used to prevent double spending of payment hashes. A hash chain commitment consists of the final hash as follow:

$$Comm_E = \{E_0\} sig_{HNO}$$

- R_broker. Each SP fixes the broker through whom they will redeem payment hashes for this visit.

The HNO is responsible for ensuring that the pricing contract is constructed correctly using a three-way handshake protocol, shown in Figure 5. In step one, each SP adds their charging details to the contract. In step two, each SP digitally signs a hash of the fully assembled pricing contract, checking that their inputs have not been altered in any way. The SP signature does not include other SP contract signatures. The signatures later prove that each SP took part in the call and is due payment. The finished contract is forwarded to each SP in step three. The completed contract is presented to the user for agreement before the payment begins. From the charging information fields, the total visit

Figure 5. Constructing pricing contract

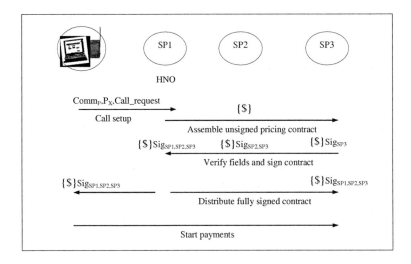

cost per charging unit is obtained. The user can verify the signatures to prove that each quote is genuine.

Payment Processes

Payment is ongoing, with the user releasing payment hashes at regular intervals. For a voice call this might be every 10 seconds, while for streaming video it might be every 500KB. In return for a valid payment, the SPs continue to provide the service they agreed on in the pricing contract. If the user does not receive these services he or she can terminate the call by not releasing any more hashes. The total call cost per unit, or per data unit transmitted, is the sum of each SP's tariff rate in the pricing contract.

Releasing payments throughout a service is shown in Figure 6. For example, every 10 seconds, the user releases a payment hash, in this case starting with P1 from a new payment chain. The HNO verifies that the payment is valid by performing one hash function on it to obtain the previous payment hash, which in this case is the starting hash P_0. The HNO forwards the payment hash and his or her own endorsement hash to the other SPs. Each SP independently verifies both the payment hash and the endorsement hash. Since the hash function is one-way, payment hashes cannot be forged, and knowledge of the payment hash is the proof of payment.

Figure 6. Mobile pays all SPs with same payment hash

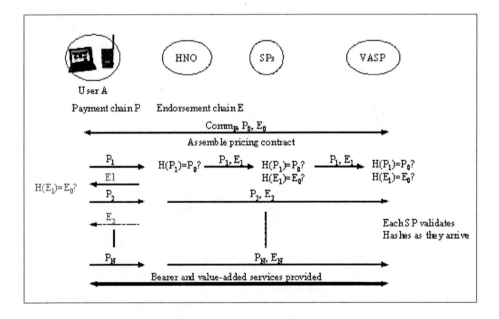

Redeeming Payment Hashes

At the end of the day, each SP will redeem the highest spent payment hash from the visit with their preferred broker. The broker will only accept a payment hash from an identified SP if a corresponding endorsement hash and pricing contract accompany it. The broker knows how much to pay each SP from the contents of the pricing contract.

Most micro-payment and electronic cash schemes require that a payee redeem payment tokens directly from the issuer, so as to prevent double spending. In a multi-party payment, the requirement that all payees must go directly to the issuing broker is a serious restriction. For geographically dispersed SPs this will introduce a communication overhead, even when performed off-line. To address this limitation the scheme proposes a network of brokers, where a payment chain may be redeemed at any broker agreed upon at the time of visit setup. When the pricing contract is constructed, each SP fixes the redeeming broker, normally a local broker, with whom he or she is going to redeem the payment chain:

{SP1: BrokerA, SP2: BrokerB, ... SPN: BrokerX}

No other brokers can now redeem the part of the chain spent during the call, and hence double redeeming is prevented.

Security Analysis

In this section we will demonstrate the security of the proposed scheme.

Outside Attacker Fraud

An attacker cannot obtain value during a payment chain purchase from a broker, cannot redeem value from a paid call, cannot impersonate a value holder to obtain free service and cannot impersonate a valid SP during a call.

The contents of the purchase request cannot be seen or altered as it is encrypted with the public key of the broker. The purchase response is the broker-signed payment commitment containing the anchor of the chain and can be obtained by an eavesdropper. Without knowledge of chain hashes, the commitment value cannot be spent. The secret chain values never leave the user until they are spent. An attacker can prevent messages reaching their destination, but a reliable transport protocol with re-transmission will handle this to a certain degree. Redeeming SPs must authenticate themselves, using a signature, to their chosen broker. Therefore, while an eavesdropper can obtain spent payment and endorsement hashes, they cannot be redeemed without breaking the authentication mechanism used with the broker. The pricing contract and endorsement hashes make payment hashes vendor-specific.

User Fraud

A user cannot spend more than the total value of a payment chain and double spend payment hashes. Payment hashes must be spent through the HNO and a chargeable service cannot be obtained for free.

The total value of the payment chain is specified in the broker-signed payment commitment. The signature prevents this value being altered. Without a valid endorsement hash matching a specific payment hash, the payment hash cannot be redeemed. If an already spent payment hash is sent to the HNO, he will detect it and can prevent double spending payment hashes. Since the user cannot double spend or overspend them, the only way to obtain services is by releasing valid payment hashes.

SP Fraud

An SP cannot obtain more value than paid by a user and cannot obtain value belonging to another SP. To increase the value per token requires the pricing contract to be altered, which is not possible without forging signatures. To obtain extra hashes requires the co-operation of both the user, for the payment, and the HNO for the endorsement. The HNO will not aid SP cheating as the HNO becomes liable for losses.

HNO Fraud

The broker records the total amount redeemed against a payment chain. When more than the total value is spent, it will be detected by the broker when redeemed. The redeemed pricing contracts are proof of the overspending, and show exactly how much each party redeemed. The overspending fraud occurred with the HNO's consent, since earlier claims showed that fraud by any entities other than the HNO was not possible. The HNO can cheat in a number of ways. User payment hashes can be obtained in a normal call with a valid pricing contract, and can then be double spent by the HNO. The worst the HNO can do is redeem the total chain value for itself, and use the chain to provide many false payments to any number of SPs. However, in each case the fraud will be detected as having been committed by the HNO and can be proved by using the HNO signatures and endorsement hashes. In such cases HNO privileges and certificates can be revoked and legal actions taken.

Broker Fraud

The amount owed to each SP by the broker can be proved to an independent third party. SPs redeem value from the broker with the pricing contract and the highest payment and endorsement hashes received. The value of each hash to the SP is stated in the contract. Therefore, any party can verify the amount owed to a specific SP. Broker payment to an SP will be an auditable business-to-business electronic payment.

Denial-of-Service Attacks

Requiring proof of payment chain ownership limits the effect of a denial-of-service attack. By invalidating a single payment hash an attacker cannot prevent the remainder of a payment chain being spent.

We showed that an unspent payment hash should accompany each new call request. The purpose of this was to prevent an attacker stealing a single token. In fact, this requirement also efficiently limits the effect of a denial-of-service attack on call setup. The payment hash in the call request proves the presence of the chain owner before the call is set up. Between calls there is always at least one payment hash used for authentication rather than payment. Unless a valid unspent token is presented, no new pricing contract is assembled. However, when the user later attempts a new call, this attack will be discovered before releasing any more tokens. Therefore, we have limited the denial-of-service attack on call setup to a single bogus contract assembly instead of possibly infinite contracts. An attack using invalid tokens will never get past the HNO. This is a vast efficiency improvement over allowing all unauthenticated call requests to assemble a fully signed contract.

Limited Anonymity

User anonymity to the broker depends on the macro-payment used. No identity information needs to be included in a payment commitment, which allows the user to be anonymous to the HNO, all SPs, and eavesdroppers.

Conclusion and Further Works

We briefly discuss some macro-payment systems and explain why they are not suitable for micro-payment. Related works on micro-payment schemes are also discussed. We emphasize the hash chain notion and evaluate several micro-payment schemes based on hash chain simply. While PayWord scheme, NetPay scheme, and Millicent scheme are all famous micro-payment schemes, they are not directly suitable for multi-party micro-payment for m-commerce. By comparing the performance of the different schemes, we know how certain micro-payment techniques perform, and which knowledge is later used in the design of multi-party micro-payment scheme for m-commerce. Finally, we introduce a new micro-payment system that is able to apply to multi-party for mobile commerce. The details of the protocol are presented and its operation in a typical multi-party mobile commerce environment is explained. The multi-party micro-payment scheme allows a roaming mobile user to pay every party involved in providing mobile communication as services are used.

In the future, a number of avenues are possible to continue the research. Firstly, we will consider more complex patterns by allowing one consumer to deploy services from several providers within a single transaction. This is applied to a concrete scenario, the interaction between customers and merchants in electronic purchases. Secondly, we will consider the heterogeneity of the electronic purchase, by allowing different existing protocols for micro-payment to be merged incrementally, as the user performs a distributed purchase on the Internet. Besides the technique based on hash chain, we will develop a new multi-party micro-payment scheme for m-commerce based on some other micro-payment techniques.

References

Ahuja, V. (1996). *Secure commerce of the Internet.* Academic Press.

Bellare, M. et al. (1995). iKP – a family of secure electronic payment protocols. *Proceedings of the 1st USENIX Workshop on Electronic Commerce* (pp. 89-106,).New York.

Boly, J.P. et al. (1994). The ESPRIT project CAFÉ-high security digital payment system. *Computer Security-ESOLICS'94, 875.*

Dai, X., & Lo, B. (1999). Netpay – An efficient protocol for micropayments on the WWW. *Proceedings of the 5th Australian World Wide Web Conference (AusWeb'99),* Southern Cross University, Lismore, Australia.

Doggest, J. (1995). Electronic check project. *Financial Services Technology Consortium (FSTC). http://macke.wiwi.hu-berlin/IMI/micropayments.html*

Ferreira, L.C., & Dahab, R. (1998). A scheme for analyzing electronic payment system. *14th Computer Security Applications Conference* (pp. 137-146).

Hauser, R., Steiner, M., & Waidner, M. (1996). Micro-payments based on iKP. *Proc. of the 14th Worldwide Congress on Computer and Communications Security Protection* (pp. 67-82).

Hwang, M.S., Lin, I.C., & Li, L.H. (2001). A simple micro-payment scheme. *The Journal of System and Software, 55,* 221-229

Lamport, L. (1981, November). Password authentication with insecure communication. *Communications of the ACM, 24*(11), 770-72.

Lee, M., & Kim, K. (2002). A micro-payment system for multiple-shopping. *The 2002 Symposium on Cryptography and Information Security Shirahama,* Japan.

Manasse, M. (1995). The Millicent protocols for electronic commerce. *Proceedings of the 1st USENIX Workshop on Electronic Commerce* (pp. 117-23). New York.

MasterCard & Visa. (1997). *Secure Electronic Transaction (SET) Specification Book 1: Business Decryption.*

Neumann, C., & Medvinsky, G. (1995). Requirements for network payment-the NetCheque perspective. *IEEE Compcon.*

Pederson, T. (1996). Electronic payments of small amounts. *Proceedings of the 4th Security Protocols International Workshop (Security Protocols), Lecture Notes in Computer Science* (vol. 1189, pp. 59-68). Berlin: Springer-Verlag.

Peirce, M. (2000). Multi-party electronic payments for mobile communications. A thesis submitted for the degree of Doctor of Philosophy in Computer Science University of Dublin, Trinity College Department of Computer Science.

Rivest, R., & Shamir, A. (1996). PayWord and MicroMint: Two simple micropayment schemes. *Proceedings of the 4th Security Protocols International Workshop (Security Protocols), Lecture Notes in Computer Science* (vol. 1189, pp. 69-87). Berlin: Springer-Verlag.

Sirbu, M., & Tygar, J.D. (1995). NetBill: An Internet commerce system optimized for network delivered services. *IEEE Personal Communications, 2*(4), 34-39.

Stern, J., & Vaudenay, S. (1997). SVP: A flexible micropayment scheme. *Financial Cryptography '97 Proceedings, Lecture Notes in Computer Science* (vol. 1318, pp. 161-171). Berlin: Springer-Verlag.

Wayner, P. (1994). Digital cash. *Byte, 19*(10), 126.

Zhu, J.M., & Ma, J.F. (2002a). An efficient micro-payment scheme for electronic commerce. *Journal of Xidian University*.

Zhu, J.M., & Ma, J.F. (2002). The Internet key exchange protocol in IP security. *The 7th International Symposium on Future Software Technology,* Wuhan, China.

Chapter XI

SeMoPS:
A Global Secure Mobile Payment Service

Stamatis Karnouskos, Fraunhofer Institute FOKUS, Germany

András Vilmos, SafePay Systems Ltd., Hungary

Antonis Ramfos, Instrasoft International, Greece

Balázs Csik, ProfiTrade 90 Ltd., Hungary

Petra Hoepner, Fraunhofer Institute FOKUS, Germany

Abstract

Many experts consider that efficient and effective mobile payment solutions will empower existing e- and m-commerce efforts and unleash the true potential of mobile business. Recently, different mobile payment approaches appear to the market addressing particular needs, but up to now no global mobile payment solution exists. SEMOPS is a secure mobile payment service with an innovative technology and business concept that aims to fully address the challenges the mobile payment domain poses and become a global mobile payment service. We present here a detailed description of the approach, its implementation, and features that diversify it from other systems. We discuss on its business model and try to predict its future impact. The aim is to provide an insight of a new mobile payment service and discuss implementation decisions and scenarios.

Introduction

The increasingly popular ownership of mobile personal, programmable communication devices worldwide promises an extended use of them in the purchase of goods and services in the years to come (Mobey Forum, 2003). Security in payment transactions and user convenience are the two main motivations for using mobile devices for payments. Authorisation in existing electronic payment systems, including ATM and credit/debit card transactions as well as online payments through a PC, is based on account-holder authentication. Account-holder authentication, however, can fail in multiple ways, of which the most usual is the case of the compromise of the user's computer, which is, typically, protected with minimal security mechanisms and processes. Moreover, existing payment networks do not always distinguish among user fraud, compromise of the user's computer, or compromise of the bank's computer. For example, in most countries, if the user claims not to have authorised a credit card transaction, the transaction has to be cancelled and the bank cannot prove that the user is not cheating. In such cases, responsibility is not necessarily allocated fairly, and non-corrupted, innocent parties may find themselves responsible for somebody else's fraudulent activity or security breach. The lack of a technical solution for preventing and resolving fraud creates substantial risk and expense for users, merchants and banks alike.

It is now well understood that a secure electronic payment transaction can only be ensured through a device that offers its own I/O interface to the user, so that the initiator of the payment transaction is clearly identifiable (Pfitzmann, Pfitzmann, Schunter & Waidner, 1999). Mobile personal devices provide a technical solution for personalised I/O interface to payment transactions since it can be safely assumed that the transaction initiator is in the majority of the cases also the owner of the mobile device. Security in payment transactions through a mobile device, therefore, is ensured by the authentication mechanisms of existing mobile devices, as a way to prevent call theft. Moreover, additional built-in mechanisms to ensure secure transaction authorisation and execution are relatively easy and inexpensive to be incorporated by device manufacturers. Therefore, payment through mobile devices benefits merchants and banks by supporting transactions where most fraud is prevented and responsibility for the remaining fraud is fairly allocated. As far as the end customer is concerned, the value of secure transactions far outweighs their possible cost.

Convenience is the other reason why people are expected to use mobile personal devices for payments. Convenience can result from people using their mobile personal device when paying for goods and services, while on foot, in cars, planes, or trains, and when authorising payment transactions at remote servers of banks, brokerages, and merchants. Payments through mobile devices will enable validation of the customer's consent to the transaction during online, by telephone or by post purchases, since the merchant and the customer are at separate locations and the merchant cannot get the customer to sign in order to authorise the payment. In addition, payment through mobile devices will enable the secured purchase of content and services delivered via the network, as well as person-to-person payments and money transfer.

SEMOPS is a secure mobile payment service with an innovative technology and business concept (Karnouskos, Vilmos, Hoepner, Ramfos & Venetakis, 2003) that aims to fully address the challenges the mobile payment domain poses, and become a global mobile payment service (Vilmos & Karnouskos, 2003). We present in the rest of the chapter a detailed description of the approach, its implementation, and features that distinguish it from other systems and make its future promising.

Mobile Payment Solutions

A mobile payment solution can be used in multiple applications and scenarios. The simplest scenario involves only the user, the device and a single payment processor, such as a mobile operator, bank, broker or an insurance company. The user identifies himself to the mobile device through secure identification mechanisms, including physical possession and password or even via biometric methods; the device then authorises the transaction to the payment processor for money transfer. More complex transactions involve at least one additional party, the merchant. In this case, the merchant may be affiliated with a different payment processor; therefore the two payment processors must be able to interoperate.

Most of the existing mobile payment solutions, such as NewGenPay (*www.newgenpay.com*) and m-pay (*www.m-pay.com*), assume that a mobile payment service is offered to the customers of a particular mobile network operator (MNO), as shown in Figure 1. These payment solutions allow customers of a particular mobile operator to perform payment transactions with merchants who are contracted by the same mobile operator (the payment processor, in this instance). In these payment

Figure 1. Existing m-payment solutions

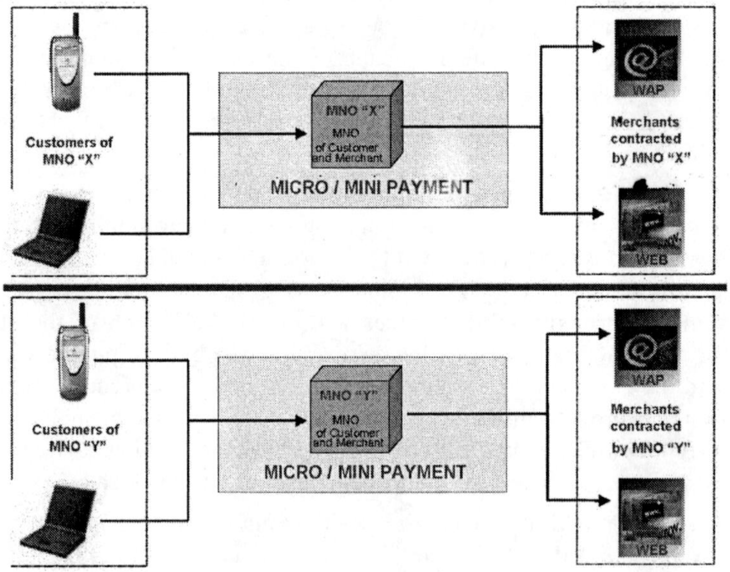

solutions, no crossover to other operators is foreseen, no direct involvement of trusted organisations, such as banks, takes place and, hence, payment transactions are limited to micro-payment transactions only, typically under $2. Although existing payment solutions have provided the critical mass for the adoption of mobile commerce, they offer limited transaction potential and limited accelerator effect to mobile commerce (Henkel, 2001).

In this chapter we present a secure mobile payment service (SEMOPS, 2003), a mobile payment solution that is capable of supporting micro, mini (e.g., between $2 and $20), as well as macro payment (e.g., over $20) transactions. It is a universal solution, being able to function in any channel, including mobile, Internet and POS; it can support any transaction type, including P2P, B2C, B2B and P2M (person to machine), with a domestic and/or international geographic coverage. As shown in Figure 2, SEMOPS enables the realisation of a mobile payment network that combines different payment processors, and, hence, it can realise a payment service with huge transaction potential, and lower user fees and large turnover (Kreyer, Pousttchi & Turowski, 2002).

As shown in Figure 2, the SEMOPS payment solution allows both mobile operators and banks to become payment processors in a mobile payment service. There can be different combinations, depending on whether the user uses his bank or MNO account and whether the merchant accepts the payment on his bank or MNO account. Furthermore, the SEMOPS model is versatile and any trusted service provider that can offer the customer an account (e.g., credit card, financial service provider) can also easily take the role of the SEMOPS payment processor.

Figure 2. SEMOPS m-payment solution

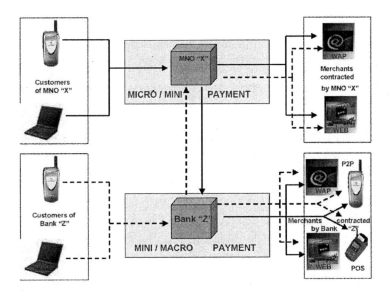

SEMOPS Transaction Architecture and Flow

As in every payment system, SEMOPS is capable of transferring funds from the customer to the merchant, or, in more general terms, from the payer to the payee. Typically, this transfer is realised via a payment processor, such as a bank or a mobile operator. The SEMOPS payment solution, however, is novel in that it enables cooperation between different payment processors, for example, cooperation between banks and mobile operators, thereby achieving a global, secure, real-time, user-friendly and profitable mobile payment service that can be used in both electronic and mobile commerce transactions.

SEMOPS supports both remote and proximity transactions. In remote transactions, which are conducted independent of the user location such as prepaid top-up services, delivery of digital services, mTickets, digital cash, peer-to-peer payments and so forth, payments may be conducted via several communication channels that include SMS, USSD, WAP push and Instant Messaging, and manual input. In case of proximity transactions, however, where both payer and payee are at the same physical location, the payer's mobile device may communicate directly, (e.g., via Bluetooth, IrDA, RF, NFC) with a POS/ATM such as payments at unattended machines, mParking, payments at traditional POS, or money withdrawal from a bank's ATM. If the technical capabilities of the involved devices do not cater for direct communication, the communication channels supported for remote payments can be used instead. Note that the payers can authorise payments by both mobile devices and Web browsers, whereas payees can participate with any sale outlet, including WAP, POS, vending machines, or Web. Moreover, SEMOPS can support mobile person-to-person (P2P) transactions with the same convenience as any other payment transaction.

In SEMOPS, payment requests are completed in real time. However, in cases where the payee is not connected to its payment processor, the payment is still going to be credited and the payee will be notified at some later time (offline payments).

The transaction flow, which is completely controlled by the payer, follows a simple credit push model. A typical SEMOPS transaction flow for a prompt payment from a customer to a merchant is discussed in the following (see Figure 3):

- The merchant (in general, any POS/VirtualPOS) provides to the customer the necessary transaction details (e.g., via IrDA, Bluetooth or even Instant Messaging) (Step 1). These data include certain static and dynamic elements that identify the merchant and the individual transaction. During the whole payment process, the customer does not identify himself to the merchant, nor does he provide any information about himself, his bank, or any other sensitive data.

- The customer receives the transaction data from the merchant (Step 2). A standard format payment request is prepared to be sent to the selected payment processor who is the trusted partner of the customer – either his bank or his mobile network

Figure 3. SEMOPS transaction architecture

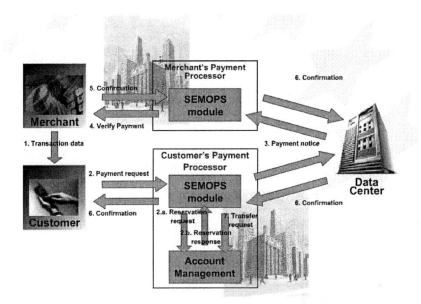

operator. When the payment request is ready for transfer, the customer checks its content, authorises it (via PIN and/or PKI), and sends the payment request to the selected payment processor.

- The customer's payment processor receives the payment request, identifies the customer and processes the payment request (Step 3). Processing includes the verification of the availability of the necessary funds, and reservation of the required amount. When the processing is completed a payment notice is prepared by the payment processor and is forwarded to the Data Center of the SEMOPS service. The Data Center identifies the addressee bank of the payment notice and forwards the message to the merchant's trusted payment processor, who again can be either its bank or mobile operator. The Data Center handles the message delivery among the payment processors. We assume that at least one Data Center per country will exist, and in case of an international transaction a second Data Center is also involved, namely the local Data Center of the foreign merchant's country. The two Data Centers cooperate and the transaction is routed accordingly.

- The merchant's payment processor receives the payment notice and identifies the merchant. The payment processor advises the merchant in real time about the payment by forwarding the payment notice (Step 4). The merchant has the chance to control the content of the payment notice and can decide whether to approve or reject the transaction. By confirming the transaction to its payment processor, (Step 5), a confirmation is forwarded to the customer's payment processor, via the Data Center (Step 6).

- When customer's payment processor receives the positive confirmation, it initiates a regular bank transfer to merchant's bank. This transfer is based on the regular well-established inter-banking procedures. In case of successful money transfer, the merchant's bank sends a notification to the merchant, and the customer's payment processor sends a notification to the customer. If for whatever reason the merchant rejects the transaction, the customer's payment processor releases the funds it has reserved for the purchase.

SEMOPS Front-End Infrastructure

Unlike the PC environment, the mobile environment presents the challenge of supporting multiple data channels and platforms. Mobile communications are characterised by the variety of data technologies, device capabilities, and standards. Shopping and payment may take place on separate channels. For example, a customer may shop via WAP or receive an actionable alert, and carry out the payment over SMS, USSD, raw GPRS or WAP to the payment processor. Therefore, in defining mobile solutions, it is important to recognise that multiple technologies coexist, and will continue to do so.

As a result, the SEMOPS infrastructure became very colourful from mobile technology point of view and combines all viable implementation possibilities. It utilizes SIM Toolkit (STK), Java phones (J2ME) and embedded operating systems (OS) as the application executing environment and various transmission technologies:

Figure 4. Base technologies of front-end modules

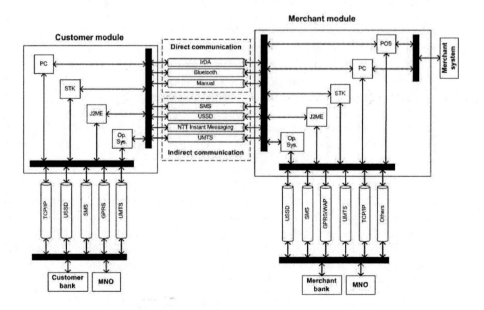

- *SIM Application Toolkit*: The SIM Application Toolkit (SIMToolkit or STK) defines the necessary set of commands and procedures required building the basic SIM Card – Mobile Equipment interface for mobile equipment independent applications running on the SIM card. The standard has broadened from data download and the proactive SIM approach to a powerful tool-set for several types of applications enabling network operators to develop competitive and differentiated applications.

- *Java 2 Micro Edition*: The Java 2 Micro Edition (J2ME) is a popular standard among major handset manufacturers. Most handset manufacturers have already launched at least one pilot mobile with J2ME capability. The mobile phones are mainly supporting the MIDP 1.0 (JSR-037) and the CLDC 1.0 (JSR-030) Java recommendation. MIDP supports the Java Sandbox Model very much like the applets that run in Web browsers. In this context each MIDlet runs in its own environment and cannot affect other MIDlets. MIDP 1.0 is capable to start HTTP connection to a server. The nature of the http connection is that the MIDP client sends GET and POST commends to get info from the server application. This means server push is not available in MIDP 1.0 (only with some tricky workarounds). MIDP 2.0 implements server push.

- *Embedded Operating System*: Most of the popular mobile phones and smartphones are using proprietary OSs today. SEMOPS focuses also on the commonly used mobile phone and PDA OSs that support Java. To our opinion only a small set of the high-end mobile phones and smartphones will use rich-feature java-enabled OSs in the next years, but in the long term this type of handset is expected to proliferate and dominate the markets.

Customer and Merchant Modules

The main modules in the SEMOPS solution are the front-end modules, namely, the customer and the merchant modules. These are designed to have extended functionality, security, openness, usability and a versatile application-executing environment. The back-end modules comprise of transaction management applications that reside in the payment processors' premises and interact with their accounting systems, as well as the Data Centre modules, which are responsible for the communication and reconciliation of transactions between involved payment processors. As shown in Figure 4, the SEMOPS front-end modules are very versatile from the mobile technology point of view and combine all viable implementation possibilities in user-process and client technologies.

- *The Customer Module*: It has two basic forms, the mobile and the Internet one. A variety of implementations exists in the mobile form, namely, a SIM toolkit (STK) based, a Java based and an operating system (OS) based module. The customer module assists the customer to carry out a payment transaction using the service. The module can be downloaded and updated over the air or from the Internet, thus avoiding the usual hassle one has to go through when subscribing for a service. The actual payment functions include communication with the merchant's systems, preparation of payment request, communication with the selected payment processor, administration of the transaction details, and notification of the user about a transaction status.

- *The Merchant Module*: It is the bridge between the payee's sales outlet and the payer, and also between the payee and the payee's payment processor. For this reason, the merchant modules include an Internet and a POS version, along with multiple mobile versions (STK, Java, OS). The merchant module receives the necessary transaction information from the merchant's sale system and transfers it to the customer. An important function of the merchant module is the approval of the transaction. The merchant's payment processor advises the merchant about the payment and the module either approves or rejects the transaction automatically based on the information it has. The merchant module features also extensive administrative functions, for example report generation, refund initiation and so forth.

Security Considerations

SEMOPS built up its security framework at the payment processors with the following considerations:

- Banks do not allow encrypted information into the intranet; therefore decryption must be done in the Demilitarised Zone (DMZ).

- Banks usually have their own authentication system; therefore SEMOPS must co-operate with existing infrastructures.

- SEMOPS uses heterogeneous channels, including more rare ones, like USSD; therefore SSL cannot be always used as encrypted channel.

- Different country regulations prohibit the usage of the same keys for encryption and signing; therefore SEMOPS must support multiple key pairs.

Based on these limitations, SEMOPS utilizes the security approach depicted in Figure 5. The termination of the physical channel and message decryption is done in the DMZ. The decrypted information reaches the SEMOPS Bank Module (residing on the Intranet of the bank) through the bank's standard authentication system, which is already used for applications, like home banking. Currently SEMOPS uses RSA encrypted XML with 3DES message keys, and also uses RSA digital signatures on the messages, but with a different key pair. The hardware security modules execute all the cryptographic operations in the system, resulting in the split security operations as depicted in Figure 6.

SEMOPS uses a dual authentication method for identity control. Depending on the payment processor's requirement it is able to use digital signatures or encrypted passphrase authentication. The payment processor can decide which authentication method to use, and in case of using digital signatures the recipient is sure that:

- The original data was not altered (data integrity);
- The message could only have been signed by the holder of that private key (entity authentication); and

Figure 5. Security infrastructure at payment processors

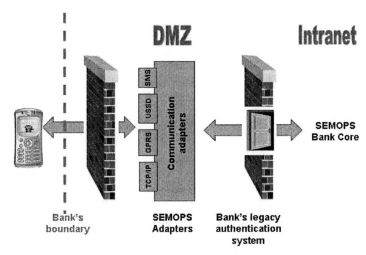

Figure 6. Split security operations of SEMOPS

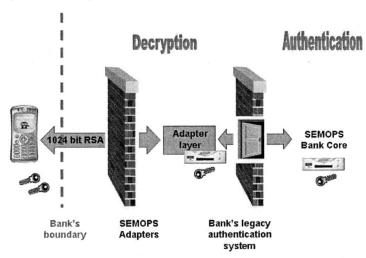

Therefore, the uniqueness of the digital signature and the underlying hash value coupled with the strength of the public key certificate provides an acceptable level of assurance to authenticate the sender and to verify that the sender was the originator of the signed data.

With the basic considerations above, SEMOPS provides a strong end-to-end encryption for transferred data and allows the usage of different authentication techniques embedded into this encryption. This seems a viable solution, but in live environments it must be adapted to the usual practices of banks, which insist on not allowing anybody else to authenticate their users, as this task has to remain within the banks' legacy procedures.

Applications and Business Scenarios

The SEMOPS solution is a universal solution that allows payment for goods and services in practically any kind of commercial situation. As shown in Figure 7, SEMOPS is a global payment service that can be a viable cash substitute for various types of e/m-commerce transactions. The *customer* (payer) and the *merchant* (payee) exchange transaction data and then the fund transfer is performed by the corresponding trusted payment processor, that is, the *customer's* and *merchant's banks,* respectively. The Data Centre simply routes the information flow between the actors and is responsible for the reconciliation of the transactions.

To understand the basic philosophy behind the operation one has to see that all transactions, irrespective of the channel, value, commercial situation and terms, are using the very same infrastructure, the same solutions and processes, and are settled and protected by one service. This uniformity allows unparalleled efficiency. The specifics of the revenue and cost side result in favourable commercial terms for the users and in high-level profitability for the operating actors.

In the following, we examine how SEMOPS operates in certain situations:

- Purchase of mobile content
- In-band transaction
- POS payment: P2M
- P2P payment
- EBPP and
- Internet payment: B2C, B2B, Auction.

Purchase of Mobile Content

Digital content will have one of the largest shares of revenue generated in mobile commerce. Important elements of this category may be ring tones, logos, games, music

Figure 7. Overview of SEMOPS (bank-based model)

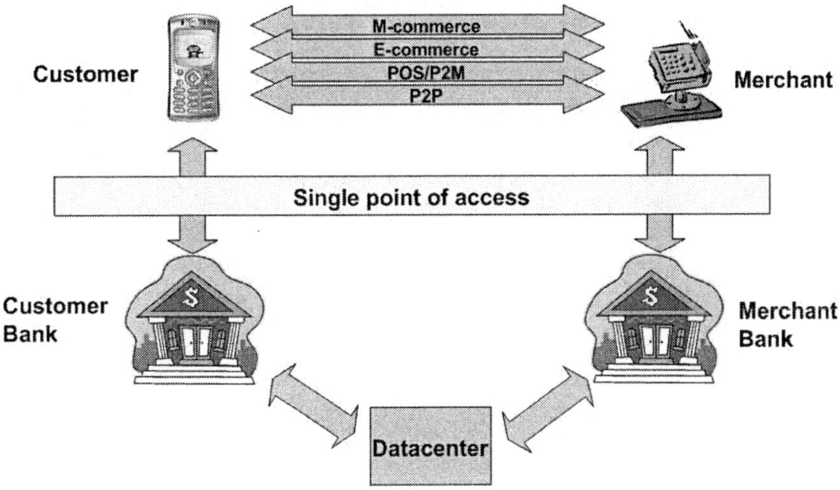

and videos, information, online gambling, and adult content. A customer browses the Web using his mobile handset and wishes to buy digital content. The customer selects the product, and pushes the payment button on the site. Having initiated the payment, the customer receives the payment information onto the handset he has used for the browsing.

Knowing that the value of digital content is quite low, the customers have the option to pay from their bank account or from the prepaid/post-paid account with their mobile operator. Having decided which account to use, the customer selects his payment processor of choice from a menu in the handset (there is always one default payment processor to accelerate the transaction flow) and prepares the payment request. After validating the transaction, for example with a PIN, the payment request is sent to the payment processor. If the transaction is approved by the merchant, then in a matter of seconds a confirmation is received by the customer that also includes a link where the content can be accessed.

In-Band Purchases

The process of making in-band payment transactions is quite similar from a technical point of view to the digital content scenario, the key difference being the value and delivery of the goods and services. In-band purchases also include widely varying products and services and the special features of these need to be taken into account. Key applications may be parking payments, various kinds of ticket purchases and payments made to online stores through a mobile device. Purchase can be made through browsing, locating the product and selecting payment as in the case of buying digital content.

Figure 8. In-band purchases in SEMOPS

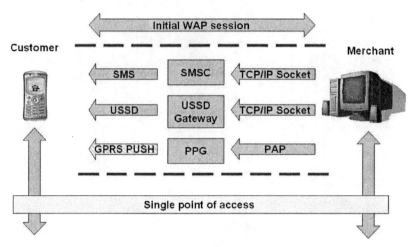

In case of payments for parking, a more convenient solution is preferred as this will usually be a repeated transaction. The customer can store details of the parking company in a template, and also the license plate of his/her car. By just sending the payment request to the payment processor the parking company is advised of the payment, and grants a parking permit for the time that the customer paid. In the confirmation received from the payment processor, the customer is also advised about the time period he has paid for. When the controller finds a car without a valid ticket, he first communicates with the central database and he may be advised that the specific car has paid for parking through a mobile device. An additional advantage of this solution is that, should the driver need to stay longer than originally expected, he can extend the validity of the permit even from a remote location, without the need to go to the car or to the parking meter.

The top up of mobile pre-paid accounts could also be considered as one type of in-band transaction. In this case the customer is practically buying airtime from the mobile operator by putting money onto the prepaid account. The customer prepares a payment request and requests from its bank, its payment processor, to send money to the MNO, the merchant, in this case. As soon as the payment information arrives to the MNO, the top up can take place and calls can be placed again. If the MNO had a service to actively inform the customers that their pre-paid balance was running low, the mobile payment could ensure continuous availability of the pre-paid phone service.

P2P Payment

Today, there is no real widely adopted solution for mobile person-to-person payments in the same currency, not to mention international transactions. Using the SEMOPS solution, payment can be made to anyone having a mobile handset in a matter of seconds and the money sent can also be available for use immediately.

Figure 9. P2P payment in SEMOPS

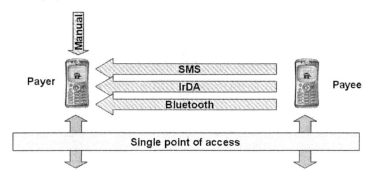

There are three basic scenarios in P2P payments:

- If the two parties are in the proximity of each other, the payee's device sends the transaction data over to the payer's handset using either IrDA or Bluetooth communication.

- If the two parties are not in the position of using direct link, the payee can send the necessary info over the air (e.g., SMS or instant messaging) to the other person.

- In certain cases, the payer initiates a transfer while the payee may not even be aware of the fact that he is going to receive money. In this case, the payer can manually input all necessary information into the handset and can start the payment process without advising the payee in advance.

Depending on the transaction value, the payer in all three cases has the option to select either one of its banks or his MNO for processing the payment. The payment processor performs the payment and the beneficiary's payment processor confirms the transaction if the payee really exists. The payee will also receive the payment notice on his mobile handset in real time, or will be notified when he turns his mobile on, if he was offline at that moment.

Point of Sale (POS) Payments

POS payments are well known for purchases made in stores where credit cards are accepted. The mobile POS version supported by the SEMOPS service is slightly different from the traditional solution. This difference, however, makes the payment considerably more secure and trusted. In the case of a SEMOPS POS transaction, the POS terminal has to be modified. Today the new EMV conformant terminals can be easily extended and have also a number of SAM card slots to allow simple programming and modifications. After having made this typically minor modification, an IrDA device is plugged into the serial port of the POS, and the POS is ready to perform mobile payments.

Figure 10. POS/P2M payment in SEMOPS

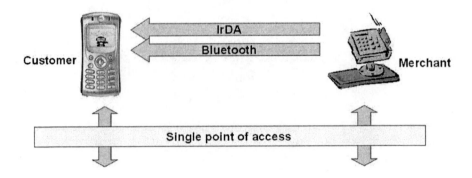

In a typical scenario, after shopping in a store, the customer goes to the cashier to pay. When the cashier finishes entering the purchased items into the merchant's system, a standard non-cash transaction is initiated. The POS receives the transaction data from the cashier either automatically or manually. At this point the customer may decide to pay using the mobile payment service. The mobile handset receives the transaction data from the POS terminal through the IrDA communication; alternatively, an SMS can also be sent to the customer's mobile if it does not have an IrDA port. Having received the necessary information, the mobile device prepares a payment request that is validated by the customer (PIN) and it is sent to the payment processor. Depending on the purchase value, the customer may decide to send this information for processing, either to his MNO or to his bank. The cashier receives the payment authorisation in the POS terminal just like in the case of traditional card transactions.

P2M (Vending Machine)

Buying from a vending machine and paying it electronically is equivalent to making a payment to an unmanned POS terminal. The only difference is the way the transaction data is forwarded to the POS terminal. In the case of a vending machine, the customer selects the product and by initiating the transaction on the vending machine the transaction data are forwarded to the handset. When the payment is performed, the vending machine receives the authorisation and provides the selected product. A similar approach is provided today by calling a premium number; however, this is product specific and not as flexible as the SEMOPS-enabled payment. The unmanned POS scenario is one that may have huge potential in future stores. Should the customer wish to avoid queuing at the cashier, he can have the purchased products valued automatically by a scanner and can make the payment without the need to communicate with the clerk at the cash register.

ATM

Even if it is assumed that a universal mobile payment solution will be used in all types of transactions, need for cash payments will still exist. Withdrawing cash from an ATM is very similar to buying a coke from a vending machine; the only difference is the type of product sold. An ATM sells cash while a vending machine sells tangible goods. The SEMOPS solution can be easily used in realising ATM withdrawals in a global base, meaning that any service user in any country at any bank can get the desired cash.

EBPP (MBPP)

Electronic Bill Presentment and Payment (EBPP) transactions with SEMOPS are placed between mobile and Internet payments. The summary of an invoice can be sent to the mobile device, whereby, if the structure of the information matches the SEMOPS required format, the customer can also pay the invoice with the regular procedure. Would, however, the customer be interested in the invoice details, he could visit a dedicated site on the Internet and perform payment online.

Internet Payments

B2B, B2C: Payments with the SEMOPS solution can also be realised on the Internet. While browsing the Web, the customer finds the desired product. After placing it into the shopping cart, the customer selects the SEMOPS payment option. The merchant e-shop provides the transaction data to the customer over the Web. The customer receives the data, and using a dedicated software application prepares a payment request on his screen. The customer authorises the payment, for example with his PIN, and sends the payment request to his bank. During the whole procedure the customer did not provide any sensitive data to the unknown Internet merchant. Through the usual SEMOPS procedure, the payment request is processed by the customer's bank.

Auction payment: A unique transaction type with increasing importance is the purchase at auction sites. The peculiarity of this type of transaction is that the customer wishes to see the product first before payment is performed, but the merchant also wants to make sure that he will receive the purchase price. The solution is the escrow service provided by the auction house to be supported by the SEMOPS payment service. In this case, a payment request contains information both about the seller and the escrow agent. The payment is processed at the customer's payment processor and the merchant receives only a conditional payment notice. The merchant will only be paid if there is no customer complaint within a limited period of time. The money in the meantime is sent to the auction house, which plays the role of the escrow agent. If there is no customer complaint, the money is forwarded automatically – without the involvement of the escrow agent – from the escrow agent's bank to the merchant's payment processor. If, however, the customer complains, payment is stopped until the escrow agent investigates the issue, and, based on its findings, the money is either refunded or paid out to the merchant.

SEMOPS Business Model

As with any other new payment solution, SEMOPS should make good economic sense for its key players. All the advantages offered to the end users, that is, the security, the convenience, and the wide range of transactions, may be in vain if there are no economic incentives for the key actors (Camponovo & Pigneur, 2002). It is also obvious that the operating actors alone cannot make a success story of the payment solution, if the users are dissatisfied either with the service, or with the usage terms (Heijden, 2002).

Actors and their Involvement and Interests

The key actors in the SEMOPS model include, as shown in Figure 11:

- *Operating actors*: International Operator (IO), Local License Holder (LLH), Data Center (DC), Risk Managers (RM) and the Local Payment Processor (LPP), which as noted before can be different entities, for example a bank, a mobile network operator (MNO) or any other service provider (OSP).

- *User actors*: Customer and the merchant (any type of real/virtual POS).

Figure 11. Business relations of the SEMOPS actors

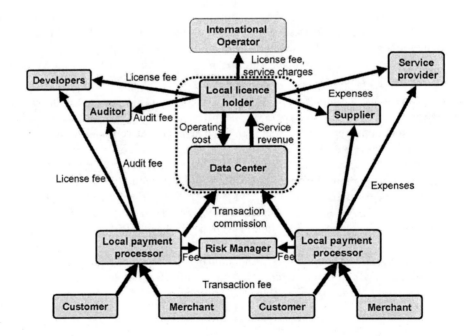

- *Additional actors*: Developers, auditors, service providers, suppliers, and so forth.

The *international operator* (IO) is the entity responsible for the coordination and development of the service on an international level. The *local license holder* (LLH) is the entity that is in charge of the local operation of the SEMOPS payment service that owns all the rights in relation to this service. The local *data center* (DC) operates the data Center module of the payment service. The *risk manager* is charging a fee to the local payment processors for the services it provides. *Local payment processors* (LPP) are entities that provide the SEMOPS service to the users. The *customers* and *merchants* are clients of LPPs. The *developers* are the software development team, providing the software modules that form the basis of the SEMOPS payment solution or its extensions.

Finally, the payment service is a complex operation that needs external services and products from a number of *service providers* and vendors, who have no affiliations with the payment service itself.

Business Concept

Primary principle of the business model of SEMOPS is that it is based on the cooperation of banks and MNOs. This situation has two consequences:

- resources can be combined, and
- net revenue has to be shared.

The business concept of SEMOPS was formed by taking into account the following considerations.

- Firstly, the banks involved in the new service already have electronic payment services, and while SEMOPS may offer increased market presence and new transaction channels, it has to be more profitable than existing services.
- The MNOs are already involved in a number of payment initiatives, or are completely disinterested in this line of business. One of the key challenges of the SEMOPS solution is to integrate micro payment services with mini and macro payments, which are typically performed via banks, into a combined payment service, a business prospect which MNOs find attractive.
- The SEMOPS service should offer increased potential for the mobile operators in terms of customer reach, product scope, and most importantly in terms of value added new revenue channels.
- Customers have the full spectrum of services and products to buy with the new payment service in a number of purchase situations and via different communica-

tion channels. This benefits the customers, but the level of this benefit differs according to each transaction type. Consequently, in certain cases purchase fees are not acceptable.

- Finally, the associated expenses keep the majority of merchants away from mobile payment schemes. Consequently, SEMOPS overall transaction costs (including set up expenses) have to be below existing levels of electronic payments, and the approach has to address as many payment procedures as possible (Kreyer et al., 2002) in order to reach the critical mass.

SEMOPS Implementation Expenses

SEMOPS has a relatively low implementation cost due to several factors.

- Firstly, the solution is fully automated and there is end-to-end electronic processing. As a result variable expenses are minimal and introductory expenses can also be well controlled through a modular and scalable implementation approach.

- The standardisation of the service processes and technology will further reduce both introductory and operating expenses.

- Installation of the new service modules is based on middleware technology, and by offering the service on a number of different operating platforms the introduction will be simple and cost efficient.

- The operation of the SEMOPS service also has a number of factors that allow optimisation of resources. The payment processing is allocated to those organisations that can perform this activity within their existing operating framework with marginal extra expenses, such as banks. To allocate micro payment to mobile operators and larger values to banks provides an operating optimum.

- Similar is the case with the data centers, whose operation, at least at the launch of the SEMOPS local services, will be performed by existing service providers. Much of the cost of operation could be incurred through communication, the settlement process and through security related solution.

- The secure process flow, the applied hardware and software solutions, the homogenous rules, regulations and processes, and the continuous audit activity will minimize the security risk and as a result reduce related expenses.

SEMOPS Revenue Generation

The potential revenue generation in SEMOPS service is based on the following considerations:

- SEMOPS customers base combines the customer base of participating banks and mobile operators.

- SEMOPS combines different transaction channels, that is, mobile (in-band), Internet, traditional (POS, P2M).

- SEMOPS combines different transaction types, that is, C2B, B2B, and P2P.

- SEMOPS combines different payment values, that is, micro, mini and macro payments.

- SEMOPS offers large geographical coverage, that is, domestic and cross border.

Figure 12 depicts the major revenue streams for the key operating actors, that is, the mobile operators and the banks. It contains only the service related revenue sources and does not include revenue streams for the associated parties. Those revenues will have to be derived from these channels. Figure 12 contains those potential revenue streams that are uniquely associated with SEMOPS. For this reason, the normal communication revenues that are associated with the use of the telecommunication infrastructure in any mobile communication activity are not shown.

Figure 12. SEMOPS revenue streams

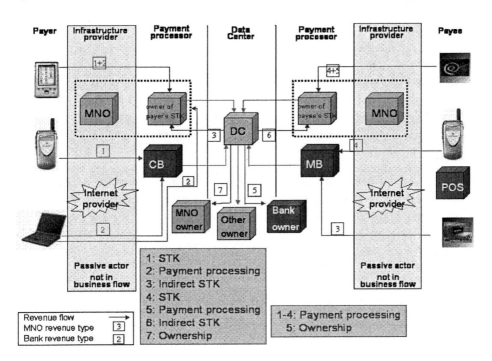

Let us note, once more, that a third party service provider (e.g., credit card companies) can easily slip into the role of banks in the SEMOPS model, and, therefore, benefit from the revenue streams mentioned previously.

Evaluation of the SEMOPS Approach

SEMOPS was designed and developed so that it can operate in commercial electronic channel on Internet and mobile infrastructure. The key features of the SEMOPS payment solution, which constitute the main differences from existing payment services, include:

- *Security, Trust and Privacy*: With existing electronic payment services, the customer provides his personal information to a merchant or to other third-party service providers without controlling the subsequent use of this information. It is of no surprise that many people avoid making electronic payments due to the imposed lack of privacy. In SEMOPS, the customer communicates only with his trusted partners, that is, his own bank or mobile network operator, and he does not provide private information either to the merchant or to any third-party operator. This prevents possible misuse of the customer's sensitive information, and the transaction cannot be repeated by anyone else, at any other time. Furthermore, SEMOPS allows the customer to retain his anonymity against the merchant, if he wishes so. In this way, anonymous payments are possible, which can be a real substitute for cash. Moreover, due to the credit push concept adopted in SEMOPS, the customer is the driver of the payment process. Nothing can happen that the customer would not approve of or agree with. The customer personally approves all transactions and sensitive personal information is not stored in the system. Transaction details are only captured at one's own payment processor.

  Furthermore, the money received or spent via the SEMOPS solution is moved always from the user's account; therefore there is no need to "preload" any money to use the service, and the money will not get lost if the user loses his device, as in e/m-wallets approaches. Trust and security is ensured on the merchant's side, as well. Although the merchant may not know who the actual buyer is, his trusted payment processor guarantees the payment to him. The merchant really does not care from whom the money is coming, but he needs a guarantee that he will be paid for a certain transaction. The SEMOPS service ensures this in real time, and as such, increases the trust in the system. Finally, SEMOPS has several security services in place in order to make the service as secure as possible, from the technology point of view. SEMOPS provides a strong end-to-end encryption for transferred data and allows the usage of efficient authentication techniques embedded into this encryption. SEMOPS also takes advantage of the "social security feeling" and existing years-long trust relationships between customer/merchant and their respective payment processors, for example, bank or MNO. There is a feeling of trust in the SEMOPS system that can substantially contribute in the rapid expansion of the service.

- *Speed*: There are many services that consider themselves electronic payment solutions; however, the speed they perform the transactions, not to mention the settlement of the transactions, is slow and inadequate even for traditional purposes. SEMOPS is different from this point of view, as the approval of the transaction is performed within seconds and in certain circumstances even the actual money is available for use immediately for the beneficiary. This speed allows the introduction of such new transaction types like P2P payments, where the beneficiary can spend the money received right away.

- *User friendliness*: Existing e-payment solutions are either cumbersome, slow, or are specifically tailored for a limited clientele, on the customer or merchant side. If someone needs to type all his payment details, and if this typing needs to happen on a handset with 12 keys, chances are that the person will think twice whether to perform the transaction. SEMOPS is very much user centered. All user-specific information can be stored locally either on one's handset or in the PC and the information stored is not sensitive. Payment is performed from a special menu that is identical both on the mobile handsets and on the PC, to ensure a homogeneous user experience. The latter is further enhanced through the fact that all different payment types supported by SEMOPS follow the same pattern and same procedure, to increase the comfort of the customers. As menus are assisting the users, the actual typing is reduced to a minimum, namely, to menu selection and the input of a PIN.

  As mentioned before, transactions can roam many devices; therefore it is possible to initiate the transaction on one device and continue it on a different one, for example, enter the transactions on one's PC and then simply activate them via one's mobile (after synchronizing with the bank). To assist conflict solving between customers and merchants a special refund function is also part of the SEMOPS service, built into the same menu that is used for payment purposes.

  In a broader sense, user friendliness also includes such aspects as ease of registration to the service, access to the service, scope of use of the service, internationalism and so forth. Although registration policy depends on the individual payment processors, theoretically electronic registration is possible, and one can start to use the service without the need to visit any branch office, or meet any customer service agent. The service is offered to the public primarily by banks and mobile operators. This concept means that not only a handful of selected ones could enjoy the benefits of SEMOPS, but it can be made available online to a wide group of people – something very interesting for people living in rural areas. This potential wide reach also ensures that a large number of merchants can be paid through this service, and also that merchants can serve a large clientele. This scope is even further increased by the fact that the service is designed for international operation allowing cross-border, international transactions to be made.

- *Cooperative approach*: Most existing electronic payment services are offered by a single entity or a closed group of entities to a limited clientele. The failure of most of these services is programmed at birth already, as this closed concept does not allow growth and market penetration, and slows down any effort to reach the critical mass. The network effect is critical in this business, which can only be realized through openness and cooperation. The SEMOPS service is built on cooperation. SEMOPS realised that a successful electronic/mobile payment service needs to assure the cooperation between banks and mobile operators. There were too many attempts on both sides to dominate the business alone without the participation of the other party, but all of them have failed. If participation is limited to a couple of players then huge segments of the population will be left out, and the service cannot reach its universal scope.

The SEMOPS service aims to establish the wide cooperation of banks and MNOs along the lines of real financial benefits. It is obvious that the banking sector has different operating specifics from those of the mobile communication sector. It is possible to elaborate an operating structure, where these specifics are combined in a way that results in operating optimum, in terms of efficiency. In the SEMOPS service banks are processing macro and mini payments, while MNOs are processing micro and mini payments. Moreover, for mini payments that are offered by both, the user is the one who decides who to select. This division of work results in substantial cost reduction, risk reduction, utilisation of a joint back end infrastructure and great market coverage. The involvement of a number of the banks and MNOs further increases the market coverage by enabling transactions between any of their clients either on the customer or on the merchant side.

- *Universality*: Most existing mobile payment services are of very specific nature. They are not suitable for micro transactions, or many of them are even more limited scope like payment for digital content, or parking services. Contrary to existing solutions, the SEMOPS service follows a universal approach that aims to both mobile and Internet transactions, it addresses domestic and cross border payments, and it can accommodate various transaction types, irrespective of value, function, time, currency and so forth. SEMOPS is account based and, therefore, can be used also by people who do not trust electronic card transactions, or for transactions that are of low value and their process is more expensive than the actual value.

- *Openness*: Existing mobile and electronic payment services are rather closed in their structure. The SEMOPS service on the other hand is explicitly open. The service itself is offered to the banks and mobile operators – the payment processors - who are providing the service to their own clients. This approach means that the actual users do not have to centrally register with any third-party entity in order to be able to use service. Furthermore there is no centralised authentication, and any client of any payment processor can perform payment to any other client of any other payment processor. When new payment processors join in the SEMOPS service the potential number of transactions increases rapidly, as all existing SEMOPS users will be able to carry out transactions with clients of the new payment processor.

- *Independence*: Existing electronic payment services are very much technology and operator dependent. The SEMOPS service is independent from technical, operational, and commercial aspects, as it provides a homogeneous layered approach to which components can be exchanged without impact on the other levels. Technical independence means that the service can be used under various technical conditions. There is communication variety, as the payment service is designed to be a used in 2G, 2.5G and 3G, as well as Internet infrastructure. There is platform independence, as there are several front-ends and modules implementations in SIMToolkit, JAVA and OS versions. Independence for the user implies that, even if all components of the service are changed, the service will not be interrupted for both the customer and the merchant. In practice, this means that the user may change country, bank, MNO or mobile device, but still receive the same service, and all the transactions that were available before are still accessible for the users.

- *State of the art technology*: The SEMOPS solution is designed with the state of the art technology in sight. The service utilises protocols like the Bearer Independent Protocol (BIP) when card based solutions are deployed, and MIDP 2.0 when the application is based on J2ME. New APIs like JSR-82 and JSR-120 are also included in the design. The IrDA, Bluetooth and RFID communication in relation with POS technology is also novel, and there are efforts to integrate Instant Messaging approaches as an extension to communication channels in all transactions. The overall design concept that is capable of managing variable communication channels and different security solutions ensures versatility for the service and easy deployment under widely differing conditions. In regards of the back-end infrastructure, the J2EE development integrated with middleware technology provides interoperability. The security services use private/public key pairs for encrypting and signing messages, and we plan also to integrate Elliptic Curve Cryptography (ECC) for better performance on the mobile devices.

Conclusion

Present electronic payment services are relatively expensive for the users. This is of no surprise if one looks at the operating conditions of the services and the security environment they have to cope with. As discussed in this chapter, the existing services target a limited clientele, they lack scale of economics and, therefore, if they want to be profitable they need to charge hefty commissions. The situation is further deteriorated by the high security expenses and risks these services are facing, either in terms of expensive complex solutions, or high fraud rate, or both.

SEMOPS aims at developing a global mobile payment system with good economical conditions both on the revenue and the cost side. Its innovative business model is based on two key concepts a) that of cooperation of banks and MNOs and b) that of social trust relationships, since each actor transacts only with his trusted bank or MNO. It is worth noting that SEMOPS features a distributed approach where banks/MNOs can dynamically join the system with their customer base and users do not have to register alone, something which will allow SEMOPS to grow fast and reach the critical mass that may establish it as a global payment service. In particular, SEMOPS presents the following advantages:

- The service relies on numerous revenue channels and large potential clientele.

- Different sales channels are combined (Internet, mobile).

- A number of different transaction types are combined (B2C, B2B, P2P, Escrow).

- Different product categories are combined (digital content, out of band, vending, gambling, parking, EBPP, traditional products, loyalty programs).

- Various commercial situations are combined (remote, proximity, POS, P2P).

- The client base of various service providers is combined (banks, mobile operators, others).

A number of factors contribute to the minimisation of cost of the SEMOPS service. Both capital and operating expenses can be kept at low levels due to the favourable environment and process flow. In particular:

- The service leverages existing infrastructure, especially in the banking environment.

- The service concept is built around the traditional financial processes, modifying them but not completely replacing them.

- The deployment of the necessary technical elements is simple as integration is built on interfaces and middleware technology.

- The use of standardised solutions in the service and in its technical environment further reduces introductory expenses.

- Personnel expenses are low due to the full automation of the service that requires manual intervention only in exceptional cases.

- Communication expenses are low as wherever it is possible the service is optimised to use those communication channels that are the cheapest.

- Risk management, and security expenses are also low, as the service relies on existing risk management practices and due to the trusted feature of the payment process good security protection can be achieved with relatively simple solutions.

- The cost of financial settlement is minimized as transactions are settled in large value batch processes.

- The fact that all different kind/type of transactions are processed on the same back end infrastructures that partially are also shared by other services substantially reduces unit cost compared to any other payment solutions.

Trial SEMOPS services have been deployed in Hungary and Greece. Future plans include extensive cross-border trials and tests, as well as the deployment of a pan-European pilot until 2005.

Acknowledgments

This chapter describes work undertaken and in progress in the context of the SEMOPS (IST-2001-37055), a 2-year project (2002-2004), which is partially funded by the Commission of the European Union. The authors would like to acknowledge all SEMOPS partners.

References

Camponovo, G. & Pigneur, Y. (2002). Analyzing the actor game in m-business. *First International Conference on Mobile Business* (pp. 8-9). *http://inforge.unil.ch/yp/Pub/02-Athens.pdf*

Heijden, H. (2002, June 17-19). Factors affecting the successful introduction of mobile payments systems. *Proceedings of the 15th International Bled Electronic Commerce Conference.*

Henkel, J. (2001). Mobile payment: The German and European perspective. In *Mobile commerce* Wiesbaden, Germany: Gabler Publishing. *http://www.inno-tec.de/forschung/henkel/M-Payment%20Henkel%20e.pdf*

Karnouskos, S., Vilmos, A., Hoepner, P., Ramfos, A., & Venetakis, N. (2003). Secure mobile payment - Architecture and business model of SEMOPS. *EURESCOM Summit 2003, Evolution of Broadband Service, Satisfying User and Market Needs.*

Kreyer, N., Pousttchi, K., & Turowski, K. (2002). Standardized payment procedures as key enabling factor for mobile commerce. In K. Bauknecht, G. Quirchmayr & A.M. Tjoa (Hrsg.), *Proceedings of the EC-WEB* (pp. 400-409).

Mobey Forum. (2003). White paper on mobile financial services. Retrieved June 2003, from *http://www.mobeyforum.org/public/material/*

Pfitzmann, A., Pfitzmann, B., Schunter, M., & Waidner, M. (1999). Trustworthy user devices. In G. Müller & K. Rannenberg (Eds.), *Multilateral security in communications, information security* (pp. 137-156). Addison-Wesley.

SEMOPS. (2003). Secure Mobile Payment Service. *http://www.semops.com*

Vilmos, A., & Karnouskos, S. (2003). SEMOPS: Design of a new payment service. *International Workshop on Mobile Commerce Technologies & Applications, in proceedings of the 14th International Conference* (pp. 865-869). IEEE Computer Society Press.

Section IV

Ad Hoc Mobile Commerce Security and Payment Methods

Chapter XII

Remote Digital Signing for Mobile Commerce

Oguz Kaan Onbilger, University of Florida, USA

Randy Chow, University of Florida, USA

Richard Newman, University of Florida, USA

Abstract

Mobile agents (MAs) are a promising technology which directly address physical limitations of mobile devices such as limited battery life, intermittent and low-bandwidth connections, with their capability of providing disconnected operation. This chapter addresses the problem of digital contract signing with MAs, which is an important part of any mobile commerce activity and one special challenging case of computing with secrets remotely in public. The authors use a multi-agent model together with simple secret splitting schemes for signing with shares of a secret key carried by MAs, cooperating to accomplish a trading task. In addition to known key splitting techniques of RSA, authors introduce similar techniques for El Gamal and DSS public key cryptosystems. The objective is to achieve a simple and ubiquitous solution by using the well-known public-key cryptosystem implementations, which conform to the established standards.

Introduction

Mobile agents (MAs) are an approach to distributed computing employing the mobile code concept. An MA is an autonomous entity, which is composed of code, data and state information. They visit hosts (e.g., servers) possibly using an itinerary, perform some execution on those hosts using their codes and migrate with their state information from host to host. They act on behalf of their owners (i.e., senders). They are autonomous in the sense that they have all the knowledge needed to perform the assigned task on behalf of their owners.

Although the MA paradigm opens many interesting applications, to validate it as an alternative to traditional client/server computing, one must address its security issues. In particular, it should demonstrate the ability to compute with secrets in remote public domains. A good example of the need for this is digitally signing a contract for m-commerce (and in general e-commerce) applications with MAs as shown by Sander and Tschudin (1998). We call this problem *remote digital signing*. In this chapter, a multi-agent architecture is used and a solution to this problem is presented. The techniques we explore and analyze are based on information dispersal in distributed system security terms as well as multisignatures and secret splitting in cryptographic terms. The idea is to devise a secure way of sharing secret keys among members of a multi-agent group and signing with shares.

Electronic Commerce and Mobile Agents

Among many application areas of MAs (such as information retrieval, e-commerce, network management, network/site security, distance education, and software distribution), e-commerce draws the most attention from both academic and industrial researchers; for example see Busch, Roth, and Meister (1998) and Klusch (1999). This is mostly due to the fact that MAs and in general agent systems have the capability of representing users (i.e., customers) in the cyberspace. Agents can effectively profile user preferences, act on behalf their owners, participate in e-auctions, watch stock prices, search for commodities and find the best offer from competing vendors, purchase goods by paying and committing to transactions, communicate and cooperate with other agents of relevant goals. Although it is now agreed that MAs are not a new enabling technology, they offer many technical capabilities together (i.e., all-in-one) over the traditional client/server computing (Chess, Grosof, Harrison, Levine, Parris & Tsudik, 1995a; Chess, Harrison & Kershenbaum, 1995b; Lange & Oshima, 1998). Mobile commerce (m-commerce), which is a rapidly growing field in e-commerce, is especially a suitable application area of MAs.

Mobile Commerce and Mobile Agents

Mobility of agents brings unique advantages to m-commerce. Mobile devices such as PDAs and laptop computers have limited battery life, intermittent and low-bandwidth connections to the fixed network. Traditional client/server computing, which was originally designed for and very well fit into the fixed wireline networks, is not suitable for m-commerce due to these limitations. MA paradigm enables disconnected operation (Chess, Grosof, Harrison, Levine, Parris & Tsudik, 1995a; Gray, Kotz, Nog, Rus & Cybenko, 1996), where a brief connection to the fixed network from a mobile device through the wireless network is sufficient to launch an MA (or MAs) to engage in a mobile commerce activity. For example, a laptop owner, which has a wireless connection to the Internet, through a cell phone, may launch an agent to search for the best offer for an airline ticket and make a purchase. While the agent working towards the goal of purchase, the owner can (or may be forced to) disconnect from the network. When the MA accomplishes the goal, it takes another brief connection to receive the agent with the results.

Mobile Agent Security in Mobile Commerce

There are two aspects of the security issues in MA technology that are known as the malicious agents problem and the malicious hosts problem. In the former case, the hosts that are to accept and execute the agents should be protected against any possible hostile behavior of agents. There are known mechanisms such as sandboxes proposed and implemented. The latter case is considered to be much more challenging due to the remote nature of the platforms where the MAs are to be run. Since these platforms are owned and operated by other parties, it is difficult to establish trust. Classical security mechanisms designed for distributed systems, including the cryptographic ones, come short for threats against the MAs due to the assumptions, which do not hold for MAs (Chess, 1998). So, protection mechanisms are needed to make MAs safe in possibly hostile environments.

E-commerce is the most security demanding application of the MA paradigm. This is not different for m-commerce, which is a special case of the broader topic of e-commerce. In fact, it can be argued that if all the security requirements of e-commerce applications are met, then the general MA security problem is solved altogether. The shopping agent application where a MA is deployed to find the best possible price for some good such as an airline ticket, flowers or CDs, and make a purchase, has become the classical problem for discussing the requirements of MA security and proposing solutions to certain aspects of the requirements (see for example, Berkowitz, Guttman & Swarup, 1998; Hohl, 1998; Yee, 1999). Hohl (1998) provides an extensive list of attacks using a shopping agent application example that could be launched against an agent.

The focus of this chapter is the remote digital signing problem for shopping agents. In any trade, principals engaged in the activity need to authenticate each other. A merchant would like to know whether the credit card presented by the buyer really does belong to the party or whether a check provided is legitimate and authentic. Customers would like to make sure they present their confidential information such as a credit card to the merchant of their choice, but not anybody else. Similarly, merchants need to authenticate the MAs and their owners. This is necessary to prevent repudiation, which could be a very simple attack to devise using MAs. Even honest users may change their minds well after the transaction took place and deny that they send any MAs to buy any such product. On the other hand, a hostile MA could masquerade as a legitimate MA and hence its owner, to engage in fake trading to harm either or both of the principals of the transaction. Therefore an MA should be capable of digitally signing a contract agreed on by both parties to authenticate themselves and their owners, remotely and publicly, meaning on the hosts they execute.

Objectives

Our first objective, in general, is to meet the requirements of solutions proposed for any aspect of MA security problem. These requirements were identified previously (Onbilger, Newman & Chow, 2001), and can be summarized as follows. First is that a solution proposed to protect MAs should not jeopardize the protection of hosts they execute on. The second one, which is directly related to this chapter, is the autonomy property of MAs. Usually, solutions proposed for MA security violate some properties of MAs, and as a result desirable benefits of MAs are diminished. For example, an MA may be required to communicate with its owner's host to perform some security sensitive operations. This violates the autonomy property of the agents, which constitute the basis of disconnected operation, which is a highly desirable mode of functioning in m-commerce.

Our specific goals in this chapter are to achieve a solution to the remote digital signing problem that should be as simple, realistic, flexible and ubiquitous as possible. With simplicity, we mean that the solution will be easy to understand and implement. By the use of already established and standardized digital signature schemes, such as RSA and El Gamal algorithms, if the original signing and verification functions can be used then specific implementation may not even be needed for our problem. To be realistic, it is meant that a proposed solution should fit into the real-world environments, where they are to be used. For example, in theory, threshold signature schemes seem to fit very well in the MA paradigm when a multi-agent model is used. However, in practice it is necessary to identify the hosts where these MAs are going to be executed. The number and location of these hosts are to be restrictive as explained in detail later. Flexibility is related to the autonomy of MAs from another perspective. Unlike some other solutions proposed, it is important to distinguish what can be done (i.e., signed) by an MA and what actually has been accomplished. Ubiquity is again related with the cryptographic functions used. Widely implemented cryptographic signature schemes improve the scalability in terms of number of hosts where MAs may need to find and use these schemes.

Background

Multiple agents have first been used by Minsky, Renesse, Schneider, and Stoller (1996) for fault-tolerant distributed computing with MAs. The proposed scheme is deploying clones of an MA to identical servers at each stage of the computation and then comparing the results. In this scheme MAs do not communicate or cooperate. The assumptions that the identical servers would be available and that they would be under different administration domains, so that they would behave independently, are not realistic. Ng (2000) used multiple agents for security purposes. In this scheme, again the agents do not cooperate; instead the task is split into multiple agents so that any agent alone would not reveal any useful information. In contrast to the multiple agent model we use, agents in this scheme visit the same hosts, and therefore they need to be completely anonymous to be able to defeat attacks. Cooperating multiple agents have been first used by Roth (1998). It is shown that two cooperating agents, under certain assumptions, can verify the path each agent takes and whether the migration patterns adhere to the itinerary of the agents.

Sander and Tschudin (1998) introduced the concept of mobile cryptography. The idea is to encrypt agents as a whole and apply computing with encrypted functions and data. Although it is limited to polynomial and rational functions, this is a good example of a software solution to the MA security problem that is based solely on cryptography. In the same paper they also introduced the concept of "undetachable digital signatures," which is based on the concept of computing with encrypted functions. They point out that this is a possible realization of "… an agent would like to use the secret in public e.g., to compute the digital signature of an order form but without disclosing the secret needed to do so". In this approach, user constraints are "glued" together with the general purpose signature function to enforce them to be a part of the signed contract; hence the term "undetachable signatures". Nevertheless, they also point out that the scheme on which their proposal is based has been successfully attacked.

Kotzanikolaou, Burmester, and Chrissikopoulos (2000) proposed a solution to the problem introduced by Sander and Tschudin (1998). They use RSA (Rivest, Shamir & Adleman, 1978), which is based on exponential functions rather than rational functions. However, as the term "undetachable digital signatures" implies, the solution given by Kotzanikolaou, Burmester, and Chrissikopoulos (2000) requires that the signature be generated by the user (i.e., owner of the agent) and given to the agent *before the mission takes place*. This contradicts MA autonomy. This is due to the fact that the purchase decision has to be made strictly before negotiation with the sellers. User constraints, which have to be signed before these negotiations, therefore need to be pure data. However, it is desirable that a decision function be executed after or during the negotiation or bargaining process. This means that agents should be capable of deciding what to buy, where to buy, under what conditions, price, type of payment, delivery options, and so forth. For example, the user demand should be able to be stated as flexibly as possible with "I would like to purchase as many blank rewritable CDs as possible and I've got $100." The result of the decision function will have a direct effect of the contract to be signed. Therefore what we need is to make the agents capable of computing with secrets in public as the quoted sentence in the previous paragraph implies. Without this capability, either the user must have a perfect knowledge of market conditions that might change rapidly, or user interaction during the mission is necessary. In the former case it is highly possible that the mission may fail; in the latter, autonomy is sacrificed. The problem arises from the fact that a malicious host should not be able to manipulate or directly use the agent in order to sign "arbitrary" documents. On the other hand, agents should also be capable of preparing the documents to be signed. The challenge is to resolve this contradiction.

A threshold signature scheme in conjunction with the use of multiple agents and an undetachable threshold signature scheme, which combines undetachable signatures with threshold signature schemes, has been proposed (Borselius, Mitchell & Wilson, 2001; and further references). While the former is vulnerable to attacks when used alone the latter still carries the concerns with threshold signatures.

First concern is that threshold signature schemes come in great variety. They are neither standardized nor widely accepted. This means that MAs may face problems in finding the hosts to execute, which would have standardized implementations of these schemes. The second concern is threshold signature schemes tacitly assume that there would be sufficient number of shareholders to sign a document. Even small values of this "sufficient number" may not be feasible for Mas, since in practice, existence of hosts for MAs to execute on, finding those hosts and location of them in the underlying network are problems, as will be explained later. So, threshold schemes are reduced to multisignature schemes by these restrictions. Nevertheless, their complexity remains.

The Multi-Agent Model

In the classical MA model, a single MA performs a single task, which we call a *mission*. The term *mission* is the counterpart of the term *session* in client/server computing. A mission can represent any session that carries out a computation such as a database search, a network management activity or an e-commerce task, and so forth, using MAs. Figure 1(a) illustrates the single agent model by showing a mission being carried out by an MA called Alice. The mission must be accomplished by visiting several hosts, which requires process migration from host to host. Alice computes (e.g., is being executed) in these hosts and returns home at the end of a successful mission in this case. Note that the illustration in Figure 1(a) is a simplified generic case of a mission. It may not be necessary for an MA to return home and a same host might be visited multiple times in the same mission.

One of the open research issues in this single MA model is the ability of computing with secrets in the public domain. Recently, the authors proposed a collaboration and execution support system for MAs (Onbilger, Newman & Chow, 2001), which addresses this security issue as well as the problem of interoperability. In this architecture, a multi-agent model for MAs is used. The multi-agent paradigm fits well with the concept of *protection of an application as a whole*. It is more difficult to compromise a task if the task is split into multiple collaborating agents. In the context of data secrecy, this is also referred to as *information dispersal for security,* which has been widely studied. The new definition of MA autonomy takes the form: "A group of agents is called 'autonomous' if they have the knowledge necessary to perform a single task, and they communicate and cooperate to perform that well-defined single task during a mission."

The multi-agent model does not differ from the classical agent model in terms of the definition of the mission. The difference is due to the definition of the autonomy property of MAs. So, in the new model, MAs are autonomous as a group but not as an individual

Figure 1. (a) Classical mobile agent model and (b) multi-agent model

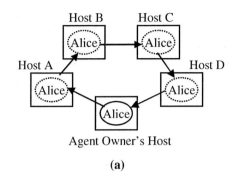

(a)

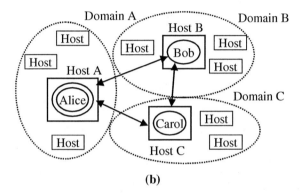

(b)

entity. The group of agents carries out a single task, which is again a mission, by communicating and cooperating.

Figure 1(b) illustrates the model using the agents Alice, Bob, and Carol executing on three hosts A, B, and C respectively. In the model, we call one of the agents the *master agent* (distinguished by double circles in the figure), who actually visits the set of hosts that are necessary to complete the mission. This set of hosts is called the itinerary of the mission. The other agents are called *support agents,* who visit only the hosts outside of the itinerary of the master agent. Note that the model that we describe here is the most generic multi-agent model. Variations of the model admit more than one master agent.

In Figure 1(b), observe that these three hosts A, B, and C reside in three different network domains, A, B, and C respectively, which are shown with dashed ovals. Note that the figure shows a snapshot of the mission at a specific time, and therefore migration of the agents is not shown. In fact, the migration of an agent or agents in a group is more complicated in this model and requires support from an underlying system that is aware of the underlying network topology.

Multiple Cryptography

Multiple cryptography, as the name implies, covers the cryptosystems that deal with more than two parties as opposed to the classical cryptography where there are only two parties: the one who encrypts or signs and the other who decrypts or verifies. In fact, there are many real-world applications that have multiple parties involved. For example, in a banking application, electronic fund transfers require approvals of bank officials of different ranks. Usually, at least two people are involved for a single transaction. Ironically, this is such an application that, in the digital world, a more realistic abstraction of the real world than the real world itself may be possible. Using the same example, a bank cannot have a signature. Only people who work for the bank have signatures, and they sign on behalf of the bank. But with multiple cryptography, it is possible to assign a key to the bank, and shares of this key with the individuals who work for the bank. When these officials sign a document like a check, the signature they generate perfectly represents the bank itself, but not the individuals who really signed the document. So as the example implies, it is possible with multiple cryptography not only to share the secrets but also to compute with them without regenerating the secrets.

Our focus in this chapter is on multiple digital signatures or *multisignatures,* which are a special case of multiple cryptography. The term refers to digital signature schemes, which enable multiple parties to sign documents or messages cooperatively but independently of each other using keys or shares of a key generated for this purpose. Boyd (1988) shows the generalization of RSA and use it as a multisignature scheme. A brief explanation of Boyd's work, which is related to our application, will be given later.

Multiple cryptography, in general, is intended for classical applications (e.g., a banking application). In these applications, shareholders are usually individuals who represent an organization or a company. There is an important distinction between these applications and the MA applications. MAs are nothing but software entities. They are neither organizations nor individuals. Moreover, they are owned by individuals or organizations. In fact, it can be argued that the MA owner and a bank have some kind of resemblance. So, the officials of the bank and the MA perform similar operations when signing a document. While this is not wrong, the actual difference comes from the fact that MA owners are active players, while organizations or companies like a bank are not. A bank is actually an abstraction and cannot for example sign a document. But in the case of a human MA owner, this individual can equally sign documents him/herself. Also, the shareholders do not always exist. They are created when necessary and after they complete their work they cease to exist.

In addition to the threshold schemes like Shamir's (1979), techniques which are known as *threshold cryptography* for the purpose of not only sharing keys but also being able to compute with them without a central authority, have been proposed. A survey of research in this area was provided by Desmedt (1997). A threshold multisignature scheme has been given by Frankel and Desmedt (1992). In this scheme, authors combine RSA signature scheme by Rivest, Shamir, and Adleman (1978) together with Shamir's (1979) threshold scheme to distribute and to sign documents with shares. It is also possible to generate the shares of a secret in a distributed fashion, which enables the shareholders to compute their own shares without the necessity of a central authority. An example using RSA is given by Boneh and Franklin (1997). The threshold multisignature schemes are in fact the generalization of the multisignature schemes. While key sharing is *k-out-of-k* in the latter, it is *t-out-of-k* in the former, which means that *t* of the total of *k* shares are enough to generate signatures.

Nevertheless, threshold schemes do not have specific advantages over simple secret splitting techniques we are using with MAs. While it is feasible to use these secret splitting schemes to both share the keys and compute with them, it is also feasible to come up with very simple techniques to create multiple combinations of keys for providing fault-tolerance, as demonstrated by Wu, Malkin, and Boneh (1999). On the other hand, in our application, secret splitting has two important advantages: simplicity and ubiquity. We use very simple secret splitting schemes, which use only addition and multiplication. The secret splitting schemes we use require nothing but the implementations of the standard public key cryptosystems, namely, de facto industry standard RSA and the official Digital Signature Standard (DSS), which is based on El Gamal public key scheme. So, these schemes do not need any new algorithms or an implementation of those algorithms. It should also be noted that what makes it possible to use these simple secret splitting schemes with the El Gamal cryptosystem and DSS is the unique property of the application that the whole secrets and all of the shares are to be computed and known by the MA owner; therefore it is possible to perform computations in advance to be used later when the complete signature is computed. Details of these computations are given in the next section.

Key Splitting and Signature Generation

Boyd (1988), by using the multiplicative property of RSA, showed that the classical RSA is actually a specialization of a general multisignature scheme. For an RSA implementation for sequential signing, we will use this property. Boyd (1989) also mentions a similar technique, which enables the performance of signature generation in parallel. This is the RSA part of the techniques we will use in parallel signing. Note that both techniques use nothing but original RSA signing and verification algorithms. The RSA implementations, which are standardized and used in practice, and their implications on remote digital signing will be discussed later in the chapter. In the following, we present techniques to do the same with El Gamal Cryptosystem, which again use original signing and verification procedures, by using a property that is unique to MAs, as explained.

Using El Gamal Public Key Cryptosystem

Here we use a variant of the original El Gamal signature scheme as given by Kaufman, Perlman, and Speciner (1995). There are two reasons to do this. First is, this scheme is simpler and it is easy to compute with partial keys. The other reason is that the scheme is actually the El Gamal version used in DSS, which in turn is based on the original idea introduced by El Gamal (1985). So this scheme will enable us an easy transition from El

Gamal to DSS. The El Gamal variant that we use is summarized next (Kaufman, Perlman & Speciner, 1995):

- Long term public key: $<g, p, T>$, secret key: S, where $g^S \bmod p = T$
- For a message m choose random number r, compute $g^r \bmod p = T_m$, and message digest d_m (digest of $m \mid T_m$)
- Sign with $X = r + d_m \, S \bmod (p - 1)$
- Verify by $g^X = T_m T^{d_m} \bmod p$

Signing in Sequence with El Gamal Signature Scheme

The El Gamal cryptosystem uses a pair of private keys as opposed to RSA's single key. The first one is the long-term key, as in the RSA. The second is a short-term, per session, private key for each message to be signed with the long-term key. We split up both of these keys as follows:

$$\text{Long-term key: } S = S_a \cdot S_b \cdot S_c \tag{1}$$

$$\text{Short-term key: } r = r_a + r_b + r_c. \tag{2}$$

Here we assume again that our MA group consists of three agents, namely, Alice, Bob and Carol. Alice is the master and the others are support agents.

To sign a message, Alice computes the message digest d_m and signs with:

$$X_a = r_a + d_m \, S_a \bmod (p-1) \tag{3}$$

Note that the message digest d_m here is the result of an appropriate cryptographic hash function H applied to the contract m concatenated with T_m:

$$d_m = H(m \mid T_m) \tag{4}$$

where $T_m = g^r \bmod p$ as given above. In sequential signing, Alice is the only agent who needs T_m and it is assumed here that she is provided by this value before the mission takes place.

Then, she sends her partial signature to Bob. Bob, upon receiving Alice's signature X_a, further signs it with his portions of partial keys as:

$$X_b = r_b + X_a\, S_b \bmod (p-1)$$
$$= r_b + S_b\, r_a + d_m S_a S_b \bmod (p-1) \tag{5}$$

Carol does the same on X_b, which represent the partial signature generated by Alice and Bob:

$$X_c = r_c + X_b\, S_c \bmod (p-1)$$
$$= r_c + r_b\, S_c + r_a S_b S_c + d_m S_a S_b S_c \bmod (p-1) \tag{6}$$

Unfortunately, this last equation, unlike the RSA counterpart, is not equal to the signature X, although the last term of the equation is nothing but the last term of the original signing equation:

$$d_m \times S_a \times S_b \times S_c = d_m S. \tag{7}$$

This leads us to the observation that the difference between the target signature X and the signature generated by the three agents X_c is:

$$X_c - X = (S_c - 1)r_b + (S_b S_c - 1)\, r_a \bmod (p-1) \tag{8}$$

Since the right hand side of the equation consists only of constants and partial private keys, it can easily be computed and given to agents before they are sent out to the network. This ability is *unique* to the application that we consider in this chapter. In the classical applications of digital multisignatures and threshold signatures, it is not possible to perform the same computation since the signatories are distinct parties and the secrets they share cannot exist in a single site as a whole. So the last agent in the row, Carol, sends the partial signature X_c to Alice. Alice computes X, the target complete signature by using the equation above. The general difference equation for n signatories is:

$$X_n - X = \sum_{t=1}^{n-1}\left(r_t\left(\prod_{k=t+1}^{n} S_k - 1\right)\right) \bmod (p-1) \tag{9}$$

Signing in Parallel with El Gamal Signature Scheme

Signing in parallel with the same variant of El Gamal cryptosystem is also possible and even easier. For this purpose we split up the keys as follows:

$$\text{Long-term key: } S = S_a + S_b + S_c \tag{10}$$

$$\text{Short-term key: } r = r_a + r_b + r_c \tag{11}$$

Then, each agent is given the partial keys as well as $T_m = g^r \bmod p$ since all of the agents will need it to compute the message digest $d_m = H(m \mid T_m)$ where m is the contract to be signed and H is an appropriate cryptographic hash function. They sign independently of each other as:

$$X_a = r_a + d_m S_a \bmod (p-1),$$
$$X_b = r_b + d_m S_b \bmod (p-1),$$
$$X_c = r_c + d_m S_c \bmod (p-1) \tag{12}$$

and the support agents send their partial signatures to the master agent. Together with the master agent's signature, the server combines the partial signatures and obtains the complete signature as follows:

$$X = X_a + X_b + X_c$$
$$= r_a + r_b + r_c + d_m S_a + d_m S_b + d_m S_c$$
$$= r + d_m (S_a + S_b + S_c) = r + d_m S \tag{13}$$

The scheme can be generalized to n signatories in the obvious way.

Transition from El Gamal Cryptosystem to Digital Signature Standard

While RSA is the *de facto* industry standard of public key cryptography, the Digital Signature Algorithm has been proposed as the official standard as Digital Signature Standard (DSS) by US National Institute of Standards and Technology. It is based on the original idea of the El Gamal public key scheme and is very similar to the variant of the El Gamal cryptosystem.

Due to space considerations, we will neither provide the details of DSS nor the details of the signature generation by partial keys. However, we will give the differences between the El Gamal scheme presented in previous sections and DSS.

The signing equation in DSS is given by:

$$X = r^{-1}(d_m + S \, T_m) \bmod q \tag{14}$$

where r^{-1} is the multiplicative inverse of $r \bmod q$. Therefore it can be calculated in advance and instead of splitting up r we can just as easily split up r^{-1}.

Signing in Sequence with DSS

The key splitting is performed as follows:

Long-term key: $S = S_a + S_b + S_c$ **(15)**

Short-term key (inverse): $r^{-1} = r_a \cdot r_b \cdot r_c$. **(16)**

The signing process is very similar to El Gamal scheme. However the difference in this case is given by:

$$X - X_c = ((r_a - 1) \, r_c r_b \, S_b + (r_b r_a - 1) \, r_c S_c) T_m$$ **(17)**

For n signatories (i.e., agents), the general difference equation is:

$$X - X_n = T_m \sum_{t=1}^{n-1} \left(\prod_{k=1}^{t} r_k - 1 \right) \left(\prod_{w=t+1}^{n} r_w \right) S_{t+1}$$ **(18)**

Signing in Parallel with DSS

The key splitting, signing and signature combination calculations here are very similar to the El Gamal scheme. However, the combined value is not equal to the target complete signature X. Therefore we call this value X' and the difference is given by:

$$X - X' = T_m \, (r_a (S_b + S_c) + r_b (S_a + S_c) + r_c (S_a + S_b))$$ **(19)**

For n signatories (i.e., agents), the general difference equation is:

$$X - X_n = T_m \sum_{t=1}^{n} \sum_{\substack{k=1 \\ k \neq t}}^{n} r_t S_k.$$ **(20)**

Overall System for
Remote Digital Signing

As presented in the previous section, there are two major multi-signature schemes: sequential and parallel. Figures 2 and 3 provide the overall system of signing and verification processes as part of an MA mission, for sequential and parallel signature generation schemes, respectively. In this section, we discuss these protocols, compare them with respect to assumptions made and the analysis of attacks possible against each scheme.

Please note that in this chapter we do not address fully the overall security issues necessary for a whole MA mission. Signature generation is actually an integral part of the whole mission. However, we provide the protection mechanisms when necessary in addition to the signature generation process to make this process more meaningful.

In both of the protocols, the first part is to obtain the bid of the server along with the signature for this offer and then verify this signature in steps 1 through 4. After Alice obtains server's signature, she sends it to both Bob and Carol. Signature verification is carried out by both Bob and Carol independently on different hosts in different domains. It would not make sense to let Alice verify the signature since Alice is under complete

Figure 2. Protocol for sequential signing with multi-agent model

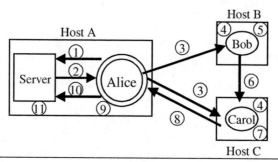

1. Alice asks the Server for a bid for her demand
2. Server provides Alice with its offer along with its signature for the contract
3. Alice sends the server's bid along with its signature to Bob and Carol
4. Bob and Carol verify the server's signature
5. Bob prepares the contract and signs it with his part of private key
6. Bob sends the partially signed contract C_B to Carol
7. Carol signs the contract, partially signed by Bob, further with her partial key
8. Carol sends the partially signed contract C_{BC} to Alice
9. Alice, with her partial key, further signs the contract and obtains the fully signed contract C_{ABC}
10. Alice delivers the signed contract C_{ABC} to the server
11. Server verifies the contract using the public key of the user

Figure 3. Protocol for parallel signing with multi-agent model

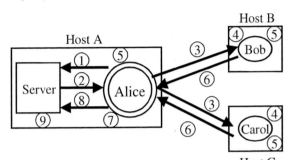

1-4. Same as Figure 2
5. Alice, Bob, and Carol prepare the contract and sign it with their part of
   private key and each obtain C_A, C_B, and C_C respectively
6. Bob sends the partially signed contract C_B to Alice, Carol does the same
   with C_C
7. Alice, combines C_A, C_B, and C_C, and obtains the fully signed contract C_{ABC}
8. Alice delivers the signed contract C_{ABC} to the server
9. Server verifies the contract using the public key of the user

control of the very same host that made the offer. Step 5 in Figure 2 contains the contract preparation process performed by Bob. The protocol assumes that Host B does not have any interest in forging the computation as does Host A. Although the chances are low, this assumption is not enough for a convincing level of security, since a denial-of-service attack by Host B is possible. This is due to the drawback of this protocol that there is no way to check whether the contract signed by the first agent in the row is correct. This is true regardless of the fact that the decision function is executed in cooperation with all the members of the group. However, this drawback does not make the protocol totally inappropriate because even though an attack cannot be prevented, it would be detected in Step 11 when the host attempts to verify the signature. Nevertheless, it is not possible to tell which host is cheating. The parallel signature generation scheme does not have this drawback, as we see next.

In Figure 3, Step 5 states that all agents prepare the contract to be signed. This is possible since Bob and Carol receive the server's offer from Alice. Furthermore, any decision function that needs to be executed to reach the decision for actual purchase is shared by three agents and executed in cooperation. However, it is also possible for any one agent to prepare the contract and communicate it to the others. Once the contract is obtained either way, agents sign it with their shares of the private key for the chosen algorithm as described previously. Step 6 says that Bob and Carol send their signatures back to Alice, and in Step 7, Alice combines them to obtain the fully signed contract. This means that combining the partial signatures takes place in the host where Alice resides. This is because there is no trusted authority to ask for this computation. But for the application under consideration, there is no need for it either, since there is no known attack possible.

Using Limited-Liability Keys and Public Key Certificates

Our multi-agent model provides a high level of security by making it difficult to compromise all the agents, which together form an autonomous group. However, the secret, which is a private key of the agent owner, is an extremely sensitive piece of information. Revealing users' shopping preferences or losing electronic cash is certainly undesirable, but in essence a part of our daily lives since we have just enough security to protect these valuables. But a forged signature under a document may mean "anything" and may not be tolerable or acceptable. So even a very small chance of the whole group of agents being compromised may not be acceptable since the consequence of this malicious action is revealing the private key of the user. Therefore we define two types of public/private key pairs as follows:

- *Long-term public/private key pairs*: These are the long-term keys, which are created, registered and assigned to the user (who becomes the owner of the keys) by a Certificate Authority (CA). The lifetime of these keys are again decided by the same authority.

- *Limited-liability public/private key pairs*: These are the short-term keys, which are created by the very same user (owner of the keys). Since the creators of the keys are the users themselves they also are the authority to decide the lifetime of the keys.

There are two limitations that can be imposed on the limited-liability keys. The first one is the lifetime of the key and the second one is what can be done (i.e., signed) with these keys. Both of these limitations can be flexible or restrictive and it is up to the owner of the keys. For example, the lifetime of a key may vary from a single MA mission, which may be limited to a couple of minutes, to a total of a couple of days that spans several different missions. Liability definition says what exactly can be signed with these keys. For example, a typical definition may say that these keys can only be used in an m-commerce transaction and the amount that could be involved in such a transaction cannot exceed $500. The other type of limitation that can be imposed is the type of the transaction. For example, it can be stated that with these keys only one mobile phone, one color printer or one DVD player purchase contract can be signed.

The problem with this scheme is the authenticity of this new pair of keys. One possible solution would be to register this pair of new keys with a CA and obtain a certificate, or ask the CA directly for a pair of new keys. Nevertheless, this solution does not make much sense, since this introduces an overhead of obtaining a new key for every single transaction from a CA, which could easily become unmanageable. Instead, the user creates this key and a certificate for this key by using his/her long-term key. The idea is that the user obtains only a single public key and a certificate for it from a CA. Using this certificate and public key, it is possible for the very same user to create and use an unlimited number of other public keys. The key point here is that these new keys are certified by their owners. That is, the user in essence becomes a CA for the agents he/she sends on missions.

It may seem at first that the scheme explained in this section provides enough security for the limited-liability private key. This is due to the fact that what can be signed by this key is restricted by the certificate provided for it. However, it is not so for two reasons. First problem is the same problem that the undetachable signature schemes have, as explained previously, which is the difference between the limitation of what can be signed and what actually is signed. A certificate can only enforce what can be signed with the key for which it is issued. But in fact, it is necessary for agents to be able to engage in transactions with the most favorable choices. For example, a certificate may allow for a purchase of up to $500. However, this should not mean that the agent would accept an offer of this amount. If the server's original bid is $300, then the server should not be able to enforce the agent to involve in an agreement for the allowed full amount of $500. The second problem is that an attack is possible by any host visited. Any such host for example might learn the complete limited-liability private key from agent Alice, and then can sign a contract to sell something. Also, even if the support agents are involved in the decision function to be executed, this is not enough since a single agent who possesses the complete key could be manipulated. In short, this scheme when used alone could open a can of worms. Therefore, the limited-liability keys are protected by splitting them up and giving them to members of a group of MAs. Their usage, on the other hand, is protected by the certificate created by the user using the long-term key.

The complete protocol for using the certificates and limited-liability keys for agents is given in Figure 4. In the protocol, P and S represent the long-term public and private keys respectively and p and s represent the limited-liability keys. The protocol assumes that user already has P and S. Note that P, S, p and s are symbols for the private and public keys; for example in the case of RSA, P and p indicate (E, N) and (e, n) respectively. The certificate contains p and the description of the liability. Any document that is signed with s and therefore can be verified by p should conform to this description to be valid.

Note that a certificate chain that would also include CA's certificate for (P, S) rules out the necessity for the server to connect the CA and ask for verification.

Now let's look at what can and cannot be accomplished with these limited time and liability keys and what can go wrong. The analysis involves three parties that can act maliciously: agent owner, the host to which a signature is provided, and third parties, which could presumably acquire the limited-liability private key. Since the private/public key pair is arbitrary, meaning that they are neither created nor registered by a CA, the host on which the transaction took place may sign a contract that states that the agent purchased 500 mobile phones for the price of $100 each. Since the host also knows the credit card information of the user, it can perform a transaction and bill the user's credit card for this transaction. The solution to the dispute requires the proof of the user's demand for this kind of purchase. But the certificate that is signed by user's long-term private key pair states that the transaction amount may not exceed $500 and it is only valid for a purchase of a single mobile phone. Therefore there is no way for the host to prove such claim.

Now, suppose that a third party was able to compromise all the agents in a group and therefore acquire the limited-liability key. Then this party could sign an arbitrary contract

Figure 4. Limited-liability key protocol

1. User creates (p, s) or uses a pre-computed pair of keys
2. User splits up s, using one of the techniques mentioned
3. User prepares a certificate and signs with S
4. Server uses P to verify the certificate and obtains the identity of the user and p
5. Agents sign the contract with their shares of s
6. Server verifies this signature using p

on behalf of the user by masquerading as the user. In this case, however, it is not possible to bind the user to this contract since there is no certificate signed by the user using the long-term private key. So, such signed document is invalid because the user can deny it rightfully.

Third attack involves a malicious user, and is known as non-repudiation problem. The user cannot deny a contract that states a purchase demand that conforms to what is stated in the certificate signed by the user's long-term private key. This is what we expect since this is the aim of the certificate and is completely legitimate. Also, the user cannot deny the legitimacy of a contract by claiming that the contract was signed after the limited-liability key had been expired. That is because agents are supposed to check whether the expiration date and time has passed. On the other hand, as explained in the previous paragraph, the user can deny any illegitimate contract signed by the limited-liability key that does not conform to the certificate. Another similar attack might be possible, if an attacker creates and uses a limited-liability key by also creating a fake long-term key without registering this long-term key by any CA. Then the attacker prepares a certificate for the limited-liability key using this fake long-term key. The last step for the attacker is to let the agents engage in transactions and then deny their existence. These transactions may or may not conform to the certificate prepared. So, the merchants/sellers should always check the legitimacy of the short-term keys by checking the certificates prepared for them, as well as the legitimacy of the certificates by checking the long-term keys used to prepare them, possibly consulting the CA, if not provided.

Practical Issues of
Remote Digital Signing

In this section we examine the issues related with using the remote digital signing in practice. First we look at the issues related with the security level and robustness of the multisignature schemes by discussing the recent theoretical advances in digital signatures, their impact on implementations in practice and particularly on remote digital signing. Then, we look at the broader picture of multiple MAs paradigm and discuss the performance issues that might arise in practice and how to address them.

Probabilistic Signature Scheme and Its Impact on Practice

Probabilistic Signature Scheme (PSS) has been proposed by Bellare and Rogaway (1996). It is applied to the hashing but the signature generation is the same. The idea is to mix the document to be signed with a random salt in a specific way and the result is a better security proof. This is due to the fact that security of PSS can be tightly related to the difficulty of inverting RSA. We refer the interested reader to Bellare and Rogaway (1996) for details. As the name implies, PSS is probabilistic rather than deterministic, which is the case for classical RSA commonly in use today. The scheme has practical importance and has been adopted by the RSA Corporation as a standard (PKCS#1, 2002).

Unfortunately, the scheme is not applicable in environments where deterministic signature generation is necessary. In our case, it is applicable to sequential signature generation using RSA since signature generation is initiated by a single agent and appropriate hashing is only performed by the same agent. The other agents (i.e., support agents) therefore need not know the random salt value used and can apply their keys to the signature function. However, parallel signature generation with RSA requires a deterministic scheme since all the agents need to know or be able to generate the same random salt. The issue is important since our main concern is to use standardized and widely implemented and used schemes like RSA. The random salt value in PSS enhances the security by providing a tighter security proof. However, in practice, randomness is not critical to security (PKCS#1, 2002). In our case, parallel RSA signature generation is still feasible by providing a fixed value to the agents or having them compute the same value and use it when it is time to generate the underlying message digest to be signed. Furthermore, in our scheme, the lifetime of the keys and their applicability can be extremely restricted due to the use of certificates issued for them. So, the probability of forging the signatures is extremely low and it is difficult to justify the efforts to do so.

Some theoretical research results, however, lead us to question the probabilistic schemes like PSS. Recently, Katz and Wang (2003) showed that an equally tight security proof of PSS could be constructed in a deterministic way. The idea is to use a single bit (0 or 1) instead of a random salt value when generating the hash value. This variant of PSS may render the current proposed standardization of the original PSS obsolete, which is not convenient in environments where random generation is not possible or is not preferred, as in the case with parallel signature generation presented.

Performance Considerations and the Big Picture

Remote digital signing is in fact a part a new computation paradigm of multiple MA systems. Among many issues of this big picture, performance considerations deserve specific attention since multiple agents introduce additional communication to the classical single agent model. The immediate result follows as more communication overhead to the underlying network and degraded performance observed by the user. Network-awareness in general and specifically network distance estimation are hot research topics and aim at assisting applications, which would benefit from being aware of the underlying network characteristics and conditions. Multiple MAs are such an application area where network-awareness as well as context-awareness, which also addresses security considerations, is important. For example, choosing hosts to send the agents randomly increases the security risk of conspiracies against them. So, hosts to be chosen need to be in different administrative domains and should not have common interests to alleviate this risk. The goal, therefore, is to find the best possible combination of available hosts under the restrictions mentioned above, which are -in terms of network distances- close to each other. This not only addresses the performance but also the security, since vulnerability of the agent communications over the network reduces.

One last remark on performance issue is the subtle difference between the client/server paradigm and the MA paradigm in general, regarding user expectations. The applications of the MA paradigm, which is in fact a special case of the multiple MAs paradigm, are not user-interactive, as is the case for client/server systems. Users do not expect immediate results from their MAs and it is in that aspect that constitutes the foundation for enabling disconnected operation. Therefore, performance penalties should be observed in a more relaxed fashion than it should be in the traditional client/server computing.

Conclusion

Mobile commerce is a rapidly developing field of electronic commerce. Mobile devices and wireless networks, which make the mobile commerce a reality, however, are not developing at the same pace. It can be expected that the limitations of these technologies will be with us several decades from now. MAs are distinguished candidates to tackle this problem. Although benefits offered by this technology are well understood by now, especially in the mobile commerce field, security and interoperability are two main concerns of this technology. It is also well understood that without proper security mechanisms in place, MAs will not be accepted. So, advances in MA security area will directly affect the future of mobile commerce applications.

This chapter carefully examines the implementation of remote digital signing, which is a special case of computing with secrets in the public domain, within a larger picture of supporting multi-agent computing. The solution approach is based on secret sharing and the concept of protection as a whole. In addition to well-known multiplicative and additive properties of the RSA, similar techniques with El Gamal public-key cryptosystem are demonstrated to show their applicability in the MA systems. Although threshold multisignature schemes fit well into the application, it may not be feasible and even reasonable to provide the implementations of these schemes to the MAs. Moreover, the advantage of the techniques we presented in this chapter is that they use nothing but original signing and verification algorithms of RSA and DSS, which are well known, standardized and widely used. In this sense, these simple schemes address the ubiquity in a large-scale MA execution environment like the Internet.

It is shown that both parallel and sequential signature generation schemes are possible. There are important properties of each scheme. The former one provides data integrity since each agent in the group signs the original document, and therefore can check its integrity. However, in this scheme there is no confidentiality for the document to be signed. The latter scheme provides data confidentiality only if signing process begins at the server, where the master agent is being executed. The other hosts, where the support agents are running, cannot see the document in clear, assuming the partially signed documents have enough strength against cryptanalysis. The schemes presented in this chapter therefore address authenticity rather than data confidentiality.

References

Bellare, M., & Rogaway, P. (1996). The exact security of digital signatures: How to sign with RSA and Rabin. In U. Maurer (Ed.), *Advances in cryptology - Eurocrypt 96 Proceedings, LNCS 1070*. Springer-Verlag.

Berkowitz, S., Guttman, J.D., & Swarup V. (1998). Authentication for mobile agents. *Mobile Agents and Security, LNCS 1419* (pp. 114-136). Springer-Verlag.

Boneh, D., & Franklin, M. (1997). Efficient generation of shared RSA keys. *LNCS 1233* (pp. 425-439). Springer-Verlag.

Borselius, N., Mitchell, J.C., & Wilson, A. (2001). On mobile agent based transactions in moderately hostile environments. *Proceedings of IFIP First Annual Working Conference on Network Security.*

Boyd, C. (1988). Some applications of multiple key ciphers. *LNCS 330, Advances in Cryptology, EUROCRYPT'88 Proceedings.*

Boyd, C. (1989). Digital multisignatures. *Cryptography and Coding*, 241-246.

Busch, C., Roth, V., & Meister R. (1998). Perspectives on electronic commerce with mobile agents. *Proceedings of 11th Amaldi Conference on Problems of Global Security* (pp. 89-101).

Chess, D., Grosof, B., Harrison, C., Levine, D., Parris, C., & Tsudik, G. (1995a). Itinerant agents for mobile computing. *IEEE Personal Communications,* 34-49.

Chess, D., Harrison, C., & Kershenbaum, A. (1995b). Mobile agents: Are they a good idea? *IBM Research Report, RC 19887*, IBM Research Division.

Chess, D.M. (1998). Security issues in mobile code systems. *Mobile Agents and Security, LNCS 1419* (pp. 1-14).

Desmedt, Y. (1997). Some recent research aspects of threshold cryptography. *LNCS 1396* (pp. 158-173). Springer-Verlag.

El Gamal, T. (1985). A public key cryptosystem and a signature scheme based on discrete logarithms. *IEEE Transactions on Information Theory, IT-31,* (4).

Frankel, Y., & Desmedt, Y.G. (1992). Parallel reliable threshold multisignature. Tech. Report. Department of E.E. and C.S., University of Wisconsin-Milwaukee, TR-92-04-02.

Gray, R., Kotz, D., Nog, S., Rus, D., & Cybenko, G. (1996). Mobile agents for mobile computing. Technical Report PCS-TR-96-285. Dept. of Computer Science, Dartmouth College.

Hohl, F. (1998). Time limited blackbox security: Protecting mobile agents from malicious hosts. *Mobile Agents and Security, LNCS 1419*, 92-113.

Katz, J., & Wang, N. (2003). Efficiency improvements for signature schemes with tight security reductions. *Proceedings of the 10th ACM Conference on Computer and Communications Security* (pp. 155-164).

Kaufman, C., Perlman, R., & Speciner, M. (1995). *Network security.* Prentice Hall.

Klusch M. (Ed.) (1999). Intelligent information agents. *Agent-based information discovery and management on the Internet.* Springer-Verlag.

Kotzanikolaou, P., Burmester, M., & Chrissikopoulos, V. (2000). Secure transactions with agents in hostile environments. *LNCS 1841*, 289-297.

Lange, D.B., & Oshima, M. (1998). *Programming and deploying Java mobile agents with aglets.* Addison-Wesley.

Minsky, Y., Renesse, R., Schneider, F.B., & Stoller, S.D. (1996). Cryptographic support for fault-tolerant distributed computing. Technical Report, TR96-1600. Dept. of Computer Science, Cornell University.

Ng, S-K. (2000). Protecting mobile agents against malicious hosts. Master's Thesis. Division of Information Engineering, The Chinese University of Hong Kong.

Onbilger, O.K., Newman, R., & Chow, R. (2001). A distributed and compromise-tolerant mobile agent protection scheme. *Proceedings of International Conference on Intelligent Agents, Web Technologies and Internet Commerce* (pp. 394-400).

PKCS#1: RSA Cryptography Standard, Version 2.1, RSA Laboratories. (2002).

Rivest, R.L., Shamir, A., & Adleman, L. (1978). A method for obtaining digital signatures and public-key cryptosystems. *Communications of the ACM, 21*(2), 120-126.

Roth, V. (1998). Secure recording of itineraries through co-operating agents. *Proceedings of 4th ECOOP Workshop on Mobile Object Systems.*

Sander, T., & Tschudin, C.F. (1998). Protecting mobile agents against malicious hosts. *Mobile Agents and Security, LNCS 1419*, 44-60.

Shamir, A. (1979). How to share a secret. *Communications of the ACM, 22*(11).

Wu, T., Malkin, M., & Boneh, D. (1999). Building intrusion tolerant applications. *Proceedings of the 8th USENIX Security Symposium* (pp. 79-91).

Yee, B.S. (1999). A sanctuary for mobile agents. *Secure Internet Programming – Security Issues for Mobile and Distributed Objects, LNCS 1603*, 261-273.

Chapter XIII

A Mobile Coalition Key-Evolving Digital Signature Scheme for Wireless/Mobile Networks

Quanxing Zhang, Auburn University, USA

Chwan-Hwa "John" Wu, Auburn University, USA

J. David Irwin, Auburn University, USA

Abstract

A scheme is proposed in this chapter to apply a secure digital signature scheme in a mobile-IP environment and treats the three entities in a dynamic path as either foreign agents (FA), home agents (HA) or mobile agents (MA), such that a coalition is formed containing each of the individual agents. Each agent has a pair of keys: one private and one public. The private key is evolving with time, and the public key is signed by a certification authority (CA). All the private keys of the three agents in the coalition are needed to sign a signature. Furthermore, all the messages are signed and verified. The signature is verified against a public key, computed as the product of the public keys of all three agents, and readily generated when a new dynamic path is formed. In addition, the key-evolving scheme prevents an adversary from forging past signatures under any circumstances. As a result of the schemes' proactive refresh capability, an adversary must simultaneously compromise each MA, FA and HA in order to forge future signatures. When a new dynamic path is formed or private keys evolve to new states, an interactive, proactive synchronization scheme is employed among the agents. Thus, the loss of a mobile device, or its information, will cause minimal information damage.

Introduction

Wireless/mobile networking is proliferating throughout the Internet and mobile computing is quickly becoming more and more popular. The number of mobile phones and PDAs has literally exploded and deployment of 2.5G and 3G networks is leading to the emergence of new e-commerce applications and services, usually referred to as mobile commerce, or m-commerce. Mobile-IP (mobile-IP, n.d.) is a means by which a mobile client can maintain a transparent end-to-end connection while seamlessly roaming among different IP networks. Mobile node, defined as a mobile agent (*MA*) in this chapter, home agent (*HA*) and foreign agent (*FA*) are three major components in mobile-IP. In mobile commerce, especially when a large monetary transaction is involved, it is crucial to ensure that all parties involved in the transaction are legitimate and the information exchanged between them emanates from the proper source and is not tampered with. Digital signature schemes provide such a guarantee provided that the underlying cryptosystem is not broken. In practice, exposure of the secret key has become the greatest threat to security in a digital signature scheme (Bellare & Miner, 1999). In an m-commerce environment, mobile/wireless devices are more vulnerable to intrusion than desktops and workstations because the connection path is dynamically transitioning during communication, wireless connections can be sniffed and the devices are easily subject to being stolen, thus making the key-exposure problem for a cryptosystem even worse. Mobile-IP protocols also have security vulnerabilities, as pointed out by Mankin, Patil, Harkins, Nordmark, Nikander, Roberts, and Narten (2001), which must be addressed in order for mobile-IP to be able to be widely adopted. In this chapter we will discuss current digital signature schemes with digital signing key security, and propose a new digital signature scheme. We will also discuss security problems regarding mobile-IP and present a solution for them while applying the proposed new digital signature scheme.

Previous Works

One solution, widely employed for the problem of key exposure, is key distribution across multiple servers via secret sharing, as outlined by Shamir (1979). Basic secret sharing has evolved into both threshold schemes by Desmedt and Frankel (1989), and proactive schemes by Ostrovsky and Yung (1991), and Herzberg, Jakobsson, Jarecki, Krawczyk, and Yung (1997). A (t_h, t_n) threshold scheme means there are t_n signers, each holding a share of the signing key, and a valid signature can only be generated by t_h or more signers, signing together. The adversary (normally represented by a female figure, "Eve") will not be able to generate valid signatures as long as the number of compromised signers is less than t_h. Thus, threshold schemes essentially provide fault tolerant protection for secrecy as well as secret key availability, in the presence of computer break-ins or any other local computer faults.

However, for some keys that are designed for long-term use, such as the key pairs employed by a well-established certification authority, an adversary may patiently try to compromise the key shares, one by one, until she eventually gets enough shares to break the cryptosystem.

Proactive schemes, as the name implies, proactively update and refresh shared keys. In this scenario, even if all the signers are compromised at some point during their lifetimes, as long as the simultaneous corruption is below the threshold, the adversary is still unable to forge a signature. One obvious drawback of this method is that an ordinary user may not be able to split his key among multiple servers because of the high cost involved. Even if keys are successfully distributed among several servers, there is another threat known as *common mode failure*. When the vulnerability of a particular operating system is exploited, all servers could be compromised at essentially the same time. Thus, an adversary will be able to forge signatures for current, past or future time provided the number of keys compromised exceeds the threshold.

The notation for forward-secure signature schemes was first proposed by Anderson (1997). He suggested that the total life span of a key pair be divided into predefined time periods and, at the end of a period, the signing key be updated to a new one using some one-way function while the old key is erased. The public key, in the meantime, remains unchanged during the life span of the key pair. Under this condition, even if an adversary learns the key for the current period, she is still unable to forge signatures for past periods. Bellare and Miner formalized forward-secure signatures by extending the security definition for the ordinary signature scheme by Goldwasser, Micali and Rivest (1988). Since then, a variety of forward-secure schemes with different flavors have emerged (Abdalla & Reyzin, 2000; Itkis & Reyzin, 2001; Kozlov & Reyzin, 2002; Krawczyk, 2000; Malkin, Micciancio & Miner, 2002). However, using this model, once an adversary compromises the current signing key, she is able to forge signatures in the future, and the public key has to be revoked to eliminate further damage.

Dodis, Kats, Xu and Yung (2002) introduced a key-insulated scheme that uses two modules: a signer and a home base. In this scheme, the life span of the key pair is also divided into predefined time periods. The signer has a temporary secret signing key for the current period, and can generate signatures on its own. At the end of each time period, the signing key expires and the signer needs to communicate with the home base to get an updated signing key for the next period. The damage caused by the loss of signing keys is limited to the periods that are compromised, and the adversary will not be able to forge signatures for any other time periods. However, if both the home base and the signer are compromised, the adversary will be able to forge signatures for the current, past and future periods. The most serious problem with this scheme is the fact that an adversary need not compromise both modules at the same time. When a signing key has been compromised, the adversary can simply keep it and wait until she breaks into the home base at a later time. At that point, she will be able to forge signatures for the past as well as the future. Therefore, when a signing key is lost, the prudent user will refrain from using the home base key and revoke the public key.

The SiBIR (signer-base intrusion-resilient) signature scheme is a new method, developed by Itkis and Reyzin (2002), that combines features from proactive security, forward security and key-insulated security to make the signature scheme more resilient to key exposure. As in the key-insulated scheme, there are two parties in the SiBIR scheme: a mobile signer and a home base. Both signer and home base update their internal states at the end of each time period. The home base sends a key update message to the signer and the signer combines this update message with its own key to form the signing key for a new period. If only the signer is compromised, an adversary will be capable of forging a signature for the current period but not for past and future periods. Within each period there is a special refresh procedure, which provides the means for proactive key security. Only when both the signer and the home base are compromised during the same period without a refresh in between can an adversary forge a signature for the future. In this case, the public key needs to be revoked. One of the major problems of this scheme is the danger that the signer and home base will lose synchronization, an event possible even if a single refresh message is lost due to network congestion or active attack from an adversary.

Mobile-IP Protocols and Security Threats

In mobile-IP terminology, the host that changes its point of attachment from one network or sub-network to another is referred to as a mobile node (*MN*) or mobile agent (*MA*). The host that communicates with an *MA* is referred to as a correspondent node (*CN*), which can be a stationary node or another MA. A *home agent (HA)* is a router on an MA's home network that maintains current location information for the MA in order to deliver packets to and from the MA when it is away from home. A *foreign agent (FA)* is a router on the network that the MA is visiting, which provides routing services to the mobile node while it is with the foreign agent.

Currently there are two mobile-IP protocols: mobile-IPv4 and mobile-IPv6, which are based on Internet Protocol v4 and v6 (IPv4 and IPv6), respectively. Mobile-IP allows a node to roam seamlessly across multiple network domains while at the same time keeping its home IP address.

In mobile-IP, an MA uses the IP address of an FA as its care-of-address (CoA) to indicate its actual point of attachment. An MA uses an agent discovery process to find the CoA when it moves to another network (Thomson & Narten, 1996). The CoA is registered at its HA, which is described as a binding update to HA in both mobile-IPv4 and mobile-IPv6. The HA will also send back a binding acknowledgment (ACK) to MA.

Once the binding is registered at HA, the communication channel between the HA and the MA works like a tunnel, which is essentially a route that the HA uses to redirect packets received from a CN for the MA on its home network to its new location. The tunnel is constructed by either a mechanism referred to as IP-within-IP (Perkins, 1996a) or other means (Perkins, 1996b). The FA de-tunnels the encapsulated packets and delivers them to the MA that is attached to it. Basic operation for this tunneling mechanism is shown

Figure 1. Basic operation of mobile-IP

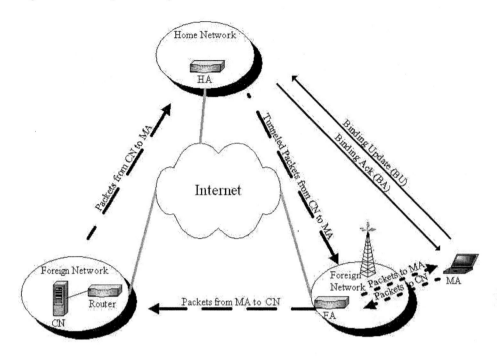

in Figure 1. From the figure, one can see that the data path between the CN and MA forms a triangle.

Imagine the case when both CN and MA are close to each other or even on the same subnet, the packets from CN still need to go through HA in order to reach MA according to Figure 1. In order to reduce the unnecessary hops, route optimization is proposed by Perkins and Johnson (2001). After the initial binding registration with HA, the MA can directly register the CoA with the CN and packets between them can be routed directly without needing to go through HA again, as is illustrated in Figure 2. Any CN can maintain a binding cache containing the CoA of one or more MAs.

The binding of CoA with the IP address of MA opens doors for different security threats against mobile-IP. Different scenarios are discussed by Mankin, Patil, Harkins, Nordmark, Nikander, Roberts, and Narten (2001). In general there are two ways an adversary can attack a mobile-IP network:

(a) *Faking home address of an MA*: A malicious MA could send a forged binding updates to a CN in which the home address is set to the address of another MA. If the binding update is accepted by the CN, it will send packets to a wrong CoA where the malicious MA is attached and as a consequence the legitimate MA will be denied packets from CN as well.

Figure 2. Basic operation of mobile-IP with route optimization (RO)

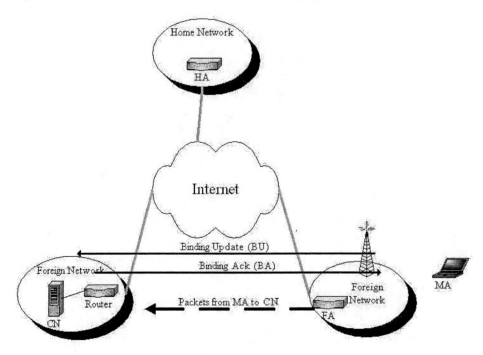

(b)   *Faking CoA*: If a malicious node sends a forged binding update message with a forged CoA, the CN will send (potentially large amount of) packets to that router who owns the CoA and cause a denial of service attack.

Obviously the authenticity of the binding update message must be guaranteed in order to avoid the attacks mentioned. Many solutions are proposed to tackle this problem (Nikander & Perkins, 2001; Nordmark, 2001; Roe, Aura, Shea & Arkko, 2002).

Our Scheme

We propose a new digital signature scheme that combines the advantages of the above-mentioned schemes and applies them in the mobile-IP framework for wireless/mobile networks. The technique involves a three-tier signature signing and key-evolving scheme, which is referred to as a *mobile coalition key-evolving (MCKE)* signature scheme. This proposed scheme maps into mobile-IP structure and thus the three entities, which form a coalition, are referred to as foreign agents (*FA*), home agents (*HA*) and mobile agents (*MA*), respectively. In our scheme, the HA can be on a router or server in the home network. Each agent has a private/public key pair. All the private keys in the

Figure 3. The three parts of the coalition in a mobile/wireless network (All other mobile clients are implicitly MAs.)

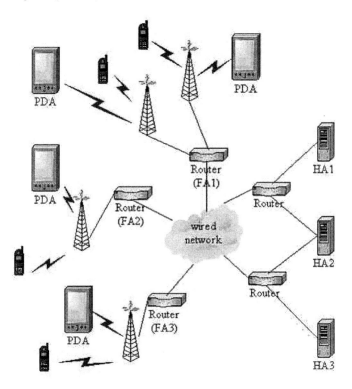

coalition are needed to sign a signature, and all the messages are signed and verified. Each coalition member is identified by an identity string, which is hashed and signed by a CA. The signed ID string is the public key for the specific agent. All the agents in the coalition must have a signed public key. This prevents an adversary from impersonating an FA or MA, which is a more prevalent scenario in a mobile/wireless environment. The signature is verified against a public key, which is the product of the public keys of all the agents. The three parts of the coalition in a mobile/wireless network are shown in Figure 3.

A proactive/interactive private key-evolving scheme is proposed to prevent an adversary from forging the future signatures unless this adversary is able to compromise all three members of the coalition. In a worst-case scenario, when all the private keys of the agents in the coalition are compromised at the same time, forward security is still preserved because an adversary cannot forge a signature that was generated in the past. We improve the scheme outlined by Itkis and Reyzin (2002) by requiring that the refresh be done interactively in order to avoid losing synchronization. The public key for the coalition is computed as the product of the public keys of each agent. Thus, the new coalition public key can be computed dynamically when an MA roams into a new FA. Proof of the security of this scheme is discussed by Zhang (2003).

The Definition of *MCKE*

The proposed signature scheme is a secure technique within the mobile-IP framework. Our definitions are based on those of the SiBIR scheme (Itkis & Reyzin, 2002), which, in turn, are based on definitions of key-insulated security by Dodis, Katz, Xu, and Yung (2002), forward security by Malkin, Micciancio, and Miner (2002) and ordinary signature schemes by Rivest, Shamir, and Adleman (1978).

In contrast to the scheme of Itkis and Reyzin (2002), where the private key is split into two parts: signer key and home-base key, the proposed scheme treats the three entities in a mobile-IP architecture as a coalition containing each individual agent. Each agent has a pair of private and public keys. The private keys of all three agents are needed to sign a signature. The signature is verified with a public key that is the product of each agent's public key.

Coalition Definition for Agents

The set of all agents is defined as A_C, where A_C can be expressed as:

$$A_c = \{FA_1, \cdots, FA_L; HA_1, \cdots, HA_M; MA_1, \cdots, MA_N\} \tag{1}$$

and L, M and N represent the total number of FAs, HAs and MAs, respectively. At any time when an MA is connected to a network, it passes through an FA to connect to an HA. These three entities constitute a coalition. Thus a coalition C is a 3-tuple defined as:

$$C = \{FA_i, HA_j, MA_k\} \tag{2}$$

C is a subset of A such that $\forall(i, j, k)$, $FA_i \in A_C$, $HA_j \in A_C$, $MA_k \in A_C$, or in other words, $C \subseteq A_C$.

Although the discussion of the signature scheme is limited to one coalition, the results can be applied to each and every other coalition. Therefore, it will not be necessary to use an index to distinguish coalitions when the context is clear.

At any given time, an MA and an HA will belong to a single coalition, while an FA may belong to more than one. An MA can move to another location at any time and connect to the network through another FA; as a consequence, a new coalition is formed.

Interaction Between Agents in a Coalition

Like the scheme of Itkis and Reyzin (2002), as well as many other signature schemes, the total lifetime for the coalition is divided into small periods, and at the end of each period each agent will update its private key. The public key for a coalition will remain the same, provided that the membership of the coalition does not change. The home agent and foreign agent send their key update messages to the mobile agent.

Within the coalition, an MA is paired with an HA, and these two entities send refresh messages between them in order to provide proactive security for the coalition. Refresh only affects the internal states of the mobile and home agents. The signing key will remain the same when the keys for the mobile agent and the home agent are combined. This process is therefore transparent to the verifier.

Let T denote the sum of the running time periods of the proposed signature scheme. Each period is a fixed interval that corresponds to a day or a few hours, based on the specific environment under which the scheme is run. Let t denote the t-th time period such that $t \subseteq \{0, 1, \ldots, T\}$.

Refresh happens during each time period, and $RN(t)$ denotes the number of refreshes that occur during time period t. Let r denote the r-th refresh such that $r \subseteq \{0, 1, \ldots, RN(t)\}$. Following the convention adopted by Bellare and Miner (1999) and Itkis and Reyzin (2001-2002), private keys are updated immediately following key generation in order to obtain the keys at $t = 1$. At the beginning of each period, a key refresh algorithm is also performed to refresh number $r = 1$. The first refresh message can be combined with the key update message so the HA need only send one message to the MA.

In the SiBIR scheme (Itkis & Reyzin, 2002), a communication failure has fatal consequences, because the signer and home base keys lose synchronization. As a result, the signer cannot compute the correct signing key and thus is unable to sign any signature. Hence, once the signer and the home base lose synchronization, the SiBIR scheme will not work for the current or any future periods and must be abandoned. Thus it is relatively easy for an adversary to defeat this SiBIR scheme by actively blocking the communication channel.

To counter this key-out-of-synchronization problem during refresh, we propose an interactive/proactive synchronization scheme. This scheme employs the following steps:

(a)   Refresh is initiated by a mobile agent that sends a refresh request, together with its index value, to its corresponding home agent at the beginning of a new period as well as during each refresh interval.

(b)   The home agent sends to the mobile agent the combined refresh and update message, provided the request is made at the beginning of a new period. Only the refresh message is sent during other refresh intervals. The home agent will also check the refresh index r to make sure the two sides are synchronized.

(c)   After receiving the refresh message, the mobile agent will send an acknowledge message to the home agent and update its private key.

(d)   After receiving the acknowledge message, the home agent erases the random number used in the refresh and updates the refresh index. However, if no acknowledge index is received from the mobile agent, the random number will be retained. When the next refresh message is received, the index will be compared again. From

Figure 4. Message flow among agents in the coalition of a dynamically forming mobile network

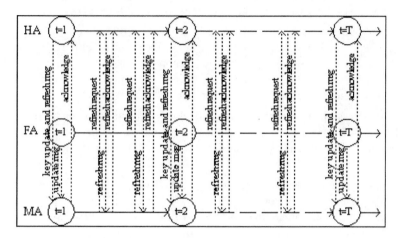

the index r, the home agent will be able to determine the reason the last acknowledge was not received and decide to either roll back the last refresh number or update the index and send a new refresh message.

The simplified message flow among the agents in the coalition is shown in Figure 4.

The Secret Key update and refresh messages, sent from both the foreign agent and home agent to the mobile agent, are denoted as $SKU_{(.)_t}$ and $SKR_{(.)_{t,r}}$, respectively, where t is the time period index and r is the index for the refresh number. For simplicity, $(.)$ is used to denote either (FA), (MA) or (HA). Furthermore, the index r is usually not included in the discussion unless the refresh algorithm is being discussed and such an index is necessary. Let $SK_{(.)_{t,r}}$ denote the private key for an agent at period t and refresh interval r. $SK_{(.)_{t,r}}$ is actually a collection of several parameters that include the signing key $\hat{s}_t$ for the current period t.

With regard to the indices, $(t,r) = (t',r')$ means both $t = t'$ and $r = r'$. Likewise, $(t,r) < (t',r')$ means that there are two possibilities: (1) $t < t'$ or (2) $t = t'$, $r < r'$.

Structural Definition of MCKE

Let $e_1, ..., e_T$ denote the RSA exponents of the underlying GQ scheme for time periods l to T. Let $B_{(.)_{[1,T]}}$ denote the base private key for an agent at time period $t = 1$, while the number of total periods is T. If $B_{(.)_{[t,T]}}$ is used to denote the evolved base private key for time period t, then $B_{(.)_{[t,T]}} \leftarrow B_{(.)_{[1,T]}}^{e_1, ..., e_{t-1}} \pmod{n}$.

Definition 1: A mobile coalition key-evolving (*MCKE*) signature scheme is a 5-tuple consisting of probabilistic polynomial-time algorithms *MCKE=(MCKE.keyGen; MCKE.Sign; MEKE.Ver; MCKE.Update; MCKE.Refresh)* (note that some of the symbols used at this point are defined in the next section).

1. *MCKE.keyGen* is the key generation algorithm.

    Input: Security parameter(s) K and l (in unary), the total number of time periods T, and identity strings for agents

    Output: Initial base private keys $B_{(\cdot)[1,T]}$, and the public key, *PK*

2. *MCKE.Sign* is the signing algorithm.

    Input: Current signing key $\hat{s}_t$ and message M

    Output: Signature (z, σ, t, e_t) on message M for time period t

3. *MEKE.Ver* is the verifying algorithm.

    Input: Message M, signature (z, σ, t, e_t) and public key *PK*

    Output: True (1) or false (0)

4. *MCKE.Update* is the key update algorithm for all agents.

    Input: Current private key $SK(.)_t$

    Output: New private key $SK(.)_{t+1}$ and the key update message $SKU(.)_t$

5. *MCKE.Refresh* is the key refresh algorithm.

    Input: Current private keys $SK_{MA_{t,r}}$ and $SK_{HA_{t,r}}$

    Output: New private keys $SK_{MA_{t,r+1}}$, $SK_{HA_{t,r+1}}$ and the corresponding key refresh message $SKR_{HA_{t,r}}$

MCKE.Update($SK_{(.)T}$) returns $SK_{(.)T+1}$ for the period $t = T+1$ when running at time $t = T$. Under our convention $SK_{(.)T+1}$ is an empty string.

Construction of the *MCKE*

The two security parameters, l and K, are also utilized in the proposed scheme. K defines the bit length of the modulus n, which is in the range of 1024 bits. l specifies the bit length requirement for the exponents $e_1, \ldots, e_T$ employed in the GQ signature scheme. The length of $e_1, \ldots, e_T$ equals $l+1$ binary bits, where $l = 128$ or $l = 160$ in order to provide sufficient security for this underlying GQ scheme.

Certificate Issuing and Key Generation

In order to ensure that all parties in the scheme are legitimate coalition members, a central authority is used to certify all the agents that participate in the *MCKE* scheme. Most of the time, this central authority is a trusted third party (TTP), such as a certification authority (CA). In this proposed scheme the CA is also involved in key generation.

First of all, as is the case with all forms of public infrastructure, the CA must generate a pair of primes p_{ca} and q_{ca} to obtain the modulus $n_{ca} = p_{ca}q_{ca}$. Then it generates a pair of keys (e_{ca}, d_{ca}). It will keep (d_{ca}, p_{ca}, q_{ca}) safe but will either publish (e_{ca}, n_{ca}) in a depository or deliver them directly to all agents in the form of a CA certificate.

To generate keys for all of the agents in the coalition, a CA does the following:

1.   Generate a modulus n: This modulo n is for all the coalitions. The CA generates random $(\lceil K/2 \rceil - 1)$ bit primes p', q' such that both $p = 2p' + 1$ and $q = 2q' + 1$ are also primes, where $\lceil . \rceil$ is used to indicate a ceiling function. Such primes are called safe primes. The modulus n for all the coalitions is computed as $n = pq$.

2.   Generate the identities for agents: Each agent has an identity string that uniquely identifies itself. Identity strings for FA, HA and MA are defined as ID_{FAi}, ID_{HAj}, ID_{MAk}, respectively. For simplicity, the indices used for identity strings are not included here, unless there is a need to recognize one agent from another. Each identity string is hashed and signed by the CA in the following manner:

$$h_{(.)} = H(ID_{(.)}) \tag{3}$$

$$P_{(.)} = h_{(.)}^{d_{ca}} \pmod{n_{ca}} \tag{4}$$

where $h_{(.)}$ is the hashed identity string for an agent, $P_{(.)}$ is the public key for each agent that is signed by a CA, $H(\ )$ is a one-way collision-resistant hash function, and d_{ca} and n_{ca} are the private key and modulus of the CA, respectively. It is a requirement that the hash function be collision-resistant so no two agents will have the same secret keys, an event which will occur if the hash function outputs collide.

The signed identity is the public key for each agent. An agent without a signed identity will not be allowed to join any coalition. A mobile agent without a signed identity will not be able to sign signatures. Public keys for coalitions are generated using the identity of coalition members, and a public key for the coalition is valid only if all members have valid signed identities.

3.   Generate exponents: Exponents e_i are generated such that $2^l(1+(i-1)/T) < e_i < 2^l(1+i/T)$ for $i = 1, 2, ...T$. The e_i's are $l+1$ bit long primes and are relatively prime to $\emptyset(n)$, which is called the Euler Phi function. Itkis and Reyzin (2001) provided a detailed discussion of the requirements for the e_is. It is assumed a seed y can be used with a function H to generate these $e_1, ..., e_T$. This y can also be saved and used later to regenerate these $e_1, ..., e_T$.

4.   Generate private keys and public keys: It is known that the public key for a coalition should stay constant while the private keys evolve with time. The signing and verifying schemes are adopted from Guillou and Quisquater (1988). $SK_{(MA)_{t,r}}$, $SK_{(MA)_{t,r}}$, $SK_{(MA)_{t,r}}$ are called secret keys in the proposed scheme. Let B be defined as the base secret key for the coalition that corresponds to the secret identification number in the original GQ scheme, and let $B_{FA[1,T]}$, $B_{HA[1,T]}$ and $B_{MA[1,T]}$ be the base secret keys for each agent in the coalition. Then these parameters satisfy the equation:

$$B \equiv B_{FA[1,T]} B_{HA[1,T]} B_{MA[1,T]} \pmod{n}. \tag{5}$$

Functionally, the base secret for the three agents in the coalition can be thought of as the GQ secret identification number B split into three parts and distributed among three agents. However, when implemented, the reverse is true; that is, each agent gets its own base secret key and the keys are combined to produce the base secret for the coalition. The base secret for the agents satisfies the following equations:

$$(B_{(.)[1,T]})^{e1e2...eT} = (P_{(.)})^{-1} \pmod{n} \tag{6}$$

These equations are RSA problems (Rivest, Shamir & Adleman, 1978) and while it is difficult for an adversary to solve them because she does not know the factors of the modulus n, the CA can solve them easily. The CA must solve Eq. (6) for each agent, because security dictates that only the CA should know the factors of the modulus n. The computed base secrets will be delivered by the CA to the corresponding agents via a secure means. Then the public key for this coalition is simply:

$$PK \leftarrow (n, v, T) \tag{7}$$

where

$$v = \frac{1}{(B_{FA_{[1,T]}} B_{HA_{[1,T]}} B_{MA_{[1,T]}})^{e_1 e_2 ......e_T}} \pmod{n} = \frac{1}{B^{e_1 e_2 ......e_T}} \pmod{n} \tag{8}$$

Therefore

$$v = P_{FA} P_{HA} P_{MA} \pmod{n} \tag{9}$$

As long as the MA is connected to the same FA, the public key remains constant for this coalition. When a MA moves to another location and a new FA replaces the old FA, a new coalition is formed and the new public key can be obtained readily using Eq. (7) and Eq. (8).

At $t = 0$ the private keys for all agents are:

$$SK_{FA_0} \leftarrow (0, T, n, B_{FA_{[1,T]}}, \psi) \qquad (10)$$

$$SK_{HA_0} \leftarrow (0, T, n, B_{HA_{[1,T]}}, \psi) \qquad (11)$$

$$SK_{MA_0} \leftarrow (0, T, n, O, B_{MA_{[1,T]}}, O, \psi) \qquad (12)$$

where O is empty at $t = 0$ and will be filled by the update message SKU. Once the keys are generated, they are immediately updated and refreshed following the convention outlined by Bellare and Miner (1999).

Private Keys Update Algorithm

Private keys for all the agents are updated at the beginning of each time period in order to provide forward security in the proposed scheme. Each agent runs the update algorithm independently. FA and HA also send update messages to the MA. The update messages include t to indicate the message time period.

The following entities are defined:

$$SK_{HA_t} \leftarrow (t < T, T, n, B_{HA_{[t+1,T]}}, \psi) \qquad (13)$$

$$SK_{FA_t} \leftarrow (t < T, T, n, B_{FA_{[t+1,T]}}, \psi) \qquad (14)$$

$$SK_{MA_t} \leftarrow (t < T, T, n, \hat{s}_t, B_{MA_{[t+1,T]}}, e_t, \psi) \qquad (15)$$

$$SKU_{FA_t} \leftarrow B_{FA_{t+1}} \qquad (16)$$

$$SKU_{HA_t} \leftarrow B_{HA_{t+1}} \qquad (17)$$

The $e_{t+1}, e_{t+2}, \ldots\ldots, e_T$ are regenerated using ψ, and then the following are computed:

$$B_{()_{t+1}} \leftarrow B_{()_{[t+1,T]}}^{e_{t+2}\ldots\ldots e_T} \pmod{n} \qquad (18)$$

$$B_{()_{[t+2,s]}} \leftarrow B_{()_{[t+1,T]}}^{e_{t+1}} \pmod{n} \tag{19}$$

$$SKU_{()_t} = B_{()_{t+1}} \tag{20}$$

$$\hat{S}_{t+1} = B_{MA_{t+1}} B_{FA_{t+1}} B_{HA_{t+1}} \pmod{n} \tag{21}$$

where equations (18)-(19) apply to all agents, Eq. (20) applies to MA and HA and Eq. (21) is performed by MA to obtain the signing key for the coalition. The update algorithm returns $SK_{()_{t+1}}$ and $SKU_{()_t}$.

Note that all these equations do not contain the refresh indices in order to simplify the notations. After the keys are updated, the old keys for the past time periods must be erased by all agents.

Private Keys Refresh Algorithm

The private key refresh provides proactive key protection against exposure. Since the refresh algorithm is conducted within a time period, t is a constant during the key refresh while r increments until it reaches $RN(t)$ for this period.

The following items are defined:

$$SK_{HA_{t,r}} \leftarrow (t, T, n, B_{HA_{[t+1,T]}}, \psi) \tag{22}$$

$$SK_{HA_{t,r}} \leftarrow (t, T, n, \hat{s}_t, B_{MA_{[t+1,T]}}, e_t, \psi) \tag{23}$$

HA computes:

$$R_{HA_{t,r}} \xleftarrow{R} Z_n^* \tag{24}$$

$$B_{HA_{[t+1,T]}} = B_{HA_{[t+1,T]}} / R_{HA_{t,r}} \pmod{n} \tag{25}$$

and returns:

$$SK_{HA_{t,r+1}} \leftarrow (t, T, n, B_{HA_{[t+1,T]}}, \varepsilon) \tag{26}$$

$$SKR_{HA_{t,r}} = R_{HA_{t,r}} \tag{27}$$

MA computes:

$$R_{MA_{t,r}} = SKR_{HA_{t,r}} \tag{28}$$

$$B_{MA_{[t+1,T]}} = B_{MA_{[t+1,T]}} . R_{MA_{t,r}} (\bmod n) \tag{29}$$

and returns:

$$SK_{MA_{t,r+1}} \leftarrow (t, T, n, \hat{s}_t, B_{MA_{[t+1,T]}}, e_t, \varepsilon) \tag{30}$$

Signing Algorithm

Signing is done by the MA and the signature is sent to a verifier for verification. Hence, an intrusion can be detected if the signature is false. For a message M, the signature is (z, σ, t, e_t). A verifier need not compute e_t by itself.

An MA computes:

$$x \xleftarrow{R} Z_n^* \tag{31}$$

$$y = x^{e_t} (\bmod n) \tag{32}$$

$$\sigma = H(t, e_t, y, M) \tag{33}$$

$$z = x\hat{s}_t^{\sigma} (\bmod n) \tag{34}$$

and returns (z, σ, t, e_t) as a signature.

Verifying Algorithm

A verifying algorithm first must verify that e_t is within the correct specified range. It must also make sure z does not equal $0 (\bmod n)$, in order to eliminate the possibility of a signer cheating by selecting the random number x as 0.

Next input $(M, PK, (z, \sigma, t, e_t))$

  if $e_t \geq 2^l (1 + t/T)$ or $e_t < 2^l$ or e_t is even, return 0

  if $z \equiv 0 \pmod{n}$, then return 0 (reject the signature)

$$y' = z^{e_t} v^{\sigma} \pmod{n} \tag{35}$$

$$\sigma' = H(t, e_t, y', M) \tag{36}$$

  if $\sigma' = \sigma$, then return 1, otherwise return 0

Theorem 1: For message M, the signature generated at time period t by the signing algorithm, listed previously, is the correct signature.

Proof: From $y' \leftarrow z^{e_t} v^{\sigma} \pmod{n}$

  generate $y' \leftarrow (x\hat{s}^{\sigma})^{e_t} v^{\sigma} \pmod{n}$

  $\leftarrow x^{e_t} (\hat{s}^{e_t} v)^{\sigma} \pmod{n}$

  $\leftarrow x^{e_t} ((B_{FA_t} B_{MA_t} B_{HA_t})^{e_t} v)^{\sigma} \pmod{n}$

  $\leftarrow x^{e_t} ((B_{FA_{[1,T]}}^{e_1 \cdots e_{t-1} e_{t+1} \cdots e_T} B_{MA_{[1,T]}}^{e_1 \cdots e_{t-1} e_{t+1} \cdots e_T} B_{HA_{[1,T]}}^{e_1 \cdots e_{t-1} e_{t+1} \cdots e_T})^{e_t} v)^{\sigma} \pmod{n}$

By definition:

$$v = \frac{1}{(B_{FA_{[1,T]}} B_{HA_{[1,T]}} B_{MA_{[1,T]}})^{e_1 e_2 \ldots e_T}} \pmod{n} \tag{37}$$

$$x^{e_t} (1)^{\sigma} \pmod{n} = x^{e_t} \pmod{n} = y \tag{38}$$

Therefore $y' = y$

Application of MCKE Scheme

The MCKE scheme can be easily applied to provide security for mobile-IP and be a very useful tool in m-commerce. First of all, we require that the binding update message be signed and the signature needs to be verified by a CN; therefore it is impossible for a malicious node that does not have a certificate to generate a legitimate binding update message.

Secondly, when creating certificates for all agents, one can construct the ID strings to include information such as IP address, location of the agent, the organization it belongs to, and so forth, to correctly identify each agent. A binding update message consists of the IP address of MA and CoA. When the binding update message is signed, the IP addresses of the signing agents are also included in the signature. A CN will check to make sure the IP addresses in the binding update message and that of the IP addresses contained in public keys of the FA and MA are the same. This way, a node with valid certificate and signing key cannot generate a binding update message using another node's IP address.

Thirdly, a mobile node cannot submit a binding update message with a CoA that is not the address of the FA, since the message is signed by the FA also. In order to generate a binding update message with the CoA of a specific FA, an MA has to physically move to the subnet where the FA is located.

In summery, MCKE scheme can effectively authenticate the binding update message and thus by combining MCKE with mobile-IP, the security threats facing mobile-IP no longer exist.

In m-commerce application, MCKE provides the strongest security against signing key compromise of all the current digital signature schemes. Forward-security mechanism in MCKE provides non-repudiation for transactions. If all the agents are compromised at time period P and at the same refresh interval, the signature at and after period P will be invalid but all the signatures signed and transactions conducted before period P will still stand; otherwise, even the future transaction will not be affected.

In a real m-commerce transaction, for example, MCKE can utilize a software mobile-agent module such as these used by Borselius, Mitchell and Wilson (2001) or Roth, Jalali, Hartman and Roland (2000). Notice that the software mobile-agent module defined by them is not the same as the MA that we defined before. To avoid confusion we will use m-agent to denote the software mobile-agent module. An m-agent can be dispatched by MA to visit different service providers to find the desired service and to ask the providers for price offers. Some of the crucial information, such as the route of the m-agent to service providers, can be signed using the public key of the MA. In the mean time, the MA can be offline and later connect to the network from another location. After the m-agent obtains all the information, it will find the new location that the MA is attached to because of mobile-IP. The MA will negotiate with the service provider that offers the best price of service and then both parties will sign the contract to finalize the transaction.

Security of MCKE Scheme

Random Oracle Model

The random oracle model will be used to show the security of our scheme. This model was introduced by Bellare and Rogaway (1993). They argue that the random oracle model, where all parties (including an adversary) have access to a public random oracle, provides a bridge between cryptographic theory and practice. Collision-resistant hash functions *H* are assumed to behave like a *truly random function* and are treated as a *black box*. A truly random function takes a value as input and generates a random value as output. This assumption is defined as the random oracle model. The key point about the random oracle is that one cannot compute the hash of a value *x* using a hash function. Instead, one has to query the hash oracle to obtain the hash value *H(x)* when running the random oracle model. Another key point is that with the same input, the hash oracle must output the same value for consistency.

The random oracle model is a useful tool for validating and constructing natural cryptographic schemes. Many signature schemes that are based on the random oracle are very efficient and some of them cannot be proven secure without the help of random oracles (Noar, 2003). No practical protocol that has been proven secure in the random oracle model has been broken when used with a "good" hash function, such as SHA-1.

Definition of Security for MCKE

Let Q be the set of valid key exposure queries at time period $t \geq 1$ and refresh number r, $1 \leq r \leq RN(t)$, we say that the scheme is (t, Q)-compromised if:

Definition 2: For any set of valid key exposure queries Q, the *MCKE* scheme is (t, Q)-compromised if:

- $("MA", t, r) \in Q$; or

- If $r > 1$ and $("refresh", t, r-1) \in Q$, and $("MA", t, r-1) \in Q$; or

- If $r = 1$, $("update", t) \in Q$, and $("MA", t-1, RN(t-1)) \in Q$; or

- $("HA", t', r) \in Q$, $("MA", t', r) \in Q$, $("FA", t') \in Q$ and $t' < t$

Based on this definition, a particular time period t is rendered insecure if either

- the mobile agent is broken into during that time period, or

- all three agents are broken into during a previous time period and prior to the time the refresh between home agent and mobile agent occurs.

If a mobile agent is compromised without a valid refresh, then it can generate a valid signature for that period only. If a mobile agent is compromised and keeps receiving valid refresh messages, then it can generate valid signatures for all future periods. Therefore, the proactive detection of a compromised mobile agent is necessary to prevent an adversary from receiving valid refresh messages. This proactive detection scheme may adopt the available intrusion detection techniques and, as a result, will be a subject for future research. It is assumed that the proactive authentication is applied to every refresh and update. Update and refresh messages, as well as the three keys, prevent the adversary from forging signatures in the proposed model, since an adversary must combine individual keys of each agent, in unbroken chains, with update and refresh messages.

In the case in which all keys of the three agents are compromised at the same time, the adversary is able to forge signatures for the future too. One goal of our scheme is to prevent an adversary from forging past signatures; hence, we consider the forward security scheme invalid when an adversary is able to forge signatures in the past.

Itkis and Reyzin (2002) have suggested using a strong adaptive adversary in the discussion of their security model. The adversary operates in an adaptive mode by querying oracles based on previously received answers in order to determine the proper keys and signatures. However, proving security against such an adversary is difficult to model. Our scheme is more complex than that of Itkis and Reyzin (2002), and it will be even harder to prove security. Nonetheless, since our scheme is an extension of a forward-secure signature scheme, the added complexity makes it more difficult for the adversary to compromise the underlying security. Although the adversary is fully adaptive and has the power to determine which agent to compromise and which messages to intercept, it will not help her forge a signature if the O_{expo} query does not result in the scheme being (t, Q)-compromised. When compared with the attacks against a standard forward-secure scheme by an adaptive adversary, it can be argued that the security of our scheme can be reduced to that of a standard forward-secure signature scheme in the case where every O_{expo} query results in a (t, Q)-compromise. Therefore, we can use the insecurity function of the underlying forward-secure scheme as the upper bound, and the attack is deemed successful if the adversary is able to forge a signature for a previous period and the message has not been used as a query in the past.

With the foregoing reasoning in mind, we model an attack by the adversary F on our scheme with the following experiment.

Experiment 1: F-$Forge(MCKE,F)$

$t \leftarrow 0; r \leftarrow 0;$

$(PK, SK_{(.)_{1,r}}) \xleftarrow{\quad R \quad} MCKE.KeyGen(T, K, l, e) \, ;$

for $t = 1$ to T

$(SK_{(.)_t}, SKU_{(.)_{t-1}} \leftarrow MCKE.Update(SK_{(.)_{t-1}}) \, ;$

for $r = 1$ to $RN(t)$

$$(SK_{(.)_{t,r}}, SKR_{(.)_{t,r}}) \leftarrow MCKE.Refresh(SK_{(.)_{t, r-1}})$$

$$d \leftarrow F^{O_{Sign}, O_{hash}, O_{expo}}(PK, t, K, RN)$$

$\qquad\qquad$ if d = breakin, go to forge phase

$\qquad\qquad$ else continue

$\qquad$ end loop

$\quad$ end loop

forge: $(M, (z, \sigma, t, e_t)) \leftarrow F\,(forge, SK_b)$

if $MCKE.Ver(M, (z, \sigma, t, e_t)) = 1$ and $1 \le b \le j$

$\quad$ and M was not in the O_{sign} in period b

$\quad$ then return 1 else 0.

$F^{O_{Sign}, O_{hash}, O_{expo}}(PK, t, K, RN)$ represents the forging algorithm with access to signing, hash and exposure oracles $(O_{sign}, Q_{hash}, O_{expo})$, and with inputs PK, t, K, and RN.

In order to break the scheme, an algorithm A is built which runs forger F as a subroutine with a random tape. While running the subroutine, the state of F is preserved and the same random tape will be played later. The adversary asks A to sign and hash queries and then outputs a value d. As long as d is not the special value breakin, the adversary moves to the next period and initiates queries using the next key. This described process is strictly ordered. Once the adversary moves to another period or enters the break-in phase, the periods visited before is not allowed to access the oracle again. At some point, the adversary will decide to use O_{expo} and is returned the key $SK_{(.)_t}$ at period t. If the adversary does not break in by the last period, she will be given a key $SK_{(.)_{T+1}}$ that is actually an empty string. Due to the design of our scheme, not every break-in results in compromising the signing key. However, in this case we can assume that m is the probability of compromising the signing key during each O_{expo}, and then the discussion will be reduced to that of a standard forward-secure signature scheme.

Security Functions for MCKE

Following the concrete security paradigm used by Bellare and Rogaway (1996), the MCKE scheme is associated with an insecurity function that generates the maximum probability of breaking the scheme. This function is defined as the maximum probability over all adversarial strategies restricted to resource bounds specified as arguments to the insecurity function.

Definition 3: Let $MCKE=(MCKE.keyGen;\ MCKE.Sign;\ MEKE.Ver;\ MCKE.Update;$ $MCKE.Refresh)$ be a mobile coalition key-evolving signature scheme with security parameters K and l, the total number of time periods T and refresh number RN. Let F be an adversary who runs a forging algorithm $F\text{-}Forge(MCKE, F)$ that returns 1 if successful and 0 otherwise. The adversary success function is defined as

$$Succ^{MCKE}(MCKE(K,l,T,RN), F) = \Pr[F.Forge(MCKE, F) = 1] \qquad (39)$$

Let the insecurity of *MCKE* be the function $Insec^{MCKE}(MCKE(K, l, T, RN), \tau, q_{sign}, q_{hash})$, which achieves the maximum value of $Succ^{MCKE}(MCKE(K, l, T, RN), F)$ over all adaptive adversaries F that run in at most time τ and ask at most q_{sign} signature queries and q_{hash} hash queries. That is:

$$In\sec^{MCKE}(MCKE(K,l,T,RN), \tau, q_{sign}, q_{hash}) =$$

$$\underset{F}{MAX}\{Succ^{MCKE}(MCKE(K,l,T,RN), F)\} \qquad (40)$$

Finally, $MCKE(K,l,T,RN)$ is defined as $(\tau, \varepsilon, q_{sign}, q_{hash})$ - intrusion-resilient if:

$$In\sec^{MCKE}(MCKE(K,l,T,RN), \tau, q_{sign}, q_{hash}) < \varepsilon \qquad (41)$$

Intuitively, the smaller the insecurity function, the more secure the scheme. To obtain an asymptotic definition of security, one would assemble polynomials that relate K, l, and T to a single security parameter, $Insec^{MCKE}$, and define the scheme to be *MCKE*-secure if the insecurity function, containing this security parameter, is negligible.

Let A be an algorithm, which the adversary runs to break the strong RSA assumption that is assumed to be a hard mathematical problem by cryptographers. The algorithm can be outlined in the following experiment:

Experiment 2: Brk-SRSA(K, l, A)

Randomly choose primes p' and q' of length $(\lceil K/2 \rceil - 1)$ each, such that $2p'+1$ and $2q'+1$ are both primes.

$$p \leftarrow 2p'+1; \ q \leftarrow 2q'+1; n \leftarrow pq$$

$$\alpha \xleftarrow{\ R\} Z_n^*; (\beta, e) \leftarrow A(\alpha, n)$$

If $1 < e < 2^{l+1}$ and $\beta^e \equiv \alpha \pmod{n}$ then return 1 else

return 0

Let $Succ^{SRSA}(K, l, A)$ denote the probability that the experiment returns 1. Let the "insecurity function" $InSec^{SRSA}(K, l, \tau)$ denote the maximum value of $Succ^{SRSA}(K, l, A)$ over all algorithms the adversary runs in at most time τ. This represents the maximum probability of an adversary breaking the strong RSA in time τ.

$$InSec^{SRSA}(K, l, \tau) = \underset{A}{MAX}\{Succ^{SRSA}(K, l, A)\} \tag{42}$$

Every cryptographer assumes that $InSec^{SRSA}(K, l, \tau)$ is negligible for a τ polynomial in K, that is, $\tau < K^C$, where C is a constant. The value l determines the length of e and thus the security level, as indicated earlier. As a result, the smaller the value of l, the weaker the assumption.

Security Theorems of MCKE

The security of the MCKE scheme is ensured by the following two theorems:

Theorem 2: Given a forger F for $MCKE(K, l, \tau, RN)$ that runs in time at most τ, asking at most q_{sign} signing queries and q_{hash} hash queries, such that $Succ^{MCKE}$ $(MCKE(K, l, T, RN), F) > \varepsilon$, we can construct an algorithm A that, on inputs n, $a \in Z_n^*$ and l, runs in time τ' and outputs (β,e) such that $1 < e \le 2^{l+1}$ and $\beta^e = \alpha \pmod n$ with probability ε', where:

$$\tau' = 2\tau / \mu + O(lT(l^2T^2 + K^2)) \tag{43}$$

$$\varepsilon' = \frac{(\varepsilon - 2^{2-K} q_{sign}(q_{hash}+1))^2}{T^2(q_{hash}+1)} - \frac{\varepsilon - 2^{2-K} q_{sign}(q_{hash}+1)}{2^l T} \tag{44}$$

m is the probability of an adversary compromising the signing key during each break-in for one time period (or query of the O_{expo} oracle).

Theorem 3: For any τ, q_{sign}, and q_{hash}

$$Insec^{MCKE}(MCKE(K, l, T, RN), \tau, q_{sign}, q_{hash})$$
$$\le T\sqrt{(q_{hash}+1)InSec^{SRSA}(K, l, \tau')} + 2^{-l}T(q_{hash}+1) + 2^{2-K} q_{sign}(q_{hash}+1), \tag{45}$$

where

$$\tau' = 2\tau / \mu + O(lT(l^2T^2 + K^2)) \tag{46}$$

Conclusion

A three-tier signature signing and key-updating scheme, referred to as a *mobile coalition key-evolving (MCKE)* signature scheme for intrusion-resilient mobile networks, has been introduced in this chapter, in order to meet the challenges facing m-commerce applications in wireless/mobile network. In this proposed scheme, three entities, FA, HA and MA, which map to the mobile-IP structure, form a coalition in a dynamically forming path. The signature is generated and verified as follows:

- Each agent has a pair of private and public keys.

- All the private keys of the three agents in the coalition are required to sign a signature.

- All the messages are signed and verified.

- Each coalition member is identified by an identity string, which is hashed using a hash function, and signed by a certification authority (CA). The signed ID string is the public key for the specific agent. All the agents in the coalition must have the signed public key in order to join the coalition.

- The signature is verified against a public key, which is the product of the public keys of all the agents.

- The public key for the coalition can be easily computed as the product of each agent's public key. This enables the new coalition public key to be computed dynamically when an MA roams into a new FA.

This procedure provides help in preventing an adversary from an impersonation using a fake FA or MA. This scheme is also useful in preventing intrusion in a mobile/wireless environment.

To prevent an adversary from forging a valid signature, the following procedures are used:

- The evolving private key is a one-way function of time and cannot be regenerated for the past; hence, the past signatures cannot be forged.

- A proactive/interactive private key-evolving scheme is proposed to prevent an adversary from forging a future signature unless this adversary compromises all three members of the coalition.

- Periodic refresh is performed interactively to avoid the problem of losing synchronization and is an improvement on the scheme proposed by Itkis and Reyzin (2002).

- For the case in which a mobile device is lost, that device may be used to generate a valid signature in a refresh period; however, it will no longer be useful since the proactive synchronization scheme is used.

In the worst-case scenario, when all the private keys of the agents in the coalition are compromised at the same time, forward security is still preserved because the adversary cannot forge a signature generated in the past. Thus, it is possible to detect intrusion into mobile networks and the moment that intrusion occurs based on valid signatures. This proposed scheme introduces only a small overhead when securing mobile networks.

This intrusion-resilient network security algorithm can accommodate dynamically forming mobile networks and enhance their flexibility. The use of this scheme provides more security for mobile-commerce applications because ordinary digital signature schemes are ineffective if the secret keys are compromised, an event that occurs more often in wireless/mobile networks than in fixed-wired networks. By employing this new scheme, an intruder can be readily detected while trying to forge a signature.

Applying this scheme to mobile-IP, it is impossible for an MA, be it benign or hostile, to generate a digitally signed binding update message with false CoA or MA address content. Thus this scheme is effective in preventing the security threats facing the current mobile-IP protocols. This scheme maintains a very high digital signature key security while at the same time allowing for great mobility of network devices. This provides a guarantee for safer m-commerce transactions.

References

Abdalla, M., & Reyzin, L. (2000). A new forward-secure digital signature scheme. In *Advances in Cryptology-ASIACRYPT*. Springer-Verlag. Full version available from the Cryptology ePrint Archive, record 2000/002, *http://eprint.iacr.org/*

Anderson, R. (1997). Invited lecture. *Fourth Annual Conference on Computer and Communications Security*. ACM References.

Bellare, M., & Miner, S. (1999). A forward-secure digital signature scheme. In M. Wiener (Ed.), *Advances in Cryptology-CRYPTO '99* (vol. 1666 of LNCS, pp. 431-448). Springer-Verlag.

Bellare, M., & Rogaway, P. (1993). Random oracles are practical: A paradigm for designing efficient protocols. In *Proceedings of the 1st ACM Conference on Computer and Communication Security* (pp. 62-73). Revised version appears in *http://www-cse.ucsd.edu/users/mihir/papers/crypto-papers.html*

Bellare, M., & Rogaway, P. (1996). The exact security of digital signatures: How to sign with RSA and Rabin. In U. Maurer (Ed.), *Advances in Cryptology-Eurocrypt 96 Proceedings, Lecture Notes in Computer Science* (vol. 1070). Springer-Verlag.

Borselius, N., Mitchell, J.C., & Wilson, A. (2001). On mobile agent based transactions in moderately hostile environments. *Advances in Network and Distributed Systems Security, Proceedings of IFIP First Annual Working Conference on Network Security*.

Desmedt, Y., & Frankel, Y. (1989). Threshold cryptosystems. In G. Brassard (Ed.), *Advances in Cryptology-CRYPTO* (vol. 435 of LNCS, pp. 307-315). Springer-Verlag.

Dodis, Y., Katz, J., Xu, S., & Yung, M. (2002). Key-insulated public key cryptosystems. In L. Knudsen (Ed.), *Advances in Cryptology-EUROCRYPT, Lecture Notes in Computer Science.* Springer-Verlag.

Goldwasser, S., Micali, S., & Rivest, R.L. (1988). A digital signature scheme secure against adaptive chosen-message attacks. *SIAM Journal on Computing, 17*(2), 281-308.

Guillou, L.C., & Quisquater, J.J. (1988). A "paradoxical" identity-based signature scheme resulting from zero-knowledge. In S. Goldwasser (Ed.), *Advances in Cryptology-CRYPTO* (vol. 403 of LNCS, pp. 216-231). Springer-Verlag.

Herzberg, A., Jakobsson, M., Jarecki, S.L., Krawczyk, H., & Yung, M. (1997). Proactive public key and signature systems. *Fourth ACM Conference on Computer and Communication Security* (pp. 100-110).

Itkis, G., & Reyzin, L. (2001). Forward-secure signatures with optimal signing and verifying. In J. Kilian (Ed.), *Advances in Cryptology-CRYPTO, of Lecture Notes in Computer Science* (vol. 2139, pp. 332-354). Springer-Verlag.

Itkis, G., & Reyzin, L. (2002). SiBIR: Signer-base intrusion-resilient signatures. In M. Yung (Ed.), *Advances in Cryptology-CRYPTO* (LNCS 2442, pp. 499-514). Springer-Verlag.

Kozlov, A., & Reyzin, L. (2002). Forward-secure signatures with fast key update. In *Proceedings of the Third Conference on Security in Communication.*

Krawczyk, H. (2000). Simple forward-secure signatures from any signature scheme. In *7th ACM Conference on Computer and Communication Security.*

Malkin, T., Micciancio, D., & Miner, S. (2002). Efficient generic forward-secure signatures with an unbounded number of time periods. In L. Knudsen (Ed.), *Advances in Cryptology-EUROCRYPT, Lecture Notes in Computer Science* (vol. 2332, pp. 400-417). Springer-Verlag.

Mankin, A., Patil, B., Harkins, D., Nordmark, E., Nikander, P., Roberts, P., & Narten, T. (2001). *Threat models introduced by Mobile IPv6 and requirements for security in mobile IPv6, Internet draft.*

Mobile-IP. (n.d). Working group on IP routing for wireless/mobile hosts. Retrieved September 30, 2003, from *http://www.leapforum.org/published/mobileIpSurvey/ split/node4.html*

Nikander, P., & Perkins, C. (2001). Binding authentication key establishment protocol for mobile IPv6. *http://draft-perkins-bake-01.txt*

Noar, M. (2003). On cryptographic assumptions and challenges. In D. Boneh (Ed.), *Advances in Cryptology-CRYPTO* (vol. 2729 of LNCS, pp. 96-109). Springer-Verlag.

Nordmark, E. (2001). Securing MIPv6 BU's using return routability (BU3WAY). Retrieved from *http://draft-nordmark-mobileip-bu3way-00.txt*

Ostrovsky, R., & Yung, M. (1991). How to withstand mobile virus attacks. *Proceedings of the 10th Annual ACM Symposium on Principles of Distributed Computing* (pp. 51-59).

Perkins, C. (1996a). IP encapsulation within IP. *RFC 2003.*

Perkins, C. (1996b). Minimal encapsulation within IP. *RFC 2004.*

Perkins, C., & Johnson, D.B. (2001). Route optimization in mobile IP. Retrieved from *http://draft-ietf-mobileip-optim-11.txt*

Rivest, R.L., Shamir, A., & Adleman, L.M. (1978). A method for obtaining digital signatures and public-key cryptosystems. *Communications of the ACM, 21*(2), 120-126.

Roe, M., Aura, T., Shea, G.O., & Arkko, J. (2002). Authentication of mobile IPv6 binding updates and acknowledgements. Retrieved from *http://draft-roe-mobileipupdateauth-02.txt*

Roth, V., Jalali, M., Hartman, R., & Roland, C. (2000). An application of mobile agents as personal assistants in electronic commerce. *Proceedings of 5th Conference on the Practical Application of Intelligent Agents and Multi-Agent Technology* (pp. 121-132).

Shamir, A. (1979). How to share a secret. *Communications of the ACM, 22,* 612-613.

Shamir, A. (1983). On the generation of cryptographically strong pseudorandom sequences. *ACM Transactions on Computer Systems, 1*(1), 38-44.

Thomson, S., & Narten, T. (1998). IPv6 stateless address autoconfiguration. *RFC 2462.*

Zhang, Q. (2003). Intrusion resilient digital signature key security in mobile/wireless networks. PhD Dissertation. Electrical and Computer Engineering Department, Auburn University.

Chapter XIV

Smart Card Based Protocol for Secure and Controlled Access of Mobile Host in IPv6 Compatible Foreign Network

R. K. Ghosh, Indian Institute of Technology, Kanpur, India

Abhinav Arora, Indian Institute of Technology, Guwahati, India

Gautam Barua, Indian Institute of Technology, Guwahati, India

Abstract

We present a proposal to combine the advantages of IPSec and smart cards in order to design a new protocol for secure bi-directional access of mobile hosts in an IPv6 foreign network using smart cards. The protocol, called Mobile Authentication Protocol (MAP), builds a security association needed for IPsec. An access router in a foreign network contacts an AAA (Authentication, Authorization and Accounting) server in order to authenticate and authorize a mobile host that approaches the router to access services. The access router then acts as a gateway for all subsequent service requirements of the mobile host. The access router interoperates between two protocols, namely,

MAP to communicate with clients, and the AAA protocol to communicate with AAA servers. MAP works at the application layer and uses UDP as the transport layer. Therefore, MAP works independently of the data link layer protocols. It also supports features to establish a Local Security Association (LSA) between an access router and mobile hosts. The LSA is used to offer keying material to protect communication between a mobile host and an access router of a visited domain. The proposed design of the access router enables it to control access using IPv6 and to act as an interface between MAP and Diameter (as the AAA protocol). The network access control is secured by using IPSec by utilizing keying material offered by the LSA.

Introduction

A major concern in mobile electronic commerce (m-commerce) is security. M-commerce refers to the use of cellular phones for accessing Internet services for commercial transactions. With the availability of GPRS and higher data rate 3G services, it is expected that IP will be available end-to-end. So most of the m-commerce traffic can then be carried over IP. The security concerns and the solutions for m-commerce and e-commerce will converge, but with the constraints imposed by the limitations of mobile devices.

IP Security (IPsec) (Kent & Atkinson, 1998c) is a technology that is being deployed in current solutions using fixed Internet devices. But successful deployment of IPSec in mobile applications needs public key infrastructure (PKI) for establishing security associations (SAs). Establishing the PKI infrastructure that includes the existence of a certification authority (CA) and distribution of keys and so forth has turned out to be a difficult task. Other major drawbacks of PKI for mobile applications are large processing power needed for key generation, and relatively high bandwidth requirement for key exchange procedures.

A related development is the adoption of smart cards as secure identification and authentication elements. Global System for Mobile (GSM) communication and its evolutions use SIM cards for authentication and authorization. Smart cards are also widely deployed in financial markets as secure, portable, identification and data storage devices. An increasing number of credit cards and debit cards are incorporating smart card technology for adding security features.

The current generation of smart cards supports only a single application. But with increase in the number of applications that uses smart cards, the need for these cards to support multiple applications is growing. Emerging mobile technologies are also expected to support such multi-application smart cards. With these technological trends in mind, it can be concluded that multi-application SIM cards will be an important part of the future mobile network security scenario. IP, and especially IPv6, will become the predominant networking technology for mobile devices. It is expected that IPSec (which is mandatory in IPv6) will play an important role in securing m-commerce transactions.

In this chapter we present a proposal to combine the advantages of IPSec and smart cards to provide a security platform for m-commerce. A protocol for security service provision and negotiation is proposed which will be able to provide the security associations needed for IPSec. Furthermore, smart cards can be used to drive them. Smart cards may support either a single application or multiple applications. These applications should be able to share credentials and keys of a single application card, for example, GSM; or be able to use secondary keys provided by the single application, for example, SIM Toolkit applications.

Any link created without some form of authentication will be vulnerable to network attacks like man-in-the-middle attacks or replay attacks. There must be some mechanism that enables gateways to reliably identify each other. Without this, they cannot trust each other and so cannot create a genuinely secure link. To build secure links, we use a system where the two systems authenticate each other using shared keys, and then negotiate their own secret keys for encryption purposes. In order to get access to a foreign network, the authentication of a client is done through an AAA (de Laat, Gross, Gommans, Vollbrecht & Spence, 2000) infrastructure provided by its home server. The AAA infrastructure allows the client to authenticate itself by providing credential data using a secret key shared by it and the home server.

To summarize, the main focus of this work is on the design and prototype implementation of a protocol called the Mobile Authentication Protocol (MAP) that allows a mobile host to gain access to a foreign network using a smart card as the security and authentication device. Therefore, the following issues were examined during the design and implementation of this protocol.

- Cryptographic functions.

- Applets for Java smart cards.

- AAA Architecture and AAA protocols.

- Access Router (AR) application design.

- Secure access control in the IP layer.

- IP security and concept of (local) security association.

- IPv6 and the stateless address auto-configuration.

- User Registration Protocol (URP).

- Linux IPSec implementation.

The rest of the chapter is organized into eight sections. The next section provides a quick review of smart card technology. It also includes a discussion on the specific advantages of Java smart cards which have led us to choose them for implementing MAP. The AAA architecture is discussed in the third section. This section also points out the advantages of choosing Diameter over RADIUS as the AAA protocol. The fourth section deals with the network security layer focusing on IPSec and related IPv6 implementation aspects over Linux. MAP as a User Registration Protocol (URP) is discussed in the fifth section, while an overview of MAP appears in the sixth section. The specification of the protocol is provided in the seventh section, and the eighth section deals with implementation. The ninth section ends the chapter with concluding remarks.

Smart Cards

A smart card is a credit card-size plastic card with an embedded integrated circuit. It has some memory capacity and limited computational capability. Since a card is self-contained, it is relatively immune to security attacks as opposed to devices that have to depend upon potentially vulnerable external resources. That is why smart cards are often used in different applications that require strong security protection and authentication. Smart cards, unlike magnetic stripe cards, carry information that can be altered. These cards can be categorized as follows, based on their capabilities.

- *Memory Cards*: A memory card can hold between 64KB to 1MB of data, but does not have a processor on it. Memory cards usually have larger storage capacity compared to smarter cards that have processing hardware. But these cards have to depend on a card reader for reading information. One of the common uses of a memory card is a pre-paid telephone card. Such cards are not really "smart". An optical memory card is more advanced than a magnetic stripe card. It can store much more information. Typically about 4 MB of data can be stored in an optical memory card. One common usage of an optical memory card is as a personal identification card.

- *Microprocessor Cards*: A microprocessor card, also known as a chip card, has greater memory storage and security of data than a traditional 125 bytes processor-less magnetic stripe card. The five main components of a chip card are the CPU, ROM, RAM, EEPROM and I/O controller. The card OS is stored in ROM. The RAM is used for working memory. Most of the data are stored in EEPROM. The CPU is usually an 8-bit processor driven by a 5 MHz clock. But the trend is toward chip cards built with 32-bit RISC processors along with math co-processors. Math co-processors are needed if there is requirement for encryption. Most cards have ROM varying from 6 KB to 24 KB, RAM varying from 0.5 KB to 1 KB, and EEPROM varying from 1 KB to 16 KB. Four types of chip cards are used, namely, contact cards, contact-less cards, hybrid cards and combi-cards. Contact cards are the ones that are most commonly used. Specifications of contact card standards are available under ISO 7816 series part 1-10. ISO 14443 standards define specifications for contact-less cards.

Java Card

The major difference between a Java smart card and a conventional smart card is that the former uses Java to implement programs, whereas the latter uses programs written in other languages.

The Java card specification enables Java technology to run on smart cards and on devices with limited resources. There are certain basic advantages of using a Java card instead of a non-Java smart card.

- The applets programmed for a Java card can run on any Java-based smart card, independent of the card's vendor or manufacturer.

- Java cards inherit the security features of the Java programming language. Multiple applications can co-exist securely on a single smart card. Applets can be confined to operate in their respective areas using an applet firewall mechanism. But at the same time, a well-defined secure object sharing mechanism also exists to support cooperative applications on a single card.

- New applications can be installed securely even after a card has been issued.

- The programs using the Java card API will run on any Java-compatible card. In contrast, non-Java smart cards can only be used in applications they are originally designed for.

Interested readers can refer to the URL: http://www.java.sun.com/ for further details concerning architecture, applet firewall mechanism for sharing and protection, and so forth, which have motivated us to choose Java smart cards for implementation of MAP.

AAA Architecture

An Authentication Authorization Accounting (AAA) (de Laat et al., 2000; Vollbrecht et al., 2000) infrastructure is required to authenticate and authorize users for use of resources. Authentication is the process of verifying an identity claimed by a user. Authorization is a right or permission granted to a user to access a system resource. Accounting monitors the consumption pattern of resources for the purposes of cost allocation, auditing, and billing.

A full-fledged discussion on AAA is beyond the scope of this chapter. Interested readers may refer to Metz (1999) for a brief tutorial on the subject. The coverage here is restricted to those features required by our scheme. The protocol needs to operate in a multi-domain environment with multiple service providers as well as entities taking on multiple roles, including that as an AAA server.

AAA servers are central repositories for storing AAA information. Sometimes multiple servers may be used for resiliency in AAA services. AAA client functions are deployed at devices acting as entry points to the network being protected. The device may be a terminal server, a network access router or just another host.

In our scheme, AAAv is an AAA server in the visited network and AAAh is an AAA server in the home network of the mobile host. The AAAh server of an access client (mobile host) has access to the AAA database that holds the authentication and authorization data of that client. The AAAv server on the other hand has to forward a mobile host's requests to its AAAh server. The most important entity in this scheme is a Network Access Server (NAS) or Access Router (AR) (Mitton, 2000). An AR serving as the network entry point provides an interface between the internal IP network and mobile hosts. Apart from providing typical routing services, an AR has to provide services on a per-user basis. Consequently, it has to interact with an AAA Server to obtain a client's authentication and accounting data.

Remote Authentication Dial In User Service (RADIUS) (Rigney, Willens, Rubens & Simpson, 2000) and Diameter (Calhoun et al., 2001) are two widely used protocols that provide AAA solutions. Initially, RADIUS was designed to provide authentication in the PPP protocol used in dial-up connections. An IETF working group formalized the protocol in 1996. The base protocol functions and message formats are documented in RFC 2138 (Rigney, Willens, Rubens & Simpson, 1997).

When compared to Diameter, RADIUS suffers from a number of shortcomings, restricting its use for roaming services, especially for mobile users. The important among these shortcomings are:

- *Low security guarantee.* RADIUS uses a client/server communication model. The communication between a RADIUS client and a RADIUS server is protected by a shared key. RADIUS provides only hop-by-hop security. So any intermediate hop can easily modify data/information without being traced. Thus, there is no end-to-end security guarantee in RADIUS. The systems based on RADIUS accounting cannot be deployed on untrustworthy proxies. Encryption of only AAA data is possible in RADIUS. RADIUS cannot prevent a replay attack. An old packet can be replayed by a malicious NAS without being detected.

- *Low scalability.* Only up to 255 outstanding requests can be handled by RADIUS. Allowing client mobility would mean introduction of more NASs. This implies that a low limit on outstanding message requests is decidedly impractical. In addition, RADIUS has no windowing support and UDP — over which RADIUS runs — cannot control the flow of messages at the transport layer. Therefore, RADIUS suffers from congestion problems. Consequently, RADIUS is recommended for only small to medium sized networks.

- *Low transmission reliability.* A client will never know the state of proxies or servers in the chain of hops that connects it to its peer. Only a timeout can recognize that some intermediate proxy is down. This causes long disruption in service. Furthermore, RADIUS silently discards messages that do not have the expected information/data. Since there is no way for a NAS to know that a request has been discarded, it may send the same request to another server, assuming the first one to be down. The second server will also silently discard the request like the first. So the process will continue until the NAS itself abandons the request.

- *Low AVP space.* Low AVP (attribute value pair) space (only 256 possible) makes it difficult to implement any local policies, including transport layer security or mobile node authentication. Vendor-specific commands also cannot be supported due to the limited AVP space.

- *Heavy processing requirement.* RADIUS does not impose any alignment requirements. This places unnecessary burden on most processors. Mobile nodes are not
  expected to be equipped with heavy processing capabilities. This inhibits use of
  RADIUS for roaming services.

Diameter as AAA Protocol

Diameter (Calhoun et al., 2001) is two times the RADIUS! It not only includes the
functionalities of RADIUS, but also has enhanced support for new technologies, and is
specifically designed for roaming services. Apart from the base protocol, Diameter
includes several extensions and applications like MobileIP (Perkins, 1996), CMS (Cryptographic Message Syntax) security, NASREQ (NAS requirements), and so forth.

As opposed to RADIUS, Diameter runs over either TCP or Stream-Control-Transmission
Protocol (SCTP). Servers have to support both protocols and the clients can support any
one of them. Both TCP and SCTP are reliable transport protocols. They provide error-free,
acknowledged transfer of packets with duplicate elimination. But both the protocols are
heavier compared to UDP and increase the amount of traffic compared to the latter. Both
SCTP and TCP support retransmission as well as windowing. The Diameter protocol
requires each node on the proxy chain to acknowledge each request and be responsible
for retransmission of unacknowledged requests. Consequently,

1. Silent discarding of packets as seen in RADIUS is not possible.
2. The connection disruption witnessed in RADIUS is by and large eliminated as
   unreachable nodes can be detected quickly.
3. Congestion is controlled by windowing flow of packets to servers.

Diameter uses a peer-to-peer communication model. Unsolicited messages can be sent
from one peer to another. This allows servers also to initiate the termination of a session.

Replay attack is eliminated in Diameter by using time stamping. Diameter provides not
only hop-by-hop security like RADIUS, but also provides end-to-end security. CMS
security operates by encapsulating CMS objects in AVPs. Since Diameter has a much
larger Attribute-Value Pair (AVP) space (2^{32}) compared to RADIUS (256), it is possible
to use AVPs to provide CMS security. CMS security secures messages by two main
techniques: (i) digital signatures (along with digital certificates), and (ii) encryption. The
former provides authentication, integrity and non-repudiation, whereas the latter provides confidentiality. Apart from this, local policies, if any, can also be implemented by
using vendor-specific commands through AVPs. Mobile IP and its requirements for
roaming can also be realized by leveraging the flexibility in the use of AVPs. This greatly
simplifies the problem of scaling up.

On top of this, Diameter insists on 32-bit alignment of information. This reduces the processing burden, as most processors work efficiently when objects are aligned to 32-bit boundaries. Thus, all the shortcomings of RADIUS are by and large eliminated or restricted in Diameter.

As should be obvious, Diameter is a considerably more sophisticated protocol than RADIUS; yet it is feasible to implement it within embedded devices primarily because of the improvements in processor speeds and the widespread availability of embedded IPsec (see the following) implementations.

Network Layer Security Using IPV6

There is a need for an access router to regulate access control at the network layer, without using some data link layer protocols like PPP (Blunk & Vollbrecht, 1998). This is to ensure the portability of the protocol across different networks working with perhaps different data link layer protocols. Thus, an access router needs to perform source address filtering securely. IP source address filtering is done by comparing every incoming IP packet's source address with a table of mobile host IP addresses, which have been granted access to network resources. If an incoming IP packet meets the access requirements, it is forwarded to its desired destination. Otherwise it gets dropped and eventually an IP control message is sent back to the sender telling that access is not granted.

IP Source Address Filtering

IP source address filtering depends on the authenticity of the source address included in an incoming IP packet. The system is vulnerable to IP spoofing (i.e., creation and sending of IP packets with spoofed source addresses) attacks if there is no way of ascertaining the real sender of a received IP packet.

In our protocol, an access router not only needs to know if an incoming packet from the network node with an IP address matches the source address in the packet, but that the packet originated from an authenticated user's host. However, when dynamic host IP address configuration is used, there is no known way to relate an IP source address to a user's identity. Therefore, the access router needs a method to securely derive a user's identity from an incoming IP packet's source address. To accomplish this, a protocol is needed which works at the IP layer and serves as a way to secure the integrity of at least the end-to-end immutable parts of the IP header. Our protocol works as an application layer protocol to securely bind a user's identity to the IP address of the mobile host he/she is using. The IP header integrity has to be protected with a shared secret known only to the sender and the recipient, in this case the access client and the access router. This renders IP spoofing useless since the attacker cannot generate valid IP packets with spoofed source addresses unless he/she has an access to the shared secret key.

IPSec

The IPSec protocol suite is a collection of security protocols that can be applied to protect network traffic at the IP layer. Beneath the essential protocols like IPSec Authentication Header (AH) (Kent & Atkinson, 1998a) and IPSec Encapsulating Security Payload (ESP) (Kent & Atkinson, 1998b), IPSec includes other protocols like IKE (Harkins & Carrel, 1998). IPSec AH is a protocol used to protect the IP header against alteration by an attacker and IPSec ESP provides a method to encrypt an IP packet's payload. Additionally, IPSec describes the management and uses of IPSec Security Associations (SA).

IPSec defines two modes to process IP traffic, namely transport and tunnel mode. In transport mode, an additional security header (AH or ESP header) is added to the IP header. The tunnel mode describes an IP-in-IP encapsulation where the outer IP header contains the AH or ESP header.

In IPSec, a security association (SA) describes the security parameters of a uni-directional IP connection between two end points. IPSec SAs are stored in a security association database (SADB) and are identified by a triple consisting of a destination IP address, a protocol identifier (AH or ESP), and a unique security parameter index (SPI). Additionally, an SA includes the IPSec mode (transport or tunnel), the keying material used for AH or ESP, the lifetime of the SA, and the optional services selected within the protocol. The SA is used by the IPSec implementation to check the validity of incoming IPSec secured IP packets, or to insert the needed IPSec extension header into outgoing IP packets. The problem of using IPSec AH tunnel mode is that it can only verify the authenticity of the remote tunnel end point (by examining the outer IP header extension header), but not that of the inner IP packet's sender.

Since our protocol establishes SAs as an end-to-end relation, IPSec tunnel mode is applied to secure network traffic between a mobile host (MH) and an access router (AR). The AR is an intermediate node and not the IP connection end point. The AR checks the validity of the incoming IPSec secured IP-in-IP packets and de-encapsulates them to forward to their respective destinations. On the other side, the AR has to encapsulate IP packets destined for the MH.

In the proposed protocol there is no explicit need for encryption, since AAA credentials and local security associations have to be secured anyway by the AAA protocol in place. Hence, IPSec AH tunnel mode is used for access control in the IP layer, and to secure the integrity of IP packets. IPSec AH makes use of an IPv6 extension header, which includes a so-called integrity check value (ICV). It is the result of a keyed MD5 hash function applied to end-to-end immutable parts of the IP packet. Additionally, AH has a sequence number to prevent replay attacks.

The Linux operating system with kernel 2.2 or higher includes IPv6 support. Unfortunately, IPsec has not been included in the network stack. The only working implementation of IPSec in Linux is Free Secure Wide Area Network (FreeS/WAN) (Gilmore, Spencer, Briggs & Redelmeier, 1996). FreeS/WAN is open source, extends the Linux Kernel to support IPSec, and includes an SADB with an interface to user processes. For implementing the proposed protocol we have used FreeS/WAN to build an IPSec tunnel between an MH and an AR.

User Registration Protocol

A User Registration Protocol (URP) (Ohba et al., 2001) allows a user to register in the network by providing his/her identity and authentication information to the local network, which validates the user, charges him/her, and authorizes the use of resources with the help of a AAA infrastructure.

Designing a URP

Most existing protocols operate at the data link layer, which makes them usable only for one specific access technology. We, therefore, designed a URP that is independent from the access network's data link layer protocols. Interoperation with AAA protocols like RADIUS or Diameter is a must for a URP. Since an access router — which is an end point for URP — communicates directly with AAA servers, there is no need for a URP to include AAA protocol functionality. The interoperation requirement, to some extent, prescribes which authentication credentials and authorization data a URP must transport between a mobile host and an access router. As no point-to-point data link layer protocol information is available at the application layer, there has to be a way for an access client to discover the location of an access router.

With IPv6, the best method for discovery of access router (AR) is to extend the use of the IPv6 stateless address auto-configuration feature. The AR location is added to router advertisement messages. A URP should also have a method to establish a local security association (LSA) (Faccin & Le, 2001) between an AR and a mobile host (MH). Additionally, it should support other features like performing LSA re-negotiation in case the lifetime of an LSA has expired. Since an LSA is established with the help of an MH and its AAA home server, re-negotiation of an LSA does not depend only on a URP. Also, URP communication has to be secure; otherwise an attacker could gain access to network resources that he/she has no permission for. In this context, secure communication means authenticated and replay attack protected communication. There is no explicit need for encryption since AAA credentials and LSA keys have to be secured by the AAA protocol anyway.

Local Security Association

SAs can be further defined as either inter-domain SAs or Local SAs (LSA). An inter-domain SA is established between entities belonging to different network domains, whereas an LSA is used between entities that are located in the same network domain. Another difference is that an LSA typically has a shorter lifetime compared to an inter-domain SA. The concept of a user-specific LSA called Temporary Shared Key (TSK) has been proposed. A TSK is established between an access client and the visited domain's AR with the involvement of the AAAh (Home AAA server of the MH). Our proposal is to establish a TSK between a mobile host and an access router to secure the network layer

Figure 1. Security associations in an AAA environment

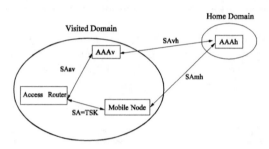

access control. Once established, the TSK is used as the IPSec SA to build an IPSec tunnel between the MH and the AR.

To build a TSK, an AAA home server AAAh has to generate a unique security key and then distribute it to the AR and the MH. Since the MH does not interface directly with the AAAh, the key has to be sent only through the AR. The key distribution has to be made as secure and as reliable as possible because if the TSK is lost the whole session will be insecure.

Figure 4 shows the pre-established SAs in a typical AAA environment. The TSK has to be sent from the AAAh to the AR in a secure manner. To accomplish this, the pre-established SAs SAvh and SAmh are used to securely transfer the TSK up to the AR. If the AR receives the TSK parameters, it has to send these parameters securely to the MH. But since the AR does not share a pre-established SA with the MH at this stage, the AR needs some more information from the AAAh server to securely distribute the TSK parameters. This extra information consists of either the SAmh parameters, or the encrypted TSK parameters using SAmh. In the latter case, the AR has to only forward the received SAmh encrypted TSK parameters to the MH. We have used this approach in developing the protocol, since it is more secure, as the AR does not need to know the SA parameters (including the long term key shared between an MH and its AAAh Server). After the MH has received the TSK parameters, the TSK between the MH and the AR is established as shown in Figure 1.

The LSA key is encrypted by using 3-DES (Karn & Simpson, 1995) with a 192-bit key. The key is generated by recursively applying an HMAC-MD5 (Rivest, 1992) hash function on the long-term shared key and by interlacing the so computed MD5 digest.

Protocol Overview

The aim of our protocol is to authenticate a mobile host roaming in a foreign network to its home server so that it can access the resources of the foreign network and develop a secure link between the mobile host and the access router. Further exchanges of messages between the two can then be safe. The protocol ensures the safety of messages from various attacks like man-in-the-middle attack, replay attack and IP spoofing. The important issue that needs to be addressed by our protocol is that there should be as few message transfers as possible between a mobile host and its home server. This is to tackle the constraints that naturally arise due to mobility and the wireless communication infrastructure. Our protocol is also designed to suit the limited processing capability of smart cards (Java card). With the resources available to a smart card, the complexity and the size of cryptographic algorithms are restricted to the extent possible.

Mobile Authentication Protocol

The URP implementation, called MAP, discussed in this section was developed covering all URP design specification requirements as stated earlier in the subsection one of the previous section. MAP is an application layer protocol. It inherits most of its features from EAPoUDP (Engelstad, 2002) (a variation of the Extensible Authentication Protocol (Blunk & Vollbrecht, 1998)), and operates on UDP in the transport layer. There are other possible choices for the transport layer protocol, like TCP or ICMP. UDP was chosen for MAP because it is the most generic delivery method among those mentioned. However, UDP is not reliable. Therefore, it introduces the need to implement retransmission and acknowledgment strategies, as it would be the case when using ICMPv6. But we do not require full TCP functionality, which introduces many overheads. Considering a MH's low processing power and low connection bandwidth, it will be better to work with a lightweight protocol.

The AAA protocol inter-operation requirement is met by using EAPoUDP parameters as AAA credentials. EAPoUDP assumes that prior to authentication the MH has configured a valid IPv6 address for itself and received the AR location during IPv6 stateless address auto-configuration (Thomson & Narten, 1998). MAP messages are secured where needed with a challenge option and authentication data, which is the result of a HMAC-MD5 one-way hash function applied to the end-to-end immutable parts of the MAP message. By doing so, man-in-the-middle attack and replay attacks are eliminated.

After a successful authentication, an MH gains access to the foreign network only for a limited time period. After the allocated time period the AAAh server sends a TSK update to the AR and the MH by providing required TSK parameters to re-establish the LSA between the MH and the AR.

The Logical Entities

The five main logical entities of the protocol and their mutual interactions have been depicted in Figure 2. MH denotes a mobile host visiting a foreign network. The access router AR allows the MH to register and be authenticated by the network. AAAv is the AAA server of the visited network, and AAAh is the AAA server in the home network of MH. The end result of the authentication procedure is that a Temporary Shared Key (TSK) is set up between MH and some agent (an access router) in the visited network.

Figure 2. Logical entities of the model

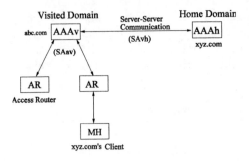

Security Elements

The security elements deployed by the proposed protocol include the security association and cryptographic algorithms. These combine together to ensure secured bi-directional access between a MH and a foreign network.

Security Associations

The security associations are put in place by the following elements and guiding principles.

- *SAvh*: MAP assumes that the AAAh and the AAAv share a long term SA, SAvh, and that it is not specific to any particular user.

- *SAav*: It is assumed that each network has its own security mechanism and an SA, SAav. It allows the entities in the same network to communicate in a secure and mutually authenticated way.

- *SAmh*: It is assumed that each user, as a part of a subscription agreement with a home domain, acquires a long-term security association (SAmh) with her/his home domain. In fact, Mobile IPv6 mandates the existence of a security association between an MH and its AAAh.

- *TSK*: For a LSA to be adopted between the user and the visited domain, the user and the visited domain must have a set of common security algorithms that can be used to support the LSA.

Cryptographic Consideration

There is no negotiation of cryptographic algorithms in our protocol. All the algorithms are pre-decided. We use 3DES in CBC mode for encryption and HMAC-MD5 for authentication. The 3DES algorithm is used for generating the keys (like TSK between MH and AR). The HMACS-MD5 is used as a one-way hash function. The 3DES algorithm uses a 192-bit key. We use the EEE approach; that is, the encryption algorithm is used three times, applying a different key each time. The HMACS MD5 algorithm uses a 128-bit key.

Security Features

As discussed earlier, the basic security features that have to be supported by MAP are: authentication and authorization, and establishing a LSA between MH and AR. When these features are guaranteed, the protocol sets up an IPSec tunnel between the access router and the mobile host.

Authentication/Authorization

Authentication is required before providing network access to the mobile user. Not only does the user need to be authenticated, the network providing the service should also be authenticated. So, the authentication mechanism which we think would be appropriate for two-way authentication is to have the network broadcast a local challenge over the access link, for example along with the router advertisement messages.

Setting Up a Local Security Association

We can improve the protocol by setting up an LSA between a user and the visited network when the user is roaming. The adoption of an LSA allows for optimizations and empowers the visited service provider to authenticate the user at any time and perform key distribution without the involvement of the home domain.

Without the use of an LSA, user authentication, network authentication, key distribution, and so forth, between the user and agents in the visited domain is usually based on the long-term SA between the user and its AAAh. When TSK is adopted, the user receives a notification that TSK is to be used. Therefore, the user would use SAav of the visited network instead of AAAh. It saves the round trip times between the visited and home networks, thus reducing time delay and the network load.

Building an IPSEC Tunnel

The protocol uses the LSA formed between a user and an access router of the visited network to form an IPSec tunnel between them, thereby securing any exchange of messages between the two.

Figure 3. Protocol specification

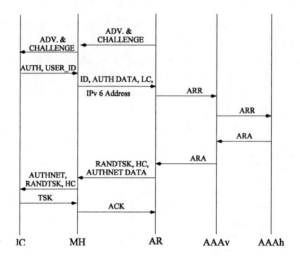

Protocol Specification

Figure 3 provides the important time-lined actions of entities for the Java card driven authentication of MHs in foreign networks.

When the user inserts the smart card in the card acceptance device, it prompts the user to enter a personal identification number (PIN). If the user enters the correct PIN then the client application running on the MH gets activated. When an MH enters a new subnet, it receives a router advertisement with a local challenge as shown. This router advertisement is broadcast periodically by an access router AR.

Request from MH

After receiving a router advertisement from an AR in the visited network, the MH sends a message to the AR seeking the services to be delivered to the access router. MH constructs a tentative IP address, called care of address (CoA), and replies with an EAP response message (Engelstad, 2002) with the following parameters:

1. *Local Challenge (LC)*: This is the value sent by the AR in the router advertisement. The LC is a random string. Its purpose is to ensure freshness of the messages exchanged so as to avoid replay attacks.

2. *Client Identifier (user_id)* consists of the client's user_id (provided by the smart card). This also contains information of the client's home network.

3. *VN_ID* is the id of the visited network and is sent in the router advertisement from where it is copied.

4. *AAA Credential Option (AUTH)* is sent by the smart card. It is constructed by concatenating all of the preceding parameters and the long-term shared key between the MH and its AAAh (SAmh) and applying the algorithm agreed upon, which in our case is HMAC-MD5:

$$AUTH = HMAC\text{-}MD5(LC, user\_id, VN\_ID, SAmh)$$

AR's Response to MH's Request

The access router (AR) first verifies the freshness of the request thanks to local challenge (LC) and then performs duplicate address detection on the care-of-address. If it fails, the AR replies to the MH with the code "ADDRESS_IN_USE". Otherwise, it creates a Diameter ARR (AAA-Registration-Request) message carrying the following information to the AAAv (containing attribute-value pairs (AVPs)):

1. *User Name AVP*: to carry the client identifier (user_id).

2. *Challenge AVP*: to carry LC for replay attack protection.

3. *EAP AVP*: to carry the authentication data AUTH, for mutual authentication.

4. *VN_ID*: the visited network's id as received from the MH.

5. *Care-of IP address*: received from the MH (MH_Ipaddr).

Actions of AAAV Server

When an AAAv receives a AAA registration request message, ARR, it verifies the message is coming from a valid AR, and forwards the message to the MH's AAAh by looking into MH's client identifier.

Actions of AAAH Server

When AAAh receives an ARR message from an AAAv, it first verifies whether the message originated from a valid AAAv, and then from the information contained in several AVPs it executes the following procedure.

1. Extracts LC, user_id, AUTH, VN_ID, and MH_Ipaddr and authenticates the user using the client identifier provided by the MH as the MH's identity, the AUTH information

sent, and the long-term shared key between the two (SAmh). That is, it checks if HMAC-MD5(LC,user_id,VN_ID,SmAh) is equal to AUTH.

2.   Stores MH_Ipaddr for future use.

3.   Generates a random number HC (home challenge) to ensure freshness of a message.

4.   Creates an AUTHNET value as follows to ensure freshness of the message to be sent: AUTHNET=HMAC-MD5(HC,user_id,VN_ID,SAmh)

5.   Creates a random number RANDTSK that is used as the basis for the session key to be defined. RANDTSK is sent encrypted as TSK as follows:

TSK = 3DES(RANDTSK, SAmh)

6.   Finally sends a Diameter ARA (AAA Registration-Acceptance) message as reply to the AAAv and this contains RANDTSK, HC, TSK, VN_ID, user_id.

Response to ARA Message by AAAV

When the AAAv receives an ARA message from the AAAh, it forwards it to the AR that sent the original request.

AR's Response to ARA Message

In response to an ARA message from the AAAv, the AR converts the message to the EAP format and sends it to the MH; this message carries:

1.   Authentication data, AUTHNET

2.   Random number HC

3.   Key generation number RANDTSK

MH's Response to ARA Message

MH sends the information received in the form of ARA message from the access router AR to the Java smart card for verification.

The Java card calculates AUTH = HMAC-MD5(HC, user_id,VN_ID, SAmh) and compares it with AUTHNET to authenticate the information. Then it calculates TSK from RANDTSK as outlined above. This is returned to the MH. MH then uses this TSK to build an IPSec tunnel between itself and the AR, and the link gets established.

Figure 4. TSK update

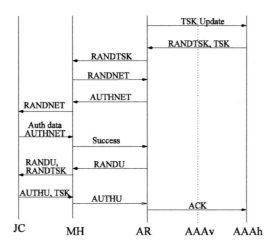

TSK Update

The TSK established between the MH and the AR usually has a limited lifetime. When this expires, the AR requests a new TSK from the AAAh via the AAAv. The actions involved in TSK update are illustrated by Figure 4. The basic procedure is similar to what has already been described.

TSK is generated using RANDTSK and Samh, which exists between MH and the AAAh server as explained earlier. The home server AAAh sends RANDTSK-AVP and TSK-AVP carrying RANDTSK and TSK to the visited network server AAAv. It waits for the acknowledgment from the AAAv server.

Implementation Details

The implementation of the proposed protocol was done by setting up an IPv6 test bed to drive the IPSec. The topology was configured as indicated by Figure 5.

FreeS/WAN (Gilmore et al., 1996) with IPv6 support (IPSec6) has to be installed in order to use MobileApplication and AccessRouter applications. Since IPSec operates at the network layer, it is flexible and can be used to secure nearly any type of Internet traffic. Two applications, however, are extremely widespread. These are:

Figure 5. Testbed configuration

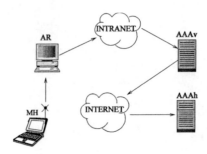

- *Virtual Private Network (VPN).* It allows multiple sites to communicate securely over an insecure Internet by encrypting all communication between the sites.
- *Road Warriors.* It connects the office from home, or perhaps from a hotel somewhere.

In our protocol, we used the Road Warrior implementation, changing it to suit our requirements. The implementation of the protocol involves the software entities described next.

Java Card Interface

Whenever the smart card is inserted in the card reader, the client application prompts the user to produce a PIN. It is checked with the PIN stored in the EEPROM of the smart card for user authentication. If the user is not authenticated then no further transactions can take place.

There will also be a method Admin(byte [ ] password) which will be used for the smart card issuer to initialize or change the crypto keys, choose the crypto algorithms, set the user ID, set the PIN, and other initialization parameters for the smart card applet. The mobile host will have an application running which will use the interface provided by the smart card to communicate with the applet inside the smart card.

Mobile Application Software

A program called MobileApplication implements the client side of MAP and has an interface to the SADB of IPSec6. If a mobile user wants to get access to the Internet, he/she will run this program with the Java Card attached to his/her machine. MobileApplication establishes an AH tunnel mode connection between the system and an access router.

Figure 6. Mobile application state machine

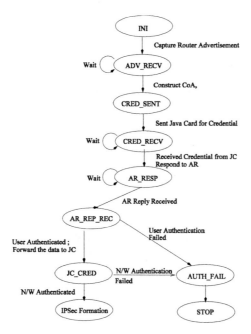

The application is written as a single threaded program in Java, which has an interface both with the Java Card and the AR.

Protocol State Machine of MobileApplication

Figure 6 shows the protocol state machine implemented in MobileApplication. It essentially implements the protocol described above.

After MobileApplication has captured a router advertisement from the AR, it sends the received information to the Java Card for credential evaluation and by that time, it configures its own care of address (CoA) using the visited network domain address. It forwards the authenticated data to AR with its own calculated IP address.

If the MH receives a positive MAP response from the AR, it forwards the intended information to the Java Card to authenticate the network. After the network authentication becomes successful, it installs the needed IPSec SAs in its SADB using the TSK included in the MAP response.

Delay Server

This application was written mainly to simulate real network conditions. It inserts virtual hops between any two different applications. This application is started by the source and waits to receive data from it, and then it inserts the required number of hops by sending data again and again to the local port before forwarding it to the destination. It provides an interface by which the number of hops to be inserted between the applications can be changed.

Access Router Application

AccessRouter is a prototype implementation of a network access server (NAS) acting as a policy enforcement point. AccessRouter application consists of four different concurrent threads as shown in Figure 7. AccessRouter implements MAP as well as an extended version of Diameter (Diameter with TSK support). Additionally, it also controls the behaviour of IPSec6 with proper interface to the kernel space.

The AccessRouterMAP threads (EAP_RECV and EAP_SEND) are responsible for the communication with an MH using MAP while the DiameterSend and DiameterReceive threads implement the communication with the AAA Server using Diameter. The dia_out_queue and the map_out_queue are both FIFO protocol messages queues used to send messages in an asynchronous manner.

Figure 8 shows the protocol state machine of AccessRouter. In the initial state of AR, it starts sending a router advertisement periodically to the network. As soon as a packet is received by AccessRouterEAP or DiameterReceive, and if the protocol message included in the packet complies with the protocol state machine, a state change including the respective action as shown in Figure 8 is executed. Otherwise, the packet gets silently discarded.

During MH authentication, AccessRouter has to establish the IPSec AH tunnel mode SAs with the help of the TSK parameters received from the AAA Server. Additionally, two entries have to be added in the database, one for inbound (Network to MH) and one for outbound (MH to Network) network traffic. The required IPSec SAs have to be added to the SADB. Since MAP runs over unreliable UDP as a transport layer protocol, it introduces the problem that an AR does not know the protocol state of an MH without the reception of an acknowledgment message.

Figure 7. Access router architecture

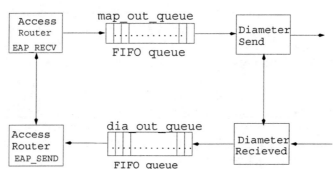

Figure 8. Access router state machine

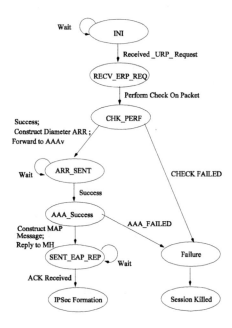

An IPsec SA needs a unique Security Parameter Index (SPI), which is a 32-bit number identifying an SA. An SA's SPI has to be same in both end systems of an IPSec connection. It is therefore necessary for the AccessRouter to send the SPI to the MH after the successful addition of the SAs to its SADB (this was not shown in the protocol description). The base SPI is the SPI of the first added SA and is used since an IPSec AH tunnel mode connection needs more than one SA to be added to the SADB. FreeS/WAN has reserved SPI numbers in the range from 0x100 to 0x1000 for manual keying, which describes the establishment of SA without IKE, which is in compliance with our protocol. Therefore, AccessRouter uses SPI values between 0x200 and 0xfff in order not to interfere with a running IKE instance and to still allow manual keying for our purpose.

User-Kernel Space Interface

There is a need to implement user-kernel space interfaces for the SADB and SPD6 from IPSec. Since the aim of our implementation is just to set up a secure connection between an MH and its home server by setting up an IPSec tunnel between the MH and an AR, user-kernel space interface can be further extended to allow proper and restricted movement of traffic between MH and AR.

Linux offers a virtual file system called /proc that enables the communication between user space processes and kernel space processes. A kernel which offers such a /proc file has to implement a read and a write file handler function for this file. If a user process reads or writes to a /proc file, the respective read or write handler function of a kernel process is called. A new IPSec6 policy can be added or deleted to the SPD6 by appropriate editing of the virtual file /proc/net/spd6. It is necessary for the application to keep track of the SPD6 rule numbers, since these numbers do possibly change after rule deletion. A user process communicates with the SADB by using a PF_KEY socket. FreeS/WAN does implement such a socket type for the Linux Operating System. PF_KEY supports only the write() and read() BSD socket routines.

Visited Network Server Application

This application implements the visited network AAA Server (AAAv). It receives packets from an AR and performs checks to determine if the packet has come from a reliable AR. If not then the packet is dropped with a failure packet sent to the source AR. If the packet passes the reliability check then it is parsed to find if it is a local request or it has to be forwarded to a server of some other domain with which it has some pre-shared contract. After the request for authentication is through then it may optionally store data for accounting purposes.

Home Server Application

This application performs as a home (AAAh) to its mobile host. It has the long-term key stored in an internal database for every mobile host (the SAmh's). If a request for authentication comes from some foreign domain, it parses the AVPs of the packet to get the credential to authenticate the user.

If authentication succeeds it calculates some other credentials to authenticate itself to the MH and also generates a TSK to be shared between MH and AR (as described in the protocol description). HomeServer application also maintains some timeout for each TSK provided to MH so that with elapsed timeout it can initiate the TSK update function (an AR can also initiate this timeout).

Conclusions

In this chapter we have described a protocol to provide secure and authenticated access to roaming mobile hosts in a foreign network using a Java smart card. The advantages of using a smart card to store security information and to implement the basic authentication functions have been exploited in this protocol. It has been designed so that it performs better in comparison to existing protocols. Limited computing power, limited battery power, and limited wireless link capacity in a mobile host have been taken into account while designing the protocol. The protocol delegates the part of the authentication function to an access router of the foreign network. This helps reduce traffic to and from the home network. The protocol uses temporary shared keys to limit the damages due to the break of a key.

MAP combines the advantages of symmetric key cryptography and the use of a temporary shared key. The implementation of the protocol, however, was mainly directed to investigate its feasibility. Yet it provides enough insight for evaluation of MAP against other protocols for secured controlled access of mobile hosts in a foreign network. PKI and IKE are two other known protocols deployed for secure access of MHs in a foreign network.

PKI versus MAP

PKI uses asymmetric key cryptography. It uses two separate keys. One of which is public, and the other is private. But in a PKI based authentication system MH and its home server would have to share the private key. The main drawback of this scheme is that after some time, an attacker can probably break the private key by eavesdropping on the communication for some time. Another limitation of PKI is the problem of communicating the secret keys between the two entities, and if the key is somehow lost then communication cannot take place. These shortcomings have been taken care of in MAP by periodically and securely refreshing the keys between MH and AR under the supervision of the home server. Furthermore, MAP uses smart cards as the medium for transporting the keys where these are hard-wired and cannot be read by any malicious user or lost. Thus both limitations of PKI are eliminated. Apart from these limitations, establishing the PKI infrastructure of a certification authority (CA) for the distribution of public keys has turned out to be a difficult task both economically and practically.

IKE versus MAP

The default IPSec key management protocol is IKE. IKE works in two phases. In the first phase, IKE can work with either main mode or aggressive mode, where it negotiates the IKE Security Associations. The main mode requires six message exchanges as compared to three message exchanges by the aggressive mode. In the second phase SAs formed are used to provide authentication, secrecy and data integrity, which again takes three more messages. Hence in all, forming the SA using IKE requires six or nine messages. Also, IKE runs on the infrastructure of PKI, which makes it computationally more expensive.

On the other hand, the process of establishing a TSK takes only three messages and this forms an SA between two entities with the same level of security. TSK sharing gives the serving system significant load control over the authentication and key distribution of a visiting MH: the key refreshing and new key distribution procedure can be based on this temporary shared key stored in the AR, thus saving round trips with the home network.

Acknowledgments

The implementation of the protocol proposal was carried out by Abhinav Arora and Deepak K. Singh at IIT Guwahati as a requirement for their major undergraduate project. The authors acknowledge the contributions of Deepak K. Singh. The authors also gratefully acknowledge the comments/suggestions of the reviewers over an earlier draft version of the chapter, which contributed to substantial improvements in overall presentation.

References

Blunk, L., & Vollbrecht, J. (1998). *PPP* extensible authentication protocol (EAP). *RFC 2284*. Retrieved from *http://www.ietf.org/rfc/rfc2284.txt*

Calhoun, P.R., Akhtar, H., Arkko, J., Guttman E., Rubens, A.C., & Zorn, G. (2001). Diameter base protocol. Internet draft, November 2001. Retrieved from: *http://www.ietf.org/proceedings/01dec/ID/draft-ietf-aaa-diameter-08.txt*

de Laat, C., Gross G., Gommans, L., Vollbrecht, J., & Spence, D. (2000). Generic AAA Architecture. *RFC 2903*. Retrieved from *http://www.ietf.org/rfc/rfc2903*

Engelstad, P. (2002). EAP over UDP. Retrieved from *http://www.ietf.org/internet-drafts/draft-engelstad-pana-eap-over-udp-00.txt*

Faccin, S.M., & Le, F. (2001). AAA local security association (LSA): The temporary shared key (TSK). Internet draft, December 2001. Retrieved from: *http://www.watersprings.org/pub/id/draft-le-aaa-lsa-tsk-00.txt*

Gilmore, J., Spencer, H., Briggs, R.G., & Redelmeier, H. (1996). Frees/wan project. Retrieved from *http://www.freeswan.org*

Harkins, D., & Carrel, D. (1998). The Internet key exchange (IKE). *RFC 2409*. Retrieved from *http://www.ietf.org/rfc/rfc2409.txt*

Karn, P., Metzger, P., & Simpson, W. (1995). The ESP triple DES transformation. *RFC 1851*. Retrieved from: *http://www.ietf.org/rfc/rfc1851*

Kent, S., & Atkinson, R. (1998a). IP authentication header. *RFC 2402*. Retrieved from *http://www.ietf.org/rfc/rfc2402.txt*

Kent, S., & Atkinson, R. (1998b). IP encapsulating security payload. *RFC 2406*. Retrieved from *http://www.ietf.org/rfc/rfc2406.txt*

Kent, S., & Atkinson, R. (1998c). Security architecture for the Internet protocol. *RFC 2401*. Retrieved from *http://www.ietf.org/rfc/rfc2401.txt*

Metz, C. (1999). On the Web: AAA Protocols: Authentication, authorization, and accounting for the Internet. *IEEE Internet Computing, 3*(6), 75-79.

Mitton, D. & Beadles, M. (2000). Network access server requirements next generation NAS model. *RFC 2881*. Retrieved from: *http://www.ietf.org/rfc/rfc2881.txt*

Ohba, Y., Kempf, J., Robert, P., Subbiah, B., Patil, B., Haverinen, H., & Soliman, H. (2001). Usage scenario of a user registration protocol (URP). Retrieved from: *http://www.watersprings.org/pub/id/draft-ohba-urp-usage-scenarios-00.txt*

Perkins, C. (1996). IP mobility support. *RFC 2002*. Retrieved from: *http://www.ietf.org/rfc/rfc2002.txt*

Rigney, C., Willens, S., Rubens, A., & Simpson, W. (1997). Remote authentication dial in user service (RADIUS). *RFC 2138*. Retrieved from *http://www.ietf.org/rfc/rfc2138.txt*

Rigney, C., Willens, S., Rubens, A., & Simpson, W. (2000). Remote authentication dial in user service (RADIUS). *RFC 2865*. Retrieved from *http://www.ietf.org/rfc/rfc2865.txt*

Rivest, R. (1992). The md5 message-digest algorithm. *RFC 1321*. Retrieved from *http://www.ietf.org/rfc/rfc1321.txt*

Thomson, S., & Narten, T. (1998). IPv6 stateless address autoconfiguration. *RFC 1971*. Retrieved from *http://www.ietf.org/rfc/rfc1971.txt*

Vollbrecht, J., Calhoun, P., Farrell, S., Gommans, L., Gross, G., de Bruijn, B., de Laat, C., Holderege, M., & Spence, D. (2000). AAA authorization framework. *RFC 2904*. Retrieved from *http://www.ietf.org/rfc/rfc2904.txt*

About the Authors

Wen-Chen Hu received a BE in computer science from Tamkang University, Taiwan (1984), an ME in electronic and information engineering from the National Central University, Taiwan (1986), an MS in computer science from the University of Iowa, Iowa City (1993), and a PhD in computer and information science and engineering from the University of Florida, Gainesville (1998). He is currently an assistant professor in the Department of Computer Science, University of North Dakota (USA). His current research interests are in the World Wide Web research and applications including information retrieval, especially electronic and mobile commerce, search engines, data mining, and databases.

Chung-wei Lee received a BS in electrical engineering from the National Tsing-Hua University, Taiwan (1987), an MS in computer science and information engineering from the National Taiwan University, Taiwan (1994), and a PhD in computer and information science and engineering from the University of Florida, Gainesville (2001). He is currently an assistant professor in the Department of Computer Science and Software Engineering, Auburn University, and a faculty of Auburn's Center for Innovations in Mobile, Pervasive, and Agile Computing Technologies (IMPACT). He is interested in mobile/wireless networks, mobile commerce, multimedia streaming, IP routing and quality of service (QoS), and network security.

Weidong Kou is dean of the School of Computer Science and Engineering, and distinguished professor of Xidian University, as well as director of the Chinese State Key Laboratory of Integrated Service Networks. Professor Kou also serves as honorary/adjunct/guest professor in more than a dozen universities, including the University of Maryland (USA) and the University of Hong Kong. Professor Kou has more than 12 years of industrial experience in IBM, AT&T, and Siemens in North America. He received various invention achievement and technical excellence awards from IBM, AT&T and Siemens. He was associate director of the E-Business Technology Institute at the University of Hong Kong. Professor Kou is founding chair of the International Symposium on Electronic Commerce (ISEC). He is a chairman of the IEEE International Conference on Dynamic E-Commerce Technology to be held in Beijing in September 2004. Professor Kou has authored/edited seven books in the areas of e-commerce, security, and multimedia technologies, and published more than 60 papers in journals/conferences. He has also authored nine US/Canadian issued and pending patents. Professor Kou is a senior member of IEEE and was elected as a member of New York Academy of Sciences in 1992.

* * *

Abhinav Arora graduated from IIT Guwahati, India, and joined Samsung India in 2003. Currently, he is pursuing graduate studies at the Seoul National University (Korea) under a sponsorship from Samsung.

Gautam Barua graduated from IIT Bombay, India. He earned his PhD from the University of California, Santa Barbara (USA). He was on the faculty with the Department of Computer Science and Engineering at IIT Kanpur (1982-1995). He has been a member of the faculty at IIT Guwahati, India. Currently, he is director of the Institute. His areas of interest are operating systems and networks.

Paolo Bellavista is a research associate of computer engineering at the University of Bologna. His research activities span from mobile agent-based middleware solutions and pervasive/ubiquitous computing to systems/service management, location/context-aware services, and adaptive multimedia. He received a PhD in computer science engineering from the University of Bologna. He is member of the IEEE, the ACM, and the Italian Association for Computing. To contact: pbellavista@deis.unibo.it

Elisa Bertino is a professor of computer sciences and research director of CERIAS at Purdue University (USA). Her research interests are in the areas of security, privacy, database systems, multimedia systems and object-oriented technology. She is a fellow member of ACM and a fellow member of IEEE. She received the IEEE Computer Society Technical Achievement Award in 2002.

Gregor v. Bochmann has been a professor at the School of Information Technology and Engineering at the University of Ottawa (Canada) since January 1998, after working 25 years at the University of Montreal. He is a fellow of the IEEE and ACM and a member of the Royal Society of Canada. He did research on programming languages, compiler design, communication protocols, and software engineering and published many papers in these areas. He was also actively involved in the standardization of formal description techniques for communication protocols and services. His present work is aimed at methodologies for the design, implementation and testing of communication protocols and distributed systems. Ongoing projects include quality of service management for distributed multimedia applications and optical networks.

Randy Chow earned his PhD in computer and information science from the University Of Massachusetts (1977). He has been on the faculty in the Computer and Information Science and Engineering Department at the University of Florida since 1981, where he is currently a professor. His research areas include distributed systems, computer networks and computer security. Dr. Chow has published more than 75 technical papers and is the author of a graduate level textbook on distributed operating systems and algorithms.

Antonio Corradi is a full professor of computer engineering at the University of Bologna. His research interests include distributed systems, object systems, mobile agent platforms, network management, and distributed and parallel architectures. He received an MS in electrical engineering from Cornell University. He is a member of the IEEE, the ACM, and the Italian Association for Computing. To contact: acorradi@deis.unibo.it

Balázs Csik is leading the mobile specification, design and development of the SEMOPS payment system. He earned his master's degree in information technology at the University of Technology at Budapest (1999). Currently he works at ProfiTrade 90 Ltd., but also acts as a PhD student and assistant researcher at University of Technology at Budapest. He is a member of the McLeod Institute of Simulation Sciences. He specializes in electronic/mobile transaction handling, payment systems, mobile technologies and simulation. He published several papers related to simulation of economic systems and virtual transaction handling. In the past he was leading several big electronic payment projects in the field of SET and 3-D secure.

Mohamed Eltoweissy is a visiting professor and associate professor of computer science at Virginia Tech and James Madison University (USA), respectively. He founded the Commonwealth Information Security Center in Virginia. His research interests include information security, wireless sensor and ad hoc networks, and group computing and communications. He has published more than 60 technical papers in the refereed journals, books, and conference proceedings. For more information, visit: www.cs.jmu.edu/users/eltowemy.

Elena Ferrari is professor of database systems at the University of Insubria at Como, Italy. She has also been on the faculty in the Department of Computer Science of the University of Milano, Italy (1998 to March 2001). She received a PhD in computer science from the University of Milano (1997). Elena Ferrari has been a visiting researcher at George Mason University in Fairfax, Virginia, and at Rutgers University in Newark, New

Jersey. Her main research interests include database and Web security, and temporal and multimedia databases. In those areas, Professor Ferrari has published several papers in all major refereed journals, and in proceedings of international conferences and symposia. She is in the editorial board of the *VLDB Journal* and the *International Journal of Information Technology* (IJIT). Professor Ferrari has served as program chair of the Ninth ACM Symposium on Access Control Models and Technologies (SACMAT'04), COMPSAC'02 Workshop on Web Security and Semantic Web, the first ECOOP Workshop on XML and Object Technology, and the first ECOOP Workshop on Object-oriented Databases. Dr. Ferrari was also general chair of the Eighth ACM Symposium on Access Control Models and Technologies (SACMAT'03) and the Software Demonstration Chair of the 10th International Conference on Extending Database Technologies (EDBT'04). She has also served as program committee member for several international conferences. Dr. Ferrari is a member of ACM and the IEEE Computer Society.

R. K. Ghosh graduated with a Master in Science from Ravenshaw College, Cuttack, India. He earned his PhD from the Indian Institute of Technology, Kharagpur, India. Currently, he is on the faculty of computer science and engineering at IIT Kanpur, India. He had been also on the faculty of computer science and engineering at IIT Guwahati, India (2002-2003). His areas of interests are mobile computing and mobile ad hoc networks.

Petra Hoepner is a senior scientist and R&D project leader for security at Fraunhofer Institute FOKUS. In this function she is concerned with project management, co-ordination and technological development, specifically in the domain of security and e-government solutions in national and international projects. Her research interests include security in distributed processing environments and service architectures, identity management, as well as security for e-government, telecommunication and electronic commerce applications and services. Prior to coming to FhI FOKUS, Ms. Hoepner worked as a system specialist at Nixdorf Microprocessor Engineering GmbH (1981-1990). She received her Diploma in Computer Science from Technical University of Berlin (1980).

J. David Irwin was born in Minneapolis, Minnesota, in 1939. He received a BEE from Auburn University, Auburn, Alabama (1961), and an MS and PhD from the University of Tennessee, Knoxville (1962 and 1967, respectively). In 1967, he joined Bell Telephone Laboratories, Inc., Holmdel, New Jersey, as a member of the technical staff and was made a supervisor in 1968. He joined Auburn University in 1969 as an assistant professor of electrical engineering. He was made an associate professor in 1972, associate professor and head of the department in 1973, and professor and head in 1976. From 1982-1984, he was professor and head of EE and CS. In 1993, he was named Earle C. Williams Eminent Scholar and head.

Sushil Jajodia is BDM international professor of information technology and director of the Center for Secure Information Systems at the George Mason University in Fairfax, Virginia. His research interests include information security, temporal databases, and replicated databases. He has authored four books, edited 19 books, and published more than 250 technical papers in the refereed journals and conference proceedings. For more information, visit: http://csis.gmu.edu/faculty/jajodia.html.

Stamatis Karnouskos holds a Diploma (summa cum laude) in computer engineering and informatics from the University of Patras in Greece. He is currently a senior scientist and R&D project manager at Fraunhofer Institute FOKUS. He is involved in several industrial and European Union projects related to mobile payments, mobile commerce, software agents, active networks, security and mobility. His contributions include project management and coordination as well as technical research and development in the aforementioned domains. His research aims at making future networks and their services more open, secure and flexible. He has authored more than 25 technical papers in international books, journals and conferences, has acted as guest editor at the *IEEE T-SMC Journal,* and participates as member of the technical program committee and reviewer in several international conferences and workshops.

Ling Liu is an associate professor in the College of Computing at Georgia Tech (USA). Her research involves both experimental and theoretical study of distributed data intensive systems, including distributed middleware systems, advanced Internet systems and Internet data management. Her current research interests range from performance, scalability, reliability, to security and privacy of Internet services, mobile and wireless computing systems, and pervasive computing applications. Dr. Liu has published more than 100 articles in international journals and international conferences. Her research group has produced a number of open source software systems, of which the most popular ones are WebCQ and XWRAPElite. She is currently a member of ACM SIGMOD executive committee, editor-in-chief of *ACM SIGMOD Record,* and on the editorial board of three international journals, and served as a vice PC chair or PC co-chair of several international conferences, including IEEE International Conference on Data Engineering (ICDE 2004), and IEEE International Conference on Web Services. Her current research is partially funded by government grants from NSF, DARPA, DoE and industry grants from IBM and HP.

Chang-Tien (C.T.) Lu received a BS in computer science and engineering from the Tatung Institute of Technology, Taipei, Taiwan (1991), an MS in computer science from the Georgia Institute of Technology, Atlanta, Georgia (1996), and a PhD in computer science from the University of Minnesota, Minneapolis (2001). He is currently an assistant professor in the Department of Computer Science at Virginia Polytechnic Institute and State University (USA). His research interests include spatial database, data mining, data warehousing, and geographic information systems.

Jianfeng Ma received a BS in mathematics from Shaaxi Normal University (Xi'an) (1985) and obtained an ME and PhD in computer software and communications engineering from Xidian University (Xi'an) (1988 and 1995, respectively). Since 1995, he has been with Xidian University as a lecturer, associate professor and professor. He is also a supervisor of PhD students in "Cryptography" and "Computers with Their Applications" at the university. From 1999-2001, he was with Nanyang Technological University of Singapore as a research fellow. He is an IEEE member and a senior member of Chinese Institute of Electronics (CIE). His research interests include information security, coding theory and network management.

Ravi Mukkamala received a PhD from the University of Iowa (1987) and an MBA from Old Dominion University (1993). Since 1987, he has been with the Department of Computer Science at Old Dominion University, Norfolk, Virginia (USA), where he is currently a professor. His research interests include distributed systems, data security, performance analysis, and PKI. His research has been sponsored by NRL, DARPA, NASA, and CISC. For more information, visit: www.cs.odu.edu/~mukka.

Seema Nambiar received a BS in computer science from the University of Bangalore, India, and spent a year and a half working as software engineer in Wipro Technologies (NYSE: WIT) for their Lucent division. Since the fall of 2001 she has been a master student of the Department of Computer Science at Virginia Polytechnic and State University.

Richard E. Newman is an assistant professor of Computer & Information Science & Engineering at the University of Florida (USA). He received a BA in mathematics from New College in Sarasota, Florida (1981) and his MS in computer science from the University of Rochester in Rochester, New York (1983), where he completed his PhD in computer science (1986). After graduation, he joined the faculty at the University of Florida. He has taught operating systems, distributed operating systems, computer networks, computer and network security, algorithms, formal languages and computation theory, and computational complexity. His research is primarily in distributed systems, computer networking and security, including industry- and government-sponsored projects on these topics that have brought in over $3 million and led to over 60 technical publications.

Oguz Kaan Onbilger received a BS from the Computer Science and Engineering Department at Hacettepe University, Turkey (1990). He received an MS in computer engineering from the Middle East Technical University, Turkey (1995). He is currently a PhD candidate in the Computer and Information Science and Engineering Department at the University of Florida. Between and during the academic programs he completed, he worked in the industry several years before he joined the doctorate program at the University of Florida. His research interests are computer networks and security, mobile code systems, and Internet/distributed computing.

Changxing Pei received a BS in wireless communication from Xidian University, Xi'an, China (1970). He is a professor with the School of Telecommunications Engineering, Xidian University, where he teaches and conducts research in wireless communications, data networks, Internet, and interference cancellation.

Antonis Ramfos joined Intrasoft International in 1997 and is currently R&D section manager. His main responsibilities include R&D strategy formulation, conception and management of R&D projects, (both externally- and internally-funded), innovation transfer to commercial solutions of the company and finally the promotion and commercial exploitation R&D results. His current research interests include knowledge and content management technologies; e-business and e-government systems; and e-commerce and m-commerce systems. Dr. Ramfos has several publications in journals, conferences and books. He holds a BSc in mathematics from the University of Sussex, UK (1983), an MSc in computing and statistics from the University of Wales, College of Cardiff, UK (1985), and a PhD in the area of distributed heterogeneous databases from the University of Wales, College of Cardiff (1991).

Anna Cinzia Squicciarini is a PhD student at the University of Milan, Italy. She received a degree in computer science from the University of Milan with full marks (July 2002). During Autumn 2003, Anna Cinzia was a visiting researcher at Swedish Institute of Computer Science, Stockholm. During Spring 2004, she also was a research scholar at Colorado State University, Fort Collins (CO) (USA). Her main research interests include trust negotiations, privacy, models and mechanisms for privilege and contract management in virtual organizations and, recently, Web services access control models.

Cesare Stefanelli is an associate professor of computer engineering at the University of Ferrara. His research interests include distributed and mobile computing, mobile code, middleware supports for adaptive services, network and systems management, and security infrastructures. He received a PhD in computer science from the University of Bologna. He is a member of the IEEE and the Italian Association for Computing. To contact: cstefanelli@ing.unife.it

András Vilmos is the project manager of SEMOPS and managing director of SafePay Systems Ltd. He has held different leading positions at major companies, as being chief controller of the national carrier, and CFO of the national grid. A few years ago, Mr. Vilmos launched his own company active in financial consulting. Being interested in telecommunication and Internet business, Mr. Vilmos was working on payment related research and eventually developed the concept that forms the bases of the SEMOPS project. Mr. Vilmos has a number of patents pending related to online payments.

Chwan-Hwa "John" Wu received a BS from the National Chiao Tung University, Taiwan, Republic of China (1980), and a PhD from the Polytechnic University, New York (1987). In 1987, he joined the faculty of Auburn University, Alabama, and is currently a professor of electrical & computer engineering. Dr. Wu is the author and co-author of over 150 scientific and technical publications.

Li Xiong is a PhD candidate in the College of Computing at Georgia Institute of Technology (USA). Her research interests are in Internet data management, electronic commerce, distributed computing and Internet security. She has published articles in international journal and conferences including *IEEE Transactions of Knowledge and Data Engineering* and *IEEE Conference on Electronic Commerce.* Previously, she received her BS and MS in computer science from the University of Science and Technology in China and Johns Hopkins University, respectively. She also had several years of industry experience working as a software engineer with companies, including Internet security systems.

Jyh-haw Yeh received a BA in applied mathematics and an MS and PhD in computer science (1988, 1993, 1999) from the National Chung-Hsing University (Taiwan), Cleveland State University, and University of Florida, respectively. Currently, he is an assistant professor in the Department of Computer Science at Boise State University, Idaho (USA). His research interests are in the areas of computer security, e-commerce, and interconnected networks. He is a member of the IEEE Computer Society and the Association of Computing Machinery.

Eric Zhen Zhang is a master's student in the computer science program at the School of Information Technology and Engineering at the University of Ottawa, after working years in telecommunication industry. He did research on wireless network, quality of service, multimedia and information security. His present work is aimed at security support for mobile user access services in ubiquitous environment.

Quanxing Zhang was born in 1962 in Shanxi province, P.R.China. He attended Northwestern Polytechnic University, Xi'an, China (1978), and graduated with Bachelor of Science in electrical engineering (July 1982). He worked in Baocheng General Electronics Corp, Shaanxi, China, as a technologist until September 1985, when he enrolled in graduate school of the same university. He graduated in April 1988 with Master of Science in Electrical Engineering and was working for the same corporation as a design engineer until he came to enroll in Auburn University. He graduated from Auburn University with a PhD in 2003.

Changhua Zhu received a BS in electromagnetic field theory and microwave technology (1995) and his MS in telecommunications and information system (2001), all from Xidian University, Xi'an, China. He was a microwave engineer at Institute of Electromechanical Information Technology, Xi'an, China (1995-1998). Now he is pursuing a PhD at Xidian University. His research interests include measurement, modeling and performance analysis of IP networks.

Jianming Zhu received a BS in mathematics from Huaibei Coal & Normal College, Huaibei, Anhui, China (1985), and obtained his ME in computers and their applications from Taiyuan University of Technology, Taiyuan, Shanxi, China (1998). Since 1989, he has been with Shanxi Finance & Taxes College (Taiyuan) as a lecturer and associate professor. Currently, he is pursuing a PhD in computers with their applications at Xidian

University, Xi'an, Shaanxi, China. His research interests include information security, cryptography and e-commerce.

Index